COLLABORATIVE NETWORKS:
REFERENCE MODELING

T0184378

COLLABORATIVE NETWORKS: REFERENCE MODELING

Edited By

Luis M. Camarinha-Matos
New University of Lisbon, Portugal

Hamideh Afsarmanesh
University of Amsterdam, The Netherlands

 Springer

Luis M. Camarinha-Matos
New University of Lisbon
Campus de Caparica
Quinta da Torre
2829-516 Monte Caparica
Portugal
cam@uninova.pt

Hamideh Afsarmanesh
University of Amsterdam
Collaborative Networks Group
Kruislaan 419, MATRIX I
1098 VA Amsterdam
The Netherlands
hamideh@science.uva.nl

Collaborative Networks: Reference Modeling
Edited By: Luis M. Camarinha-Matos and Hamideh Afsarmanesh

ISBN-13: 978-1-4419-4638-6   e-ISBN-13: 978-0-387-79426-6

Printed on acid-free paper.

9 8 7 6 5 4 3 2 1

springer.com

TABLE OF CONTENTS

REFEREES

The following people helped with the revision of the various chapters:
Servane Crave
Ekaterina Ermilova
Nathalie Galeano
Iris Karvonen
Toni Jarimo
Simon Msanjila
Wico Mulder
Alexandra Pereira-Klen
Michel Pouly
Ricardo Rabelo
Iiro Salkari
Ingo Westphal

ECOLEAD REVIEW TEAM

The following members of the European Commission Review Team followed the development of the ECOLEAD project where this work was developed and contributed with very useful guidance for its improvement:
Jorge Grazina
Alberto Bonetti
Bernhard Koelmel
Jorge Pinho Sousa
Norman Roth

SPONSOR

ECOLEAD
European Collaborative Networked Organizations Leadership Initiative
IST IP 506958 project
www.ecolead.org

Foreword

The field of Collaborative Networks has seen a remarkable progress during the last 10 – 15 years in terms of research and practical applications. Nevertheless the ongoing consolidation of the area as a new discipline requires more efforts on establishing its theoretical foundation. This book is a contribution in this direction.

Particular emphasis is put on modeling multiple facets of collaborative networks and establishing a comprehensive modeling framework that captures and structures diverse perspectives of these complex entities. Further, a contribution to the definition of reference models for Collaborative Networks is introduced.

This work was mostly developed in the context of the ECOLEAD project, a large 4-year European initiative including 28 academic, research, and industrial organizations from 14 countries in Europe and Latin America, within which the authors had major leading responsibilities. In addition to the contribution from the authors, some other colleagues have also contributed to some chapters, namely with provision of some modeling examples, as indicated in the corresponding sections.

We would like to also thank those colleagues who acted as referees reviewing earlier versions of this manuscript and making valuable contribution to its improvement.

Finally we expect this work to effectively contribute to the establishment of comprehensive reference models for Collaborative Networks, and thus to offer a basis for researchers and practitioners interested in the field.

Luis M. Camarinha-Matos
New University of Lisbon, Portugal

Hamideh Afsarmanesh
University of Amsterdam, The Netherlands

PART 1

INTRODUCTION

1.1
Overview

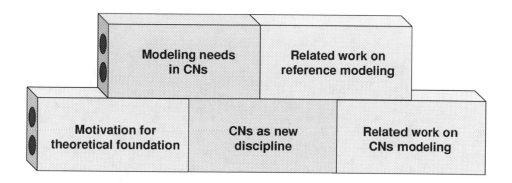

The area of collaborative networks is already extended over two decades of research and development since the first results on virtual enterprises were published. A large number of research projects and pilot applications contributed to the worldwide establishment of the area since then, generating a vast amount of concepts, mechanisms, models, systems, approaches, etc. In order to facilitate its smooth progress, it is necessary to invest on a theoretical foundation that gives a solid basis for further developments.

The motivation for this foundation and the need for recognition of collaborative networks as a new discipline are introduced in this section.

Main modeling needs and an overview of related work on modeling CNs are also discussed, giving the baseline for the technical propositions appearing in the following sections of the book.

1.2
Motivation for a theoretical foundation for collaborative networks

A growing number of collaborative networks can be observed in many domain areas. However, the developments and even the understanding of these cases have suffered from ad-hoc approaches, being urgent to establish a proper theoretical foundation for the area. Furthermore, the fast developments in the area and the nature of the paradigm configure the emergence of a new discipline, which needs to be built on a sounder theoretical basis.

1. INTRODUCTION

The rapid progress on computer networks and pervasive computing has offered the base conditions for the establishment of a networked society where new forms of collaboration are being explored. In fact a large variety of collaborative networks have emerged during the last years as a result of the challenges faced by the business, social, and scientific worlds and enabled by the fast progress in the information and communication technologies. Advanced and highly integrated supply chains, virtual enterprises / virtual organizations, virtual (professional) communities, virtual laboratories / e-science, are illustrations of a major trend in which entities seek complementarities and join efforts that allow them to better participate in challenging and competitive opportunities (Fig. 1) (Camarinha-Matos, Afsarmanesh, 2007). In particular for industrial societies composed mostly of small and medium enterprises (SMEs), as is the European case, the involvement in a collaborative network represents not only a survival factor but also a competitive advantage in face of turbulent market scenarios. Market turbulence in this context is characterized by complexity as well as the speed of change in interactions and inter-dependencies in the socio-economic environment.

In addition to industry, many similar cases can be found in other domains, namely in the service sector. For instance, the concepts of virtual organization and virtual community are entering the elderly care sector (Camarinha-Matos, Afsarmanesh, 2004b) as a way to facilitate a smooth interaction and collaboration among all actors involved in an integrated elderly personal wellness system. The logistics and transportation sector is another example where new synergies are being created through collaborative processes among a diversity of actors (Osorio et al., 2005).

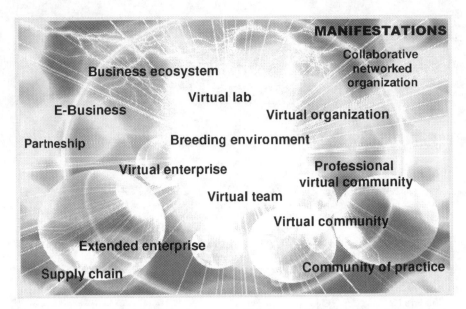

Figure 1 – Some "manifestations" of collaborative networks

A large number of research projects have been carried out worldwide in the last decades and a growing number of practical implementations showing different forms of collaborative networks are being reported. This trend has so far led to an extensive amount of empirical base knowledge that now needs to be organized and leveraged.

The initial investments on Virtual Organizations led, in most cases, to highly fragmented and case-based approaches. For many years, one of the main weaknesses in the area has been the lack of appropriate theories, consistent paradigms definition, and adoption of formal modeling tools. Often the project of a new case of collaborative network is conducted from scratch, without benefiting from previous experiences because knowledge from past cases is not properly organized and made widely accessible. Dramatically enough, there is not yet a common definition of basic concepts such as virtual organization, collaborative networks, or virtual enterprise. This situation constitutes a major obstacle for interaction among experts from multiple disciplines, involved in this area, and creates an obstacle for the recognition of collaborative networks as a new scientific paradigm. Based on the acquired experiences, it is now urgent to consolidate and synthesize the existing knowledge, setting a sounder basis for the future.

As in any other scientific discipline or engineering branch, collaborative networks (CNs) require the development of formal theories and models, not only as a help to better understand the area, but also as the basis for the development of methods and tools for better decision-making. In fact decision-making in all phases of the future CNs life cycle needs to be based on well argued and verified models and methodologies. These models and methodologies constitute the basis for the ICT-based support for business and organizational development and operation, as well as the base for education, training, and effective management and operation of CNs.

After an initial phase in which, mostly biased by traditional business practices, the very first infrastructures and pilot cases were developed, there is at present a vital need to focus more on fundamental research in order to understand both the architectures and the emerging behavior as well as to support the design of new collaborative organizational forms. The establishment of a theoretical foundation for collaborative networks needs to proceed in two directions:

1 - <u>Consolidation</u> / structuring of the large body of existing empirical knowledge.

2 - Adoption / extension of theories and modeling tools developed elsewhere, in order to <u>understand and explore</u> emerging forms of collaborative networks and their behavioral patterns.

Existing knowledge on diverse manifestations of "traditional" collaborative networks is in fact quite fragmented, being urgent to proceed with an integration and formalization effort. Nevertheless, purely formal methods in addition to being hard to apply are also difficult to follow by those not familiar with such methods. This might suggest, in some cases, the appropriateness of semi-formal methods.

On the other hand, new forms of collaborative networks and new patterns of behavior are being invented and explored. As illustrated in Fig. 2, it is typical that emerging CNs are first perceived and explained through informal descriptions. Only when more cases become available and sufficient experience is accumulated an effort to consolidate the acquired knowledge through formal modeling methods starts.

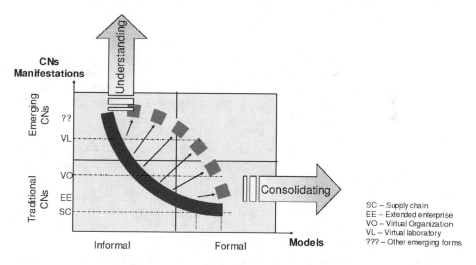

Figure 2 – Evolution of modeling approaches

Furthermore, new CN forms correspond to complex phenomena that require new ways of analysis and proper modeling tools. These phenomena show characteristics such as complexity, emergence[1], self-organization, dynamics, interaction of social

---

[1] A property studied in the Theories of Complexity

networks with organization networks, etc.   As new collaboration-support infrastructures and tools become available, new behavioral patterns emerge, even in traditional collaborative networked organizations. In this context, new ways of collaboration, new forms of organizing the collaborative networks, even new institutions, and new roles for participants are being rapidly developed while not being yet well understood. Therefore, a theoretical foundation is necessary, not only to consolidate the existing empirical knowledge, but also as a basis for perceiving and understanding emerging collaborative forms.

In order to establish a theoretical foundation for CNs inspiration and help can be sought in other areas. Some theories and paradigms defined elsewhere (see part 3 of this book) have been suggested by several research groups as promising tools to help understand and characterize emerging collaborative organizational forms. Nevertheless, it is unlikely that any of these theories and modeling methods will cover all modeling needs of CNs; they can be used as a starting point but extensions or adaptations are needed. In fact, there is no single (formal) modeling tool / approach that adequately covers all perspectives – i.e. no "universal language" for all modeling problems in this area. For instance, typical works on networking and social networks consider, for sake of simplicity, just one kind of links among network members, while practical methods for CNs need to consider a diversity of link types (and different strengths for each link). Furthermore, interoperability of different modeling tools and approaches is needed for a comprehensive definition and modeling of this paradigm.

2. TOWARDS A NEW DISCIPLINE

CNs are complex systems and consist of many facets whose proper understanding requires the contribution from multiple disciplines. In fact the various manifestations of this paradigm have been studied by different branches of science, including the computer science, computer engineering, management, economy, sociology, industrial engineering, law, etc., to name a few. The 1990s and early 2000s correspond to the stage that Kuhn would call a pre-paradigmatic phase (Kuhn, 1975), in which the collaborative networks phenomenon has been described and interpreted in many different ways, depending on the background of the researcher.

The acceptance of a new paradigm is not a pacific process (Kuhn, 1975), as the established sciences and paradigms tend to resist the introduction of another "competitor", and rather prefer to extend the existing sciences or fields and their associated rules to explain the new phenomena. For instance, virtual enterprises have been studied, in a quasi independent way, by the engineering and management communities with almost no mutual recognition. This tension situation is further increased by the multi-disciplinary nature of the phenomena, namely in the case where multiple traditional disciplines / branches of organized knowledge and professionals compete to claim and master the new area. This is the clear case we have observed for collaborative networks.

As a good example of this strained behavior, so far several of the established branches of science have tried to use / extend their definition and behavioral model of the single enterprise paradigm to explain the collaborative networks; e.g. the attempts in the direction of "enterprise engineering" and "enterprise architecture", among others. Considering a virtual enterprise as just another form of an enterprise naturally leads to consider that extending the existing models of a single enterprise would be a promising approach. However, *anomalies* appear when the existing enterprise-centric models and their extensions fall short of capturing the key facets and specificities intrinsic in networked organizations, as well as when realizing that the base facilities of the applied discipline are not sufficient to properly represent and model all aspects of the behavior of collaborative networks. Instead of focusing on the internal specificities and tight interconnections among the internal components of an enterprise, *the focus* in collaborative networks must be directed to the external interactions among autonomous (and heterogeneous) entities (e.g. interoperability mechanisms and tools), the roles of those entities (e.g. coordinator, member, cluster-manager, broker), the main components that define the proper interaction among entities (e.g. common ontologies, contracts, distributed business processes, distributed multi-tasking, collaborative language), the value systems that regulate the evolution of the collaborative association (e.g. collaborative performance records), and the emerging collective behavior (e.g. trust, teamwork), among others.

In the history of science, the recognition and acknowledgement of *anomalies* has resulted in "crises", that are the necessary preconditions for the emergence of novel theories and for a paradigm change or even the rise of a new discipline. As in other past paradigm changes, considerable research efforts have been focused on identification of "anomaly" aspects for CNs, i.e. the identification of what is new in the collaborative networks in reference to the established body of knowledge, that has itself lead to the induction and progressive characterization of a new scientific paradigm. CNs cannot be seen as proprietary to any one of the single contributing disciplines, rather representing a new emerging discipline of its own (Camarinha-Matos, Afsarmanesh, 2005). A **new discipline** emerges once: (i) the new paradigm is adjusted to cover the various manifestations of the emerging collaborative forms, (ii) the consolidated set of basic knowledge is organized, and (iii) the various multi-disciplinary researchers involved in this work start to identify themselves as members of this new community, rather than experts doing research on collaborative networks while staying as members of their original communities and disciplines. Fig. 3 illustrates the foundation for the CNs discipline.

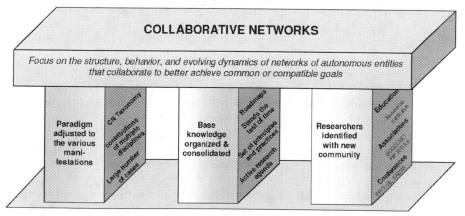

Figure 3 – The foundation of a new discipline

Adjustment to manifestations.
An ordered set of principles and practices form the foundation of a discipline (Liles et al., 1995). In the case of Collaborative Networks and their manifestations, a large number of R&D projects and practical implementations have been developed during last years. Particularly in Europe, more than 100 projects have been supported by the European Commission, in addition to various national initiatives. However, each one of these efforts has only addressed particular facets of the CNs, leading to some fragmentation of research. Furthermore most of the early initiatives were of an ad-hoc nature, not relying on sound theories and principles. In spite of this ad-hoc and fragmented research situation, a growing set of principles and practices has been collected in many projects and pilot applications. In this way, the paradigm is progressively better characterized.

At present, the main phases of the life cycle of a CN are intuitively understood and the primary required support functionalities have been identified. It is also nowadays a widely accepted principle that the effective establishment of dynamic VOs requires an underlying breeding environment (or cluster network). A variety of such breeding environments or clusters can already be identified for instance in Europe (Plüss, Huber, 2005), Japan (Kaihara, 2004), Brazil (Vargas, Wolf, 2006), and Mexico (Flores, Molina, 2000). CNs is therefore seen as the paradigm that gives the base framework for all such manifestations.

On the other hand, disciplines, like the proposed one, are frequently based upon other disciplines that can be called the reference disciplines or adjacent disciplines (Liles et al., 1995). Developments in CNs have benefited from contributions of multiple disciplines, namely computer science, computer engineering, communications and networking, management, economy, social sciences, law and ethics, etc. Furthermore some, theories and paradigms defined elsewhere have been suggested by several research groups as promising tools to help define and characterize emerging collaborative organizational forms.

Base knowledge organized and consolidated.
A scientific discipline for Collaborative Networks is characterized by the existence of an active research agenda where many fundamental questions are being tackled and studied. In principle, the existence of an active research agenda is revealed if the following three main characteristics exist (Liles et al. 1995): (1) It stands the test of time, (2) It is complex and substantial enough to be subdivided into different research directions, and (3) Multiple fundamental questions / approaches are raised and formulated to guide the research in the area. In the case of collaborative networks the following situation holds:

1. *It stands the test of time.* CNs represent an active research area for more than 15 years. During this time a growing number of research projects have been launched world-wide and many pilot application cases are being developed in different regions for a variety of application domains. Definition of challenges and the research questions are becoming more precise and detailed, and their dimension more evident as the knowledge about the area accumulates. The application domains are also growing. In addition to industry, forms of collaborative networks can now be found in services, governmental

organizations, elderly care, energy management, etc. It is therefore becoming clear that this is not a temporary *fashion* but rather a major area of research that continuously grows.

2. *It is complex, and substantial enough to be subdivided into different research directions.* CNs represent a vast area of research that requires a subdivision into a number of research areas in order to be studied and handled. This subdivision can be based for instance, on the type of manifestation (VE/VO, Professional Virtual Communities, Collaborative Virtual Laboratories, etc), or on different technical perspectives (e.g. socio-economic focus, management focus, ICT infrastructure focus, ICT support services focus, theoretical foundation focus).

3. *Multiple fundamental questions/approaches are raised and formulated to guide the research in the area.* A large and growing number of open issues and research challenges are being identified in the various manifestations of the CNs and their focus areas. These questions are illustrated by a number of research roadmaps related to collaborative networks, that are elaborated, namely in Europe (Camarinha-Matos, Afsarmanesh, 2004a).

An example of a comprehensive research agenda for CNs is given by the VOmap roadmap for advanced virtual organizations (Camarinha-Matos, Afsarmanesh, 2003), (Camarinha-Matos et al, 2005). VOmap aimed at identifying and characterizing the key research challenges needed to fulfill the vision, required constituency, and the implementation model for a comprehensive European initiative on dynamic collaborative virtual organizations (VO). The VOmap vision is that of an effective transformation of the landscape of European industry into a society of collaborative relationships. In order to be efficient and competitive in their operation, VOs of the future have to rely on solid bases and strong methodological approaches. This roadmap, which includes contributions from about 100 experts from industry and academy, identifies a large number of the main challenges for research and development in this area, and suggests a time frame for the proposed research actions.

Other roadmaps have also been proposed, addressing some of the related research challenges to collaborative networks. For instance, the COCONET roadmap (Schaffers et al., 2003) is focused on virtual communities and their cooperation environments, the IDEAS roadmap (Chen, Doumeingts, 2003) addresses needs for supporting interoperability of ICT infrastructures, the Semantic Grid roadmap (Roure et al., 2001) focuses on e-Science and GRID infrastructure needs, and the Assembly-net roadmap (Onori et al., 2003) discusses research challenges in advanced collaborative manufacturing systems.

A new research community.
Community development through education and professional associativism is essential to the widespread recognition of a discipline. Several activities that have taken place during last years have contributed to the establishment of a significant community of professionals involved in collaborative networks. Examples are:

▪ *Education activities.* Some universities already offer courses on virtual organizations / virtual enterprises (Klen et al., 2005). For instance, the New University of Lisbon (Portugal) offers a 1-semester course on Virtual Enterprises to the 5th year students of Electrical and Computer Engineering since 2002

(Camarinha-Matos, Cardoso, 2004). Similarly the Federal University of Santa Catarina (Brazil) and the Costa Rican Institute of Technology (Garita, 2004) started offering VE/VO courses to their students. Other universities are designing similar courses or including CN-related modules in their existing curricula (Klen et al., 2005). Other similar example courses are being developed in Europe at the Master program level. A proposal for a reference curriculum for CN education at the university level was developed by the ECOLEAD project (Camarinha-Matos et al., 2008).

▪ *Scientific associations.* Scientific associations play an important role as facilitators and promoters of collaboration among professionals involved in a specific discipline. Some initiatives in this area have been launched in recent years. For instance, at IFIP (International Federation for Information Processing) level, a Working Group on Infrastructures for Virtual Enterprises and e-Business (COVE - CO-operation infrastructure for Virtual Enterprises and electronic business) was established under its Technical Committee 5. The SOCOLNET Society of Collaborative Networks started in 2006 and aims at promoting and stimulating the scientific research, teaching, technological development, technical and scientific interchange between researchers in the Collaborative Networks area, including virtual organizations, virtual enterprises, virtual laboratories and related areas. Another example is the ESoCEnet (European Society of Concurrent Enterprising Network) established in Italy.

▪ *Conferences.* Professional and scientific conferences provide a forum to discuss current thoughts and experiences, as well as a channel to publish emerging ideas. The IFIP/SOCOLNET Working Conference series PRO-VE [www.pro-ve.org], the first yearly conference focused on Virtual Enterprises started in 1999, and since then has established itself as the reference conference and most focused scientific event on collaborative networks, attracting a good number of professionals from academia and industry. CTS is an American annual conference devoted to Collaborative Technologies and Systems. BASYS is an IFIP conference series focused on Information Technology for Balanced Automation Systems that devotes a track to collaborative networks. Another related event, more focused on the Concurrent / Collaborative Engineering aspects is the ICE conference.

These elements are evidence of the establishment of Collaborative Networks as a new discipline. As such, CN require a sound theoretical basis to support its continued development.

3. CONCLUSIONS

The large diversity of existing and emerging collaborative forms and related experiences and empirical knowledge require a consolidation effort in order to:
- better understand the paradigm and its manifestations, and
- facilitate new developments.

A theoretical foundation supported by adequate modeling tools is also important to help understanding the new collaboration forms and thus support a more rational design, analysis and management.

Furthermore, as the CNs phenomenon is not "property" of any single established discipline, it clearly requires a multi-disciplinary approach. Progressively, the area of CNs has been turning itself into a distinct discipline. Further developments of the discipline require a sounder holistic modeling effort.

The following chapters of this book represent a contribution to this modeling effort. Complementarily, in (Camarinha-Matos et al., 2008) a comprehensive collection of methods and tools for collaborative networks also developed in the ECOLEAD project are presented.

Acknowledgements. This work was funded in part by the European Commission through the ECOLEAD project.

4. REFERENCES

1. Camarinha-Matos, L.M.; Afsarmanesh, H. (2003). A roadmap for strategic research on virtual organizations. In *Processes and Foundations for Virtual Organizations*, Kluwer Academic Publishers, Boston.
2. Camarinha-Matos, L.M.; Afsarmanesh, H. (Ed.s) (2004a). *Collaborative networked organizations – A research agenda for emerging business models*, Kluwer Academic Publishers, Boston.
3. Camarinha-Matos, L.M.; Afsarmanesh, H. (2004b). TeleCARE: Collaborative virtual elderly care support communities, *The Journal on Information Technology in Healthcare*, Vol. 2, Issue 2, pp 73-86, ISSN 1479-649X, London, Apr 2004.
4. Camarinha-Matos, L.M.; Afsarmanesh, H. (2005). Collaborative networks: A new scientific discipline, *J. Intelligent Manufacturing*, vol. 16, N° 4-5, pp439-452.
5. Camarinha-Matos, L.M.; Afsarmanesh, H. (2007). Classes of Collaborative Networks. In Encyclopedia of Networked and Virtual Organizations (G. Putnik, M. M. Cunha, Ed.s), Idea Group, Dec 2007.
6. Camarinha-Matos, L.M.; Afsarmanesh, H., Cardoso, T., Klen, E. (2008). A reference curriculum for education in CNOs. In *Methods and Tools for Collaborative Networked Organizations*, Springer, 2008.
7. Camarinha-Matos, L.M.; Afsarmanesh, H., Ollus, M., (Ed.s)(2008). Methods and tools for collaborative networked organizations. Springer.
8. Camarinha-Matos, L.M.; Cardoso, T. (2004). Education on Virtual Organizations: An experience at UNL. In *Virtual Enterprises and Collaborative Networks*, Kluwer Academic Publishers, Boston.
9. Chen, D.; Doumeingts, G. (2003). Basic Concepts and Approaches to develop interoperability of enterprise applications. In *Processes and Foundations For Virtual Organisations*, Kluwer Academic Publishers, Boston.
10. Flores M., Molina A., "Virtual Industry Clusters: Foundation to create Virtual Enterprises", in *Advanced in Networked Enterprises - Virtual Organizations, Balanced Automation and Systems Integration*, L.M. Camarinha-Matos, H. Afsarmanesh, Heinz-H. Erbe (Eds.), Kluwer Academic Publishers, 2000, pp. 111-120.
11. Garita, C. (2004). A case study of VO education in Costa Rica. In *Virtual Enterprises and Collaborative Networks*, Kluwer Academic Publishers, Boston.
12. Kaihara, T. (2004). A challenge towards the Japanese industry: Industrial cluster. In Collaborative Networked organizations – A research agenda for new business models, Springer 2004.

13. Klen, E., Cardoso, T., Camarinha-Matos, L. M. (2005). Teaching Initiatives on Collaborative Networked Organizations, in *Proceedings of 38th CIRP - International Seminar on Manufacturing Systems*, May 16-18, Florianópolis-SC, Brazil.
14. Kuhn, T. S. (1975). *The structure of scientific revolutions*. Univ. of Chicago Press, 2nd edition.
15. Liles, D.; Johnson, M.; Meade, L.; Underdown, D. (1995). Enterprise Engineering: A discipline?, Society for Enterprise Engineering (SEE) Conference, Orlando, FL, http://www.webs.twsu.edu/enteng/ENTENG1.html.
16. Onori, M.; Barata Oliveira, J.; Lastra, J.; Tichem, M. (2003). European Precision Assembly – Roadmap 2010, Assembly-Net, ISBN 91-7283-637-7.
17. Osorio, A.L., Camarinha-Matos, L.M., Gomes, J.S. (2005) – A collaborative network case study: The extended "Via Verde" toll payment system. In Collaborative Networks and their Breeding Environments, Springer.
18. Plüss, A., Huber, C. (2005). "VirutelleFabrik.ch – A Source Network for VE in Mechatronics. In *Virtual Organizations Systems and Practices*. Edited by L.M. Camarinha-Matos, H. Afsarmanesh and M. Ollus. Springer, pp. 255 – 264.
19. Roure, D.; Jennings, N.; Shadbolt, N. (2001). Research Agenda for the Semantic Grid: A future e-Science infrastructure, EPSRC/DTI Core e-Science Programme.
20. Schaffers, H.; Ribak, A.; Tschammer, V. (2003). COCONET: A roadmap for context-aware cooperation environments. In *Processes and Foundations for Virtual Organizations*, Kluwer Academic Publishers, Boston.
21. Vargas, R., Wolf, P. (2006). "Virtual Collaboration in the Brazilian Mould and Die Making Industry" in *Real-Life Knowledge Management: Lessons from the Field*, KnowledgeBoard. Abdul Samad Kazi & Patricia Wolf (Eds.), ISBN: 9525004724. April 2006, pp. 323 – 333.

1.3
Related work on reference modeling for collaborative networks[*]

Several international research and development initiatives have led to development of models for organizations and organization interactions. These models and their approaches constitute a background for development of reference models for collaborative networks. A brief survey of work on modeling the enterprises, enterprise architectures, and early contributions to reference models of virtual enterprises is provided. Finally an identification of the main modeling requirements for collaborative networks is made.

1. INTRODUCTION

Some authors see the roots of the Virtual Organization / Virtual Enterprise paradigm, which constitutes one of the first manifestations of the Collaborative Networks, in the early works of economists such as Oliver Williamson in the 1970s. Along his very prolific work, and in particular in the "Markets and Hierarchies" (Williamson, 1975), Williamson established the study of Transaction Cost Economics as one of the first and most influential attempts to develop an economic theory of organizations. He defends that manufacturing firms should make much greater use of externally purchased goods and services, rather than those internally supplied. Williamson also discusses the business transaction costs at the same level as the production costs. While production costs are considered as being analogous to the costs of building and running an "ideal" machine, transaction costs cover those that incur by deviation from perfection. For instance, he argues that the lack of information about the alternative suppliers might lead to paying too high a price for a good or service. Through identifying the important variables that determine the transaction costs, the work of Williamson contributed to the better understanding of business interactions among enterprises.

These ideas had a more evident impact with the booming of the "outsourcing" wave in the 1980s. Outsourcing became very attractive when managers had to reduce the organization overheads and eliminate the internal inefficient services, the so called lean manufacturing, as it transfers the problem to the outside, namely other efficient service providers. For many enterprises, outsourcing some services allows them to concentrate on their core competencies. For others, outside contractors simply provide complementary services for which the company lacks adequate internal resources or skills. In the same line but with a focus on the management

[*] *By H. Afsarmanesh, L. M. Camarinha-Matos*

and financial activities is the off shoring movement. Among many factors that justify the outsourcing strategy, the reduction of costs, and elimination of poor performance units, can be pointed out, particularly in the case of those units that do not represent core capabilities or when better and cheaper alternatives can be identified in the market. In parallel with the outsourcing tendency, another transformation can be observed in large companies that reorganize themselves in terms of their production lines, leading to some "federation" of relatively autonomous departments.

These transformations, putting the emphasis on networking and partnership / cooperation have raised a large interest for new disciplines such as the coordination theory, organizational theory, and sociology of the industrial organizations.

The idea of virtual enterprise (VE) / virtual organization (VO) was not "invented" by a single researcher, rather it is a concept that has matured through a long evolution process. Some of the early references first introducing the terms like virtual company, virtual enterprise, or virtual corporation go back to the early 1990s, including the work of Davidow and Malone (1992), and Nagel and Dove (1995). Since then, a large but disjoint body of literature has been produced mainly in two communities, the Information and Communications Technology community and the Management community.

Generalized access to Internet that is available through multiple channels and the fast developments around the world-wide-web have led to the proliferation of many terms such as the e-commerce, e-business, e-work, e-government, etc. To put it in a more emphatic way, it seems that in the first years of this decade everything became e-something. Similarly, Business-to-customer (B2C) and Business-to-Business (B2B) are other examples of popularized terms.

So a question arises: since virtual organizations are also supported by the Internet and the web, where do they fit in this "e-movement"? Fig. 1 shows an attempt to put things into perspective, showing that e-Commerce is mostly about B2C relationships and mainly concerned with buy-sell transactions among the involved entities. Virtual organizations on the other hand, go far beyond simple transactions, and are focused on collaboration among a number of enterprises and doing things together (Camarinha-Matos, Afsarmanesh, 2005).

However, concepts and definitions related to the VE/VO paradigm are still evolving, and the terminology is not yet fixed. There is still not even a common definition for the VE/VO that is agreed by the community of researchers in this area.

Most developments in the area are of ad-doc nature, i.e. focused on solving specific application cases. Only a few contributions to a sounder basis can be found in the literature. For instance, one of the first references to a (partial) theoretical foundation for virtual organizations comes from Appel and Behr (1998) which however limit their approach to the application of the transaction-costs theory. Ahuja and Carley (1998) focused on the structural aspects of the collaborative networks.

An attempt to organize and categorize reference models for VOs can be found in Tolle, Bernus, and Vesterager (2002), and Zwegers, Tolle and Vesterager (2003) as a result of the GLOBEMEN project.

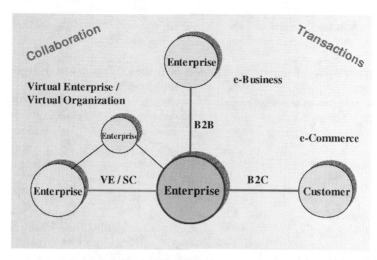

Figure 1 – Virtual Organization and e-Commerce

The THINKcreative project was one of the first initiatives to introduce the concept of Collaborative Networked Organization (CNOs) as a more general concept to encompass various collaborative forms such as virtual organization, virtual enterprise, professional virtual community, etc (Camarinha-Matos, Afsarmanesh, 2004a). This project also clearly identified the need for a sound theoretical foundation for CNOs (Camarinha-Matos, 2003), (Camarinha-Matos, Abreu, 2003). Furthermore THINKcreative identified and briefly analyzed some potential theories and approaches developed in other disciplines that could form the basis for the desired theoretical foundation (Camarinha-Matos, Afsarmanesh, 2004b,c). THINKcreative also discussed the concept of emergence in complex self-organizing systems and briefly analyzed the potential contribution of areas such as theories of complexity, multi-agent systems, self-organizing systems and evolving networks, and holistic approaches. Sustainable development of collaborative networked organizations needs to be supported by fundamental research leading to the establishment of Collaborative Networks as a <u>new scientific discipline</u> (Camarinha-Matos, Afsarmanesh, 2004e). However, THINKcreative was not a development project and this study was confined to a first identification of needs, potential contributions, and generation of research recommendations.

Another initiative, the VOmap roadmapping project, also pointed out the importance of a theoretical foundation for advanced virtual organizations (Camarinha-Matos, Afsarmanesh, 2003, 2004d), (Camarinha-Matos et al., 2004). This project aimed at identifying and characterizing the key research challenges needed to fulfill the vision, required constituency, and the implementation model for a comprehensive European initiative on dynamic collaborative virtual organizations. In the elaboration of the roadmap five focus areas were considered: Socio-economic, VO management, ICT infrastructure, ICT support services, and Formal models and theory. Establishing a formal theoretical foundation and methodology for modeling dynamic virtual organizations, defining basic formal reference models for collaborative networks, elaborating soft modeling approaches as well as approaches for models interoperability, are among the recommended research actions proposed by VOmap. Another recommendation for investing on a theoretical foundation for collaborative networks can be found in the work of Eschenbaecher and Ellmann (2004).

One example of effort to systematize and consolidate the existing empiric knowledge on virtual organizations, mainly based on the achievements of a large number of European projects, was carried out by the VOSTER project (Camarinha-Matos et al., 2005). It is also important to mention the role of the IFIP PRO-VE series of conferences, started in 1999, in the development and consolidation of the area.

Proper understanding of collaborative networks, due to their complexity, requires the contribution from multiple disciplines. A typical tendency when a new paradigm emerges is that each contributing discipline tries to extend its boundaries in order to capture the facets of the new phenomena. As a good example of this behavior, so far several of the established branches of science have tried to use / extend their definition and model of the single enterprise paradigm (Noran, 2003) to explain the collaborative networks; e.g. the attempts in the direction of "enterprise engineering" and "enterprise architect", among others. Understanding a VE/VO as just another form of an enterprise naturally leads to consider that extending the existing models of a single enterprise would be a promising approach. However, the existing enterprise-centric models and their extensions cannot adequately capture all key facets and specificities intrinsic in networked organizations.

For instance, in relation to the Collaborative Networked Organizations, past studies and developments have primarily focused on the internal aspects of an "organization", rather than on "collaboration" among enterprises, which is of a totally different nature, and requires innovative approaches to solve its many problems.

To clarify this issue and motivate this problem area, let us look at a metaphoric example that is easier to describe.

Consider the case of "collaboration among a number of people" who aim to achieve certain goals, e.g. to organize a party, to write a research proposal, to produce an innovative product, or even to build a house together. Here the constituents of this "collaboration network" are humans. How to model this situation? Certainly, the study of human body and the function of its internal organs has long been achieved through the research on human anatomy, and has lead to the elaboration of detailed models of various systems related to the human body (e.g. nervous system, and circulatory system) in terms of their composition, inter-relationships, flows, etc. Although the human anatomy studies is necessary and very useful in some contexts (e.g. for disease diagnosis in medicine), they are not appropriate and at best minimally relevant to the understanding of neither the potential nor the behavior of social groups of people, or even for understanding the behavior of a single individual within a social collaborative group (Fig. 2).

Figure 2 - Human anatomy vs. Understanding of social behavior

Similarly, for a CNO, although the detailed study of its constituents, namely the "organizations" is achieved by some research in the past, and proves to be very valuable, it is in fact not addressing the "collaboration" and or "networking" problem areas and focus.

Finally it shall be mentioned that although there are not many contributions to the holistic understanding of collaborative networks, there are many publications that contribute to the advances in certain specific facets, whose full account is out of the scope of this chapter, but some main contributions are addressed in different chapters of this book. Perhaps surprisingly, some important contributions to the study and understanding of complex dynamic networks during the last five years come from the area of Physics (Barabási, 2002), (Dorogovtsev, Mendes, 2003).

There are also many developments in other disciplines that can contribute to the start of a foundation for collaborative networks, e.g. in complexity theories, game theory, multi-agent systems, graph theory, formal engineering methods, federated systems, self-organizing systems, swarm intelligence, and social networks. The theoretical foundation work in the ECOLEAD project took the mentioned early works as a baseline.

2. A BRIEF SURVEY OF RELEVANT WORK

The following sections give a brief overview of relevant elements from some important attempts to establish reference models. As none of the early initiatives covers the necessary scope for CN reference models, the cases included here are mainly to illustrate the conceptual approaches and give the reader a synthetic overview of the state of the art and trends.

2.1 Zachman framework

Purpose and scope. The Zachman Framework for Enterprise Architecture (Zachman, 1987) is an approach for documenting and/or developing a enterprise-wide information systems architecture. This framework provides multiple perspectives of the overall architecture of an enterprise and a categorization of the artifacts of the architecture. It establishes a common vocabulary and a set of perspectives to *describe* and *design* complex enterprise systems. Thus, Zachman reference framework is useful to define suitable architectures of complex systems for enterprises.

Highlights of the model. The Zachman Framework constitutes a matrix of 36 cells, covering the Who, What, Where, When, Why, and How questions in regards to an enterprise. The enterprise is then split into six perspectives, starting at the highest level with business abstraction, passing through intermediate level of details (i.e. conceptual, logical, etc.), and going all the way down to implementation. Such objects or descriptions of architectural representations are usually referred to as Artifacts. The framework can contain global plans as well as technical details, lists, and charts. Any appropriate approach, standard, role, method or technique may also be placed in it.

Zachman basically supports two important actions for an enterprise namely: The creation of a new enterprise and the evolution of an existing enterprise. The support and management aspects are based on the interrogation of perspectives subjected to the abstractions. The interrogatives are used for deciding about what must be included in the enterprise when creating a new enterprise. Also, they are used to decide about what must be changed when an enterprise must evolve. Therefore, in general, the interrogative abstractions are applied for the management of the enterprise complexity. On the other hand, this perspective allows dealing with the rate of change; in fact it brings the engineering disciplines to the management and the priority of change. This provides guidelines from the abstract description to the detailed level of implementation.

Useful elements for CNs. Zachman architecture represents one enterprise properly. Clearly enough, CNs cannot be treated the same as a single organization; in fact, members of a CN are all independent and autonomous entities. However, it would be interesting and challenging to consider the application of Zachman to CNs in relation to the following aspects:
- Similarities between running an enterprise and the operation of a CN shall be studied.
- Similarities between the evolution of an enterprise as supported by Zachman and the creation, evolution, dissolution and metamorphosis stages of CNs shall be studied.

Also, considering the life cycle of CNs and the application of Zachman in these phases may be useful:
- Investigating the necessary elements when creating an enterprise can be used to study what needs to be included in the architectures for CNs.
- Investigating what needs to be changed when an enterprise has to evolve, change or dissolve, can be used for issues of CN evolution and metamorphosis.

2.2 SCOR

Purpose and scope. The SCOR (Supply-Chain Operations Reference-model) has been developed / endorsed by the Supply-Chain Council. It is a process-based model developed as a standard diagnostic tool for supply-chain management in industry. Considering all stakeholders involved in the supply-chain, SCOR provides an environment for their interaction/communication, enabling users to address, improve the management of supply-chains (Barnett, Miller, 2000).

Highlights of the model. Since the development of SCOR, this model has been successfully used, providing a base for projects of any size, from small projects specific to a site, to large and global projects. The SCOR-model, focused on satisfying customer demands, facilitates the modeling and description of all business activities associated with different phases of the supply chain developments. It uses a set of process building blocks and a common set of definitions to model and describe activities of both simple and complex supply-chains. As a result, independent, heterogeneous, and geographically distributed industries can be simply linked within any supply chain.

Useful elements for CNs. As a supply chain is a particular case of CN, SCOR is an adequate reference model for the functional / process perspective of this organizational form.
When it comes to other classes of CNs however, it is necessary to consider that:
- While providing a comprehensive reference-model for relatively stable environments; SCOR is not tailored for dynamic environments of many CNs.
- SCOR cannot capture / measure performances with soft factors related to the collaboration, for instance the trustworthiness of organizations.
- SCOR requires major efforts in configuring the Supply-Chain, and therefore prohibits the agility needed in configuration of ad-hoc or dynamic collaborative networks, for instance VOs for emergency management.

2.3 VERAM

Purpose and scope. The Virtual Enterprise Reference Architecture and Methodology (VERAM) primarily aims to increase the preparedness of entities involved in the networks for efficient creation of virtual enterprises (VEs). The VERAM facilitates the modeling process through provision of guidelines on how to build the models and how to identify the common characteristics of the VEs and networks (Zwegers et al. 2003). It offers a blueprint that can be followed by organizations for setting up VEs (Tølle and Bernus 2003). VERAM provides a generalized model for the desired properties of VE. It specifically addressed the involved entities in creation, operation, and dissolution of VEs (Tølle and Bernus 2003).

Highlights of the model. Three main layers can be identified in VERAM (Zwegers et al. 2003):
1. The *Concepts* of VE and network;
2. The *Reference Architecture* for Concepts;
3. The *Components* of the Reference Architecture.
The concepts address for example the network, the competencies, the customers, etc. The reference architecture presents a three dimensional view, with dimensions of *life-cycle phases*, *generality*, and *modeling views*. Furthermore, the components of VERAM are divided into five categories of: 1) contingency factors, 2) modeling, 3) applications and infrastructures, 4) methodology, and 5) VE implementation.

Useful elements for CNs. The emphasis of VERAM on comprehensively representing the characteristics and elements common to all aspects of the VE is also important for general CNs modeling, due to their complexity. The identification of the lifecycle stages in VERAM is also important for CNs and their life cycle stages. But for example the Reference Architecture of VERAM with its three dimensions, mainly borrowed from the GERAM (TFAEI, 2003), makes the model more difficult to understand and utilize. For instance it seems that by eliminating the *generality* dimension, perhaps the VERAM model can be simplified

2.4 EGA – Enterprise Grid Alliance

Purpose and scope. The Enterprise Grid Reference Model developed by the Enterprise Grid Alliance (EGA, 2005) defines the terminology and glossary of grid computing and identifies various components, interfaces, interactions and data models. It is intended that such reference model enables interoperability among heterogeneous grid applications or products and improve integration of grid applications or services, thereby improving the opportunities for the effective use of grid computing within the enterprise, to the benefit of both vendors and users of such technology.

Highlights of the model. The reference model provides a specific context for describing requirements, standards, comparing technologies and implementing grid solutions. The model delivers a framework and a set of customer-based requirements needed to accelerate enterprise grid adoption. Included in its three main components are: a **glossary** providing a common lexicon of grid terms; a **model** that classifies the management and lifecycles of the components required for enterprise grids; and a set of **use cases** that demonstrate the requirements for enterprise grid computing.

The principal aim of the glossary is not to define new terms rather it is to provide some precision around terms in common use but which are directly applicable to the work of the area. Some terms which have specific meaning within the EGA are also defined. The model itself is concerned with providing a context for the grid components including attributes and properties, life cycle and classification and also a management entity called GME – Grid Management which is responsible for ensuring that the various grid components meet their goals. Finally the set of use cases provide the overall customer or user centric view of the sets of problems that the EGA intends to address such as: the set of commercial enterprise community-centric use cases and consistent and relevant requirements for partner SDOs (Standards Development Organizations) and all other enterprise Grid stakeholders.

Useful elements for CNs. Similarly to EGA, in CNs we need to define the base concepts, relationships and interfaces. Some elements from EGA regarding resources management can also be useful to CNs.

2.5 FEA – Federal Enterprise Architecture

Purpose and scope. The development of the Federal Enterprise Architecture (FEA, 2005) by the US Office of Management and Budget (OMB) started on February 6, 2002. The purpose of this effort is to identify opportunities to simplify processes and unify work across the agencies and within the lines of business of the US Federal government.

The FEA, a business-based framework for government-wide improvement, has the aim of transforming the US Federal government to one that is citizen-centered, customer-focused, results-oriented, market-based, and that maximizes technology investments to better achieve mission outcomes.

Highlights of the model. The FEA consists of a set of interrelated "reference models" designed to facilitate cross-agency analysis and the identification of duplicative investments, gaps and opportunities for collaboration within and across agencies. Collectively, the five reference models comprise a framework for describing important elements of the FEA in a common and consistent way. Through the use of this common framework and vocabulary, IT portfolios are expected to be better managed and leveraged across the federal government. The FEA Reference models are:
- Performance Reference Model (PRM);
- Business Reference Model (BRM);
- Service Component Reference Model (SRM);
- Technical Reference Model (TRM);
- Data Reference Model (DRM).

As FEA adopts an entirely business-driven approach, its foundation is the Business Reference Model, which describes the US government's Lines of Business and its services. This business-based foundation provides a common framework for improvement in a variety of key areas such as: Budget Allocation, Information Sharing, Performance Measurement, Budget / Performance Integration, Cross-Agency Collaboration, E-Government, and Component-Based Architectures.

Useful elements for CNs.
The use of a set of interrelated reference models seems to be a practical approach. Putting the center of gravity on the Business Reference Model (BRM) may also be a good alternative for the CNs Reference Model. The FEA BRM provides a framework that facilitates a functional (rather than organizational) view of the federal government's lines of business, including its internal operations and its services for citizens, independent of the agencies, bureaus and offices that perform them. The BRM describes the federal government around common business areas instead of through a stove-piped, agency-by-agency view and thus promotes agency collaboration (collaborative e-government);
- The development of a process for maintaining and evolving the FEA reference models is very relevant. The continued maintenance of the reference models is critical to the implementation and usage of the corresponding architecture.

3. MODELING NEEDS

On modeling. *Models* and *modeling* are an integral part of the human understanding and thinking processes. Since reality is usually too complex to understand and influence directly, we develop models of reality either on our minds (mental models) or formally / semi-formally using drawings or other representations including mathematical and computer (simulation) models.

A model is an abstract representation of reality and as such should exclude details of the world which are not of interest to the modeler or the ultimate user of the model. This justifies that even in a given field (e.g. computer science) there are various modeling approaches, which very much depend on the modeling purpose. For instance, when we are interested in the dynamics of a system our focus is on the processes rather than on the structure of the system.

On the other hand, modeling is a kind of *art* that very much relies on the "eyes of the modeler". Although some modeling tools and methodologies try to constrain / guide the modeling process, the outcome greatly depends on the experience of the modeler and even his/her aesthetic preferences. The same applies, to some extent, to the choice of the modeling tools and formulation to apply.

On systems perspective. Modeling is one of the key activities in understanding, designing, implementing, and operating systems. Modeling is at the very heart of any scientific and engineering activity.

A major output of the process of designing a new system is a model or set of models of the system to be implemented. The abstract representation of the intended system will then be used to guide the implementation. Furthermore, a model is also very useful in order to supervise (manage) the operation of the developed system during its life cycle. Complementarily, a model can also be used to predict the behavior of the system being developed or managed. And yet, from a systems perspective, it is important to set the purposes for each model. As Shannon clearly noted:

> "The tendency is nearly always to simulate too much detail rather than too little. Thus, one should always design the model around the questions to be answered rather than imitate the real system exactly".

On modeling CNs. As in any other scientific discipline or engineering branch, collaborative networks require the development of models, not only as a help to better understand the area, but also as the basis for the development of methods and tools for better decision-making.

It is however important to note that modeling is not only necessary for building software systems; in the context of a complex system like a CN, modeling is fundamental for understanding, managing, simulating / predicting the behavior of the network and its members, and certainly also for software development. For instance, in the VOSTER project (Loeh, Zhang, Katzy, 2005), the following purposes for modeling in this domain were considered:

- Support the development and understanding of the organizational structure and processes for the management;
- Define and document ways how partners collaborate in virtual organizations for the human actors involved;
- Support enterprise and business process reengineering;
- Document the solution domain (e.g. actors, objects, standard processes);
- Document software requirements (e.g. system processes, entity relationships);
- Document computer systems (e.g. system architecture, system objects);
- Allow computer enactment of the models;
- Define standards for data exchange and process behaviors;
- Establish system interoperability requirements.

A previous work from Presley at al. (2001), although biased by a process-view of virtual enterprises (a popular view after the "boom" of the business process re-engineering methods), also recognized the need to consider multiple views for modeling collaborative networks. Even for the very particular case of traditional supply chains, a quite simple case of CN, Kim et al. (2004), in an extensive state-of-the-art analysis of the best practices in the area, identified the need to consider several modeling methods (in addition to the traditional process-based SCOR model), such as for example: Deterministic analytical models, Stochastic analytical models, Economic models, and Simulation models. Furthermore, they also mentioned the need for models involving multi-functional issues such as location/routing, production/distribution, location/inventory control, inventory control/ transportation, and supplier selection/inventory control.

In fact in the late 1990's several works tried to extend SCOR to cope for the new needs of more dynamic supply chains, but still limited to a process view. Another example is given by the work of Barnett and Miller (2000) that introduced extensions to support discrete event simulation but also resorting to other developments such as the HLA (High Level Architecture) of the Department of Defense.

After 2000 the research community gradually became more aware of the need to also consider other modeling perspectives. As an example, Goranson (2003), although discussing a process view (and defending PSL), recognizes the need to go much further, including:

- Federated approaches;
- Multi-level control to consider both operational processes and business processes;
- Multi-agent based models;
- Introduction of the notion of fractional value;
- Soft modeling - support for uncertain and unknown facts and dynamics; situation theory; and
- Metaphors.

Modeling purposes. Based on a number of workshops organized by the ECOLEAD project, Figure 3 illustrates some of the questions a modeler may pose when attempting to model a VO Breeding Environment (VBE).

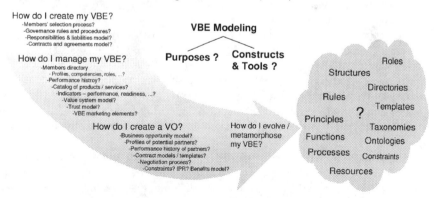

Figure 3 – Examples of modelling purposes in VBE

Certainly many other relevant questions may be asked in relation to a VBE. Similarly, for VO management a large number of modeling purposes are typically considered (Fig. 4).

In the same way many purposes are identifiable for PVCs and other forms of CNs.

Given this large diversity of modeling purposes, which also leads to different types of models, it is important to establish a framework for modeling. A proposal for a more comprehensive framework is discussed in chapter 2.4 of this book.

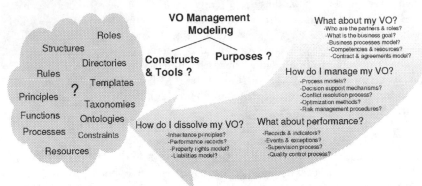

Figure 4– Examples of modelling purposes in VO management

On perspectives and tools. Proper understanding and analysis of a complex system such as a CN requires the consideration of many facets. However, an analysis of past modeling efforts indicates that practitioners and researchers are not fully aware of a comprehensive spectrum of suitable modeling processes, tools, and methodologies. For instance, very often modeling is restricted to a "processes view" (e.g. SCOR type of models for traditional supply chains). Or they stick – often out of principle – with one approach such as using UML even though it might not be the most appropriate approach for all or a part of the modeling effort.

This situation is however improving and lately some theories and paradigms defined elsewhere have been suggested by several research groups as promising tools to help understand and characterize emerging collaborative organizational forms. Nevertheless, it is unlikely that any of these theories and modeling methods will cover all needs of CN; they can be used as a starting point but extensions or adaptations are needed.

Furthermore, existing knowledge on diverse manifestations of "traditional" collaborative networks is quite fragmented, being urgent to proceed with an integration and formalization effort. Nevertheless, purely formal methods in addition to being hard to apply are also difficult to follow by those not familiar with such methods.

As mentioned above, dissemination, education, and communication is one important purpose for modeling CNs. As such, we must acknowledge that this area is addressed by a large variety of people with different backgrounds; not all of them possess a strong formal background, and even many of the ICT practitioners do not have a formal education on computer engineering or computer science. This might suggest, in some cases, the appropriateness of semi-formal methods.

On the other hand, new forms of collaborative networks and new patterns of behavior are being invented and explored, for which it is not feasible to develop fully consistent formal models at start. In these cases, semi-formal models, or even informal analogies as represented by metaphors, can provide valuable insights towards a preliminary level of understanding of new collaborative forms.

4. CONCLUSIONS

Along the history of collaborative networks a few projects, e.g. VOSTER, THINKcreative, and VOmap among others, made some contributions to the systematization of existing empirical knowledge in the area. Some works also emphasized the need for a sounder theoretical and modeling foundation for CNs.

Earlier works on enterprise modeling have produced some well-known modeling frameworks and reference models that various researchers tried to extend to cover networks of enterprises. However, while those approaches were focused on the "internals" of the enterprise / organization, the needed focus here should be on the "collaboration" and "networking / interactions" among autonomous entities with some temporary common interests. Full understanding of these aspects requires an extensive modeling effort and thus the development of a specialized modeling framework.

Acknowledgements. This work was funded in part by the European Commission through the ECOLEAD project. The authors thank the contributions from E. Ermilova, S. Msanjila, F. Ferrada, F. Graser, A. Pereira-Klen, and T. Jarimo.

5. REFERENCES

Ahuja, M. K.; Carley, K.M. (1998). Network Structure in Virtual Organizations, Journal of Computer-Mediated Communication, Vol. 3, issue 4, Jun 1998. http://www.ascusc.org/jcmc/vol3/issue4/ahuja.html.

Appel, W.; Behr, R. (1998). Towards the theory of virtual organisations: A description of their formation and figure. Virtual-Organization.Net Newsletter, 2(2):15-36, June 1998. http://virtual-organization.net/news/nl_2.2/nl_2-2a4.pdf .

Barabási, A.-L. (2002). Linked: The New Science of Networks, Perseus Books Group.

Barnett, M. W.; Miller, C. J. (200). Analysis of the virtual enterprise using distributed supply chain modeling and simulation: An application of e-SCOR, Proceedings of the 2000 Winter Simulation Conference, J. A. Joines, R. R. Barton, K. Kang, and P. A. Fishwick, eds.

Camarinha-Matos, L.M. (2003). New collaborative organizations and their research needs, in Proceedings of PRO-VE'03 – Processes and Foundations for Virtual Organizations, Kluwer Academic Publishers, Oct 2003.

Camarinha-Matos, L.M.; Abreu, A. (2003). Towards a foundation for virtual organizations, in Proc.s of Business Excellence 2003 – 1st Int. Conf. on Performance measures, Benchmarking, and Best Practices in New Economy, Guimarães, Portugal, 10-13 Jun 2003.

Camarinha-Matos, L.M.; Afsarmanesh, H. (Ed.s) (2004a). Collaborative networked organizations – A research agenda for emerging business models, Kluwer Academic Publishers, ISBN 1-4020-7823-4, Mar 2004.

Camarinha-Matos, L.M.; Afsarmanesh, H. (2004b). Emerging behavior in complex collaborative networks, in Collaborative Networked Organizations – A research agenda for emerging business models, cap. 6.2, Kluwer Academic Publishers, ISBN 1-4020-7823-4, 2004.

Camarinha-Matos, L.M.; Afsarmanesh, H. (2004c). Formal modeling methods for collaborative networks, in Collaborative Networked Organizations – A research agenda for emerging business models, cap. 6.3, Kluwer Academic Publishers, ISBN 1-4020-7823-4, 2004.

Camarinha-Matos, L.M.;   Afsarmanesh, H. (2004d). A roadmapping methodology for strategic research on VO, in Collaborative Networked Organizations – A research agenda for emerging business models, chap. 7.1, Kluwer Academic Publishers.

Camarinha-Matos, L.M.; Afsarmanesh, H. (2004e). The emerging discipline of collaborative networks, in Proceedings of PRO-VE'04 – Virtual Enterprises and Collaborative Networks, Kluwer Academic Publishers, ISBN 1-4020-8138-3, pp 3-16, 23-26 Aug 2004.

Camarinha-Matos, L.M.; Afsarmanesh, H. (2005). Brief historical perspective for virtual organizations. In Virtual Organizations – Systems and Practices, Springer.

Camarinha-Matos, L.M.; Afsarmanesh, H.; Loeh, H.; Sturm, F.; Ollus, M. (2004). A strategic roadmap for advanced virtual organizations, in Collaborative Networked Organizations – A research agenda for emerging business models, chap. 7.2, Kluwer.

Camarinha-Matos, L.M.; Afsarmanesh, H.; Ollus, M. (2005). Virtual Organizations: Systems and Practices, Springer.

Davidow, W.; Malone, T. (1992). The virtual corporation. Harper Business.

Dorogovtsev, S. N.; Mendes, J. F. (2003). Evolution of networks - From Biological Nets to the Internet and WWW, Oxford University Press.

EGA (2005). Enterprise Grid Alliance Reference Model, 13 Apr 2005. http://www.gridalliance.org/en/workgroups/ReferenceModel.asp

Eschenbaecher, J.; Ellmann, S. (2003). Foundation for networking: A theoretical view on the virtual organization, in Processes and Foundations for Virtual Organizations, Kluwer Academic Publishers, (Proceedings of PRO-VE'03).

FEA (2003). FEA Consolidated Reference Model, May 2005, http://www.whitehouse.gov/omb/egov/documents/CRM.PDF

Goranson, H. T. (2003). Architectural support for the advanced virtual enterprise, Computers in Industry, Volume 51, Issue 2, June 2003.

Noran, O. (2003) – A mapping of individual architecture frameworks (GRAI, PERA, C4ISR, CIMOSA, ZACHMAN, ARIS) onto GERAM, in Handbook on Enterprise Architecture, P. Bernus, L. Nemes, G. Schmidt (Ed.s), Springer

Kim, C.-S.; Tannock, J.; Byrne, M.; Farr, R.; Cao, B.; Er, M. (2004). Techniques to model the supply chain in an extended enterprise – State-of-the-art review, VIVACE Deliverable D2.5.1_1, University of Nottingham.

Löh, H.; Zhang, C.; Katzy, B. (2005). Modeling for virtual organizations, in Virtual Organizations – Systems and Practices, Springer.

Nagel, R., Dove, D. (1995). 21st Century Manufacturing Enterprise Strategy. Bethlehem: Iaccoca Institute, Lehigh University.

Presley, A.; Sarkis, J.; Barnett, W.; Liles, D. (2001). Engineering the Virtual Enterprise: An Architecture-Driven Modeling Approach, The International Journal of Flexible Manufacturing Systems, 13: 145–162.

TFAEI (2003). GERAM – The generalized enterprise reference architecture and methodology, IFIP-IFAC Task Force on Architectures for Enterprise Integration, in Handbook on Enterprise Architecture (P. Bernus, L. Nemes, G. Schmidt, Ed.s), ppm22-63, (Springer, Heidelberg).

Tolle, M.; Bernus, P.; Vesterager, J. (2002). Reference models for virtual enterprises,   in Collaborative business ecosystems and virtual enterprises, L. M. Camarinha-Matos, Editor, Kluwer Academic Publishers.

Williamson, O. E. (1975). Markets and Hierarchies: Analysis and Antitrust Implication. New York, Free Press.

Zachman, J. A. (1987). A Framework for Information Systems Architecture. IBM Systems Journal, vol. 26, no. 3.

Zwegers, A.; Tolle, M.; Vesterager, J. (2003). VERAM – Virtual enterprise reference architecture and methodology, in Proceedings of GLOBEMEN – Global Engineering and Manufacturing in Enterprise Networks, VTT Symposium 224.

PART 2

TOWARDS A CN REFERENCE MODEL

2.1
Overview

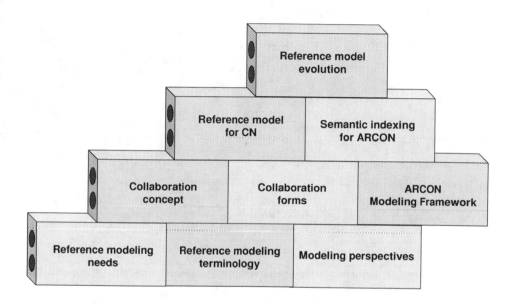

A reference model for collaborative networks can be a very important instrument to both the education of the newcomers as well as facilitation of communication among researchers and practitioners involved in the area, and thus contributing to its smooth development and evolution. This section offers a contribution to the elaboration of a comprehensive reference model for CNs.

In the second chapter motivation and a set of basic needed terminology are introduced, together with a brief historic overview.

The third chapter proposes a taxonomy of collaboration forms and offers working definitions for each class, complemented by examples of the most common cases. The very concept of collaboration is also discussed.

The fourth chapter introduces the ARCON modeling framework. It covers three modeling perspectives (environment characteristics, life cycle, and modeling intent). For the environment characteristics, both the Endogenous Elements (Structural, Componential, Functional, and Behavioral dimensions) and the Exogenous Interactions (Market, Support, Societal, and Constituency dimensions) are covered.

ARCON provides a comprehensive framework for the organization of the various elements of the proposed reference model.

The fifth chapter applies the ARCON modeling framework to structure the set of concepts and entities proposed for the generic level of the reference model. A bottom up approach is followed, i.e. concepts are first collected for specific classes of CNs, namely VO Breeding Environments, Professional Virtual Communities, Virtual Organizations and Virtual Teams, and then generalized to a common set of concepts.

Sixth chapter complements the ARCON modeling framework by proposing a more formal representation, i.e. a semantic indexing schema for the various components of the reference model.

Finally, as the establishment of a reference model is a long-term process, the seventh chapter introduces a set of guidelines for the evolution and improvement of the ARCON model.

2.2
Reference modeling:
Needs and basic terminology

A reference model for collaborative networks is a fundamental instrument for the smooth development of the area. It is therefore important to understand the reference modeling process and associated terminology. This chapters makes a brief historic analysis, introduces basic concepts and perspectives for reference modeling.

1. INTRODUCTION

Lack of reference models for collaborative networks or even to some of their manifestations (such as virtual enterprises) is an issue frequently mentioned in the literature, being also pointed out as an obstacle for a more consistent development of the area. The difficulties are found namely in the used terminology and associated meanings, which leads to frequent misunderstandings among members of the community with a different original background.

When a team of researchers or system designers develop a new system the output of the design phase is a model or set of models of the system to be implemented. A model, i.e. an abstract representation of the intended system, will then be used to guide the implementation. Due to a number of practical reasons the implemented system might show some (minor) differences regarding the original model (usually the case). A model is also very useful in order to guide (manage) and analyze the operation of the developed system during its life cycle.

Further to the models of specific systems we can also elaborate reference models. A reference model is a generally accepted framework for understanding the significant concepts, entities, and relationships of some domain, and therefore a "foundation" for the considered area.

If the design process starts without a reference model commonly used by all team members, what is typical in new areas, a larger effort is necessary to integrate the contributions of the various designers (Fig. 1.a). On the other hand, if all designers share a common reference model and a common set of definitions then the semantic gap is substantially reduced and the process can be much smoother (Fig. 1.b). A reference model can then be intuitively understood as a general (rather abstract) model that provide guidelines to effectively support designing and understanding a large variety of other more specific models for different target systems.

As also illustrated in Fig. 1), models can also be used as a basis for simulation and evaluation of the target system, even before its implementation (Camarinha-Matos, Afsarmanesh, 2006, 2008).

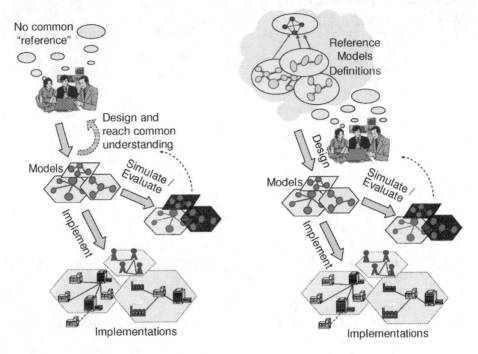

Figure 1 - a) Models and implementations   b) Design based on reference models

Past projects on collaborative networked organizations mostly followed Fig.1.a as no general and commonly accepted reference model is available.

How can a reference model be generated?
If a reference model is supposed to be used as a guiding framework for the design of multiple systems then it shall in fact be an abstract representation of a large number of possible systems. Therefore, in the beginning of a new area such as CNs for which no reference model is available yet, reference models can be built via observation / analysis and abstraction of properties from emerging manifestations of the new area (Fig. 2). Complementarily, scenarios of envisaged / future CNs can also be used as input to inspire the design of a reference model. Finally, the design of a reference model can also get inspiration in other areas / theories developed elsewhere that show a good analogy with the CNs domain.

Establishing a reference model for a new entity is not an easy task since only partial inputs are available. In this context the reference model shall play a guiding / visionary role.
    Once established, the reference model defines a common basis for understanding and explaining (at least at a high abstraction level) the different manifestations of the paradigm. It shall facilitate the development of particular models for specific CNOs

(Figure) (Camarinha-Matos, Afsarmanesh, 2006, 2008). These particular models will drive the implementations and also serve to simulate / evaluate the networks.

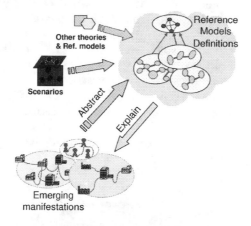

Figure 2 – Elaboration of reference models

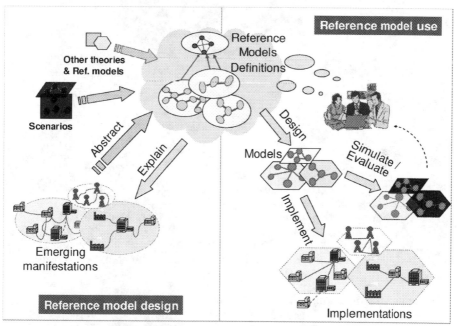

Figure 3 – Reference models in a context

2. EARLY CONTRIBUTIONS

When attempting to establish a reference model it is fundamental to consider the potential inputs and partial contributions from previous works. In fact some previous projects have tried to contribute to reference models of some manifestations of collaborative networks, namely for Virtual enterprises / virtual organizations.

Fig. 4 illustrates the diversity of sources which can potentially be used as inputs to this activity (Camarinha-Matos, Afsarmanesh, 2006, 2008). As shown, there are two main streams:

- Enterprise-centric stream, which starts from the extensive past modeling activities at enterprise level and try to incrementally extend / adapt such models to the context of networks of enterprises.
- Network-centric stream, which puts the emphasis primarily on the networks and their properties, rather than on the characteristics of the individual elements.

These streams are not totally disjunctive and several initiatives show in fact partial elements of the two perspectives.

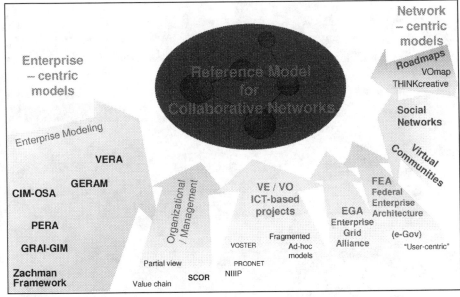

Figure 4 – Main inputs to the design of a CNO reference model

The approaches to modeling very much depend on the dominant background of people involved in each initiative. Three main groups or "schools" encompass most of the past VE/VO related developments:

i) Enterprise modeling, based on the underlying "culture" represented by the Zachman framework (Zachman, 1987), GRAI-GIM (Doumeingts et al., 1993), PERA, CIM-OSA (Vernadat, Kosanke, 1992), GERAM (IFIP-IFAC, 2003) (Noran, 2003), and related developments.

ii) Organizational / management school, which departs from traditional organizational structures such as supply chains and the corresponding SCOR model (Huan, 2004), and tries to reason about emerging organizational patterns in new collaborative forms.

iii) VE/VO ICT-based projects, which put a strong emphasis on the ICT tools and infrastructures to support collaboration. A large number of projects have been carried out in this area that, although showing a "fragmented" and mostly ad-hoc approach, contribute with partial elements to better understand CNOs, their modeling needs and possible approaches.

Some survey works analyzing early contributions namely in the areas i) and iii) above can be found in the literature, such as (Tolle, Bernus, Vesterager, 2002), (Tolle, Bernus, 2003). The PRODNET project (Camarinha-Matos, Afsarmanesh, 1999) or the VITE model (Chalmeta 2000) are examples of ICT-driven initiatives. An example survey under perspective ii) was conducted in the VOSTER project (Katzy, Zhang, Loeh, 2005), which also included some analysis of ICT developments and common practices on VE/VO implementation (Camarinha-Matos, Afsarmanesh, Ollus, 2005). Other areas of interest include:

iv) Grid community, which has moving towards virtual organizations and is trying to consider a business perspective, as in the case of the Enterprise Grid Architecture initiative (EGA 2005).

v) E-Government, which is a wide area but has some common elements when it addresses the cooperation among different governmental organizations, as illustrated by the Federal Enterprise Architecture (FEA 2005).

vi) Social networks and virtual communities are areas that although not yet offering much in terms of reference models, have developed considerable background in terms of basic properties of networks with a strong basis on graph theory.

vii) Collaborative networks roadmapping initiatives such as THINKcreative, VOmap and others which have contributed to the identification of the research challenges in the area (Camarinha-Matos, Afsarmanesh 2004).

Fig. 5 tries to put into a simplified historic perspective some of the key initiatives and events that represent a substantial input to a better understanding of collaborative networks and therefore offer base material for the elaboration of reference models for CNs (Camarinha-Matos, Afsarmanesh, 2006, 2008).

The lower half of the diagram in Fig. 5 includes major representatives of the enterprise integration and modeling area that were particularly active in the 80s and 90s. A parallel initiative, from a different area but that can also give some hints for some cases of virtual organizations, is the Project Management Body of Knowledge (PMI 2004).

The upper half of the diagram shows initiatives that are more directly related to collaborative networks. Of particular relevance here is the heritage of a large number of VE/VO projects. VOSTER represented an attempt to synthesize part of this heritage. The PRO-VE series of conferences and the corresponding proceedings have also played a major role in the consolidation of knowledge in the area and contributing to establish some (progressive) consensus, important elements towards the definition of reference models.

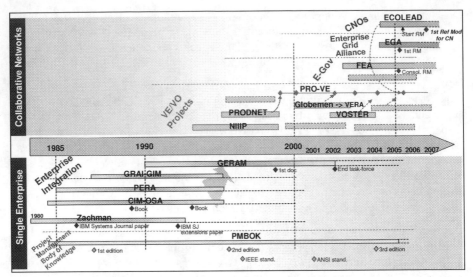

Figure 5 – Towards a CN reference model - A simplified historic perspective

The relevance given to the FEA and EGA projects in this diagram is due to being recent initiatives, almost contemporary of ECOLEAD, have published preliminary versions of reference models for their specific domains.

3. BASE CONCEPTS

The establishment of reference models for CNs is frequently pointed out as a major need for the consolidation and sustainable development of the area. However, it seems that there is not so much consensus on what this term exactly means. In fact it seems that it represents quite different things for different people and consequently it raises quite different expectations regarding its utility. It is therefore necessary to revisit the concept of reference model and its purpose.

What is a reference model?
> *"An authoritative basis for the development of specific models / systems".*
> *"An authoritative basis for the development of standards". "Generic conceptual model that formalizes recommended practices for a certain domain" (Rosemann, van der Aalst, 2007).*
> *"Provides a conceptual framework that should facilitate the creation of domain-specific application models, or descriptions of specific application domains" (Misic, Zhao 99).*

What is the purpose of a reference model?
> *"The main objective of a reference model is to streamline the design of particular models by providing a generic solution". "Reference models accelerate the modeling process by providing a repository of potentially relevant business processes and structures" (Rosemann, van der Aalst, 2003).*

"Reference models would be needed to foster common understanding and communication amongst members of the scientific community". "A reference model documents the emerging consensus within the scientific and industrial community, but should no constrain future work. It therefore is by nature generic and not applicable to a concrete case" (Katzy, Zhang, Loeh, 2005).

Based on these example definitions, two main "anchors" can be associated to a reference model: Authority and re-use (Fig. 6).

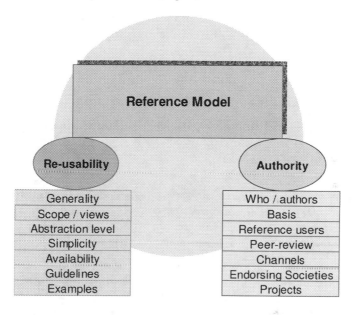

Figure 6 – Key anchors in a reference model

Establishing a model as an authoritative reference depends on a number of factors, including the authorship, i.e. the reputation / prestige of the involved contributors, the adopted bases and referenced sources, the list of early adopters or reference users, the quality of the peer reviewing process, and also the dissemination channels, professional societies and projects involved in its dissemination.

Re-usability of the elements of a reference model, with the objective of streamlining the design and development of particular models, also depends on a number of factors, including: the generality of the model, its scope and covered views, the abstraction level and simplicity, the forms of availability / easiness of access to supporting information, the existence of guidelines for use and examples of application to typical cases.

The clarification of the base concepts is however not that easy as the literature in this area is full of confusing terminology. To refer only a few, it is common to find terms such as reference architecture, reference framework, architectural framework, system architecture, etc. often used with similar or largely overlapping meanings (Fig. 7).

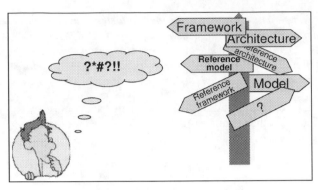

Figure 7 – Confusing terminology

For illustration purposes, let us consider a few examples:

*"An abstract **model** (or conceptual model) is a theoretical construct that represents physical, biological or social processes, with a set of variables and a set of logical and quantitative relationships between them" (Wikipedia).*

*"A **reference architecture** …is, in essence, a predefined architectural pattern, or set of patterns, possibly partially or completely instantiated, designed, and proven for use in particular business and technical contexts, together with supporting artifacts to enable their use" (RUP).*

*"A **system architecture** is an abstract description of a specific system. By indicating the functions of the system components, their interactions, and constraints, it helps to (re-)develop the system. The architecture depends on engineering principles and available technology."*
*"A **reference architecture** refers to coherent engineering and design principles used in a specific domain. A reference architecture aims at structuring the design of a system architecture by defining a unified terminology, describing the responsibilities of components, providing standard (template) components, giving example system architectures, defining a development methodology, etc." (Wyns, van Brussel, Valckenaers, Bongaerts,1996)*

*"**Architecture**: The structure of components, their relationships, and the principles and guidelines governing their design and evolution over time." (DoD Integrated Architecture Panel, 1995, based on IEEE STD 610.12)*

*"An **architecture** is the fundamental organization of a system embodied in its components, their relationships to each other, and to the environment, and the principles guiding its design and evolution." (IEEE STD 1471-2000)*

*"An **architecture framework** is a tool… It should describe a method for designing an information system in terms of a set of building blocks, and for showing how the building blocks fit together. It should contain a set of tools and provide a common vocabulary. It should also include a list of*

recommended standards and compliant products that can be used to implement the building blocks." [TOGAF 8, OpenGroup]

In some other works it is possible to find some attempts to clarify the meaning of the used terms, as in the following examples:

- In software engineering:

*"A (software) **reference model** is a description of all of the possible software components, component services (functions), and the relationships between them (how these components are put together and how they interact"*
*"An **architecture** is a description of a subset of the reference model's component services that have been selected to meet a specific system's requirements. In other words, not all of the reference model's component services need to be included in a specific architecture. There can be many architectures derived from the same reference model"*
*"**Implementation** is a product that results from selecting (e.g. Commercial-off-the-shelf), reusing, building and integrating software components and component services according to the specified architecture" [TAFIM, Carnegie Mellon University, 2004]*

- In computer integrated manufacturing and shop floor control:

*"A **system architecture** is the manner in which the components of a specific system are organised and integrated".*
*"A **reference model** is a generic manner to organize and integrate system components".*
*"A **reference architecture** is used for the framework in which system related concepts are organized". "An enterprise reference architecture is a framework in which enterprise related concepts are organized" (Zwegers 1998).*

In order to facilitate the following work it is important to clarify these concepts in our context. Therefore, without the aim of giving a "final" definition, the following working definitions are currently established in ECOLEAD:

♦ **Model**: A model is an abstract representation of an environment, system, or entity in the physical, social, or logical world.
Typically a model refers only to some aspects of the phenomenon being modeled, and two models of the same phenomenon may be essentially different. This may be due to: different requirements, differences in conceptual approaches, esthetic preferences, and also different past experiences. Therefore, users of a model need to understand the model's purpose and the assumptions or limits of its validity. Furthermore there can be models at various levels of abstraction, from very abstract theoretical constructs, to (detailed) representations very close to the modeled entity or implementation.

♦ **Framework**: In general a framework is a structure for supporting or enclosing something else. In the modeling area, a framework can be seen as an "envelope" that might include a number of (partial) models, collections of templates, procedures and methods, rules, and even tools (e.g. modeling languages).

♦ **Reference model**: A reference model is a generic abstract representation for understanding the entities and the significant relationships among those entities of some area, and for the derivation of other specific models for particular cases in that area. Preferably a reference model is based on a small number of unifying concepts and may be used for education, explaining purposes, and systems' development.

A **CN reference model** is thus a generic conceptual model that synthesizes and formalizes the base concepts, principles and recommended practices for collaborative networked organizations. It is intended as an authoritative basis (guide) to streamline or facilitate the creation of focused models for the various manifestations of CNs as well as architectures and implementation models for particular systems development. A reference model is generic and not directly applicable to concrete cases but rather provides the basis for the development (derivation) of other models closer to those concrete cases.

♦ **Architecture**: An architecture is an abstract description of a specific system, i.e. a particular model that even at a logical level tends to indicate the system structure, functions of its components, their interactions, and constraints, and can be used to develop the system. Architecture is focused on "building a system" and must be complete at its level of abstraction; therefore not all models are architectures. Although there is a difference between engineering and architecture (compare with roles of civil engineer and building architect), to some extent the architecture depends on engineering principles and available technology. An architecture can be formulated in a descriptive or in a prescriptive style. Descriptive style defines an enumeration of design elements and formal "arrangements" between them. Prescriptive style establishes constraints, namely by limiting the possible design elements and their "arrangements".

♦ **Reference architecture**: A reference architecture aims at structuring the design of architectures for a given domain by defining a unified terminology, describing the functionality and roles of components, providing template components, giving example architectures, and defining a development methodology. It corresponds to architecture as a style or method in the sense that it may represent a coherent set of design principles to be used in a specific area. The reference architecture is the basis for designing the specific architectures for particular instances of systems in the class of systems covered by the reference architecture.

In the CNO domain, a reference architecture for VO management systems would represent the "structure" and principles to be followed by particular architectures of concrete VO management systems. The concept of reference architecture also induces the creation of generic re-usable "building blocks".

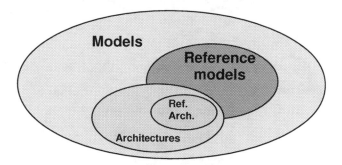

Figure 8 – Relationships among concepts

It is also important to distinguish between reference models and standards. Both share some common aspects, namely aiming at simplifying the creation of new systems and providing some stable conceptual background or building blocks. Regarding the process, both start with building consensus but then they evolve into different directions:

- Standards are basically focused on "normalizing existing knowledge" and thus tend to be conservative.
- Reference models, on the contrary, aim at "pointing a direction" and providing guidelines, and thus tend to be more visionary.

However the differences and commonalities between the two concepts depend on the level of maturity of the area. For instance, in the domain of enterprise modeling – a very old domain since enterprises exist for a long time – it took many years to distil some consensus among proponents of alternative reference models (as shown in Fig. 3). Ultimately these initiatives contributed to some standards. In the case of CNs, a much younger field in which many examples and forms of collaboration are only emerging, it does not make sense to put the emphasis, at this moment, on "standardization" but rather on providing a "direction".

4. PERSPECTIVES AND APPROACHES

Lenses or perspectives
A complex entity such as a collaborative network can be observed and analyzed through different lenses or perspectives (Fig. 9).

Each lens can provide complementary elements that help in achieving a better understanding of the paradigm. It is however important to note that lenses might also cause distortions. Particularly if one tries to explain all aspects of CNs through the perspective of a single lens, not only it leads to dangerous over-simplifications, but even introduces some misconceptions. Therefore a holistic perspective is needed.

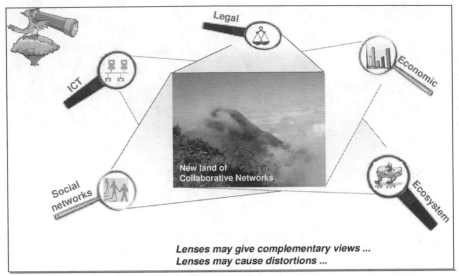

Figure 9 – CNs viewed from different lenses

Most of the previous publications towards a reference model for a CN (or some of its manifestations) are either technology-biased (e.g. Tolle, Bernus, 2003), or business-biased (e.g. Katzy et al, 2005). A holistic approach, combining both perspectives (Fig. 10) would guarantee a better alignment of business (including economic, legal, and ecosystem aspects) and technology.

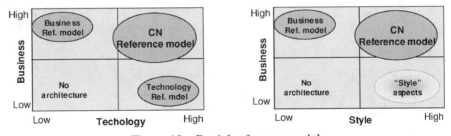

Figure 10 – Partial reference models

On the other hand, we shall not ignore other aspects such as culture, values, norms and principles, trust, etc. (often addressed in the social networks and ecosystems works) that can represent another dimension – the "style"[1] of the CN. These aspects are less addressed in previous modeling works but shall be considered in a holistic reference model for CNs.

Therefore, Fig. 11 gives a qualitative idea of the main perspectives that need to be considered on a holistic development of a CN reference model. The colored small cube is the target positioning for such model.

---

[1] A term borrowed from the area of architecture / civil construction.

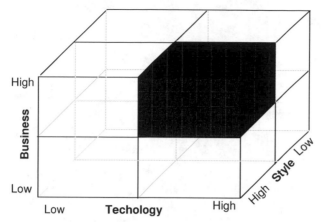

Figure 11 – A simplified holistic reference model frame

ECOLEAD does not cover all fields of expertise, namely in some areas of the *style* dimension, and the development of a full scale reference model is certainly a long term goal. Nevertheless the performed activities had this frame as guidance.

Scope or entities

Collaborative networks manifest in a diversity of forms including virtual organizations, virtual organization breeding environments, professional virtual communities, virtual teams, etc. As a first priority, general abstract models are needed in order to capture the most fundamental underlying concepts and principles of collaborative networks.

A related issue is the number of reference models: does it make sense to pursue a single global reference model or various (more focused and less general) reference models (Fig. 12)?

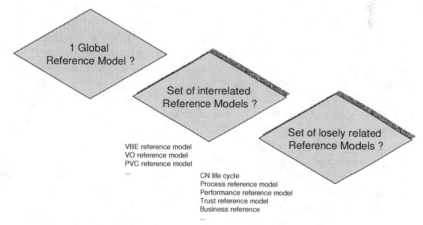

Figure 12 – One or various reference models

As suggested by Fig. 13, it is justifiable to have intermediate reference models for the entities VBE, PVC, VO, and VT as they correspond to different sectors of the represented "cube".

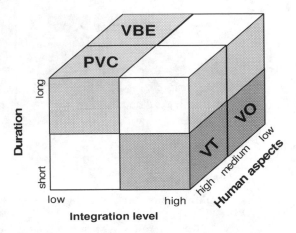

Figure 13 – Base entities and their relationship

There are, however, some common elements to the various entities, which are not evident in this cube, (e.g. actors, inter-relations, life-cycle, etc.) and therefore it makes sense to also think of a higher level of abstraction including all common features.

Target users
The nature and form of representation of a reference model (including the modeling formalisms used) depend on the target users.

The addressed user groups considered in this work are mainly researchers, educators, and other experts in the area of collaborative networks. Although one of the general goals for any reference model is to contribute to the consolidation of knowledge and to facilitate the communication among the actors involved in a specific area, the reference model itself shall not be misunderstood as a text book. Therefore, the users of the CN reference model(s), whereas researchers, engineers, or decision makers (e.g. coordinators of SME networks), are expected to have basic knowledge on the area.

The general public, workers and other professionals without background on CNs will require simplification of the model and basic intuitive representations, which will be out of the scope of the current work.

Elements of a reference model
A simple analysis of reference models developed in other areas makes it clear that there are a large number of potential elements to consider in a reference model (Fig. 14). These include elements related to the structure and behavior of the CN, but possibly also supporting elements (e.g. software systems' architecture), or elements related to applicability and life cycle of the reference model itself.

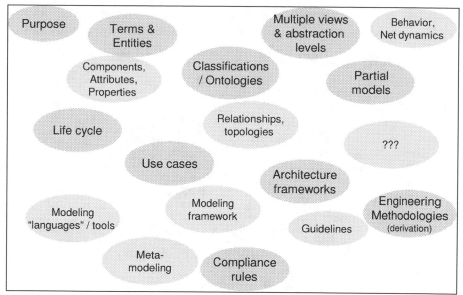

Figure 14 – Which elements for a CN reference model?

The elements exemplified above belong clearly to <u>two distinct groups</u>:
- "Logistics" of the reference model, e.g. purpose, modeling language/tools.
- Reference model purposes, e.g. terms and entities, behavior, life cycle, relationships.

The second group comprises four major **modeling dimensions**:
- <u>Structural dimension</u>, addressing the elements of structure of the CN such as actors and roles, relationships.
- <u>Componential dimension</u>, covering resources, ontologies, and (represented) data and knowledge.
- <u>Functional dimension</u>, which includes functions, processes, procedures and methodologies.
- <u>Behavioral dimension</u>, including the various elements of behavior and what constrains or "gives form" to that behavior (e.g. policies, contracts, agreements).

Level of granularity

In addition to the modeling dimensions presented above, it is necessary to consider, for instance, which modeling sub-dimensions shall be considered and at what level of detail. More detailed models are potentially closer to a practical use, but they tend to become too complex, reducing their understandability and thus their acceptance. Very detailed models also tend to become less general. The degree of integration among the various perspectives / dimensions is another relevant question.

Time horizon

The ECOLEAD project activities on reference models as part of its contribution to the theoretical foundation for CNs - and that are the basis for this work - is just one step in a longer term process. If we take as reference the history of the development of reference models for enterprises (considered in isolation), an effort that spanned over more than 20 years, it becomes clear that it would be unrealistic to expect that in the life span of ECOLEAD a fully developed reference model could be developed for this emerging paradigm.

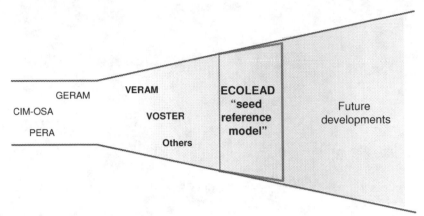

Figure 15 – Time horizon for CN reference models development

The goal was therefore the elaboration of "seed" reference model(s), based on the existing knowledge, and the establishment of the basis for future refinements and further detailing of the initial models.

Level of completeness
The discussion on the time horizon rules out the hypothesis of aiming at reference models with a high degree of completeness. In addition to the time constraints, it is also necessary to consider the limits of the available expertise and the set of CN cases considered in the project. However, ECOLEAD was driven by a holistic perspective and therefore the reference model(s), at some (high) level of abstraction, should be comprehensive and covering multiple focus areas and their inter-relationships.

A seed reference model, on top of which further developments can be pursued in the future, shall be defined at a high level of conceptualization. This model(s) shall not be confused with architectures which are more "static" and closer to implementation of systems. In an analogy, the seed reference model can be seen as a kind of "constitution". Like in country's governance, the constitution provides the global principles and has to be then instantiated in concrete laws and directives (equivalent to architectures and implementation models).

Endorsement
Although not playing the role of a standard, a reference model shall seek some level of endorsement from relevant actors and institutions in order to get wider acceptance. The aim, in the current phase of the developments of the area, is not to seek the support of a standardization body. However the support from specialized working groups (working in the area) in the framework of professional and scientific societies such as IFIP WG5.5 or SOCOLNET is important.

In the current phase, the developed modeling framework and reference models were extensively discussed in the technical events organized by the mentioned societies.

The ARCON modeling framework and the ARCON reference model (Camarinha-Matos, Afsarmanesh, 2007, 2008) for collaborative networks introduced in the following chapters of this book were driven by these general principles.

5. CONCLUSIONS

A reference model for collaborative networks synthesizing and organizing the base concepts, principles and recommended practices, is a fundamental instrument for the growth of the area.

Clearly the establishment of a reference model for CNs is a long term goal that goes well beyond the duration of a single research project, as demonstrated by many other large initiatives in related areas. Furthermore, the establishment of such a model needs a comprehensive modeling framework able to capture the multiple perspectives under which collaborative networks can be considered.

Acknowledgements. This work was funded in part by the European Commission through the ECOLEAD project.

6. REFERENCES

Camarinha-Matos, L.M.; Afsarmanesh, H. (Editors) (2004). Collaborative Networked Organizations – A research agenda for emerging business models, Kluwer Academic Publishers / Springer.

Camarinha-Matos, L.M.; Afsarmanesh, H. (2006). Towards a reference model for collaborative networked organizations, in Proceedings of BASYS'07 , *Information Technology for Balanced Manufacturing Systems* (W. Shen, Ed.) (Springer), Niagara Falls, Ontario, Canada, 4-6 Sep 2006. IFIP Series, Vol. 220, ISBN: 0-387-36590-7.

Camarinha-Matos, L.M.; Afsarmanesh, H. (2008). On reference models for collaborative networked organizations, to appear in *International Journal Production Research*.

Camarinha-Matos, L.M.; Afsarmanesh, H.; Ollus, M. (Editors) (2005). Virtual Organizations – Systems and Practices, Springer.

Chalmeta, R. (200). Virtual transport enterprise integration *Transactions of the SDPS*, Vol.4, N.4, Dec 2000. http://www.sdpsnet.org/journals/vol4-4/Ricardo-4.pdf

Doumeingts, G., Chen, D., Vallespir, B., Fénié, P., Marcotte, F., (1993). GIM (GRAI Integrated Methodology) and its Evolutions - A Methodology to Design and Specify Advanced Manufacturing Systems. In *Proceedings of the JSPE/IFIP TC5/WG5.3 Workshop on the Design of Information Infrastructure Systems for Manufacturing*, IFIP Transactions; Vol. B-14, pp 101-120, North-Holland.

EGA (2005). Enterprise Grid Alliance Reference Model, 13 Apr 2005. http://www.gridalliance.org/en/workgroups/ReferenceModel.asp

FEA (2005). FEA Consolidated Reference Model, May 2005, http://www.whitehouse.gov/omb/egov/documents/CRM.PDF

Huan, S. H. (2004). A review and analysis of supply chain operations reference (SCOR)

        model. *Supply Chain Management: An International Journal*, **9**(1), 23-29, (Emerald).
IFIP-IFAC TFAEI, GERAM (2003). The generalized enterprise reference architecture and
        methodology, IFIP-IFAC Task Force on Architectures for Enterprise Integration, in
        Handbook on Enterprise Architecture (P. Bernus, L. Nemes, G. Schmidt, Ed.s),
        ppm22-63, 2003, (Springer, Heidelberg).
Katzy, B.; Zhang, C.; Loeh, H. (2005). Reference models for virtual organizations. In *Virtual
        organizations: Systems and Practices*, L. M. Camarinha-Matos, H. Afsarmanesh, M.
        Ollus (Editors), Springer.
Misic,V. B.; Zhao, J. L. (1999). Reference Models for Electronic Commerce, *Proceedings of
        the 9th Hong Kong Computer Society Database Conference - Database and
        Electronic Commerce*, Hong Kong, May 99, pp. 199-209.
Noran, O. (2003). A mapping of individual architecture frameworks (GRAI, PERA, C4ISR,
        CIMOSA, ZACHMAN, ARIS) onto GERAM, in *Handbook on enterprise
        architecture*, P. Bernus, L. Nemes, G. Schmidt (Ed.s), Springer.
PMI (2004). Guide to the Project Management Body of Knowledge, A (PMBOK Guide),
        paperback, Third Edition, Project Management Institute.
Rosemann, M.; van der Aalst, W. M. P. (2007). A Configurable Reference Modelling
        Language, *Inf. Syst.* 32(1): 1-23.
Stewart, G. (1997). Supply-chain operations reference model (SCOR): the first cross-industry
        framework for integrated supply-chain management. *Logistics Information
        Management*, **10**(2), 62-67, (Emerald).
Tolle, M.; Bernus, P. (2003). Reference models supporting enterprise networks and virtual
        enterprises, *International Journal of Networking and Virtual Organisations*, Vol. 2,
        No.1 pp. 2 – 15. http://www.inderscience.com/storage/f161185104291237.pdf
Tolle, M.; Bernus, P.; Vesterager, J. (2002). Reference models for virtual enterprises,   in
        Collaborative business ecosystems and virtual enterprises, L. M. Camarinha-Matos,
        Editor, Kluwer Academic Publishers.
Vernadat, F., Kosanke, K. (1992). CIM-OSA: A Reference Architecture for CIM. In
        *Proceedings of the IFIP TC5 / WG5.3 Eight International PROLAMAT Conference on
        Human Aspects in Computer Integrated Manufacturing*, IFIP Transactions; Vol. B-3,
        pp 41-48, North-Holland.
Wyns, J.; van Brussel, H.; Valckenaers, P.; Bongaerst, L. (1996). Workstation Architecture in
        holonic manufacturing systems, *28th CIRP International Seminar on Manufacturing
        Systems*, May 15-17, Johannesburg, South Africa, p220-231. "*CIRP Journal on
        Manufacturing Systems*" Vol.26, No 4.
Zachman, J.A. (1987). A Framework for Information Systems Architecture. *IBM Systems
        Journal*, **26**(3), 276-292.
Zwegers, A. (1998). On systems architecting – a study in shop floor control to determine
        architecting concepts and principles", PhD thesis, Technische Universiteit Eindhoven.

2.3
Collaboration forms

In order to facilitate a better understanding among professionals involved in collaborative networks, a clarification of the base concepts of networking, coordination, cooperation, and collaboration is made. A taxonomy of the main organizational forms of collaborative networks is introduced and working definitions for those forms are proposed.

1. INTRODUCTION

Collaborative networks appear in a diversity of forms and show a variety of behavioral patterns, what leads to some difficulties both in terms of characterization of the paradigm and communication among experts.

For instance, in terms of structure, three collaborative network topologies seem to appear frequently in literature (Katzy et al., 2005) (Fig. 1): a) chain topology, as in the case of supply chains in manufacturing industries, b) star topology (dominant member), which is typically the case in construction or automotive industries, and c) general network topology, as in creative and knowledge industries. In a chain topology, the partners' interaction pattern mainly follows a value-chain. In a star topology, partners interact with one central hub or strategic center, while partners in general network topology have multiple relationships among all nodes without hierarchy. In the last case we can have not only a peer-to-peer kind of interaction but also a more general form involving several partners, or even all of them.

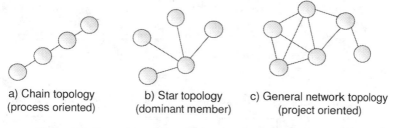

a) Chain topology (process oriented)   b) Star topology (dominant member)   c) General network topology (project oriented)

Figure 1 – Examples of topologies of collaborative networks

In terms of duration, we can find short-term networks, typically triggered by a collaboration opportunity, as the case of a virtual enterprise, and long-term networks, as the case of strategic alliances or supply chains. Furthermore, applications in different domains introduce specific terminology for that domain, what increases the difficulties of mutual understanding in an area that is of a multi-disciplinary nature. In order to cope with such situation, this chapter tries to clarify the basic concepts and introduces a taxonomy of collaborative networks forms.

2. COLLABORATION CONCEPT

This section addresses the base concepts involved in collaboration, and classifies them in a hierarchy to distinguish their differences.

2.1 Ambiguities and working definitions

In order to properly understand and model collaborative networks it is necessary to first focus on the very notion of collaboration (Camarinha-Matos, Afsarmanesh, 2006, 2007a). Although everybody has an intuitive notion of what collaboration is, this concept is often confused with cooperation. For many people the two terms are indistinguishable. Even when a distinction is made, there are many different uses of the term collaboration in the current literature.

The ambiguities reach a higher level when other related terms are considered such as networking, communication, and coordination (Himmelman, 2001), (Pollard, 2005), (Denise, 1999). Although each one of these concepts is an important component of collaboration, they are not of equal value neither one is equivalent to it.

In an attempt to clarify the various concepts, the following working definitions can be proposed:

Definition 2.1: **Networking** – involves communication and information exchange for mutual benefit.

It shall be noted that this term is used in multiple contexts and often with different meanings. For instance, when people refer to "enterprise network" or "enterprise networking" the intended meaning is probably "collaborative network of enterprises".

> *Example: A simple example of networking is the case in which a group of entities share information about their experience with the use of a specific tool. They can all benefit from the information made available / shared, but there is not necessarily any common goal or structure influencing the form and timing of individual contributions.*

Definition 2.2: **Coordinated Networking** – in addition to communication and exchanging information, it involves aligning / altering activities so that more efficient results are achieved. Coordination, that is, the act of working together harmoniously, is one of the main

> *Example: An example of coordinated networking activities happens when it is beneficial that a number of heterogeneous entities share some information and adjust the timing of, for example, their lobbying activities for a new subject, in order to maximize their impact. Nevertheless each entity might have a different goal and use its own resources and methods of impact creation.*

components of collaboration.

Definition 2.3:
Cooperation – involves not only information exchange and adjustments of activities, but also sharing resources for achieving compatible goals. Cooperation is achieved by division of some labor (not extensive) among participants.

> *Example: A traditional supply chain based on client-supplier relationships and pre-defined roles in the value chain, is an example of a cooperative process among its constituents. Each participant performs its part of the job, in a quasi-independent manner (although coordinated with others). There exists however, a common plan, which in most cases is not defined jointly but rather designed by a single entity, and that requires some low-level of co-working, at least at the points when one partner's results are delivered to the next partner. And yet their goals are compatible in the sense that their results can be added or composed in a value chain leading to the end-product or service.*

Definition 2.4: **Collaboration** – a process in which entities share information, resources and responsibilities to jointly plan, implement, and evaluate a program of activities to achieve a common goal. This concept is derived from the Latin *collaborare* meaning "to work together" and can be seen as a process of shared creation; thus a process through which a group of entities enhance the capabilities of each other. It implies sharing risks, resources, responsibilities, and rewards, which if desired by the group can also give to an outside observer the image of a *joint* identity. Collaboration involves mutual engagement of participants to solve a problem together, which implies mutual trust and thus takes time, effort, and dedication.

> *Example: A collaboration process happens for instance in concurrent engineering, when a team of experts jointly develop a new product. From this example it can be noticed that although some coordination is needed, collaboration, due to its joint creation facet, involves seeking divergent insights and spontaneity, and not simply a structured harmony.*

As presented in the given definitions and depicted in Fig. 2, each of the above concepts constitutes a "building block" for the next definition. In other words, coordination extends networking; cooperation extends coordination; and collaboration extends cooperation.

As we move along the continuum from networking to collaboration, we increase the amounts of common goal-oriented risk taking, commitment, and resources that participants must invest into the joint endeavor. In this sense, these various interaction levels can also be seen as a kind of "**collaboration maturity level**". In other words, this organization of "building blocks" can be a basis to define the level of maturity of an organization towards involvement in a collaboration process.

In the rest of this chapter we focus on collaborative networks which subsume all other forms.

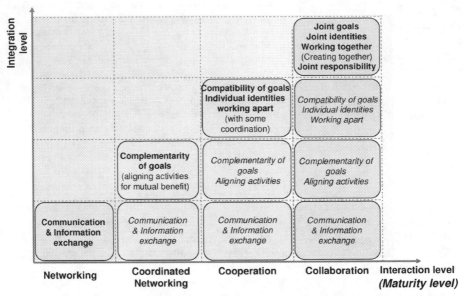

Figure 2 – Examples of joint endeavor (Camarinha-Matos, Afsarmanesh, 2007a)

Even with these definitions, in practice the distinction between collaboration and cooperation is not always very clear. In fact, in a collaborative network, collaboration in its strict sense does not happen all the time. For example, in the manufacturing alliances, very often there are phases of intense collaboration, e.g. design and planning phases of a project, intermixed with periods when the participants work individually and independently on their assigned tasks. Then from time to time they "come together" (physically or virtually) to integrate their results and continue the joint problem solving. Therefore, a collaboration process clearly involves periods of only cooperation. Understanding and supporting collaboration, which is the most demanding joint endeavor, also leads to understanding and supporting the other less demanding forms of interaction.

In collaboration, parties are more closely aligned in the sense of "working together" to reach the desired outcome, rather than that outcome being achieved through "individualistic" participation constrained by contextual factors such as those imposed by client-supplier relationships.

2.2 Requirements for collaboration

Collaboration is a difficult process and thus the chances for its success depend on a number of requirements:
  • Collaboration must have a purpose – usually translated to a joint / compatible goal or problem to be solved. It is not enough that parties have their own individual goals.

- Basic requirements or pre-conditions for collaboration include (Giesen, 2002), (Brna, 1998):
  - Parties mutually agree to collaborate, which implies accepting to share.
  - Parties know each other's capabilities.
  - Parties share a goal and keep some common vision during the collaboration process towards the achievement of the common goal.
  - Parties maintain a shared understanding of the problem at hands, which implies discussing the state of their progress (state awareness of each other).

  Sharing involves shared responsibility for both participation and decision making, shared resources, and shared accountability for the outcomes, both in terms of rewards and liabilities, as well as mutual trust. However we shall notice that sharing does not imply equality. Different parties might have different "amounts" of involvement according to their roles and commitment.
- As a process, collaboration requires setting a number of generic steps (Giesen, 2002):
  - Identify parties and bring them together.
  - Define scope of the collaboration and define desired outcomes.
  - Define the structure of the collaboration in terms of leadership, roles, responsibilities, ownership, communication means and process, decision-making, access to resources, scheduling and milestones.
  - Define policies, e.g. handling disagreements / conflicts, accountability, rewards and recognition, ownership of generated assets.
  - Define evaluation / assessment measures, mechanisms and process.
  - Identify risks and plan contingency measures.
  - Establish commitment to collaborate.
- Collaboration requires a "collaboration space", i.e. an environment to enable and facilitate the collaboration process. The characteristics and nature of this "space" depend on the form of collaboration. Collaboration can take place at the same time (*synchronous collaboration*) or at different times (*asynchronous collaboration*). It may also occur in the same place (*collocated collaboration*) or in different places (*remote* or *virtual collaboration*) (Winkler, 2002). Remote collaboration is the most relevant case in collaborative networks, which may involve both synchronous and asynchronous interactions.
- Some major points of difficulty in collaboration include (Wolff, 2005): resources, rewards, commitments, and responsibilities:
  - Resources – ownership and sharing of resources is a typical difficulty, whether it relates to resources brought in by members or resources acquired by the coalition for the purpose of performing the task.
  - Rewards – finding a fair way of determining the individual contributions to joint intellectual property creation is a rather challenging issue. Intellectual property creation is not linearly related to the proportion of resources invested by each party. At the very base of this issue is the need to reach a common *perception* of the exchanged values, which requires the definition of a benefits model and a system of incentives, based on a common value system.

    o <u>Commitments</u> – whenever there is an attack or any other obstacle to the collaboration do parties respond as a whole, facing the consequences together, or do each one try to "save its neck"?

    o <u>Responsibilities</u> – a typical phenomenon in collective endeavors is the dilution of responsibility. A successful collaboration depends on sharing the responsibilities, both during the process of achieving the goal, and also the liabilities after the end of the collaboration.

Therefore all these issues must be settled by a set of common working and sharing principles.

In spite of the difficulties of this process the motivating factor is the expectation of being able to reach results that could not be reached by parties working alone.

2.3 Collaboration and competition

To better understand collaboration it is also useful to put it in contrast with competition. Competition has been seen as one of the most successful basic mechanisms in the struggle for survival, namely in case of scarce resources. It is interesting to note that even Economics is defined as the study of "the efficient allocation of scarce resources among competing uses", and Politics is understood as "the relations between special interest groups competing for limited resources" (Kangas, 2005).

In fact, the formation of cooperation and collaboration alliances has emerged to allow more efficient competition against other entities or groups. This is typically what leads SMEs to join efforts in order to survive in turbulent markets. Also in Nature we find natural alliances that compete with others for survival – the species (Kangas, 2005). The stronger the threat is, the higher is the internal cohesion and sense of group identity.

But even inside a friendly group we often find the interplay between collaboration and competition. Internal competition happens as the means to gain more power, status, or material resources. On the other hand, if we consider the creative facet of collaboration – creating together – we can also find the interplay among the two concepts (Denise, 1999). In fact innovation very often results from healthy confrontation of different ideas and perspectives. A fruitful collaboration space shall allow for some degree of divergence. Often enough creativity is resulted from challenges to the current directions, norms, or assumptions. It is however fundamental that such divergences do not undermine the basic foundations of the group cohesiveness, such as trust, fairness, and sharing.

Finding the right balance between collaboration and competition in order to not only efficiently react to external threats or opportunities but also to excel individual capabilities and breed innovation is a major challenge for the definition of the governance policies, working/sharing principles, and supporting tools and infrastructures for collaborative networks.

3. BASE COLLABORATIVE ORGANIZATIONAL FORMS

Given the large diversity of manifestations of collaborative networks in different application domains, often using different terminologies, it is important to define a taxonomy of the various organizational forms (Camarinha-Matos, Afsarmanesh, 2005, 2006a, 2007a, b) as well as providing a working definition, though informal of the terms used. Below we provide a set of definitions (referred to as *Definitions 3.1 to 3.22*), addressing different kinds of collaborative networks, as also indicated in Figure 3.1. The remaining elements of this Figure are also defined within the text of this section.

Definition 3.1: A **collaborative network** (CN) is a network consisting of a variety of entities (e.g. organizations and people) that are largely autonomous, geographically distributed, and heterogeneous in terms of their operating environment, culture, social capital and goals, but that collaborate to better achieve common or compatible goals, and whose interactions are supported by computer network.

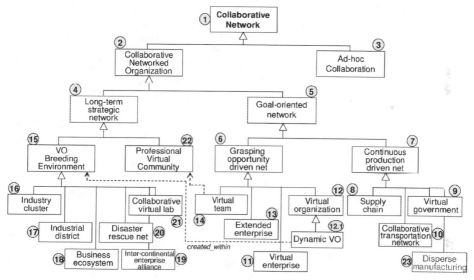

Figure 3 - Examples of Collaborative Networks

Although not all, most forms of collaborative networks imply some kind of *organization* over the activities of their constituents, identifying roles for the participants, and some governance rules. Therefore, we can consider:

Definition 3.2: **Collaborative networked organization** (CNO) – a collaborative network possessing some form of organization in terms of structure of membership, activities, definition of roles of the participants, and following a set of governance principles and rules.

Definition 3.3: **Ad-hoc collaborative** – a "spontaneous" form of collaboration

*Example: various **ad-hoc collaboration processes** can take place in virtual communities, namely those that are not business oriented – e.g. individual citizens contributions in case of a natural disaster, or simple gathering of individuals for a social cause. These are cases where people or organizations may volunteer to collaborate hoping to improve a general aim, with no pre-plan and/or structure on participants' roles and how their activities should proceed.*

without a precise structure or pre-defined organization.

Among the CNOs, we can distinguish between long-term strategic alliances and goal-oriented networks:

> *Definition 3.4*: **Long-term strategic network** or **breeding environments** – a strategic alliance established with the purpose of being prepared for participation in collaboration opportunities, and where in fact not collaboration but **cooperation** is practiced among their **members**. In other words, they are alliances aimed at offering the conditions and environment to support rapid and fluid configuration of collaboration networks, when opportunities arise.

> *Definition 3.5*: **Goal-oriented network** – a CN in which intense **collaboration** (towards a common goal or a set of compatible goals) is practiced among their **partners.**

Goal-oriented networks can themselves be sub-divided into:

> *Definition 3.6*: **Grasping opportunity driven network** – a CN driven by the aim of grasping a single (collaboration) opportunity and that dissolves after the goal is accomplished.

> *Definition 3.7*: **Continuous *production* driven network** – a CN driven by or oriented to continuous production / service provision activities.

In goal-oriented networks, the case of ***Continuous-production driven*** includes those networks that have a long-term duration and remain relatively stable during that duration, with a clear definition of members' roles along the value chain. Typical examples include:

> *Definition 3.8: **Supply chains*** – a stable long-term network of enterprises each having clear roles in the manufacturing value chain, covering all steps from initial product design and the procurement of raw materials, through production, shipping, distribution, and warehousing until a finished product is delivered to a customer.

Example: This is the most classical example of networks of enterprises that work in a cooperative way. Examples can be found in all industrial sectors.

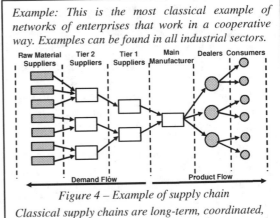

Figure 4 – Example of supply chain

Classical supply chains are long-term, coordinated, and quasi-static structures.

> *Definition 3.9: **Virtual government*** – an alliance of governmental organizations (e.g. city hall, tax office, cadastre office, and civil infrastructures office) that combine their services through the use of computer networks to provide

integrated services to the citizen through a common front-end.

More recently the principles of collaboration are being applied in other domains leading to new collaboration forms, such as:

> *Example: Most of the so-called e-government initiatives do not correspond to this concept as they basically provide access to government services through the web but do not integrate services involving various governmental organizations. A real collaborative network in e-government should "hide" from the "customer" (i.e. the citizen) the actual organizational structure of the various governmental entities and provide a unique "front-end" to the citizen.*

Definition 3.10:
Collaborative transportation networks – a long-term CN involving a diversity of actors such as road management entities, logistic operators, parking management entities, gas stations, banks, etc. in order to provide integrated transportation services.

> *Example: The "Via Verde" organization in Portugal is an example of such innovative network (Osorio, Camarinha-Matos, 2006).*

The other case of CNOs within the Goal-oriented networks is labeled as **Grasping-opportunity driven** CNOs, which are dynamically formed to answer a specific collaboration opportunity and will dissolve once their mission is accomplished. Examples include (Camarinha-Matos, Afsarmanesh, 1999, 2005):

*Definition 3.11: **Virtual enterprise** (VE) – represents a temporary alliance of enterprises that come together to share skills or core competencies and resources in order to better respond to business opportunities, and whose cooperation is supported by computer networks.*

> *Example: A temporary consortium of independent companies involved in a major construction (e.g. new bridge) and that use a computer network and ICT tools to support their collaboration and dissolve after the delivery of the construction product.*

It shall be noted that the term "virtual enterprise" has been often used in the literature with slightly different meanings. For instance, some authors also include in the definition the long-term strategic alliances.

*Definition 3.12: **Virtual Organization** (VO) – represents a concept similar to a virtual enterprise, comprising a set of (legally) independent organizations that share resources and skills to achieve its mission / goal, but that is not limited to an alliance of profit enterprises. A virtual enterprise is therefore, a particular case of virtual organization.*

*Definition 3.12.1: **Dynamic Virtual Organization** – typically refers to a VO that is established in a short time to respond to a competitive market opportunity, and has a short life cycle, dissolving when the short-term purpose of the VO is accomplished.*

Definition 3.13: **Extended Enterprise** (EE) – represents a concept typically applied to an organization in which a dominant enterprise "extends" its boundaries to all or some of its suppliers. An extended enterprise can be seen as a particular case of a virtual enterprise (in case of a temporary and goal-oriented extended enterprise) or of a supply chain (in the case of a long-term structure).

> *Example: A typical example of extended enterprise can be found in the automotive industry. The car maker, which is mainly responsible for the final assembly, has a dominant role over its network of suppliers. This dominance is reflected in the imposition of tough contractual conditions, namely in terms of quality, delivery times, etc, but also in terms of tools and methods to be used.*

Definition 3.14: **Virtual team** (VT) – is similar to a VE but formed by humans, not organizations, a virtual team is a temporary group of professionals that work together towards a common goal such as realizing a consultancy job, a joint project, etc, and that use computer networks as their main interaction environment.

> *Example: A group of free-lancing engineers based in different geographical locations can be organized as a virtual team in order to jointly perform a consultancy project.*

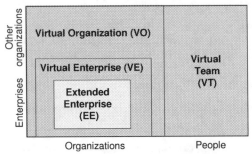

Figure 5 - Grasping-opportunity CNs

The term "virtual" in the above organizations comes from the fact that these networks act or appear to act as a single entity, thanks to their organized communication and coordination mechanisms enabled by computer networks, although they are (usually) not a single legal entity, they may not have a physical headquarter, and are typically geographically distributed.

Examples of **long-term strategic networks** include *VO breeding environments* (Camarinha-Matos, Afsarmanesh, 2003, 2005a, 2005b), (Afsarmanesh, Camarinha-Matos, 2005) and *professional virtual communities*.

Definition 3.15: **VO Breeding environment** (VBE) – represents an association of organizations and a number of related supporting institutions, adhering to a base long term cooperation agreement, and adoption of common operating principles and infrastructures, with the main goal of increasing their preparedness towards rapid configuration of temporary alliances for collaboration in potential Virtual Organizations. Namely, when a business opportunity is identified by one member (acting as a broker), a subset of VBE organizations can be selected to form a VE/VO.

Earlier cases of VBEs were mostly focused on a regional basis, e.g. industry clusters, industry districts, and business ecosystem. Besides the production / services focus, a large number of more recent VBEs focus in new areas, e.g. science and virtual laboratories, crises management (Afsarmanesh, Camarinha-Matos, 2007). Some examples include:

> *Example: A well known example of VBE is Virtuelle Fabrik which is a network of about 70 small and medium enterprises in the metal-mechanics sector, located in Switzerland. A basic ICT infrastructure is used as a communications platform and some level of commonality of business practices and agreed cooperation rules. When a business opportunity if found by any member, acting as a broker, a virtual enterprise is formed with a selected subset of enterprises.*
>
> *Another interesting example is the Swiss Microtech that involves a sub-network of SMEs in Europe and a complementary sub-network of organizations in China.*
>
> *Other relevant examples include IECOS (Mexico), ISOIN (Spain), CeBeNetwork (Germany), Supply Network Shannon (Ireland), etc.*

Definition 3.16: **Industry cluster** – is one of the earliest forms of VO breeding environments, consisting of a group of companies, typically located in the same geographic region and operating in a common business sector, that keep some "binds" with each other in order to increase their general competitiveness in the larger area. These binds may include sharing some buyer-supplier relationships, common technologies and tools, common buyers, distribution channels or common labor pools, all contributing to some form of cooperation or collaboration when business opportunities arise. Earlier forms of clusters did not require a strong ICT infrastructure but more and more collaboration resorts to such support.

> *Example: The cluster of mould makers in Portugal. Being located in the same geographical region (Marinha Grande), these companies show some similarity in terms of practices, methods of work, used tools, etc. Often they collaborate in joint projects (workload sharing), but they are not yet organized as a full VBE.*

Definition 3.17: **Industrial district** – is a term mostly used in Italy that represents a concept quite similar to an industry cluster. It can be focused on one single sector or cover a number of sectors in a given region.

> *Example: The textile district of Lecco, Italy, which brings together companies specialized in the production of furnishing fabrics, especially jacquard and velvets, that aim at keeping high quality standards, propensity for innovation, strong interaction between firms and take advantage of the significant territorial centralization.*

Another organizational structure that shares some characteristics with the above examples is the case of **incubators**. An incubator (of new companies) represents a pool of small companies in their early phase, co-located in the same geographical space, possibly covering different sectors, and that share some basic infrastructures (communications and other generic services) as well as consultancy support in order to evolve towards mature organizations. However, traditional incubators are not yet real VBEs as they usually do not collaborate much in joint business opportunities. Nevertheless it would be reasonable to imagine a next generation of incubators "absorbing" the goals, principles and mechanisms of a VBE.

> *Definition 3.18: **Business ecosystems** –* also sometimes called digital ecosystem, is similar to a cluster or industry district, although it is not limited to one sector but rather tends to cover the key sectors within the geographical region. A business ecosystem is inspired by the mechanisms of the biological ecosystems, try to preserve local specificities, tradition, and culture, and frequently benefit from (local) government incentives. In most aspects business ecosystems simply represents a renaming of the industrial district concept. Namely, differences are subtle and can perhaps be found only in a clearer emphasis on the involvement of a diversity of their actors – the *living forces* of a region – in addition to companies, and a more intense use of advanced ICT tools to support collaboration.

> *Definition 3.19: **Inter-continental enterprise alliance** –* a special case of VBE involving sub-networks of enterprises in different continents.
>
> *Example: The association of the Swiss Microtech network with a Chinese network (DecoChina) is an example of intercontinental VBE.*

> *Definition 3.20: **Disaster rescue networks** –* a strategic alliance of governmental / non-governmental organizations specialized in rescue operations in case of disasters is another recent form of VBE aimed at facilitating a rapid and well-coordinated response in case of a disaster. This VBE could have a local / regional coverage or a global geographic span.

> *Definition 3.21: **Virtual Laboratory (VL) / e-science networks** –* represent the alliance of autonomous research organizations, each having their own resources (equipments, tools, data and
>
> *Example: The VL-e project is an example of a large Dutch initiative to develop support models and tools and establish virtual labs for e-science.*
>
> information related to their past experiments, etc.), enabling their researchers, located in different geographically-spread centers to be recognized and considered for taking part in potential opportunity based problem-solving collaborations (forming a kind of VO for each problem solving). During a problem-solving collaboration process, it is typical that some expensive lab equipments owned by one or more organizations is made available for (remote) use by the other collaboration partners.

VBE is thus the more recent term that was coined to cover these cases and clearly extends their scope to both regional / global coverage, single / multi-specialty sector, and for-profit / non-profit organizations.

A graphical illustration of the coverage of these organizational forms is shown in

Fig. 6 and Fig. 7 (improved from Camarinha-Matos, Afsarmanesh, 2007b).

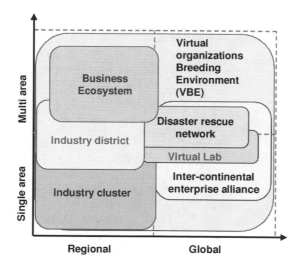

Figure 6 – Examples of long-term strategic alliances

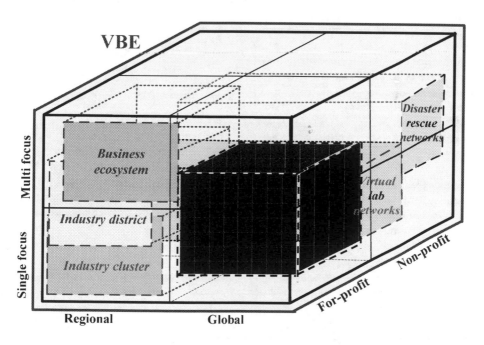

Figure 7 – Long-term strategic alliances – various views

A similar long-term organization is the Professional virtual community, as defined below.

*Definition 3.22: **Professional virtual community** -* an alliance of professional individuals, and provide an environment to facilitate the agile and fluid formation of Virtual Teams (VTs), similar to what VBE aims to provide for the VOs.

When a business opportunity happens (e.g. a design project or consultation activity), similarly to the VO creation, a temporary coalition of experts – a Virtual Team (VT) – can be rapidly formed according to the specific needs of that business opportunity.

> *Example: Associations of free-lancer knowledge workers (e.g. engineers, consultants).*
> *One such case is the PROJEKTWERK, founded in 1999, that includes about 4500 freelancers and small enterprises. This organization offers functionalities to: Publish profiles, Submit bid invitations, Search for cooperation, and Partners search.*

Simultaneously at the shop-floor level a convergent phenomenon is observed. More and more manufacturing systems are composed of autonomous (progressively more intelligent) components / resources, interconnected by computer networks (a truly ubiquitous computing and sensing environment) forming "coalitions" that need to be easily re-configured as driven by the needs of flexibility and agility. The traditional paradigm of control systems is giving pace to other mechanisms (e.g. coordination, negotiation, fuzzy reasoning, contracting) that are characteristic of collaborative networks, as seen in the most innovative recent proposals for advanced **evolvable manufacturing systems** architectures (Onori et al, 2006), (Frei et al, 2007).

> *Example: The COBASA architecture applies the collaborative networks paradigm to re-configurability of manufacturing shop-floors (Barata, Camarinha-Matos, 2003).*

Several other forms of collaborative networks are emerging as a result of both the progress on the information and communication technologies and the progress on the understanding and definition of collaboration mechanisms and supporting frameworks. New manifestations of CN might require revision of the taxonomy. For instance, the term **disperse manufacturing network** is being used to represent networks of manufacturing entities that can be seen as partly supply chain and partly VBE, depending on the particular instantiation.

Therefore, the paradigm of **Collaborative Networks** and the corresponding new discipline (Camarinha-Matos, Afsarmanesh, 2005) provides a uniform paradigm to address such complex and highly dynamic systems.

4. CONCLUSIONS

With the fast developments in collaborative networks, it is becoming very relevant to make an effort to systematize and structure the existing knowledge, first in order to facilitate mutual understanding among the members of this community; second as a step towards the elaboration of a sound theoretical foundation to boost the developments of collaborative networks and better support their management and operation. Such effort includes both a clarification of the base concepts and the elaboration of a taxonomy of collaborative forms. A number of European projects such as THINKcreative, VOSTER, ECOLEAD and others have been contributing towards this aim. The definitions and taxonomy presented in this article are a partial result of these efforts. Nevertheless, they should be considered as "working definitions" since new developments and further progress in the theoretical foundation will certainly lead to more refined propositions.

Acknowledgements. This work was funded in part by the European Commission through the ECOLEAD project.

5. REFERENCES

1. Afsarmanesh, H., Camarinha-Matos, L.M. (2005). A framework for management of virtual organizations breeding environments. In Collaborative networks and their breeding environments, Springer, pp. 35-48.
2. Afsarmanesh, H., Camarinha-Matos, L.M. (2007). Towards a semi-typology of virtual organization breeding environments. In Proceedings of COA'07 – 8th IFAC Symposium on Cost-Oriented Automation, Habana, Cuba, 12-14 Feb 2007.
3. Barata, J.; Camarinha-Matos, L. M. (2003). Coalitions of manufacturing components for shopfloor agility, in Int. Journal of Networking and Virtual Organizations, Vol. 2, Nº 1, 2003, pp 50-77.
4. Brna, P. (1998). Models of collaboration. *In Proceedings of BCS'98* - XVIII Congresso Nacional da Sociedade Brasileira de Computação 3rd-7th August 1998, Belo Horizonte, Brazil.
5. Camarinha-Matos, L. M. & Abreu, A. (2003). Towards a foundation for virtual organizations. In Proceedings of Business Excellence 2003 – 1st Int. Conference on Performance measures, Benchmarking, and Best Practices in New Economy, Guimarães, Portugal, 10-13 Jun 2003.
6. Camarinha-Matos, L. M. & Afsarmanesh, H. (2004). Formal modeling methods for collaborative networks. In L. M. Camarinha-Matos & H. Afsarmanesh (Eds.): Collaborative Networked Organizations – A research agenda for emerging business models, cap. 6.3. Boston, USA: Kluwer Academic Publishers.
7. Camarinha-Matos, L. M. & Afsarmanesh, H. (2005). Collaborative networks: A new scientific discipline. *J. Intelligent Manufacturing, 16(4-5)*, pp439-452.
8. Camarinha-Matos, L. M.& Afsarmanesh, H. (2006a). Collaborative Networks – Value creation in a knowledge society. In K. Wang, G. Kovacs, M. J. Wozny, & M. Fang (Eds.): *Knowledge Enterprise: Proceedings of Prolamat 2006*. Boston, USA: Springer.
9. Camarinha-Matos, L. M. & Afsarmanesh, H. (2006b). A modeling framework for collaborative networked organizations. In L. M. Camarinha-Matos, H. Afsarmanesh, & M. Olus (Eds.): *Network-centric collaboration and Supporting Frameworks*. Boston, USA: Springer.
10. Camarinha-Matos, L. M. & Afsarmanesh, H. (2007a). Concept of Collaboration. In: Encyclopedia of Networked and Virtual Organizations (G. Putnik, M. Cunha, Eds.), Idea Group Inc.
11. Camarinha-Matos, L. M. & Afsarmanesh, H. (2007b). Classes of collaborative networks. In: Encyclopedia of Networked and Virtual Organizations (G. Putnik, M. Cunha, Eds.), Idea Group Inc.

12. Denise, L. (1999). Collaboration vs. C-Three (Cooperation, Coordination, and Communication). In *INNOVATING*, 7(3), Spring 1999.
13. Frei, R.; Barata, J.; Di Marzo Serugendo, G. (2007). "A Complexity Theory Approach to Evolvable Production Systems", In Proceedings of the International Workshop on Multi-Agent Robotic Systems (MARS 2007), Peter Sapaty and Joaquim Filipe (Eds), INSTICC Press, pp 44-53, May 2007, Portugal.
14. Giesen, G.(2002). *Creating collaboration: A process that works!,* Greg Giesen & Associates.
15. Himmelman, A. T. (2001). On Coalitions and the Transformation of Power Relations: Collaborative Betterment and Collaborative Empowerment. In *American Journal of Community Psychology, 29(2).*
16. Kangas, S.(2005). Spectrum Five: Competition vs. Cooperation. In "The long FAQ on Liberalism", http://www.huppi.com/kangaroo/LiberalFAQ.htm#Backspectrumfive.
17. Katzy, B.; Zang, C.; Löh, H. (2005). Reference models for virtual organizations. In *Virtual Organizations – Systems and practices*, Springer.
18. Onori, M. and Barata, José A. and Frei, R.. 2006. Evolvable Assembly Systems Basic Principles. In: BASYS'06 , Information Technology for Balanced Manufacturing Systems, 04-06 Sep 2006, Ontario, Canada.
19. Osório, A.L.; Camarinha-Matos, L. M. (2006). Towards a distributed process execution platform for collaborative networks. In: Proceedings of BASYS'07, Information Technology for Balanced Manufacturing Systems (W. Shen, Ed.) (Springer), Niagara Falls, Ontario, Canada.
20. Pollard, D. (2005). Will That Be Coordination, Cooperation, or Collaboration? Blog, 25 Mar 2005. http://blogs.salon.com/0002007/2005/03/25.html#a1090
21. Winkler, R. (2002). Keywords and Definitions Around "Collaboration". *SAP Design Guild*, Edition 5, 12 Sep 2002.
22. Wolff, T. (2005). Collaborative Solutions – True Collaboration as the Most Productive Form of Exchange. In *Collaborative Solutions Newsletter*, Tom Wolff & Associates.

2.4
The ARCON modeling framework [*]

A framework is defined for ARCON reference modeling, introducing multiple modeling perspectives of: Environment characteristics, life cycle stages, and modeling intents. This novel modeling framework takes into account contributions from previous related works, mainly on enterprise modeling, and extends them further to the context of collaborative networked organizations, aiming at provision of a comprehensive environment for modeling the variety of cases of collaborative, namely the VO Breeding Environment, Virtual Organization, Professional Virtual Community, and Virtual Team.

1. INTRODUCTION

Modeling complex systems requires a proper framework to capture their complexity. Collaborative Networks (CNs) inherit their complexity from both aspects related to **collaborations** and aspects related to **networks**, and thus are no exception to this rule. Inspired by the modeling frameworks introduced earlier in the literature related to these two areas (Camarinha-Matos, Afsarmanesh, 2007), (Katzy, Zhang, Loeh, 2005), (Tolle, Bernus, Vesterager, 2002), and considering the complexity of CNs (Camarinha-Matos, Afsarmanesh, 2005a, 2005b, 2004), as well as their wide variety of aspects, features, and constituting elements, the ARCON (<u>A</u> <u>R</u>eference model for <u>C</u>ollaborative <u>N</u>etworks) modeling framework is developed. In order to comprehensively and systematically cover all relevant aspects of the CNs, the framework of ARCON divides this complexity into a number of perspectives, as addressed in details in Section 2.

The vision behind the development of ARCON reference model for collaborative networked organizations is to develop a generic abstract representation – intended as an authoritative basis - for understanding the involved entities and significant relationships among these entities. The reference model is also intended to be used as a basis for derivation (specialization) of other specific models for particular cases in various manifestations of CNs (Camarinha-Matos, Afsarmanesh, 2007).

In other words, the aim of developing the reference model for CNs, and more specifically to the most relevant case of collaborative networked organizations (CNOs), and the specific derivations/specializations to its variety of cases is to enhance the understandability of its related concepts for the purposes of discussion among researchers, education, as well as for designing architectures for its system

[*] By *H. Afsarmanesh, L. M. Camarinha-Matos*

development. Considering this aim, preferably the ARCON reference model shall be based on a *small number of unifying concepts* addressing the most generic elements for modeling different CNOs.

In ideal terms, the most important attributes characterizing a reference model for a complex system such as ARCON, shall include:

- **Simplicity** (to increase its usability by CNO's stakeholders) – easy to understand, clear, not technical, and purely logical.
- **Comprehensive capturing of the unifying concepts** (towards holistic understanding of CNOs) – as much as possible addressing the CNO in its entirety; so that any element can be mapped against it to understand where they fit within the context of the CNO as a whole.
- **Neutrality** (applying a base uniform presentation of CNO notations) – being defined totally independent of the tools or methodologies that can further model or implement different aspects of CNOs, and such that any tool or any methodology can be mapped against it, in order to understand their implicit trade-offs (what they can or cannot do).

Stakeholders
In the development of ARCON, the following main stakeholders are considered:

- Researchers – The main target group for ARCON are CNs researchers that may use the reference model as a consolidated basis for further conceptual developments.
- Engineers and other practitioners – Professionals with a reasonable background and experience on CNs can also use the reference model as a basis for their practical developments as it is supposed to clarify the main concepts and their inter-relationships. However, clearly the ARCON alone cannot be used as a text book by people not familiar with the area of CNs.
- Decision makers – The most general components of ARCON, i.e. high level definitions of main concepts, are also useful to provide background knowledge about the area to industrial decision makers and other development policy makers.
- Educators – Similarly to researchers, educators can use ARCON models as a basis for introduction of concepts and preparation of focused training material.

Limitations
Next to the high level aims considered for developing ARCON, it is necessary to also address and consider the following limitation. Provision of theoretical definitions for ARCON components, although could support the verification of their consistency and correctness, are not fruitful at this stage of ARCON's life cycle due to the following main reasons:

1) It would not be suitable for supporting the majority of the current ARCON's stakeholders,

2) At the current stage of the CNO's reference model definition, many of the ARCON's concepts are either being introduced for the first time or are only semi-formally defined, and thus require further elaboration and research, before finalization.

2. MODELING PERSPECTIVES

For the purpose of modeling all features of the CNO components, at the highest level of abstraction, three perspectives are identified and defined in the ARCON framework, as represented in Figure 1.

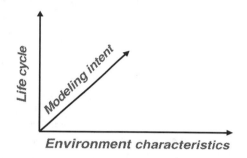

Figure 1 – Modeling perspectives in ARCON

The first defined perspective addresses the timing cycle of different CNO life stages. This perspective captures the evolution of CNOs and the diversity during their entire life cycle, represented by the vertical axis, labeled as "Life cycle stages". The second defined perspective focuses on capturing the CNO environment characteristics, represented by the horizontal axis, labeled as "Environment characteristics". This perspective further includes two subspaces (points of view) that comprehensively cover, the internal elements characteristics (labeled "Endogenous Elements") of CNOs, as well as the external interactions characteristics (labeled "Exogenous Interactions") that address the logical surrounding of the CNOs. The third defined perspective for ARCON reference modeling is related to the different intents for the modeling of CNO features, represented by the diagonal axis, labeled as "modeling intents". This perspective addresses the three possible modeling stages for CNO elements, from the general representation, to the specific models (e.g. using a specific modeling approach or theory), and finally to the detailed specification of the implementation architecture for CNO element. These three perspectives are further described below.

When planning these three perspectives, the following main usages were considered for the ARCON development:
- o Providing a model that can be instantiated to capture the definition of all potential CNOs.
- o Supporting the reusability and portability of its defined concepts.
- o Facilitating the co-working and co-development among the stakeholders.
- o Providing the high level base for design and building of the architectural specifications of modular CNO components.
- o Providing insight into the modeling tools/theories that are appropriate for mapping different CNO components (in further research).

3. LIFE-CYCLE PERSPECTIVE

In a typical (long-term) organization, usually its operation stage constitutes its entire livelihood. In other words most successful organizations spend only a negligible fraction of their life time on setting up and dissolution stages. Therefore, earlier research on reference modeling of enterprises did not need to elaborate much on its life cycle perspective. But unlike single organizations, for a wide variety of classes of CNOs (e.g. the state of the art in emerging clusters/networks of organizations in manufacturing industry) their creation stage, as well as their dissolution or metamorphosis stages, are complex and take up considerable effort. This is certainly not a negligible fraction of time, and due to the involved complexity, it requires receiving proper attention during the build up of the reference model. Our earlier study of the life cycle stages for CNOs has revealed 5 main common stages for the CNO's life cycle. These stages also match some typical pattern of the self-organizing systems in chaordic systems of thinking (van Eijnaten, 2005), as presented on the left side of the Fig. 2. Therefore, presence of the CNO's life cycle as a perspective in the ARCON reference modeling framework is justified, to guarantee the coverage of all stages of its life span.

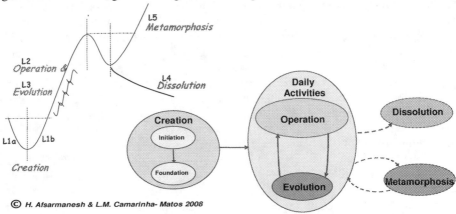

© *H. Afsarmanesh & L.M. Camarinha- Matos 2008*

Figure 2 – CNO's life cycle stages

As illustrated in Fig. 2, the **CNO-Life-Cycle** perspective consists of a number of stages:
- **L1. Creation** – The creation stage deals with incubation, system parameterization, databases creation, generation and definition of ontology, data/information loading, etc., and can be divided into two phases, namely:
  - ○ (i) **L1a. Initiation and Recruiting**, dealing with the strategic planning and initial incubation of the CNO, and
  - ○ (ii) **L1b. Foundation**, dealing with the constitution and start up.
- **L2. Operation** – Certainly the most important phase, when the CNO actually operates towards achieving its goals. Depending on the type of CNOs, different tasks will be executed at this stage. For example, during this stage, the Virtual organizations Breeding Environments – VBEs (Afsarmanesh, Camarinha-Matos, 2005), involve in member registration, establishment/maintenance of partners directory of profiles/competencies, VO establishment and contracting, etc. But

the VOs during this stage are mostly focused on co-developing their aimed products/services.

- *L3. Evolution* – During the daily operation stage of a CNO, it becomes necessary to make some changes to the CNO, e.g. to its membership, structural relationships, roles of its members, etc. Therefore, the CN can go through daily adjustment or evolution process simultaneous to its operation stage.

- *L4. Dissolution*– A short-term CNO, such as a Virtual Organization (VO), will typically dissolve after accomplishing its goals.

- *L5. Metamorphosis* – In the case of a long-term alliance, e.g. a VBE or PVC – Professional Virtual Communities (Bifulco, Santoro, 2005), considering its valuable bag of assets gradually collected during its operation, its dissolution is very unusual. Usually instead of dissolution, it is much more probable that such a CNO goes through a *metamorphosis* stage, where its general form and/or purpose can evolve. Therefore, metamorphosis may be considered as a *huge evolution leap* within the CN. Such stage may involve the transfer of collected knowledge/information, as well as the members to a third party.

4. ENVIRONMENT CHARACTERISTICS PERSPECTIVE

The reference model for CNs or more specifically collaborative networked organizations (CNOs) shall comprehensively represent its environment characteristics, including both its internal aspects, as well as the influence/interaction from the external aspects in its environment (Fig. 3). Namely, to understand and model the network both from inside (as in the traditional systems modeling) addressing its *Endogenous elements*, and from outside (i.e. the interactions between the CNO and its surrounding environment) addressing its *Exogenous Interactions* (Camarinha-Matos, Afsarmanesh, 2006a, b). Therefore, these endogenous and exogenous aspects constitute two subspaces of the CNO's environment characteristics, as further addressed below.

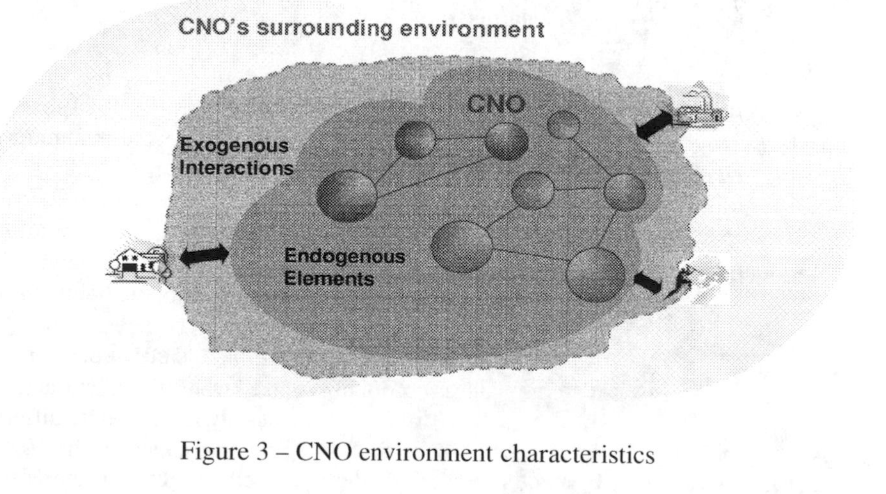

Figure 3 – CNO environment characteristics

Endogenous Elements (Endo-E) subspace. This subspace of the CNO's *environment characteristic* perspective aims at the abstraction of its characteristics *from inside* (Fig. 4), namely the identification of the main set of elements/properties that can together capture and represent CNOs. As discussed earlier, abstraction and classification of CNO's Endo-E is challenging due to the large number of their distinct and varied entities, concepts, functionality, rules and regulations, etc. inside the CNOs. In addition to various tangible elements and resources, in some forms of CNOs, e.g. the Virtual Organization Breeding Environments (VBEs), the reference model shall also capture and represent the networks of organizations configured/established within this CNO, in which every CNO participant can play a specific role and have heterogeneous relationships with other CNO participants. Furthermore, there are certain rules of behavior that either constitute the norms, or shall be obeyed by the CNO participants, and needless to say that in every CNO there are a set of activities and functionalities that also need to be abstracted in its reference model. To better characterize these diverse set of aspect, **four dimensions** are proposed and defined to cover all elements of the Endo-E subspace within the reference model, as follows:

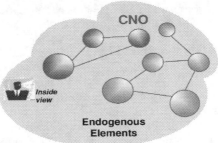

Figure 4 – Endo-E view

• E1 - Structural dimension.

The structure/composition of the constituting elements of CNOs, namely its participants and their relationships, as well as the roles performed by those elements, and any other compositional characteristics of the network such as its typology, etc. are addressed by this dimension. This perspective is introduced and applied in many disciplines (e.g. systems engineering, software engineering, economy, politics, cognitive sciences, manufacturing, etc.), although with different "wording" and diversified tools.

• E2 - Componential dimension.

The individual tangible/intangible elements in the CNO's network, e.g. different resources such as the human elements, software and hardware resources, as well as information and knowledge are addressed by this dimension. Not all these elements are "physical" or tangible in a strict sense; in fact some are conceptual, e.g. the collected knowledge in CNOs. Nevertheless, these elements together represent the "things" or components out of which the network is built. Furthermore, the componential dimension also consists of the intangible ontology and the

description (meta-data) of the information/knowledge repositories that pertain to the CNO.

• E3 - Functional dimension.

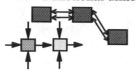
The "base functions / operations" running/supported at the network, and time-sequenced flows of executable operations (e.g. processes) related to different phases of the CNO's life cycle are addressed by this dimension.
The methodologies and procedures running at the CNO are therefore also addressed by this dimension.

• E4 - Behavioral dimension.

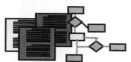
The principles, policies, and governance rules that either drive or constrain the behavior of the CNO and its members over time, are addressed by this dimension.
Included here are elements such as the principles of collaboration and rules of conduct, principles of trust, contracts, conflict resolution policies, etc.

The four specific dimensions introduced above are chosen for the reason of their "near-orthogonality" in the sense that (i) they completely cover all aspects of importance for modeling the Endo-E elements of the CNO, (ii) they are primarily disjoint in dividing this sub-space, and (iii) that if elements in different dimensions are bound to each other, then changes in one dimension can only weakly affect the elements of the other dimensions, across some region of relevance. For example in a CNO, drastically reducing the "number of workers" in one organization below certain level (a componential element in the model of an organization) may affect its nature and the "role" of this organization in the network (a structural element in the model of that organization).

It is therefore the case that in ARCON, with these four dimensions every CNO can be comprehensively defined (modeled) in relation to its Endo-E, by the collection of its four models for the dimensions, as well as a set of (weak) bindings defined across the constituents of those four models. Every such model will then represent certain set of specific (and orthogonal) aspects related to that perspective/dimension of a CNO.

An example binding that can be defined for all types of CNOs is the one addressing the dependency between the CNO's componential components (e.g. the personnel) and its structural model counterpart (e.g. the role and skill of the personnel) within a CNO. Another example binding that applies to VOs is the one addressing the connection between an organization's structural component (e.g. rights/duties of the organization in a VO) and its behavioral model counterpart (e.g. the organization's contract components in the VO).

Fig. 5 crosses the life-cycle perspective and Endogenous Elements, and exemplifies some elements of each dimension.

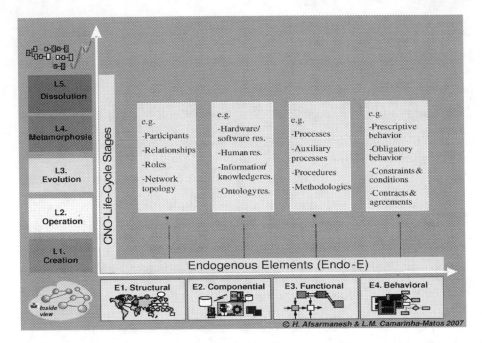

Figure 5 – Crossing CNO life cycle and the Endogenous Elements perspective

Exogenous Interactions (Exo-I) subspace. This subspace of the CNo's *environment characteristic* perspective aims perspective aims at reaching an abstract representation of the CNO as seen *from the outside* (Fig. 6), i.e. which characteristic properties the CNO reveals in its interaction with its "logical" surrounding environment. The purpose here is not to model the surrounding environment but focus on the interactions between the CNO and this environment. A CNO as a whole might interact with, influence, and be influenced by a number of "interlocutors", e.g. customers, competitors, external institutions, potential new partners. The interactions between the CNO and these external entities are quite different, the same as the way each of these entity groups looks at the CNO.

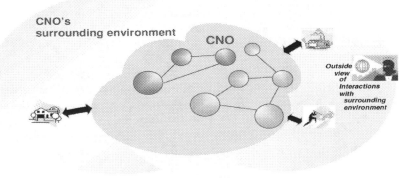

Figure 6 – Exo-I view

In order to better characterize these interactions, the following additional modeling dimensions – I1-Market, I2-Support, I3-Society, I4-Constituency - are proposed for the external or Exogenous Interactions perspective:

• I1 - Market dimension.

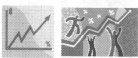

Issues related to both the interactions with "customers", representing potential beneficiaries, and "competitors" are covered by this dimension. Facets related to customers include elements such as the transactions and established commitments (contracts with customer), marketing and branding, etc. On the competitors' side issues such as market positioning, market strategy, policies, etc. can be considered. Also part of this dimension are the purpose / mission of the CNO, its value proposition, joint identity, etc.

• I2 - Support dimension.

Those issues related to support services provided by the third party institutions (outside of the CNO) are to be considered under this dimension. The Certification services, auditing, insurance services, training, accounting, and external coaching are among example related issues.

• I3 - Societal dimension.

Issues related to interactions between the CNO and the society in general are captured by this dimension. Although this perspective can have a very broad scope, the idea is to model the impacts that CNO has or potentially can have on the society, for example its impact on employment, economic sustainability of a given region, potential for attraction of new investments, as well as the constraints and facilitating elements (e.g. legal issues, public body decisions, education level) the society provides to the CNO development.

• I4 - Constituency dimension.

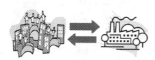

The interaction with the universe of potential new members of the CNO, i.e. the interactions with those organizations that are not part of the CNO but that the CNO might be interested in attracting them, are focused in this dimension. Therefore, general issues like sustainability of the network, attraction factors, what builds / provides a sense of community, or specific aspects such as rules of adhesion and specific "marketing" policies for members, are considered here.

Fig. 7 crosses the life-cycle perspective with the Exogenous Interactions, and exemplifies some elements of each dimension.

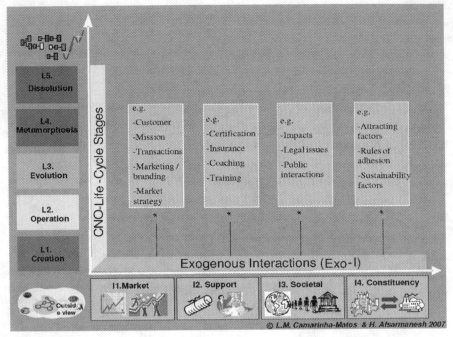

Figure 7 – Crossing CNO life cycle and Exogenous Interactions perspective

5. MODEL INTENTS PERSPECTIVE

In addition to these perspectives, a CNO reference model can be defined at multiple
levels of abstraction. Following the research practices in modeling, the following
three layers are considered in ARCON:

- **General Representation (GR) layer** – that includes the most general concepts
  and related relationships, common to all CNOs independently of the application
  domain (e.g. all kinds of VBEs independent of the area).
- **Specific Modeling (SM) layer** – an intermediate level that includes more
  detailed models focused on different classes of CNOs (the CNO typology).
- **Implementation Modeling (IM) layer** – that represents models of concrete
  CNOs.

Each of these modeling layers crosses with all of the elements in the other two
perspectives. We will further address the role of modeling intents in Section 6. Fig.
8 crosses the environment characteristics with the model intents.

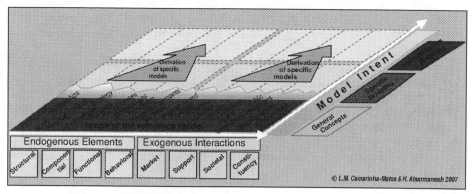

Figure 8 – Modeling intents and scope for reference model

6. THE ARCON MODELING FRAMEWORK

A comprehensive framework is thus developed for the reference modeling of CNOs that captures all of its complexity through the definition of all specific elements needed related to cross section of its three perspectives, as explained below.

Fig. 9 crosses the three perspectives addressed above in one 3D diagram.

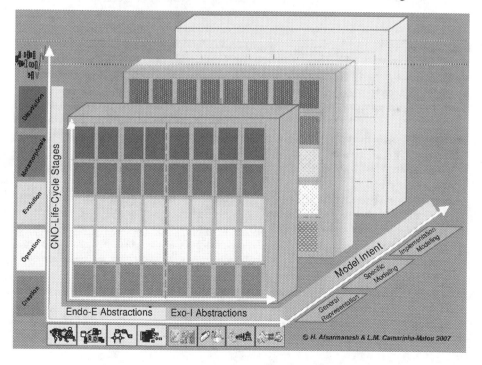

Figure 9 – ARCON Reference modeling framework

In this matrix, for the two subspaces of the *Endogenous Elements* and *Exogenous*

Interactions within the CNO **Environment characterization perspective,** their respective dimensions (E1 to E4 and I1 to I4, addressed in Section 4) are depicted as different columns. Similarly, for the CNO **Life-Cycle stages perspective**, each stage of the life cycle (L1 to L5, addressed in Section 3) is depicted as one row. The **Model Intent perspective** constitutes the third axis of the matrix, with its three respective elements addressed in 5. Each cell in the ARCON reference table therefore, represents the intersection of a particular life cycle stage with one dimension (either within the *Endogenous Elements* or *Exogenous Interactions)*, and for one specific model intent.

What will be recorded in each cell determines the "subjects" (kinds of element) that needs to be addressed and modeled in relation to these three axes. Without the proper perspectives representing each cell, the information recorded in them cannot be properly interpreted. In other words, by elimination of any of the three perspectives introduced for ARCON (from the mind), trying to describe a CNO may lack some of its aspects. Namely, this framework suggests that a CNO can be properly and comprehensively described with these three perspectives.

Each of the two environment characterization subspaces (i.e. *Endogenous Elements* and *Exogenous Interactions*) defines a point of view or a level of abstraction for the information contained in its related cells. For example, if we consider all of the cells in the single *Endogenous Elements* sub-space, we will have the abstraction of all the *subjects* that need to be defined and considered from the *Endogenous Elements'* perspective of one kind of CNO.

At the same time, the subjects contained in all the cells within a single row, such as the life cycle stage of "evolution" will provide a complete description of the CNO from that perspective. Similarly, each column in each of the two sub-spaces (e.g. the behavioral dimension of the *Endogenous Elements'* sub-space, or the constituency dimension of the *Exogenous Interactions'* subspace) captures the CNO subject for that particular dimension through the entire life cycle stages of the CNO.

For any kind of CNO, e.g. **VBE, VO, PVC**, etc., and with the model intent of **General Representation (GR)**, through the definition/representation of each *individual subject* related to all cells in this layer of its ARCON modeling framework, its *comprehensive definition*, and thus its **reference model**, can be achieved.

Furthermore, for each individual subject defined in every cell of the GR layer (e.g. the cell representing the evolution stage of the constituency Exo-I element in Figure 10) of a CNO's ARCON matrix, a number of specific models can be formalized for it, and represented at its **Specific Modeling (SM)** layer. And in the same way, if desired, one or more architectural models can be defined for any *specific model* (defined within a cell in the SM layer of the ARCON matrix, e.g. the evolution stage of the constituency Exo-I element in Figure 4.10) that will be then represented in its corresponding cell within the **Implementation Modeling (IM)** layer of the CNO's ARCON matrix.

Fig. 10 depicts the inter-relationships among the three layers of modeling intent, in relation to different models that represent the same subjects.

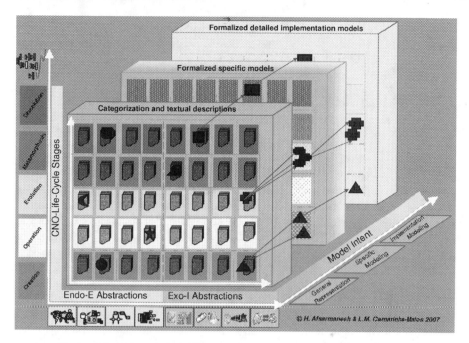

Figure 10 – Three Model intent layers and their inter-relationships

Given the base definition of reference models presented earlier, the scope of a CNO's reference model covers mainly the "General Representation" layer and it can as examples also represent some elements from the "Specific Modeling" layer. In other words, at the current stage of development of the CNO area, the first priority for a reference model for CNOs is to consolidate its most general aspects that are common to all types of CNOs. With further progress in this area of research, CNOs are better defined gradually. Therefore, it is important to also support the "maintenance of the reference model for CNOs", such that in time it can progressively and incrementally consolidate more and more specific models, as each major class of CNOs will become well developed. Chapter 2.7 of this book addresses this issue further.

In terms of representation, and considering the arguments presented above and earlier in this chapter, for the definition of the **CNO reference model** at its General Representation layer, the most **neutral** means of **textual representation** is chosen for ARCON to represent its detailed elements. Nevertheless, a structured object is further defined for each dimension, e.g. for the dimensions in the Endo-E subspace, the structured object includes: Active entity, Passive entity, Action, and Concept, as addressed in details in Chapter 2.6 of this book), where further details about the elements of CNO reference model will be textually defined.

For the other two levels of the ARCON modeling intent, depending on the specific subject/feature (e.g. within each of the cells) that need to be represented, and depending on the nature and complexity of the subject/feature, other suitable modeling tools/systems/theories shall be chosen for such representations. For example, depending on the subject/feature, the set theory, graph theory, Petri nets, deontic logic, complexity theories, multi-agent systems, federated systems, etc., can be suitable for representation of its Specific Modeling level. Similarly for the Implementation Modeling level of a subject/feature, the UML, Flowcharts, workflows, etc. can be considered.

7. COMPARISON WITH OTHER FRAMEWORKS

When attempting to establish a reference model, it is fundamental to consider the potential inputs and partial contributions from previous related works to reference modeling (Noran 2003). In the investigation and definition of the proposed modeling framework for ARCON, several relevant previous approaches introduced by other initiatives were considered. Although most related work in this area fall within the enterprise-centric stream, e.g. Zachman (Zachman 1987), VERAM (Tolle, Bernus, 2003) – that includes elements from PERA (Williams 1994), CIMOSA (Vernadat, Kosanke, 1992), and GERAM (IFIP-IFAC TFAEI, GERAM, 2003) – there are also works in this area that fall within the network-centric stream, e.g. the FEA (FEA 2005) and EGA (EGA 2005), and with SCOR (Huan 2004), (Stewart 1997), located somewhere in between, since it mostly addresses the value chain.

However, our conclusion of this study showed that for the purpose of CNO reference modeling, although the related previous works have provided valuable contributions to the understanding of several aspects of this area, they are limited when a holistic modeling is pursued. As an illustration, Table 1 summarizes the results of our analysis of the main relevant initiatives, in comparison with the needs identified for the ARCON reference modeling framework, as represented by: positive coverage (+), moderate coverage (~) and negative coverage (-) .

Table 1 – Brief summary analysis of other modeling frameworks

ARCON-Purpose Model	Modeling Target	Modeling Framework	Modeling Scope
Zachman Framework	- Single enterprise (not CNOs)	+ Good set of "dimensions" ~ different emphasis (e.g. location) ~ not clear, Endo-E / Exo-I are mixed - Confusing rows (levels, life cycle, actors)	+ Most needed modeling dimensions - Little focus on behavior within Endo-E of CNO - Little focus on Exo-I of CNO (some aspects in "Purpose")
SCOR	~ Only supply chain (no other CNOs)	+ Simple composition (client-supplier) and multi-abstraction level - Limited in terms of generality	- Can cover only process sub-dimension & performance indicators in Endo-E of CNO. - Not addressing Exo-I of CNO

ARCON-Purpose / Model	Modeling Target	Modeling Framework	Modeling Scope
VERAM[1]	~ Manufacturing CNOs (no PVC and other CNOs)	+ Good set of dimensions and abstraction levels ~ Limited in life cycle - Confusing / complex generality	+ Most modeling dimensions - Little focus on behavior within Endo-E of CNO - Little focus on Exo-I of CNO
EGA	- Grid enterprise infrastructure focus	+ Inclusion of glossary ~ Multiple levels of abstraction - Very limited in terms of generality	- Only part of the functional dimension within Endo-E of CNO - Not addressing the Exo-I of CNO
FEA	~ Governmental organizations focus	+ Inclusion of glossary + Customer orientation - Limited in terms of generality	+ Some aspects of Exo-I of CNO - Only process sub-dimension within Endo-E of CNO

8. CONCLUSIONS

Definition of a comprehensive modeling framework for CNOs is a first step in the development of a reference model for collaboration networks - ARCON. As such the ARCON modeling Framework acts as the base for consolidation of existing knowledge in this area, as well as the facilitator for its consistent further progress. This chapter offers a contribution to this purpose, by introducing a multi-perspective modeling framework for CNOs. The necessity of each of the three perspective, i.e. the environment characteristics, the life cycle stages, and the modeling intents are addressed and when applicable contrasted with other modeling frameworks. Detailed elements of each perspective are further described and exemplified. Furthermore, the visual presentation of the three dimensional ARCON reference modeling framework is illustrated and its usage for the definition of reference models for different kinds of CNOS, e.g. VBE, PVC, VO, etc. are briefly addressed. Finally, to benefit from the knowledge generated by other related research in this area, the most relevant other modeling frameworks are mentioned, and a summary of their analysis is presented, when addressing the important features required for the purpose of ARCHON modeling framework.

Acknowledgements. This work was funded in part by the European Commission through the ECOLEAD project.

---

[1] VERAM includes elements from PERA, CIMOSA and GERAM.

9. REFERENCES

Afsarmanesh, H.; Camarinha-Matos, L.M. (2005). A Framework for Management of Victual Organization Breeding Environments. In *Proceedings of PRO-VE'05 – Collaborative Networks and their Breeding Environments*, Valencia, Spain, 26-28 Sept 2005, (Springer: Boston).

Bifulco, A.; Santoro, R. (2005). A conceptual framework for professional virtual communities. In *Collaborative Networks and their Breeding Environments*, pp. 417-424, IFIP Vol. 186, 2005, (Springer: Boston).

Camarinha-Matos L.M., Afsarmanesh H. (2007). A comprehensive modeling framework for collaborative networked organizations. In *the Journal of Intelligent Manufacturing*, Springer publisher. Volume 18, Number 5, pp. 527-615, October 2007.

Camarinha-Matos, L.M.; Afsarmanesh, H. (2005-a). Collaborative networks: A new scientific discipline, *J. Intelligent Manufacturing*, 16(4-5), pp439-452.

Camarinha-Matos, L.M.; Afsarmanesh, H.; Ollus, M. (Editors) (2005-b). *Virtual Organizations – Systems and Practices*, (Springer: Boston).

Camarinha-Matos, L.M.; Afsarmanesh, H. (Editors) (2004). *Collaborative Networked Organizations – A research agenda for emerging business models*, (Springer: Boston).

EGA (2005). Enterprise Grid Alliance Reference Model, 13 Apr 2005. http://www.gridalliance.org/en/workgroups/ReferenceModel.asp

Van Eijnatten, F.M.; Putnik, G.D. (2005). A Different View of Learning and Knowledge Creation in Collaborative Networks. In *Proceedings of PRO-VE'05 – Collaborative Networks and their Breeding Environments*, Valencia, Spain, 26-28 Sept 2005, (Springer: Boston).

FEA (2005). FEA Consolidated Reference Model, May 2005, http://www.whitehouse.gov/omb/egov/documents/CRM.PDF

Huan, S. H., A review and analysis of supply chain operations reference (SCOR) model. In *Supply Chain Management: An International Journal*, 9(1), 2004, (Emerald).

IFIP-IFAC TFAEI (2003). GERAM – The generalized enterprise reference architecture and methodology, IFIP-IFAC Task Force on Architectures for Enterprise Integration, in *Handbook on Enterprise Architecture* (P. Bernus, L. Nemes, G. Schmidt, Ed.s), (Springer, Heidelberg).

Katzy, B.; Zhang, C.; Loeh, H. (2005). Reference models for virtual organizations. In *Virtual organizations: Systems and Practices*, L. M. Camarinha-Matos, H. Afsarmanesh, M. Ollus (Editors), (Springer: Boston).

Noran, O. (2003). A mapping of individual architecture frameworks (GRAI, PERA, C4ISR, CIMOSA, ZACHMAN, ARIS) onto GERAM. In *Handbook on enterprise architecture*, P. Bernus, L. Nemes, G. Schmidt (Ed.s), (Springer: Boston).

Stewart, G. (1997). Supply-chain operations reference model (SCOR): the first cross-industry framework for integrated supply-chain management. In *Logistics Information Management*, 10(2), (Emerald).

Tolle, M.; Bernus, P. (2003). Reference models supporting enterprise networks and virtual enterprises, *Int. Journal of Networking and Virtual Organisations*, 2(1), pp. 2 – 15.

Tolle, M.; Bernus, P.; Vesterager, J. (2002). Reference models for virtual enterprises. In *Collaborative business ecosystems and virtual enterprises* (L. M. Camarinha-Matos, Editor), (Kluwer Academic Publishers: Boston).

Vernadat, F.; Kosanke, K. (1992). CIM-OSA: A Reference Architecture for CIM. In *Proceedings of the IFIP TC5 / WG5.3 Eight International PROLAMAT Conference on Human Aspects in Computer Integrated Manufacturing*, FIP Transactions; Vol. B-3, (North-Holland).

Williams, T.J. (1994). The Purdue Enterprise Reference Architecture. In *Computers in Industry*, 24, (2-3) pp. 141-58.

Zachman, J. A. (1987). A Framework for Information Systems Architecture. In *IBM Systems Journal*, 26(3).

2.5
ARCON reference models
for collaborative networks

L. M. Camarinha-Matos, H. Afsarmanesh,
E. Ermilova, F. Ferrada, A. Klen, T. Jarimo

*Following the ARCON modeling framework, a comprehensive set of concepts
and entities, covering both the Endogenous Elements and Exogenous
Interactions perspectives of collaborative networks, are collected and defined.
Such collection represents a first proposal for a reference model for
collaborative networks. The establishment of a recognized reference model is
certainly a long-term activity of which this work represents a first step.*

1. INTRODUCTION

A reference model for collaborative networks (CNs) is a generic conceptual model
that synthesizes and organizes the base concepts, principles and recommended
practices for such networks. Considering the ARCON modeling framework
(Camarinha-Matos, Afsarmanesh, 2006, 2007, 2008), the reference model
corresponds basically to the "General Representation" layer (Fig. 1).

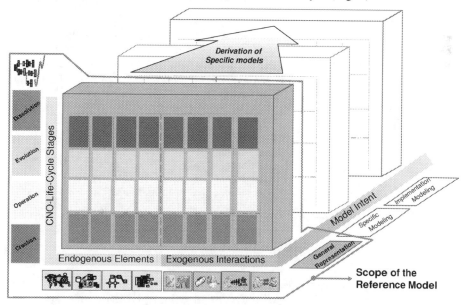

Figure 1 – Reference model in the ARCON framework context

The reference model is generic and not directly applicable to concrete cases. It rather provides the basis for an organized derivation of other specific models closer to these concrete cases. It is therefore intended as a basis or guide to facilitate the understanding of the area of CN and to streamline the creation of focused models for its manifestations.

The elaboration of a reference model for CN is a long-term task. Taking as example the case of reference modeling for single enterprises, it can be noticed that those initiatives that gained some success (e.g. CIM-OSA, GERAM, Zachman) took many years to develop (Noran, 2003), (Tolle, Bernus, 2003), and decades to get known by their target communities. Therefore, this work can only be considered as a first attempt to establish a reference model for CN. Although a large number of experts contributed, directly or indirectly, to the refinement of the concepts here presented, considerable research effort will be needed in the future. Nevertheless it is our belief that this proposal constitutes an instrument to facilitate a common understanding of the paradigm and a comprehensive starting basis for further developments.

2. APPROACH TO IDENTIFY GENERAL CONCEPTS

Departing from the ARCON modeling framework (Camarinha-Matos, Afsarmanesh, 2007), it is now necessary to identify and model the elements that should go into each "cell" of this framework for CNs. For this purpose, a "bottom-up" approach was applied (Fig. 2): We first applied (and validated) the framework to various CN cases, more specifically collaborative networked organizations (CNO), namely the virtual organization breeding environment (VBE), virtual organization (VO), professional virtual community (PVC), and virtual team (VT), the specific cases studied in the ECOLEAD project (Camarinha-Matos et al, 2005). In this way the knowledge developed in the various technical focus areas of the project was organized and integrated. Furthermore, by extraction of the "common" elements and concepts out of these individually developed models, we gradually build the elements of the higher level, i.e. the proposed reference model for CNs.

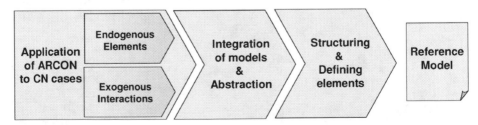

Figure 2 – Towards a CNO reference model

Therefore, as a first step of this bottom up approach, some reference tables were developed for the various classes of CNs studied in ECOLEAD and other past projects such as THINKcreative, VOSTER, or VOmap (Camarinha-Matos, Afsarmanesh, 2004), (Katzy et al., 2005). Specifically, four tables were filled out for the cases of VO Breeding Environment, VO, PVC, and Virtual Team. Afterwards a general (more abstract) table was then synthesized based on these examples, leading to the identification of a set of general (common) concepts that are at the base of the CN reference model (Fig. 3).

Figure 3 – Main classes of collaborative networks considered in this study

With this approach, i.e. resorting to previous work in ECOLEAD and other past projects, we tried to reduce the time needed for this ambitious task.

3. GENERAL CONCEPTS

3.1 Main elements according to the Endogenous Elements perspective

This section collects the main elements of the Endogenous Elements subspace for the CN's reference model, through the integration of elements found in VBEs with PVCs (Table 1), and in VOs with VTs (Table 2).

It is assumed that such lists of concepts and entities evolve, namely when more experience is collected from practice. Therefore, this set is to be understood solely as a starting basis.

For the *Endogenous Elements perspective,* the elements that are defined in each of its dimension (E1 to E4), are classified into the following four categories according to their nature. This serves to better represent their modeling semantics:

- **Active entity** – a tangible object that can behave and/or perform an action in the CN, e.g. an organization, or an individual, e.g. the CN member/partner organizations.

- **Passive entity** – a tangible object that cannot behave and/or perform any action in the CN; rather it is a "object" on top of which actions can occur, e.g. an information resource, or an ICT resource.

- **Action** – a procedure or operation that is executed within the CN, e.g. the CN's member registration, competency management, contract negotiation, conflict resolution processes.

- *Concept* – an intangible aspect in the CN that can be also associated with Active/Passive Entities or Actions, e.g. the role (associated with an organization in the CN), brokerage principles (associated with the VO creation processes), or conflict resolution policies (associated with the CN operation management processes).

Table 1. Main Endogenous Elements for long-term strategic alliances (LA)

E1. Structural	E2. Componential	E3. Functional	E4. Behavioral

Active entity
- **Actor**
  - Primary-entity
  - Support-entity
 	
Passive entity
--- 	
 	
Action
--- 	
 	
Concept
- **Role**
  - LA member
    - Administrator
    - Adviser
    - Support provider
    - VO/VT broker
    - VO/VT planner
    - Sub-network's actor
  - Spot member
 	
- **Relationship**
  - Trusting
  - Cooperation
  - Communication / information flow
  - Exchange / sharing
  - Socializing
  - Control/supervision
 	
- **Network**
  - LA-self network
  - Sub-network
	Active entity
	--- 	
	
	Passive entity
	- **Domain specific device**
	  - Manufacturing machinery
	
	- **ICT resource**
	  - Hardware
	  - Internet
	  - Software
	    - LA Management System
	
	- **Human resource**
	  - Contact person for Network
	  - Contact person for an Actor
	
	- **Info / knowledge / asset resource**
	  - Profile/ competency data
	    - Actor's profiles data
	    - Network's profiles data
	  - Inheritance information
	    - LA inheritance
	    - Sub-network inheritance
	  - Ontologies
	    - LA's common ontologies
	    - Domain ontologies
	  - Bag of assets
	    - LA Governance info.
	    - Value System Info.
	    - Sharable SW tools
	    - LA doc. repository
	    - Templates
	
	- **Network result**
	  - VO characterization
	  - VT characterization
	
	Action
	--- 	
	
	Concept
	--- 	
		Active entity
		--- 	
		
		Passive entity
		--- 	
		
		Action
		- **Fundamental process**
		  - LA management process
		    - Membership management
		    - Profile and competency management
		    - Trust management
		    - Sub-network Inherit./ performance managem.
		    - Value System info. management
		    - Support institution info. management
		    - Bag of Assets management
		  - Participants operational processes
		    - Member enrolment
		    - Roles/responsibility update request
		    - Participants trust assessment
		    - Sub-network creation
		    - Sub-network registration
		
		- **Background process**
		  - LA management process
		    - Creation of repositories
		    - Setup LA management system
		    - Bulk registration of founding participants
		    - LA inheritance management
		    - Decision support management
		    - Members' rewarding
		    - Ontology adapt/evolution management
		    - Performance measurem.
		    - IP Management
		
		Concept
		- **Methodology & Approach**
		  - Network setup handling
		    - Governance rules / value system definition
			Active entity
			--- 	
			
			Passive entity
			--- 	
			
			Action
			--- 	
			
			Concept
			- **Prescriptive behavior**
			  - Cultural principles
			    - Regional traditions
			    - Business culture
			    - NGO culture
			  - Governance principles
			    - LA general principles
			    - Domain specific principles
			  - Incentive policies and rewarding
			
			- **Obligatory behavior**
			  - LA bylaws
			    - Conflict Resolution Policy
			    - Security issues policy
			    - Bylaw amendments policy
			    - Membership policy
			    - Financial policies
			    - Contract enforcement policy
			  - Internal regulations
			    - ICT Use Guideline
			    - Sanctions Principles
			  - General law
			
			- **Contract & agreement**
			  - LA adhesion agreement
			  - Agreement amendments
			
			- **Constraint &**

		- LA network set up	**condition**
		- Sub-network set up	▪ Confidentiality
		▪ Network operation	constraints
		handling	▪ Legal constraints
		- Participant's registration	▪ Standards
		- Participant's recruiting	constraints
		- Members' information	▪ Internal normative
		quality assurance	constraints
		- LA's info. / policy	▪ Physical constraints
		transparency	
		- Interactions w/ support	
		institutions	
		- Sub-network coordination	
		selection	
		- Social processes	
		- Governance rules updating	
		- Role/right assignment	
		- Risk management	
		- Conflict resolution	
		- IP management	
		- Technology adoption	
		- Ontology management	
		and updates	
		- Sub-network's inheritance	
		handling	
		▪ LA evolution/	
		metamorphosis handling	
		- Revision of gathered	
		knowledge	
		- Transition to new	
		organizational structure	
		▪ LA dissolution /	
		inheritance handling	
		- Transfer of knowledge	
		and assets	
		- Re-defining of roles	

Table 2. Main endogenous elements for goal-oriented networks

E1. Structural	**E2. Componential**	**E3. Functional**	**E4. Behavioral**
Active entity	*Active entity*	*Active entity*	*Active entity*
▪ **Actor**	---	---	---
▪ Primary-entity			
▪ Support-entity	*Passive entity*	*Passive entity*	*Passive entity*
	▪ **Appli./Dom. specific**	---	---
Passive entity	**device**		
---	▪ Manufacturing	*Action*	*Action*
	machinery	▪ **Fundamental process**	---
Action	▪ **ICT resource**	▪ Network management	
---	▪ Hardware	process	*Concept*
	▪ Internet	- Purpose characterization	▪ **Prescriptive**
Concept	▪ Software	process	**behavior**
▪ **Role**	- VO/VT Management	- Tasks plan. & scheduling	▪ Cultural principles
▪ Partner	System	process	- Regional traditions
- Coordinator		- Roles/responsibility	- Business culture
- Support provider	▪ **Human resource**	assignment	- NGO culture
- Broker	▪ Of Network	- Trust management	▪ Governance
- Planner	▪ Of Actor	- Evolution process	principles
▪ Spot member		- Dissolution process	- Network general
		- Data/Knowledge	principles

- **Relationship**
  - Peer-peer
  - Client-supplier
  - Trusting
  - Collaboration
  - Communication / information flow
  - Exchange & sharing
  - Socializing
  - Control/supervision
  - Product/services flow
  - Monetary flow

- **Network**

- **Info / knowledge / asset resource**
  - Profile/ competency data
    - Actor's profiles (history) data
  - Inheritance information
  - Ontologies
    - Network ontology
    - Actor's ontology
    - Domain's ontology
  - Data/knowledge repositories
  - Templates

- **Network result**
  - Tangible product
  - Service

Action

Concept
---

management
- **Participants operational processes**
  - Mediation/agreement process
  - Negotiation process
  - Roles/responsibility update req.
  - Business process

- **Background process**
  - Network management process
    - Creation of repositories
    - Setup of management system
    - Network inheritance handling
    - Decision support management
    - Ontology management
    - Ontology evolution management
    - Performance measurement
    - IP Management

Concept
- **Methodology & Approach**
  - Network setup handling
    - Governance rules / value system def.
  - Network operation handling
    - Members' information quality assurance
    - Network's info. / policy transparency
    - Social processes
    - Governance rules updating
    - Risk management
    - Conflict resolution
    - IP management
    - Technology adoption
    - Ontology management & updates
  - Network evolution handling
    - Revision of gathered knowledge
    - Transition to new organizational structure
  - Network dissolution / inheritance handling
    - Transfer of knowledge and assets
    - Re-defining of roles

- Domain specific principles
- Incentive policies and rewarding

- **Obligatory behavior**
  - Network bylaws
    - Conflict Resolution policy
    - Security Issues policy
    - Amendments to Bylaw policy
    - Financial Policies
    - Contract enforcement policy
  - Internal regulations
    - ICT Use Guideline
    - Sanctions Principles
  - General law

- **Contract & agreement**
  - Coalition agreement
  - Agreement amendments
  - Individual partner agreements

- **Constraint & condition**
  - Confidentiality constraints
  - Legal constraints
  - Standards constraints
  - Internal normative constraints
  - Physical constraints

By comparing the two tables, a large commonality can be extracted at this level of abstraction. Therefore a set of common endogenous elements are identified for each dimension (Table 3).

Table 3. Common endogenous elements for the CN reference model

E1. Structural	E2. Componential	E3. Functional	E4. Behavioral
Active entity ▪ **Actor** 　▪ Primary-entity 　▪ Support-entity *Passive entity* --- *Action* --- *Concept* ▪ **Role** 　▪ Participant 　　- Administrator 　　- Support provider 　　- Broker 　　- Planner 　▪ Spot member ▪ **Relationship** 　▪ Cooperation / 　　Collaboration 　▪ Trusting 　▪ Communication / 　　information flow 　▪ Exchange& 　　sharing 　▪ Socializing 　▪ Control/ 　　supervision ▪ **Network**	*Active entity* --- *Passive entity* ▪ **Domain specific device** 　▪ Manufacturing 　　machinery ▪ **ICT resource** 　▪ Hardware 　▪ Internet 　▪ Software 　　- CNO Management 　　　System ▪ **Human resource** 　▪ HR of Network 　▪ HR of Actor ▪ **Info / knowledge / asset resource** 　▪ Profile/ competency 　　data 　　- Actor's profiles data 　▪ Inheritance 　　information 　▪ Ontologies 　　- Network ontology 　　- Domain's ontology 　▪ Data / knowledge 　　Repositories 　▪ Templates ▪ **Network outcome** *Action* --- *Concept* ---	*Active entity* --- *Passive entity* --- *Action* ▪ **Fundamental process** 　▪ Main network 　　management process 　　- Roles /responsibility 　　　management 　　- Trust management 　　- Data/Know. 　　　management 　▪ Participants operational 　　processes 　　- Roles/ responsibility 　　　update request ▪ **Background process** 　▪ Network management 　　process 　　- Creation of 　　　repositories 　　- Setup of management 　　　system 　　- Bulk registration of 　　　founding participants 　　- Network inheritance 　　　management 　　- Decision support 　　　management 　　- Members' rewarding 　　- Ontology management 　　- Ontology evolution 　　　management 　　- Performance 　　　measurement 　　- IP Management *Concept* ▪ **Methodology& Approach** 　▪ Network setup handling 　　- Governance rules / 　　　value system def. 　▪ Network operation 　　handling	*Active entity* --- *Passive entity* --- *Action* --- *Concept* ▪ **Prescriptive behavior** 　▪ Cultural principles 　　- Regional 　　　traditions 　　- Business culture 　　- NGO culture 　▪ Governance 　　principles 　　- Network general 　　　principles 　　- Domain specific 　　　principles 　▪ Incentive and 　　rewarding policies ▪ **Obligatory behavior** 　▪ Network bylaws 　　- Conflict 　　　Resolution 　　　Policy 　　- Security Issues 　　　policy 　　- Bylaw 　　　amendments 　　　policy 　　- Financial Policies 　　- Contract 　　　enforcement 　　　policy 　▪ Internal regulations 　　- ICT Use Guideline 　　- Sanctions 　　　Principles 　▪ General law ▪ **Contract & agreement** 　▪ Network adhesion /

		- Members' information quality assurance - Network's info. / policy transparency - Social processes - Governance rules updating - Risk management - Conflict resolution - Technology adoption - Ontology management & updates ■ Network evolution handling - Revision of gathered knowledge - Transition to new organizational structure ■ Network dissolution / inheritance handling - Knowledge & assets transfer - Re-defining roles	coalition agreement ■ Agreement amendments ■ **Constraint & condition** ■ Confidentiality constraints ■ Legal constraints ■ Standards constraints ■ Internal normative constraints ■ Physical constraints

3.2 Endogenous Elements definition for the CN reference model

This section includes textual definitions of common elements in the endogenous perspective of the CN reference model. Later, in Section 5.3 these elements are crossed against the life cycle stages of the CN reference model.

E1. Structural dimension

Active entity

■ **Actor**
Entity identifying all the participating actors (nodes) in the network. The actors can be enterprises, other types of organizations, or people.
An actor can have the *role* and *relationship* properties.
Two (or more) actors can be linked through a number of different types of relationships.

■ Primary-entity
An actor that can have a direct participation in the main business processes leading to the products or services that can be produced in the scope of the network's domain.

■ Support-entity
An actor not directly involved in the "production" processes but that performs supporting services to facilitate / enable the normal operation of the CNO.

Concept

- **Role**

  Concept describing and characterizing the roles that can be performed by the actors in the network. A role defines an expected behavior for an actor in a given context.

  - Participant

    The basic role played by any actor that is registered as member of the CNO and is willing to participate in the CNO's activities. Since at different times an actor may assume different roles, and as each of these roles requires assigning different proper rights/responsibilities, e.g. for access to information and services provided, it is necessary to distinguish among these more specific roles.

    - Administrator

      The role of the CNO actor responsible for the network's operation and evolution as well as for promoting cooperation / collaboration among its actors. Also responsible for filling in the skill/competency gaps by searching and recruiting/inviting new organizations into the network. It is also responsible for daily management of the general processes of the CNO, conflict resolution, etc. In the case of a goal-oriented network this role is often designated as *coordinator*.

    - Support provider

      A role typically performed by support-entities, although it can also be played by primary entities, and that represents the responsibility of providing support services and support tools and mechanisms for the operation of the CNO.

    - Broker

      Role played by an actor when engaged in identifying and acquiring collaboration opportunities (business opportunities or others), by marketing CNO competencies and assets and negotiating with (potential) customers. Also responsible for interacting with (potential) customers, on behalf of the CNO, during the early phases of response to these opportunities. In some cases there is also the possibility of this opportunity brokerage role being played by an outside entity, as a service to the CNO.

    - Planner

      Also known as business integrator, it covers the design, planning, and launching of a new goal-oriented network (typically in response to a collaboration opportunity identified by the broker). It involves the identification of the necessary competencies and capacities, selection of an appropriate set of partners, and structuring the new network. In many cases the roles of broker and planer are performed by the same actor.

    - Spot member

      Refers to a temporary participant that was invited into the CNO for a specific participation. This member usually has limited rights and will not stay as member during the full life cycle of the network.

- **Relationship**

  Any kind of logical or physical connection or association, usually referring to some form of interaction, between / among two or more actors. In the case of CNOs several relationships can be defined between participants. For each type of relationship and the involved participants a specific network topology (graph) can be represented.

- Cooperation / collaboration

Used to reflect that two actors have a joint cooperation or collaboration activity. In the case of a long-term alliance we find typically cooperation relationships. In goal-oriented networks we might have collaboration or cooperation relationships depending on the way the network and the work are organized.

- Trusting

To represent levels of trustworthiness between actors.

- Communication / information flow

An association between two or more actors for the purpose of information exchange. In CNOs this case can be used to represent the flows of information in the network.

- Exchange & sharing

Association to represent the exchange or sharing of some resource or goods among actors.

- Socializing

Represents any connection of a social nature. Useful, for instance, to represent situations in which actors are engaged in joint social, cultural, or sport events.

- Control/supervision

When an actor controls or supervises another actor. Useful to represent the power structures in the network.

- **Network**

Concept representing the CNO as a whole, through its main properties, e.g. *identity*, *size*, *location*, *participants*, *topology*.

E2. Componential dimension

Passive entity

- **Domain specific device**

Entities characterizing the production equipment needed for the specific application domain of the CNO. In the case of industry networks it can include the layout of the shared facilities as well as the logistics networks.

- Manufacturing machinery

In the manufacturing domain this refers to the equipment that is used to manufacture products.

- **ICT resource**

Entities characterizing the ICT equipment, software, and infrastructures used / shared in the network. It can include the architecture of the computer network supporting the collaboration.

- Hardware

Refers to the computer hardware infrastructure available to the network.

- Internet

Represents the specific Internet-based networking infrastructure and corresponding tools available to the CNO.

- Software

Refers to the common software tools available to the network.

- CNO management

A specific software resource aimed at supporting and facilitating the management of the activities of

system	the network and its members along all phases of its life cycle. In addition to management services, it often includes collaboration support functionalities.
▪ **Human resource**	A characterization of the human resources available in the network, namely in terms of their competencies, profile, potential roles they can perform, etc.
▪ HR of network	Refers to the individuals that perform general functions at the CNO level (e.g. brokerage, management). These resources can be specifically hired for the network (namely in the case of long-term alliances) or being part of a specific member organization but assigned a network-level responsibility.
▪ HR of actor	Refers to the individuals within an organization member of the CNO.
▪ **Information / knowledge / asset resource**	Entities including the repositories of information and knowledge that are shared by the network members or that support the collaboration processes and the networked organization.
▪ Profile / competency data	A set of structured information describing the CNO and its participants, including its competencies. An actor's competency is the actor's capability to perform (business) processes (in collaboration with partners), having the necessary resources (human, technological, physical) available, and applying certain practices, with the final aim to offer certain products and/or services to the customers.
▪ Actor's profile data	A set of structured information describing the CNO participant. This profile can be sub-divided into public profile and private profile (available CNO participants or administrator only).
▪ Inheritance information	Represents a set of documents/information and assets which are inherited from past collaboration cases. It can represent, for instance, a record of past performance, a set of learned lessons, etc. For instance, when a VO is dissolved, part of this information is inherited by the underlying VBE. The same for a VT dissolution and the PVC.
▪ Ontologies	Entities representing the main (common) ontologies used in the network and that facilitate the mutual understanding among the network members. One example can be the ontology of competencies available in the network.
▪ Network ontology	The high level ontology representing the concepts common to all members of the network.
▪ Domain's ontology	Specific ontology related to the domain of Network's activities..
▪ Data / knowledge repositories	Refers to concrete repositories of data and knowledge such as databases, knowledge bases, available to the members of the CNO or to actors playing some specific roles for the CNO (e.g. administrator, broker, or planner).
▪ Templates	In general it is a form, mold, or pattern used as a guide to making something. Often it is a model or

reference document which includes an intended format but leaves empty slots or variables to be filled in when the template is instantiated into a concrete document for a specific use case. A CNO can build and use as an asset a repository of templates of contracts, main processes, VO/VT structures, etc. The use of such templates is aimed at reducing the effort of generating concrete documents / structures.

- **Network outcome**

Refers to the results of the CNO operation, such as Products or Services in the case of goal-oriented networks, and VOs or VTs in the case of long-term alliances.

E3. Functional dimension

Action

- **Fundamental process**

Concerned with the processes involved in the main line of activities of the collaboration. Processes represent the main structured part of the operational activities of the network. An example is the distributed business processes in a business oriented CNO.

- Main network management process

Concerned with the main activities related to the management of the CNO along its life cycle, towards the achievement of the network's mission. This process may resort to a number of auxiliary processes.

  - Roles / responsibility management

Responsible for keeping track and assigning roles and responsibilities to the CNO participants.

  - Trust management

Devoted to promote the establishment of trust relationships among CNO participants, including the assessment of the trust level among members and between members and the CNO as a whole. It also includes the definition of the trust assessment criteria.

  - Data / knowledge management

Responsible for the management of the data and knowledge repositories hold by the CNO.

- Participants' operational processes

Refers to a set of processes to be carried out by participants during the operational phase of the CNO. These processes are quite varied according to the type of network. In the case of long-term alliances there might be processes for member's enrolment, trust assessment, creation of sub-networks, etc. In the goal-oriented networks there might be business processes (related to the achievement of the network's goal), negotiation processes, mediation / agreement reaching processes, etc. In both classes of networks there might be a process for requesting change / update of roles and responsibilities.

  - Roles / responsibility update request

A sub-type of the participant's operational processes aimed at requesting, from the network administration, the change/update of the roles and responsibility of the participant.

- **<u>Background process</u>** | Including those processes that are designed to assist the CNO in terms of its maintenance and improvement of operations.

- <u>Network management process</u> | Covering the preparatory and administrative activities necessary for the proper operation of the network.

  - <u>Creation of repositories</u> | Responsible for the creation and initial population of the various repositories needed for the operation of the CNO – databases, knowledge bases, templates, etc.

    - <u>Setup of management system</u> | Configuration and parameterization of the various components of the CNO management system in order to tune it according to the chosen policies.

  - <u>Bulk registration of founding participants</u> | Responsible for the registration in the corresponding repositories, of the initial / founding members of the CNO, including the introduction of their profiles and competencies.

    - <u>Network inheritance management</u> | Responsible for handling the various activities involved in processing the inheritance elements. For instance, when a VO dissolves, this process will handle the inherited information and assets from the VO and "registers" them in the corresponding VBE repositories.

    - <u>Decision support management</u> | Collection of sub-processes supporting various decision making actions. Examples of such sub-processes include: determination of warning levels (e.g. low trustworthiness level), assistance in determining competencies gap, assistance in evaluating members' readiness to participate in a collaboration opportunity, etc.

    - <u>Member's rewarding</u> | Process implementing the determination and assignment of rewards to CNO members according to the adopted incentives and rewarding policies. For instance, this process can involve processing various items recorded in the CNO repositories that are relevant to determine the merit of each partner.

    - <u>Ontology management</u> | Responsible for the definition, maintenance and access to common ontologies. It may involve semi-automatic ontology extraction (e.g. from corpora text) or simply support manual definition of the ontologies.

    - <u>Ontology evolution management</u> | Organizes and orchestrates the activities involved in the evolution of common ontologies, including consistency checking.

    - <u>Performance measurement</u> | Responsible for performance measurement at the network level, through the determination of a set of performance indicators. This process also involves the distributed data acquisition for the computation of these indicators.

    - <u>Intellectual Property management</u> | Set of activities responsible for the various aspects of intellectual property management, including methods for determination of property ownership, supporting value assignment to the members, protection mechanisms, etc.

Concept

- **Methodology and approach**

  Typically less formalized and conveying less detailed information than processes, represent the body of practices, procedures, and rules used mainly by human actors in a CNO. They are frequently represented as a semi-structured set of steps (informal enumeration of activities) combined with some structured representation of input / output information. Although giving a sequence of steps, they are not very strict in terms of schedule, indication of involved resources, etc. as it can be expected in a process definition. An example can be the methodology to be followed by a broker to announce a business opportunity to the CNO members.

- Network setup handling

  Set of procedures and practices involved in the set up phase of the network's life cycle (the last stage of the network's creation), including the final setting up of the governance rules, value systems, configuration of infrastructures, etc.

  - Governance rules / value system definition

    Refers to the methodology involved in the definition and agreement on the governance rules to be applied to the network as well as its value system.

- Network operation handling

  Set of methods, the underlying rationale, recommended practices and supporting tools to deal with the network's operation. A large number of methodologies and approaches can be included under this item in order to cover for the large set of activities and events that happen during the operational phase of the CNO.

  - Member's information quality assurance

    Approaches and methods used to check for the quality of information provided by network members. For instance, it is important to assess the accuracy of the profile and competencies information provided by participants in order to reduce the subjectivity.

  - Network's information / policy transparency

    Approaches, supporting methods and mechanisms to deal with the information visibility levels and transparency in the CNO. Transparency is a fundamental concept in order to guarantee the sustainability of a collaborative network.

  - Social processes

    Refers to a number of practices and guidelines related to social activities organized by and for the network participants, namely with the purpose of reinforcing the team spirit.

  - Governance rules updating

    Methodology to be followed when there is an intention to change or update the governance rules of the CNO. It shall define the protocols to be followed as well as the participants that shall be involved in each phase.

  - Risk management

    Approaches and methods to deal with risks in the CNO, including risk analysis and estimation, methods for fair distribution of risk consequences, risk avoidance measures, etc.

  - Conflict

    Methodology and recommended practices to be adopted in case of conflicts in the network at the

	resolution	various levels of the CNO coordination structure.
▪	IP management	Methods, decision making guidelines, and identification of external supporting entities to be used in the management of the intellectual property in the CNO.
▪	Technology adoption	Recommended practices to be followed in the case of introduction of new technologies that affect the whole CNO or several of its members.
▪	Ontology management & updates	Methodological guidelines, protocols and supporting tools to be adopted in the management and updating of the common ontologies, namely changing/extending the classification of entities/concepts in use in the network.
▪	Network evolution handling	Methodology and approaches to be used when it is necessary to make significant changes in the network in terms of membership, organizational and coordination structure, roles, and responsibilities.
▪	Revision of gathered knowledge	An auxiliary methodology to be used during the network's evolution stage to deal with the re-organization and consolidation of the knowledge acquired during the previous operational phase, in order to start with a cleaned up version in the next stage of the CNO.
▪	Transition to new organizational structure	Guidelines and recommended practices to be adopted when a CNO goes through a metamorphosis, i.e. a major change, turning into a new kind of organization. Not only the re-design / planning of the new organizational structure, but also the temporary aspects and liabilities coming from the past organization need to be properly handled.
▪	Network dissolution / inheritance handling	Approaches and support methods to use when the network dissolves and how to handle its inheritance. It shall include a clear identification of the inheritance elements (assets, liabilities), the corresponding owners / responsible participants, who will inherit them, under which conditions the transfer will be made, etc.
▪	Knowledge & assets transfer	Refers to a particular aspect of the network's inheritance, dealing with the transference of acquired / gathered knowledge and other valuable assets when the CNO dissolves.
▪	Re-defining roles	Guidelines and recommended practices for the re-definition of roles of participants when the CNO dissolves or evolves to a substantially different structure.

E4. Behavioral dimension

Concept

▪	**Prescriptive behavior**	A set of concepts capturing the elements that lies down or prescribes normative guidelines or rules for the proper behavior of the CNO such as (general)

principles, strategies, and protocols. An example is a recommendation for CNO members to give preference to network peers when searching for partners for a business opportunity. Another example could be the recommended protocol when negotiating a contract.

- Cultural principles

Those guidelines and principles generally accepted and promoted by a given group or society, and that are in general practiced by the accepted members of that group or society. Being the CNO immersed in a given "society", such general principles shall be followed in order to guarantee a good acceptance by the surrounding environment.

- Regional traditions

Includes the cultural specificities of a particular geographical region. For instance, in a given region it might be considered as appropriate social behavior that organizations operating in that region sponsor (or facilitate the participation of employees in) the local festivities.

- Business culture

Captures the set of practices followed by the business sector in which the CNO operates, i.e. "the way actors in this business sector do business".

- NGO culture

Captures the set of practices and guidelines usually followed by (philanthropic) non-governmental organizations, whose value systems are substantially different from business-oriented entities. A CNO devoted to disaster rescue management will naturally follow this particular culture.

- Governance principles

Refers to set of norms to be followed in order to effectively manage and monitor (through policy) the operation according to the strategy and goals of the CNO. These principles shall also reflect the value system and ethical code of the network.

- Network general principles

Set of elements defined as the result of a vision, ethical code, values and principles the CNO wants to follow and that may include cases such as:
  - Honesty and integrity
  - Trust and accountability
  - Openness
  - Well performance
  - Professionalism
  - Mutual respect
  - Commitment to Network
  - Code of ethics
  - IPR Policy.

- Domain specific principles

Set of principles that are adjusted to the common practices in the specific domain of operation of the CNO. These principles may include:
  - Leadership role principles
  - Interoperability principles
  - Decision-making principles
  - Etc.

- Incentive & rewarding policies

Set of principles and mechanisms to create incentives for pro-active engagement of participants in the fulfillment of the CNO's objectives, including a list of rewards and their granting rules.

- **Obligatory**

A set of concepts describing those rules and principles

behavior	that are mandatory to be followed inside the network. This includes policies, governance values and associated rules, and enforcement steps. An example can be the internal rules used for distribution of benefits or for sharing the operational costs of the network.
▪ Network bylaws	Formalizes the regulations that CNO adopts that set forth duties, limit authority and establish orderly procedures for conducting business (internal affairs).
▪ Conflict resolution policy	The policy to workout emerging problems among participants during CNO activities, in charge of a CNO board headed by network manager. Examples of relevant cases that could introduce conflicts to the CNO are: Breach to a contract, disclose of confidential information, use the CNO means for approaching particular interests external to the network, Intellectual Property Rights misuse (in case of patents), among others.
▪ Security issues & policy	Regulations regarding the safeguard the confidentiality of exchanged information and obtained knowledge that must be defined prior to operations of the CNO.
▪ Bylaw's amendments policy	Specify the policy to be followed in the revisions/modifications to bylaws. For instance, notice of proposed changes in the rules should be circulated to all CNO participants with a considerable time in advance of the decision making point.
▪ Financial policies	The set of policies for payments and an accounting in order to guarantee a potential growth of the network at economic level and the satisfaction of its members in compliance with the law.
▪ Contract enforcement policy	The set of policies to enforce the fulfillment of contracts and agreements, either internal or between the network and its customers, including the monitoring mechanisms and sanctions.
▪ Internal regulations	Formalize a set of operational regulations, in complement of the bylaws, defining responsibilities (rights and duties) of all CNO participants, communication mechanisms, reporting protocols, as well as prioritization of actions and some related functions.
▪ ICT use guideline	Regulate the use of technology as a mean to disclose and share the information, respecting the policies and rules, according to the ethical and behavioral code.
▪ Sanctions principles	Sanctions are negative/punitive actions referred to members and taken under a performance assessment, which is given through definition and measurement of indicators.
▪ General law	Refers to the applicable law of the country or region in which the CNO operates. When a CNO spans over different countries, its members typically agree on using the law of one specific country or region.
▪ **Contract & agreement**	A set of concepts covering both the contracts between the CNO and external customers and the internal contracts and cooperation agreements among the network members. These models may include both

representations understandable to humans and to software systems.

- Network adhesion / coalition agreement

A formal document defining the conditions and relations that shall prevail between the CNO and a new participant joining the network. It typically specifies the rights and duties of both parties and identifies the background knowledge and assets brought in by the new member.

- Agreement amendments

Formal changes to agreements that need to be defined according to the established amendment policy or procedures.

- **Constraint & condition**

A set of concepts representing those "environmental features" that limit the context of operation of the CNO and its members. An example is a set of restrictions on the use of intellectual property of one member by other members of the network.

- Confidentiality constraints

Constraints regarding the (non-)disclosure of information imposed either by the customer or by CNO participants.

- Legal constraints

Refers to the constraints imposed by law.

- Standards constraints

Refers to constraints derived from existing national or international standards in the domain of the CNO.

- Internal normative constraints

Constraints that derive from the internal agreements and regulations.

- Physical constraints

Refers to physical or geographical constraints imposed by the specific nature of the domain of the CNO. For instance, a CNO in the civil construction domain will require that most participants have some performance in the same physical place i.e. the construction site.

3.3 Main elements according to the Exogenous Interactions perspective

This section collects the main elements of the Exogenous Interactions subspace for the CN reference model, through the integration of elements found in VBEs with PVCs (Table 4), and VOs with VTs (Table 5). Similar to the Endogenous tables, it is assumed that such lists of concepts and entities evolve, namely when more experience is collected from practice. Therefore, this set is to be understood as a starting basis.

The Exogenous Interactions perspective captures the aspects related to the interactions between the CN, as a whole, and its surrounding environment. Therefore three main groups of elements are considered for each dimension:

- *Network identity*, defining the general *positioning* of the CN in the environment or how it presents itself to the environment;
- *Interaction parties*, identifying the relevant entities the CN interacts with;
- *Interactions*, listing the various transaction types between the CN and its interlocutors.

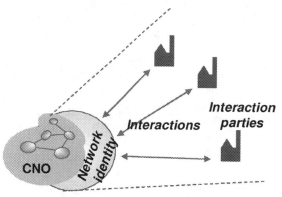

Figure 4 - Exogenous interactions

Table 4. Main exogenous interactions for long-term strategic networks

I1. Market	I2. Support	I3. Societal	I4. Constituency

Network identity
 ▪ Mission statement
   - (General) Strategy
   - (Long term) Goals
 	
 ▪ References /
   testimonials
 	
 ▪ Network profile
   - Who we are
   - How to contact us
 	
 ▪ Market strategy
   - Marketing strategy
   - Branding strategy
	Network identity
	 ▪ Network's social nature
	   - Profit
	   - Not for profit
	   - Governmental
	   - NGO
		Network identity
		 ▪ Legal status
		   - Legal entity
		   - Informal entity
		
		 ▪ Values & principles
			Network identity
			 ▪ Attracting & recruiting
			   strategy

Interaction parties
 ▪ Customers
   - Strategic customers
   - Potential customers
 	
 ● Competitors
   - Direct competitors
   - "Indirect" competitors
 	
 ▪ (Potential) Suppliers
	Interaction parties
	 ▪ Certification entities
	   - National institutions
	   - International institutions
	
	 ▪ Insurance entities
	   - Private institutions
	   - Public institutions
	
	 ● Logistics entities
	
	 ● "Standard" registries
	   - Clearing centers
	   - Master data providers
	
	 ▪ Financial entities
	   - Banks
	   - Investors
	   - Sponsors
	
	 ● Coaching entities
	   - Advisers
	   - Individual external
	     experts
	
	 ▪ Training entities
	   - Advisers
	   - Professional association
	   - Individual external
	     experts
		Interaction parties
		 ▪ Governmental
		   organizations
		   - Social security
		   - City hall
		   - Civil defense
		
		 ▪ Associations
		
		 ▪ Interest groups
		   - Supporters
		   - Opponents
		
		 ▪ Regulatory bodies
		
		 ▪ Other entities
			Interaction parties
			 ▪ Business organizations
			   - Private institutions
			   - Individual experts
			
			 ▪ Public institutions

	Research entities - Universities - Research institutes		

Interactions
• Advertising
  - Broadcast
  - Direct
• Bidding
• Handling inquiries
	Interactions
	• Service acquisition
	  - Financial relation
	  - Technological service
	  - Training action
	  - Coaching action
	  - Guarantee action
	  - Knowledge transfer
	  - Consulting service
	• Agreement
	establishment
		Interactions
		• Political relations
		• Seeking support
		• Information transfer
		  - Broadcast
		  - Direct
		• Social relations
		  - Cultural
		  - Patronage
			Interactions
			• Member searching
			  • Invitation
			  • Solicitation
			• Receiving applications

Table 5. Main exogenous interactions for goal-oriented networks

I1. Market	I2. Support	I3. Societal	I4. Constituency

Network identity
• Goal
• References /
testimonials
(of core partners)
• Network profile
  - Who we are
  - How to contact us
• Market strategy
(product/service)
  - Marketing
  - Branding
	Network identity
	• Network's social nature
	  - Profit
	  - Not for profit
	  - Governmental
	  - NGO
		Network identity
		• Legal status
		  - Legal entity
		  - Informal entity
		• Values & principles
			Network identity
			• Strategy for inclusion of
			external members

Interaction parties
• Customers
  - Known
  - Un-known
• Competitors
• Suppliers
	Interaction parties
	• Certification entities
	  - National institutions
	  - International
	   institutions
	• Logistics entities
	• "Standard" registries
	  - Clearing centers
	  - Master data providers
	• Insurance entities
	  - Private institutions
	  - Public institutions
	• Financial entities
	  - Banks
	  - Investors
	  - Sponsors
	• Coaching entities
	  - Advisers
	  - Individual external
	   experts
	• Training entities
	  - Advisers
	  - Professional
	   association
	  - Individual external
	   experts
		Interaction parties
		• Governmental
		organizations
		  - Social security
		  - City hall
		  - Civil defense
		• Associations
		• Interest groups
		  - Supporters
		  - Opponents
		• Regulatory bodies
		• Other entities
			Interaction parties
			• Business organizations
			  - Private institutions
			  - Individual experts
			• Public institutions

	Research entities - Universities - Research institutes		
Interactions	***Interactions***	***Interactions***	***Interactions***

■ Advertising
  - Broadcast
  - Direct
 	
■ Customer-oriented
transactions
 	
■ External suppliers-
oriented
transactions
	■ Service acquisition
	  - Financial relation
	  - Technological
	    service
	  - Training action
	  - Coaching action
	  - Guarantee action
	  - Knowledge
	    transfer
	  - Consulting
	    services
	
	■ Agreement
	establishment
		■ Political relations
		
		■ Seeking support
		
		■ Information
		transfer
		  - Broadcast
		  - Direct
		
		■ Social relations
		  - Cultural
		  - Patronage
			■ External members
			search
			  - Invitation
			  - Solicitation
			
			● Receiving
			applications?

Comparing the two tables, a quasi-total similarity can be found. In fact, at this level of abstraction the differences are mainly at the level of importance of the various concepts and entities. For instance "attracting and recruiting" new members may be a key aspect in a long-term alliance, while the inclusion of external members in a goal-oriented network typically only happens when the current members in the underlying breeding environment cannot adequately satisfy the requirements.

Other differences may though exist, even when the same terms are used. For instance, external suppliers are a quite normal party that a goal-oriented network needs to interact with. For the long term alliances, this concept is not so relevant, as these networks are not involved in any real production activity. Therefore, for long term alliances we can talk of potential suppliers, instead of actual suppliers. Another example of difference is the concept of "goal", which is a fundamental characterizing element of the goal-oriented networks. For a long-term alliance it is more reasonable to think in terms of "mission statement", which includes "generic" long-term goals and strategies.

Finally there are some concepts / entities that are important for one class of networks while they are not so important for the other class. As an example, "competitors" are important in the Market dimension for long-term alliances; for goal-oriented networks they may be negligible, especially in those cases the networked is driven by a firm contract with the customer. In the cases that a goal-oriented networked is created to develop a product/service to put in the market (i.e. not ordered by a concrete customer), then it also makes sense considering competitors.

Nevertheless, although being a bit excessive in some cases, it is reasonable to consider a common table of exogenous elements for the CN reference model, at the general concepts modeling level.

Table 6. Common exogenous elements for the CN reference model

I1. Market	**I2. Support**	**I3. Societal**	**I4. Constituency**

Network identity
■ Mission
  - Strategy
  - Goals
	Network identity
	■ Network's social
	nature
		Network identity
		■ Legal status
		  - Legal entity
		  - Informal entity
			Network identity
			■ Members' attracting &
			recruiting strategy

▪ References / testimonials
 	
▪ Network profile
  - Who we are
  - How to contact us
 	
▪ Market strategy
  - Marketing strategy
  - Branding strategy
	- Profit
	- Not for profit
	- Governmental
	- NGO
		▪ Values & principles	

Interaction parties
▪ Customers
  - Strategic customers
  - Potential customers
 	
● Competitors
  - Direct competitors
  - "Indirect" competitors
 	
▪ Suppliers
	Interaction parties
	▪ Certification entities
	  - National institutions
	  - International institutions
	
	▪ Insurance entities
	  - Private institutions
	  - Public institutions
	
	● Logistics entities
	
	● "Standard" registries
	  - Clearing centers
	  - Master data providers
	
	▪ Financial entities
	  - Banks
	  - Investors
	  - Sponsors
	
	● Coaching entities
	  - Advisers
	  - Individual external experts
	
	▪ Training entities
	  - Advisers
	  - Professional association
	  - Individual external experts
	
	▪ Research entities
	  - Universities
	  - Research institutes
		Interaction parties
		▪ Governmental organizations
		  - Social security
		  - City hall
		  - Civil defense
		
		▪ Associations
		
		▪ Interest groups
		  - Supporters
		  - Opponents
		
		▪ Regulatory bodies
		
		▪ Other entities
			Interaction parties
			▪ Business entities
			  - Private institutions
			  - Individual experts
			
			▪ Public institutions

Interactions
▪ Advertising
  - Broadcast
  - Direct
 	
▪ Customer/supplier-oriented transactions
  - Bidding
  - Reporting
  - Asking quotation
 	
▪ Handling inquiries
	Interactions
	▪ Service acquisition
	  - Financial relation
	  - Technological service
	  - Training action
	  - Coaching action
	  - Guarantee action
	  - Knowledge transfer
	  - Consulting service
	
	▪ Agreement establishment
		Interactions
		▪ Political relations
		
		▪ Seeking support
		
		▪ Information transfer
		  ▪ Broadcast
		  ▪ Direct
		
		▪ Social relations
		  - Cultural
		  - Patronage
			Interactions
			▪ Member searching
			  ▪ Invitation
			  ▪ Solicitation
			
			▪ Receiving applications

This set of concepts is certainly <u>not complete</u> and <u>will evolve</u> with the emergence of new collaborative forms and the evolution of the markets and society. Nevertheless they give a good indication of relevant aspects to consider relative to the interactions between the CNO and its surrounding environment.

3.4 Exogenous Interactions definition for the CN reference model

This section includes textual definitions of common elements in the exogenous perspective of the CN reference model. Later, in Section 5.3 these elements are crossed against the life cycle stages of the CN reference model.

I1. Market dimension

Network identity

- Mission

  Typically includes the mission statement of the CNO, representing its purpose for existence. Of relevance to the market it shall include the target market, range of products / services, geographic domain, and expectations. It can be divided into "strategy" and "goals". In the case of goal-oriented networks it might be reduced to the definition of the specific goal that triggered the creation of the coalition.

- References / testimonials

  List of relevant past successful collaboration stories and / or short testimonials from customers, attesting the level of competence / professionalism of the CNO.

- Network profile

  Brief information about the members of the CNO ("who we are") and contact information.

- Market strategy

  Defines how the CNO plans to engage customers, prospects and competitors in the market arena for the success of its mission. It involves elements such as:
  - Marketing strategy – defining how the CNO concentrates its resources on the most relevant opportunities for achieving its goals and a sustainable competitive advantage.
  - Branding strategy – in order to create a unique identity for the CNO that will differentiate it from the competition and allow (potential) customers to easily associate it with the network. It also defines how the identities of the individual members are related to the common identity of the CNO.

Interaction parties

- Customers

  Identifies those entities that can order / receive the products or services produced by focused alliances of network members. In the case of long-term alliances this term refers to the potential customers through which CNO brokers can find collaboration opportunities. For goal-oriented networks it represents those entities that have put the order that triggered the formation of the VO/VT or the entities that will be targeted as potential clients for the product / service being developed by the consortium.

- Competitors

  Represents the networks or single organizations that compete with the CNO in the same market arena.

- Suppliers

  Refers to the external entities, not members of the CNO, that might provide raw materials, components, or base services on top of which the CNO builds its own products / services. In the case of long-term alliances this means the set of potential suppliers while in the case of goal-oriented networks it refers to actual suppliers.

Interactions

- Advertising

    Refers to the actions devoted to deliver information about the competencies and (potential) products / services to the market in order to attract customers. Various mechanisms can be applied including broadcasting to the target market actors or direct contacts with specific potential customers.

- Customer/supplier-oriented transactions

    Includes the set of interactions with potential or actual customers and/or external suppliers. Examples of such interactions are:
    - Bidding – when the CNO (or a subset of its members) sends a bid in response to a call for tenders or auction issued by an actor in the market.
    - Reporting – in case of an already acquired contract with a customer, several reporting actions take place according to the agreements established with this customer.
    - Asking for quotation from external suppliers.

- Handling enquiries

    Refers to the reception of inquiries from (potential) customers about the potential interest of the CNO in a specific business opportunity or about the competencies of the network. It also includes the provision of answers to those inquiries.

I2. Support dimension

Network identity

- Network's social nature

    Represents the "identity" of the CNO in terms of its social and economic objectives. Various options can be considered:
    - A profit-oriented organization, the typical case in business scenarios.
    - A not-for-profit organization.
    - A governmental organization (which is typically a not-for-profit organization).
    - A non-governmental organization (which is also typically a not-for-profit organization).

    The interactions with a number of support entities will depend on the nature of the CNO (e.g. there might be special incentives such as tax reductions when dealing with not-for-profit organizations).

Interaction parties

- Certification entities

    Those entities that are entitled to issue certificates of compliance with establish regulations or norms. For instance, certifications of quality, such as compliance with ISO 9000. These entities can operate at national or international level.

- **Insurance entities**

Including insurance companies or associations of insurance companies that can provide specific insurance policies for the CNO and its members. A special case would be new forms of social security, namely for the case of professional virtual communities.

- **Logistics entities**

The entities that manage and control the flow of goods, energy, information and other resources (materials, products, etc.) along a value chain. These operators, if not part of the CNO, are important support entities for the operation of a geographically distributed network.

- **«Standard» registries**

Entities that keep centralized formal records of information such as brand names, official registration numbers, domain entities (Internet), copyrights, etc. Examples of such entities include:

  - Clearing centers – locations for clearing permissions.

  - Master data providers – offering reference data for specific business branches.

- **Financial entities**

Those entities that can give financial support to the CNO, either in business terms or as a sponsoring action. This group includes banks, investors, and sponsors (either private or governmental).

- **Coaching entities**

Refers to entities, either people or organizations, which can help the network members in operating as a collaborative organization. Not to be mistaken with network management, they focus on non-directive questioning, provoking and helping network members to analyze and solve their own challenges.

- **Training entities**

Organizations or people that can support the CNO by providing (on demand) training on specific technical subjects of their operating domain (e.g. new processes, new technologies) and therefore contributing to enrich the set of competencies of the network.

- **Research entities**

Institutes (public or private) and universities that can offer targeted research activities in support of the CNO, although they are not part of the network.

Interactions

- **Service acquisition**

Involving a large set of interactions between the CNO and the support institutions for acquisition of specific services. According to the various supporting parties, there could be acquisitions of:
  - Certification services
  - Financial support
  - Technological services
  - Training actions
  - Coaching actions
  - Guarantee services
  - Knowledge transfer
  - Consulting services
  - etc.

- **Agreement establishment**

Refers to the protocols and actions involved in the established of agreements between the CNO and support institutions. Unlike a specific service acquisition, these agreements typically refer to a longer-term cooperation arrangement.

I3. Societal dimension

Network identity

- Legal status

  Gives indication of the particular place of the CNO in the society, relative to the law, which determines the laws that affect or regulate the existence and operation of the network. This status depends on the particular legal provisions existing in each country or geographical region where the network operates. Some CNOs may constitute a legal entity, in one of the available forms (e.g. association, joint venture, etc.), or be an informal association.

- Values & principles

  This element states the value system and the ethical, moral, and social principles that guide the behavior of the CNO. This gives the society an indication of what can be expected from the network. Such values & principles are closely related to the mission statement and represent a complementary perspective of the CNO's identity.

Interaction parties

- Governmental organizations

  Are the set of governmental institutions and departments that the CNO might need to interact with. It includes central, regional, and local government related entities such as ministries, city hall, regional development agencies, social security, civil defense entities, etc.

- Associations

  Includes industry and commerce associations, professional associations, chambers of commerce, etc. The CNO might interact with them in terms of getting support, access to information dissemination channels, etc.

- Interest groups

  Are relevant, formal or informal, groups in society that are organized to defend specific economic, cultural, or social interests and that might play a role of supporters or opponents of the CNO.

- Regulatory bodies

  Public or private entities that issue regulations and standards on how businesses and some professions can be practiced. Examples include the standardization organizations, some professional associations, national strategic infrastructures regulators (e.g. tele-communications, energy).

- Other entities

  Any other relevant entity that plays a significant role in the local society where the CNO operates and that might affect or influence the network.

Interactions

- Political relations

  Relates to the interactions with the power groups, often as a lobbying activity, in order to influence political decision making in the domains that affect the CNO.

- Seeking support — Actions in order to get direct or indirect support for the CNO from the relevant actors in society.

- Information transfer — Includes all exchanges of information between the CNO and the social actors. Some of these interactions have the objective of raising awareness for the activities of the CNO and their importance to the (local) society and, as such, constitute also a mechanism to indirectly seek support.

- Social relations — Relate to the contributions of the CNO to activities of benefit to the society in general. Examples include sponsoring cultural activities, being the patron of events, scholarships, regional publications, sport activities, etc.

I4. Constituency dimension

Network identity

- Members' attracting & recruiting strategy — An important element of the "identity" of the CNO, defining rules for membership, attraction mechanisms for engaging new members, as well as the recruiting mechanisms. In the case of long-term alliances it means the policies to get new entities adhering to the principles of the established breeding environment or professional virtual community. In the case of goal-oriented networks it defines general principles for resorting to external members when there are no appropriate candidates in the breeding environment.

Interaction parties

- Business entities — Refers to the recruitment universe for business-oriented CNOs. This universe includes business organizations (e.g. enterprises), and/or individual professionals.

- Public institutions — Refers to the universe of public institutions that might be interesting to attract to the CNO. In case of collaborative e-government, these institutions are the natural members. In the case of business oriented CNOS, public institutions can typically participate as supporting members.

Interactions

- Member searching — Interactions with the constituency actors in order to identify and select potential new members for the CNO. This can involve a number of mechanisms such as direct invitation, open solicitation / calls, etc.

- Receiving applications — Actions related to the reception of applications for membership and sending the corresponding response after a decision is made.

4. CONCEPTS ALONG THE LIFE CYCLE

The following two tables show how the identified elements appear / are used along the life-cycle of the CN.

Table 7. Endogenous elements along the CN life-cycle

E1. Structural	c o e m d	E2. Componential	c o e m d	E3. Functional	c o e m d	E4. Behavioral	c o e m d
Active entity		*Active entity*		*Active entity*		*Active entity*	
Actor		---		---		---	
Primary-entity		*Passive entity*		*Passive entity*		*Passive entity*	
Support-entity		**Domain specif. dev**		---		---	
Passive entity		Manufacturing machin		*Action*		*Action*	
---				**Fundam. Process**		---	
Action		**ICT resource**		Main CNO manag proc		*Concept*	
---		Hardware		- Roles/respons. Mng.		**Prescript. behavior**	
Concept		Internet		- Trust management		Cultural principles	
Role		Software		- Data/Know. Manag.		- Regional traditions	
Participant		- CNO Manag. System		Particip. operat. proc.		- Business culture	
- Administrator				- Roles/resp. Update rq.		- NGO culture	
- Support provider		**Human resource**				Governance principles	
- Broker		HR of Network		**Backgr. Process**		- Net. gen. principles	
- Planner		HR of Actor		Network manag. proc.		- Domain specif. princ.	
Spot member				- Creation reposit.s		Incent.&reward. policy	
		Info/knowl./asset r.		- Manag. Sys. Setup			
Relationship		Profile/compet. data		- Bulk regist. particip.s		**Obligatory behavior**	
Cooperation/Collaborat.		- Actor's profiles data		- Net. Inherit. mang.		Network bylaws	
Trusting		Inheritance information		- Decis. support man.		- Conflict resol. policy	
Communication /info flow		Ontologies		- Members' rewarding		- Secur. issues policy	
Exchanging & sharing		- Network ontology		- Ontology manag.		- Bylaw amend.s pol.	
Socializing		- Domain's ontology		- Ontol. Evolution man.		- Financial policies	
Control/supervision		Data/knowl. Reposit.s		- Performance man.		- Contract enfor. pol.	
		Templates		- IP Management		Internal regulations	
Network						- ICT Use Guideline	
		Network outcome		*Concept*		- Sanctions principles	
				Methodo.&Approach		General law	
		Action		Net. setup handling			
		---		- Govern/valu sys def		**Contract&agreeme.**	
		Concept		Net. operation handling		Net adhesion/coal. agr.	
		---		- Members' info quality		Agreement amendm.s	
				- Net's info./policy tr.			
				- Social processes		**Constraint&condit.**	
				- Govern. rules updat.		Confidentiality constr.s	
				- Risk management		Legal constraints	
				- Conflict resolution		Standards constraints	
				- IP management		Internal norm. constr.s	
				- Technology adoption		Physical constraints	
				- Ontol. manag.&updates			
				Net. evolution handling			
				- Rev. gathered knowl.			
				- Trans. to new o. str.			
				Net. Dissolut./inherit.			
				- knowl.&assets transfer			
				- Re-defining roles			

■ Very important
▨ Moderately important
☐ Not so important

c- creation o- operation e- evolution m- metamorphosis d- dissolution

Table 8. Exogenous interactions along the CN life-cycle

1. Market	c o e m d	2. Support	c o e m d	3. Societal	c o e m d	4. Constituency	c o e m d
Network identity		**Network identity**		**Network identity**		**Network identity**	
Mission		CNO's social nature		Legal status		Attract.&recruit. Strat.	
References/testimonials				Values & principles			
Network profile							
Market strategy							
Interaction parties		**Interaction parties**				**Interaction parties**	
				Interaction parties			
Customers		Certification entities		Governmental organ.s		Business entities	
Competitors		Insurance entities		Associations		Public institutions	
Suppliers		Logistics entities		Interest groups			
		Standard registries		Regulatory bodies			
		Financial entities		Other entities			
		Coaching entities					
		Training entities					
		Research entities					
Interactions		**Interactions**		**Interactions**		**Interactions**	
Advertising		Service acquisition		Political relations		Member searching	
Customer/supplier-oriented transactions		Agreement establishment		Seeking support		Receiving applications	
Handling inquiries				Information transfer			
				Social relations			

■ Very important   c- creation o- operation e- evolution m- metamorphosis d- dissolution
▨ Moderately important
☐ Not so important

5. CONCLUSIONS

The large scope and multi-disciplinary nature of collaborative networks require an urgent systematization of concepts and empiric knowledge in order to facilitate the progress of the discipline. In this direction, this chapter introduced an organized set of definitions classified according to the ARCON framework. These definitions are not given using any formal representation but rather simple textual descriptions, as they are mainly intended for human communication and understanding.

The approach was therefore to use textual descriptions at the level of "General Representation", while formal models apply to the following layers of the ARCON framework ("Specific Modeling" and "Implementation Modeling") for which some examples in part 3 of this book.

Nevertheless it is proposed that this organized body of knowledge constitutes a first attempt to have a reference model for collaborative networks. Reference modeling is certainly a long-term activity and further iterations and extensions will naturally be required as the area becomes more mature.

Acknowledgements. This work was funded in part by the European Commission through the ECOLEAD project. The authors thank the contributions of their colleagues in the project and other researchers, with special reference to Andrew Kusiak, Hermann Kuhenle, Falk Graser, Dario Franco, Antonio Abreu.

6. REFERENCES

1. Camarinha-Matos, L. M.; Afsarmanesh, H. (2004). Collaborative networked organizations – A research agenda for emerging business models, Springer.
2. Camarinha-Matos, L. M.; Afsarmanesh, H. (2006). Towards a reference model for collaborative networked organizations. In *Proceedings of BASYS'06, Information Technology for Balanced Manufacturing Systems (W. Shen, Ed.)* (Springer), Niagara Falls, Ontario, Canada, 4-6 Sep 2006. IFIP Series, Vol. 220, ISBN: 0-387-36590-7.
3. Camarinha-Matos, L. M.; Afsarmanesh, H. (2007). A comprehensive modeling framework for collaborative networked organizations, *Journal of Intelligent Manufacturing, Volume 18, Number 5 / October, 2007, pp 527-615.*
4. Camarinha-Matos, L. M.; Afsarmanesh, H. (2008). On reference models for collaborative networked organizations, L.M. Camarinha-Matos, H. Afsarmanesh, to appear in *International Journal Production Research.*
5. Camarinha-Matos, L. M.; Afsarmanesh, H.; Ollus, M. (2005). ECOLEAD: A holistic approach to creation and management of dynamic virtual organizations. In *Proceedings of PRO-VE'05 – Collaborative Networks and their Breeding Environments,* Springer, pp. 3-16, Valencia, Spain, 26-28 Sep 2005.
6. Katzy, B.; Zhang, C.; Loeh, H. (2005). Reference models for virtual organisations, in *Virtual organizations: Systems and Practices*, L. M. Camarinha-Matos, H. Afsarmanesh, M. Ollus (Editors), Springer.
7. Noran, O. (2003). A mapping of individual architecture frameworks (GRAI, PERA, C4ISR, CIMOSA, ZACHMAN, ARIS) onto GERAM, in *Handbook on enterprise architecture*, P. Bernus, L. Nemes, G. Schmidt (Ed.s), Springer.
8. Tolle, M.; Bernus, P. (2003). Reference models supporting enterprise networks and virtual enterprises, *International Journal of Networking and Virtual Organisations - Vol. 2, No.1* pp. 2 – 15. http://www.inderscience.com/storage/f161185104291237.pdf

2.6
A comprehensive semantic-indexing schema for ARCON

E. Ermilova, H. Afsarmanesh

In order to formally and systematically address the elements in the ARCON models for CNs, a schema of their unique identification needs to be developed. This chapter introduces an approach for comprehensive and semantic "indexing" of both meta-elements, e.g. the Componential dimension of the Endogenous sub-space of ARCON's reference modeling framework, , and each individual element, e.g. the specific resource or market strategy belonging to the ARCON reference model of the CN. The main contribution of the introduced semantic indexing-schema is to the formalization process of the ARCON m. Furthermore, the indexing schema facilitates: (1) dynamic systematic evolution, (2) organized physical storage, (3) semi-automated processing and derivation of both elements and meta-elements of ARCON.

1. INTRODUCTION

A comprehensive abstract model representation for Collaborative Networks (CNs) is strongly required for the new paradigm of CN that is widely emerging in the market and society. An earlier work in this area (Camarinha-Matos, Afsarmanesh, 2006) provides the following definition for the CNs:

A Collaborative Network (CN) is a network consisting of a variety of entities (e.g. organizations and people) that are largely autonomous, geographically distributed, and heterogeneous in terms of their operating environment, culture, social capital and goals, but that collaborate to better achieve common or compatible goals, and whose interactions are supported by computer network.

CNs are complex systems, emerging in many forms and in different application domains. They consist of many facets whose proper understanding requires the contribution from multiple disciplines [Camarinha-Matos, L. M., Afsarmanesh, H., 2007]. As addressed in Chapters 2.3 and 2.5 of this book, a number of different types of CNs can be identified, however research in the area has mostly concentrated on the description of the Collaborative Networked Organizations (CNOs), which itself consists of the long term strategic alliances such as the Virtual Organizations
Breeding Environments (VBEs) (Afsarmanesh, Camarinha-matos 2005), (Afsarmanesh, et. al. 2007), and Professional Virtual Communities (PVCs) (Bifulco, 2006), as well as the sort-term goal-oriented consortiums such as the Virtual Organizations (VOs) (Ollus, 2006), and the Virtual Teams (VT) (Bifulco, 2006).

Development of the CN reference framework, such as ARCON, facilitates the understanding, instantiation, management, and simulation of the CNs (Tolle, M., Bernus, 2003) (Katzy et al, 2005). It shall also facilitate the development of information systems and the required supporting software tools both for the existing and for the emerging CNs.

In (Camarinha-Matos, Afsarmanesh, 2007) the reference framework for ARCON is introduced. The ARCON (A Reference model for COllaborative Networks) is developed as an evolving system, which itself constitutes of two parts:

- o *ARCON reference modeling framework,* which in this chapter is referred to as generic **ARCON meta-model**, and

- o a set of *ARCON reference models* generated within this framework to represent different kinds of CNs, for instance the VBEs, VOs, VTs, etc., which in this chapter are referred to as **ARCON models.**

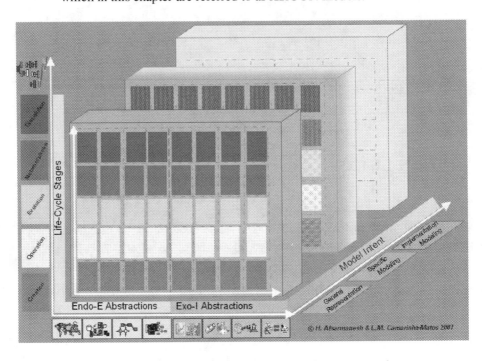

Figure 1 – ARCON Reference modeling framework

The ARCON meta-model comprehensively addresses the heterogeneous elements of different CN environments from three different near-orthogonal perspectives, namely the Environment Characteristics perspective, the Life Cycle Perspective, and the Model Intent perspective, constituting the three axes of the ARCON three dimensional (3D) matrix, as also illustrated in Figure 1. Furthermore, the organization of this matrix is further clarified in Table 1. Please note that the concepts presented in Table are further heavily used in section 2. This chapter however does not cover the detailed definitions of all concepts introduced in the ARCON meta-model, since except for the concept of "Nature of elements" that is described in the next paragraph, all other concepts are addressed in Chapters 2.4 and 2.5 of this book.

Table 1 – Structure of the 3D matrix of the ARCON meta-model

Perspectives	Sub-spaces	Dimensions		Nature of elements			
x-axis: Environment Characteristics	Endogenous Elements	Structural Dimension		Active Entity		28 sections	420 cells
				Passive Entity			
				Action			
				Concept			
		Componential Dimension		Active Entity			
				Passive Entity			
				Action			
				Concept			
		Functional Dimension		Active Entity			
				Passive Entity			
				Action			
				Concept			
		Behavioral Dimension		Active Entity			
				Passive Entity			
				Action			
				Concept			
	Exogenous Interactions	Market Dimension		Network Identity			
				Interaction Party			
				Interaction			
		Support Dimension		Network Identity			
				Interaction Party			
				Interaction			
		Societal Dimension		Network Identity			
				Interaction Party			
				Interaction			
		Constituency Dimension		Network Identity			
				Interaction Party			
				Interaction			
y-axis: Life Cycle stages	Creation					5 sections	
	Operation						
	Evolution						
	Metamorphosis						
	Dissolution						
y-axis: Model Intent	General Representation					3 sections	
	Specific Modeling						
	Implementation Modeling						

In the first perspective (i.e. x-axis), the CN elements are grouped into two different "subspaces" (i.e. the "*CN Endogenous Elements*" subspace and the "*CN Exogenous Interactions*" subspace), and further each subspace is divided into four different "dimensions" (i.e. the *structural, componential, functional* and *behavioural* dimensions for the "CN Endogenous Elements" subspace, and the *market, support, societal* and *constituency* dimensions for the "CN Exogenous Interactions" subspace), that together represent the CN environment characteristics.

Furthermore, while for simplicity reasons, Figure 1 only represents the meta-elements specified above, and therefore their intersection represents only 144 cells (6*8*3), in ARCON, elements within the two subspace are further categorized according to their different *nature*. Table 1 illustrates this fact. The CN elements belonging to any dimension within the "*CN Endogenous Elements*" subspace, are further categorized into "*active entities*", "*passive entities*", "*actions*", and "*concepts*", constituting its three nested subsections. In the same manner, the CN elements belonging to any dimension within the "*CN Exogenous Interactions*" subspace, are further categorized into "*network identity*", "*interaction parties*", and "*interactions*".

In the second perspective (i.e. y-axis), the CN elements are related to the five stages of the CN life cycle (i.e. the *creation, operation, evolution, metamorphosis* and *dissolution* stages), where during each stage different set of CN elements are typically activated.

In the third perspective (i.e. z-axis), the CN elements are modelled with three different levels of details/abstraction (i.e. *general modelling, specific modelling* and *implementation modelling*), depending on the specific intent of a model, e.g. if the model of the CN is intended to be only descriptive – related to the general modelling level – or if the model is intended to provide specifications for development of CN elements – related to the implementation modelling level. In chapter 2.5, the ARCON models for a number of different kinds of CNs are represented in the form of "reference tables".

Each ARCON model is an instantiation of the ARCON meta-model addressed above, within the 3D matrix, with a set of potential values related to each of the **420** (28 x 5 x 3) individual *cells* in this matrix. Table 1 also represents the number of sections that can be identified within the 3D matrix of ARCON as **36** (28+5+3) *sections*. Furthermore, we introduce the following two notations:

- Each *section* (i.e. a perspective), sub-section (e.g. a subspace or a dimension), and each cell (i.e. the result of the intersection/nesting of all sections and sub-section) within this matrix are further referred in this chapter as **ARCON-meta-elements**.

- The content of each *cell* in the Matrix, e.g. the cell "*Passive Entity of the Componential dimension of Endogenous Elements of the Environment Characteristics*", is typically a number of real modeling elements (e.g. textual descriptions, graphs, algorithms, etc.) that will be defined specifically for each CN type. These elements are further referred in this chapter as **ARCON-elements**.

Please note that the ARCON-meta-elements appear in both the ARCON meta-model as well as in all ARCON models. However, the ARCON-elements belong to and appear only in the ARCON models.

As also addressed in Chapters 2.4 and 2.5 of this book, at the current stage of the development of the ARCON reference models for CNs:

- Every meta-element of the ARCON meta-model is well described and exemplified.

- All elements of ARCON models, for the complete first layer, i.e. – *General Representation layer* – are defined for the four specific CNs, namely the VBE, PVC, VO and VT, as well as three generic CNs, namely Long-term Alliance – LA (that is a generalization of VBE and PVC), Goal-oriented network - GO (that is a generalization of VO and VT), and CNO (that is a generalization of LA and GO).

Nevertheless, the ARCON meta-model is the framework that can be used to develop reference models for any kind of CNs, as represented in the taxonomy of CNs (Camarinha-Matos, Afsarmanesh, 2006) illustrated in Figure 2, e.g. for Virtual government, Ad-hoc networks, etc., and at the three different levels of details (abstraction), as represented by the three model-intents defined for it. Please note that more details related to the CN typology are addressed in Chapter 2.3 of this book.

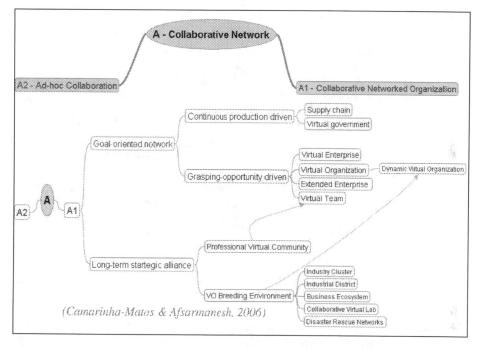

Figure 2 – Partial taxonomy of Collaborative Networks

Since collaborative networks as a new discipline is currently an active area of research and development, both the ARCON meta-model as well as the ARCON models for variety of CNs are active and evolving systems. Consequently, we foresee that while the ARCON meta-model is reaching its near-maturity stage (if not already fully mature), in the coming years, a large number of ARCON models for different kinds of CNs will be developed and thus undergo a number of improvement/extension releases.

Furthermore, both the ARCON meta-model and the ARCON models represent large multi-dimensional and multi-elemental structures, which make it challenging to support their evolution, their physical storage with different versions, and their semi-automatic processing. For example during an **evolution** process, when a "marketing" dimension of a specific CN model is being developed/edited, its developers typically does not need to work with the entire CN model, rather only with one specific part of it (i.e. only with the "marketing" dimension). Usually the developer of one element may not even need to know about the development of the other parts (i.e. about existence of "componential" dimension). Thus, the ARCON model can benefit from dispersed storage of its elements as a *set of information units*, which can be evolved / developed distinctly. Furthermore, such division and dispersed storage can also support separate versioning of different information units in the ARCON models, which can enhance and secure the process of ARCON models evolution. Additionally, this divided physical storage of the ARCON models also facilitate **semi-automated processing** of the ARCON elements, for example the processing of a hierarchy of the VBE member's roles needed during VBE instantiation/operation.

Such **physical storage** for ARCON models is currently challenging, hence an approach for: (1) a clear and formal division of each ARCON model into a set of independent, but complementary information units, and (2) a further loss-less assembly of this model out of its units, needs to be developed.

At present, the ARCON models, as defined in Chapter 2.6, do not support solving the above challenges. For example, even referring to a specific element in any of ARCON models (e.g. to a specific role for the CN members) is not straightforward. To refer to an element, either (i) a long enumeration of sub-dimensions and sections, where the element is located in the ARCON model, or (ii) even pointing to a specific place in the figure/table illustrating that ARCON model, is needed.

One solution to the above challenge is through the introduction of **formalization** for different information units in the ARCON.. As a first step in this direction, definition of unique formal identifiers is introduced. For this purpose, our approach suggests further ARCON's formalization through development of a **semantic-indexing-schema**.

The remaining part of this chapter is structured as follows: section 2 introduces the details of our indexing approach. First, we define *compound indexes* to refer to every meta-element within the ARCON meta-model, namely the meta-element-index, and then we define *compound indexes* to refer to every specific ARCON element, namely the element-index. Then Section 3 introduces the index-based representation of all elements in the ARCON models. Section 4 addresses two index-based representations for the ARCON models. Section 5 addresses one specific derivation/reasoning mechanism developed for the ARCON models, on top of its indexing approach, and section 6 concludes this chapter.

2. INDEXING APPROACH

As addressed above, the elements of the ARCON models are by nature of two different kinds, namely they represent the ARCON-meta-element (i.e. sections and cells of the ARCON matrix) and the specific ARCON-elements (i.e. specific elements of any specific ARCON model), and therefore as addressed in details below, they are also indexed as such, namely:

       o   *ARCON meta-element-index*
       o   *ARCON element-index.*

For the purpose of introducing unique formal identifiers in ARCON, instead of introducing an ad-hoc indexing system, e.g. a set of unique superfluous/artificial names for each cell in the matrix, or using a *numbering systems*, e.g. from 1 to *N*, we introduce semantic/mnemonic set of unique identifiers as indexes for all information units in ARCON. For example, the **semantic-index** defined for each ARCON element, semantically represents all related details defined for its x, y, and z characteristics, e.g. uniquely identifying one cell in the ARCON matrix. Furthermore, the introduced semantic-index consists of the two parts of: (1) a *unique semantic representation,* and (2) a *name/label.* To put it simply, the semantic-index in ARCON is a notation, based on the concatenation of all the *elemental characteristics of the unit* a name introduced for it. As such, the indexes are referred to as *compound indexes* and are semantic.

2.1. ARCON Meta-element-indexes

Below in Table 2 we present *five elemental characteristics* (i.e. **M, S, D, N,** and **L**) identified for the ARCON-meta-element-indexes (as also addressed in Figure 3). These characteristics are needed to build the *unique semantic representation* part of the indexes, for all *meta-elements*, i.e. all sections, sub-sections, and cells in the ARCON matrix (see Table 1) follow:

Table 2: Elemental characteristics of ARCON-meta-elements included to their indexes

Model Intent	M
Sub-space	S
Dimension	D
Nature of element	N
Life Cycle stage	L

Figure 3 gives a formalized definition and examples of the meta-element-indexes. It introduces a "formula" on top, for each meta-element-index written in the style of *normal forms definition.* The Figure also represents the definition of all the elements in this formula one by one, e.g. **M, S, D,** etc, where the description of each introduced symbol is also provided with a "*" character. It finally gives the example indexes for two real meta-elements at the bottom, namely for the perspective of "General representation" and for the dimension of "Market".

Please note that depending on the section or cell of the ARCON matrix being indexed, not all elemental characteristics may appear in the resulting index. For example in the index for the entire "General representation" section of the matrix, namely the "GR: General Representation", does not include any of the other elemental characteristics, e.g. the S, D, N and L labels are absent from this semantic-index.

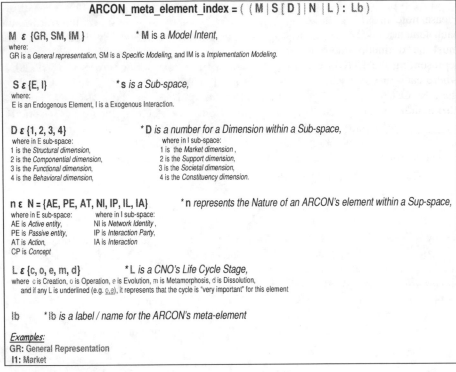

ARCON_meta_element_index = ((M | S [D] | N | L) : Lb)

M ε {GR, SM, IM }   * M is a *Model Intent*,
where:
GR is a *General representation*, SM is a *Specific Modeling*, and IM is a *Implementation Modeling*.

S ε {E, I}   * s is a *Sub-space*,
where:
E is an Endogenous Element, I is a Exogenous Interaction.

D ε {1, 2, 3, 4}   * D is a number for a *Dimension within a Sub-space*,
where in E sub-space: where in I sub-space:
1 is the *Structural dimension*,   1 is the *Market dimension*,
2 is the *Componential dimension*,   2 is the *Support dimension*,
3 is the *Functional dimension*,   3 is the *Societal dimension*,
4 is the *Behavioral dimension*,   4 is the *Constituency dimension*.

n ε N = {AE, PE, AT, NI, IP, IL, IA}   * n represents the Nature of an ARCON's element within a Sup-space,
where in E sub-space: where in I sub-space:
AE is *Active entity*,   NI is *Network Identity*,
PE is *Passive entity*,   IP is *Interaction Party*,
AT is *Action*,   IA is *Interaction*
CP is *Concept*

L ε {c, o, e, m, d}   * L is a *CNO's Life Cycle Stage*,
where c is Creation, o is Operation, e is Evolution, m is Metamorphosis, d is Dissolution,
    and if any L is underlined (e.g. o,e), it represents that the cycle is "very important" for this element

lb   * lb is a label / name for the ARCON's meta-element

Examples:
GR: General Representation
I1: Market

Figure 3 - Semantic-indexing for meta-elements in the ARCON framework

Besides the unique representation part, please also notice that the semantic-index of each meta-element must also have a **Mnemonic-Label (Lb).** This label is introduced to better represent the role of the meta-element in the ARCON model.

2.2. ARCON Element-indexes

An ARCON reference model for a specific type of CN (e.g. for a VO, VT or VBE), is an instantiation of the ARCON meta-model, and provides specific **content** within that framework, to comprehensively capture all aspects of that type of CN. The six elemental characteristics (i.e. **C, M, SD, N, E,** and **Ls**), needed to build the *unique semantic representation* part of the indexes for all *elements* in the ARCON model, are addressed in Table 3:

Table 3: Elemental characteristics of ARCON-elements included to their indexes

CN-type	C
Model Intent	M
Sub-space Dimension	SD
Nature of element	N
Relative-order-number	E
Life cycle stages	Ls

Please note that all elemental characteristics, defined above, must be defined for each semantic-index of each element. For example, for each ARCON element the **Ls** must be defined, where **Ls** is an ordered subset of the **{c, o, e, m, and d}** representing the CNO's Life cycle stages (where c is Creation, and so forth), and where each of these set elements can be present in the semantic-index definition of the ARCON element. Specification of a **Mnemonic-Label** for the element **(Lb)** is also mandatory to complete the index definition.

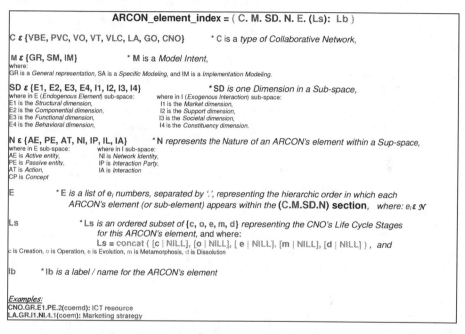

Figure 4 - Semantic-indexing for elements in the ARCON reference models

A formalized description and examples of element-indexes are illustrated in Figure 4. Similar to Figure 3, Figure 4 also introduces a "formula" on top, for each element-index. It further defines all parameters in this formula one by one. It finally provides example indexes for two real ARCON elements at the bottom, namely the indexes for "ICT resource" and for "Market strategy". Please note, that relative-order-numbers of elements identify certain CN elements in case they are located within the same cell of the ARCON framework For example, as also addressed further in Figure 7, the ARCON CNO model's cell called "CNO.GR.E1.PE.2(coemd) ICT resource", with order number 2 represented for "E" in its index, includes an entire hierarchy of ICT resources, such as "CNO.GR.E1.PE.2.1(coemd) Hardware", "CNO.GR.E1.PE.2.2(coemd) Internet", "CNO.GR.E1.PE.2.3(coemd) Software"., Furthermore, pay attention that the "Software" class (with order number of 2.3) has also a subclass, as follows "CNO.GR.E1.PE.2.3.1 (coemd) CNO Management System", etc.

3. INDEX-BASED REPRESENTATION OF ARCON ELEMENTS IN ARCON MODELS

After addressing the indexing schema for meta-elements and elements in ARCON, this section focuses on ARCON elements themselves, and providing an *index-based representation of ARCON elements* in the ARCON models. In addition to the element-indexes, described in section 2, for comprehensive representation, two other aspects of the ARCON elements need to be addressed and formulated. Namely, we must address the semantic-indexing of two other aspects of the ARCON elements as follows:

- o   representation of the *potential relationships* that can be defined between different ARCON elements, and

- o   representation of the *specific model (also called the model-representation-extension)* being defined/developed for an element in the ARCON reference model of a CN,

Introducing semantic-indexes addressing these two other aspects of the ARCON elements is necessary for full representation of these elements with all their potential characteristics and features. Figure 5 represents a formalized definition and examples of these two characteristics, completing the description of ARCON elements. As such these two aspects extend the ARCON-element-index definition, as provided in Figure 4. The definitions of **Relationships** of each ARCON element with other elements **(Rs)**, as well as the **Model representation Extension** of each element **(X)** are therefore addressed in Figure 5.

The Model-representation-extension represents a specific model of the element, depending on its modeling intent, e.g. a semantic-index must be generated for the *textual definition* generated for an ARCON element at its "General representation" modeling intent level.

In the same style of Figures 3 and 4, Figure 5 first provides a "formula" on top, for each ARCON element. It further defines all elements in this formula one by one. It finally illustrates two example elements at the bottom, namely the extensions for the "ICT resource" and for the "Market strategy" ARCON elements.

Please note that while the formula on top represents the complete semantic index for each ARCON element, e.g. including the set of relationships, as well as the specific model (or a pointer to the specific model) within the defined index, the example at the bottom of the figure, only exemplifies these two potential extensions of the ARCON element in a table format. Therefore, please do not confuse the representation of these examples with the format for representation of the semantic-index for the ARCON elements.

ARCON_element = (ARCON_element_index, Rs, X)

Rs   * *Rs is a set of tuples for relationships defined between this element and other ARCON elements, where for each* r ε Rs
     r = (**r_name, ARCON_element_index**) *, and*
       r_mane *is the mnemonic name for a relationship with another ARCON's element*

X   * *X is the model for the ARCON's element, where for each* x ε X
    x = **textual_definition** *if* M=GR, x = **specific_model** *if* M=SM, x = **implementation_ model** *if* M=IM

Examples of ARCON's CNO reference model elements for the GR model intent:

ARCON_element_index	R	X
CNO.GR.E1.PE.2(coemd): ICT resource	4. is related to Actor, CNO.GR.E1.AE.1(coemd): Actor 5. is related to Network, CNO.GR.E1.CP.1(coemd): Network	Entities characterizing the ICT equipment, software, and infrastructures used / shared in the network. It can include the architecture of the computer network supporting the collaboration.
CNO.GR.I1.NI.4.1(coem): Marketing strategy	6. is defined for Customer, CNO.GR.I1.IP.1(coemd): Customer	Marketing strategy – defining how the CNO concentrates its resources on the most relevant opportunities for achieving its goals and a sustainable competitive advantage.

Figure 5 - ARCON element representation

4. INDEX-BASED REPRESENTATION OF ARCON MODELS

With the use of the semantic-indexing, it becomes possible to produce a two dimensional (2D) representation of the ARCON reference models from the 3D representation of the ARCON matrix, through *folding* aspects related to one of its 3 dimensions. This section addresses this potential for the semantic-indexing mechanism, to be used for comprehensive representation of ARCON elements/meta-elements.

A visual 2D representation of the ARCON model is partially illustrated in Figure 6, related only to the General Representation (GR) model-intent layer of the framework, for a specific type of CNs, namely the CNOs. This object-oriented diagram exemplifies some elements (related to the GR layer) for the CNO reference model, through their indexes. The diagram also illustrates a part of the ARCON meta-elements, through their indexes. Here a new concept can be observed, related to the so-called *Index-inheritance,* which is represented explicitly among the ARCON elements, and represented implicitly from the ARCON meta-elements to the ARCON elements. Please notice that only the upper part of this figure represents the entire 2D model. However since it complete diagram cannot be represented and readable in one page of the book, instead we have expanded one part of it, as presented in the figure.

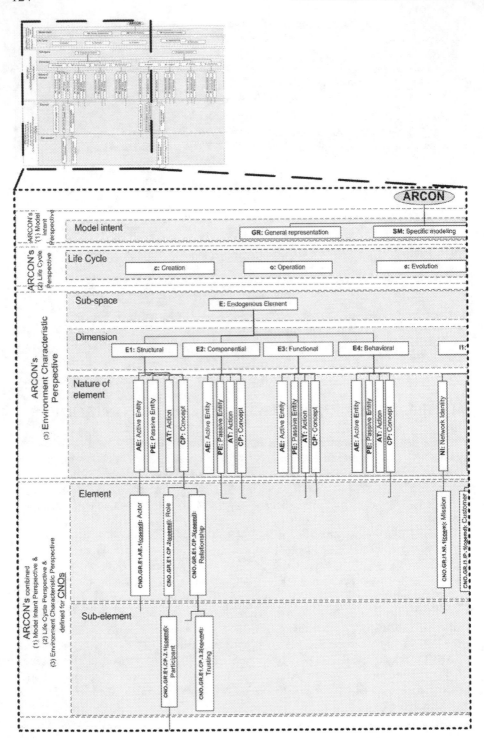

Figure 6 – Partial index-based CNO reference model

As you can also observe in Figure 6, with the possibility provided by the introduced semantic-indexing mechanism, we can include any and all life cycle stages related to an ARCON element as a part of its semantic-index at once, i.e. using the *"(coemd)"* in its index. Consequently, we can "fold" the 3D appearance of the ARCON elements through the index-based representation of ARCON reference models for CNOs to a 2D diagram. For instance, in the 2D diagram, for the "Trust relationship" (at the lower middle part of this diagram), we are in fact folding the appearances of this element in all the cells within the "column" that represents the *structural dimension of the Endogenous sub-space,* and can represent every Model-Intent layer in which it may appear, i.e. the example in the lower middle part of the diagram shows the General Representation Model-Intent layer.

Furthermore, please also note in Figure 6 that every element/sub-element (in the green area – represented by the lowest two horizontal sections of this diagram) has many links to different stages of the Life Cycle, as well as to different Model Intent perspectives. However since this is a 2D representation, the need for the visualization of all these links to the other two dimensions of the Life Cycle and the Model Intent are in fact replaced by their representation within the semantic-indexes. Please note further that for example, at the General Representation model of CNOs all elements/sub-elements in the (green area) lowest two horizontal sections of this diagram should have their textual description in order to become completely defined.

Additionally, besides the 2D representation of the ARCON reference modeling framework, we can also use the semantic-indexing of ARCON elements for their tabular representation. Figure 7 represents two example tabular representations related to the ARCON reference model of CNOs, illustrating partially the content of the reference tables presented in chapter 2.5. In addition to the previously defined ARCON elements, in these tables we also address the semantic-indexes of these elements.

The alternative presentations of the CNO model presented above also imply approaches for comprehensive storage of the ARCON models. For instance, while the indexes are semantically inter-related in the 2D visual presentation, their specific *model presentations* (e.g. a *piece of text* representing a *GR model* for an index, or a *flowchart* representing the *IM model* for an index) can be stored in the ARCON database as *blobs*, for which links/pointers will then be included within the indexes. Similarly in the tabular representation format, the links to such blobs can be introduced within the semantic-indexes.

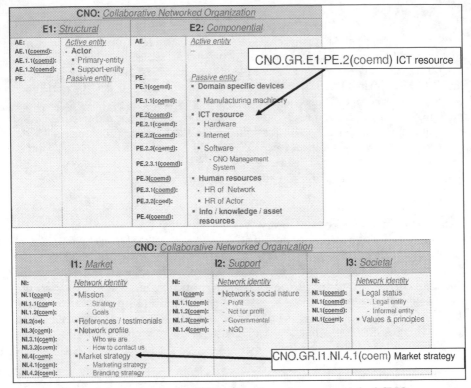

Figure 7 - Example ARCON tables for reference model of CNOs

5. INDEX-BASED OPERATIONS –
DERIVATION OF ARCON REFERENCE MODELS

Consider the simple generalization/specialization hierarchy defined among some kinds of CNs, for example the specialization of the CNOs into the VBEs and PVCs. As explained in chapter 2.5, a bottom up approach can be applied for the development of reference models for those CNs located at the higher level of the CN-taxonomy (e.g. for CNOs), from the reference models of their lower level, more specialized CNs (e.g. from Goal-oriented networks - GOs and Long-term strategic networks - LAs). Applying this approach, usually the "common" elements from the more specific CNs are extracted and used to gradually build up the elements of their generalized CNs.

Figure 8 represents a *formalized general derivation rule* that can be defined and applied to the indexed ARCON elements at the lower level CNs in order to derive their common elements for building the reference model of their higher level CN.

This figure also represents an example of how this formalized general derivation rule can be applied for the derivation of the CNO reference model out of the two reference models for *LA* and *GO*. With this general derivation rule, we can in fact formally reason about derivation of common elements for building the reference models for the generic CNs.

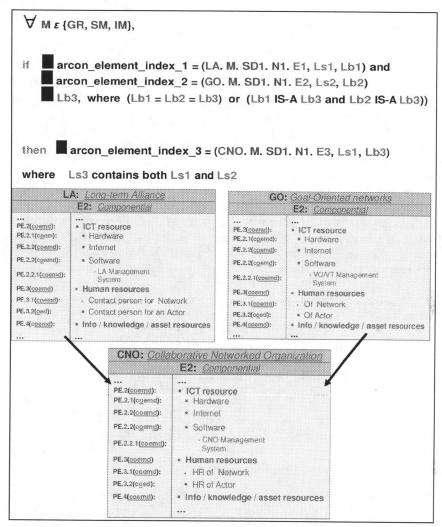

Figure 8 - Common elements' derivation rule (based on their indexes) for CNO reference modeling

Specifically this derivation rule emphasizes that if the LA reference model and the GO reference model, in the same ARCON cell (e.g. in "GR.E2.PE"), have corresponding ARCHON elements (i.e. "LA.GR.E2.PE.2.2.1: LA Management system" and "GO.GR.E2.PE.2.2.1: GO Management system"), then clearly the CNO reference model must also have this ARCON element in that cell, and then the mnemonic labels of these two ARCON elements shall be generalized (i.e. "LA Management system" and "GO Management system" can be generically called "CNO Management system"), and thus the CNO reference model will include this derived ARCON element (i.e. "CNO.GR.E2.PE.2.2.1: CNO Management system").

6. CONCLUSIONS

This chapter presented the motivations and an approach for development of a comprehensive indexing-schema for the ARCON models. The introduced indexing-schema first provides a unique semantic reference to all generic meta-elements in the ARCON meta-model, as well as to all specific elements in the ARCON models. Second it formalizes the representation of all aspects and features related to the ARCON models that in turn supports the systematic evolution of these models as well as support for development of software tools to process the ARCON model elements/meta-elements.

With the presented semantic-indexing-schema, each element of any ARCON model is associated with a specific compound index. This index has several parameters, called elemental characteristics, through which it can support users to properly locate this element in the multi-dimensional ARCON model, as well as for definition of semantic relationships among these elements. The indexing-schema also facilitates alternative form for representation of the elements in the ARCON's CN reference models, namely a 2D object-oriented representation, in addition to the 3D matrix.

Additionally, this chapter has introduced a formalized and generic index-based derivation rule for deriving reference models of more generalized CNs from reference models of their more specialized CNs. The derivation rules are specifically exemplified for the derivation of the generic ARCON reference model for CNOs from two of its specialized ARCON models, one being a reference model for Long-term alliances (LA), and the other a reference model for Goal-oriented networks (GO).

Acknowledgements. This work was funded in part by the European Commission through the ECOLEAD project.

7. REFERENCES

Afsarmanesh, H., Camarinha-Matos, L.M. (2005): A framework for management of virtual organization breeding environments, *in Collaborative Networks and their Breeding Environments*, Springer, pp. 35-49.
Bifulco, A., Santoro, R. (2005): A Conceptual Framework for "Professional Virtual Communities", *IFIP International Federation for Information Processing*, Volume 186, Pages 417 – 424
Camarinha-Matos, L.M., Afsarmanesh, H. (2006): Collaborative Networks: Value creation in a knowledge society. *In knowledge enterprise: Intelligent strategies in product design, manufacturing and management*. Springer, page 26-40
Camarinha-Matos, L.M., Afsarmanesh, H. (2007): A comprehensive modeling framework for collaborative networked organizations. *At the Journal of Intelligent Manufacturing*, Springer.
Katzy, B.; Zhang, C.; Loeh, H. (2005): Reference models for virtual organisations, *in Virtual organizations: Systems and Practices*, L. M. Camarinha-Matos, H. Afsarmanesh, M. Ollus (Editors), Springer.
Ollus, M. (2006): Towards Structuring the Research on Virtual Organizations, *in "Virtual Organizations Systems and Practices"*, Part 5, Springer US, pages 273-276, ISBN 978-0-387-23755-8
Tolle, M.; Bernus, P. (2003): Reference models supporting enterprise networks and virtual enterprises, *International Journal of Networking and Virtual Organisations* 2003 - Vol. 2, No.1 pp. 2 – 15.

2.7
Further steps on CN reference modeling

Establishing a reference model for Collaborative Networks is a long-term endeavor. The ARCON proposal is a first contribution for a comprehensive model but it needs to be continued and improved. A set of guidelines for an evolution process are defined and potential participants in this process are identified.

1. INTRODUCTION

Reference modeling in a complex area such as collaborative networks (CNs) is not a short term task. A clear indication is given by the reference modeling activities for single enterprises, a process that took about 20 years to reach its maturity, including significant milestones such as CIM-OSA (Vernadat, Kosanke, 1992), Zachman (Zachman, 1987), PERA (Williams, 1994), and GERAM (Bernus et al., 1995), (Noran, 2003).

In addition to the design of the reference model itself, it is necessary to get it accepted / recognized by the relevant stakeholders, which is also a long term process. ARCON (Camarinha-Matos, Afsarmanesh, 2006, 2007) was originated in a context of a large project involving a significant number of stakeholders from academia and industry. Many other researchers and practitioners were involved to some extent in the refinement of the concepts through discussions held in international workshops and conferences. Nevertheless further dissemination actions and feedback collecting actions are needed.

On the other hand, the area of CNs is rapidly evolving with new forms of collaboration emerging in different domains as knowledge and best practices become more consolidated and available. Technological evolution naturally induces new forms and suggests new collaboration mechanisms.

Therefore, reference modeling for collaborative networks should not be considered a one-shot initiative. There is a need for continuing refining and improving it along with accommodating the new collaborative cases. The components included in this book are thus a starting basis, which need to be complemented and improved by the CN community in the future. This chapter drafts the guidelines for such evolution process.

2. REFERENCE MODEL EVOLUTION

The purpose of this section is to recommend a process for maintaining and evolving the ARCON reference model. Collaborative Networks is a young field and new organizational forms and collaboration practices are emerging at a fast pace. Therefore, although a base reference model is fundamental to give the area a basis to support a more coherent development, it is clear that a complete model cannot be developed at this stage in time. Some perspectives have been more intensively addressed in the past than others. For instance, the endogenous perspective has received much more attention than the exogenous one in most of the past projects. Similarly, in the scope of the endogenous perspective, most modeling efforts have focused on the structural and functional dimensions, while the behavioral dimension has received very little attention. Therefore, the level of maturity of the elements currently included in ARCON reference model is quite diverse and the reference model shall be seen as an evolving construct that shall be incrementally improved in time.

The following actors are considered to play a major role in this process:
- **CN community** – all professionals, researchers, educators, and practitioners, involved in the development and implementation of collaborative networks.
  - o **Submitter** – referring to a member of this community that suggests revisions & modifications to specific aspects of the reference model.
- **AMC** – ARCON Maintenance Committee – a group of experts in CN who take the responsibility for maintenance and evolution of this model.
  - o In the previous stage this role was performed by a sub-group of ECOLEAD.
  - o After ECOLEAD this mission shall be transferred to a dedicated group of experts, in the context of the SOCOLNET (Society of Collaborative Networks).
  - o The AMC may appoint some temporary **Revision Teams** to deal with specific revision proposals.

The following high-level phases are also considered for the maintenance process:
- **Submission** – Submitters suggest revisions / modifications to the reference model. The AMC itself shall encourage the CN community to periodically discuss the model and elaborate well-structured proposals for modification.
- **Evaluation** – The AMC evaluates the proposals in terms of global consistency and compliance with ARCON as well as the trends in the field in order to decide if it is worthwhile to consider the suggested revision.
- **Revision** – The AMC selects a team to proceed with the revision and to collect feedback from the stakeholders (e.g. through surveys, workshops, meetings).
- **Approval** – The AMC reviews the final version of the reference model and either approves it or returns it to the revision team for further refinement.
- **Rollout** – Upon final acceptance of a revision / modification, a publication and dissemination plan is defined, and the new version of the CN reference model is released.

In order to reach the widest acceptance of the reference model, the AMC might establish alliances with the most relevant initiatives (e.g. research projects, other international initiatives and special interest groups and societies) on Collaborative Networks active in each moment.

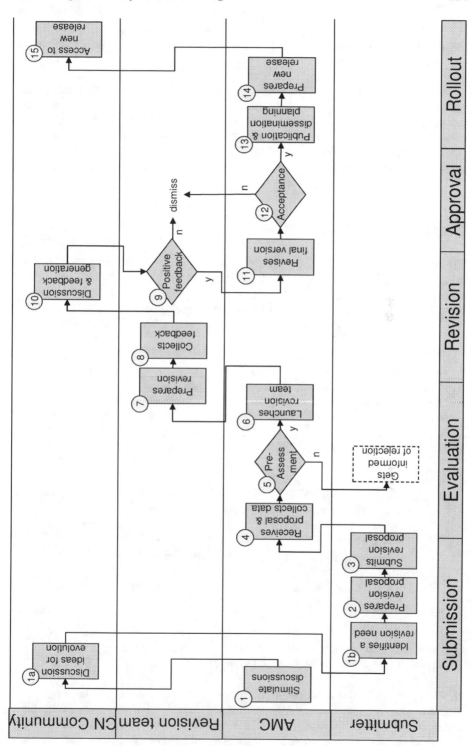

Figure 1 – A simplified view of the ARCON updating process

The diagram of Fig. 1 (inspired from the FEA process (FEA, 2005) illustrates the main steps of the suggested evolution process.

In the long term, after partial maturity is achieved, besides seeking acceptance within the research community, two other following directions shall be pursued for making ARCON recognized and accepted as the reference model for CNs.
- Seeking **Fitness Evaluation** for ARCON by real case applications, targeting & knowledge dissemination among existing and emerging CNs.
- Attempt towards wide recognition of ARCON and its endorsement by authorized bodies, e.g. IFIP and others.

3. THE ROLE OF SOCOLNET AND IFIP

Although ARCON was initiated in the framework of the European ECOLEAD project, once the project is finished the continuation of this work shall be pursued under the framework of international organizations such as SOCOLONET (Society of Collaborative Networks) and IFIP (International Federation for Information Processing) WG 5.5 (COVE: Cooperation Infrastructure for Virtual Enterprises and electronic Business).

According to its bylaws, SOCOLNET has the objective of promoting and stimulating the scientific research, teaching, technological development, technical and scientific interchange between researchers in the Collaborative Networks area, including virtual organizations, virtual enterprises, virtual laboratories and related areas. In order to achieve its objectives, the association aims to:
   a) Promote the interchange of ideas and experiences among its members as well as between them and the scientific community in order to increase the knowledge of the area;
   b) Promote activities, namely periods of training, seminars, courses, colloquia, congresses, conferences, meetings and exhibitions;
   c) Promote and sponsor the edition of publications according to the objectives of the Association;
   d) Propose curricula in Collaborative Networks to be used in educational institutions;
   e) Promote studies and carry out scientific research actions in the area of Collaborative Networks;
   f) Collaborate with official entities or entities of public interest.
Therefore, SOCOLNET, as an open international society whose membership originates in a large variety of fields, offers the proper organizational framework for the establishment of the ARCON Maintenance Committee.

The IFIP WG5.5 has a scope more focused on ICT, aiming to promote and encourage research and technological development on many aspects of business practices, advanced tools and mechanisms, and forthcoming standards, in the areas of virtual organizations, virtual enterprises, and advanced electronic business models. Furthermore, it aims to contribute to the harmonization and knowledge dissemination of world-wide research results on virtual organizations and collaborative networks, and to foster needed collaborative developments.

As for the scope of activities, COVE includes:

- Reference architectures for virtual organizations including life cycle models
- Collaboration models in networked organizations
- Interoperability infrastructures in collaborative web-based environments
- Safe communications and authentication frameworks
- Distributed/federated information and knowledge management
- Assessment of the role of ontology and standards
- Planning and supervision of distributed business processes
- New value systems and assessment methods
- Collaboration coordination and management
- Supporting functions for the full life cycle of virtual organizations
- Novel paradigms and methods to support distributed collaborative processes.

Therefore, contributing to reference models on collaborative networks is in the realm of COVE and a close interaction between COVE and SOCOLNET shall be pursued.

A significant part of the Collaborative Networks community, including most of the members of SOCOLNET and COVE, meet annually around the PRO-VE international conference where progress on reference modeling is discussed and assessed.

In addition to the evolution of ARCON, a number of complementary activities also need to be pursued in order to better support the dissemination and application of the model. These include:

- Elaboration of a number of instantiation examples to facilitate training actions.
- Definition of an instantiation method and associated guidelines to help deriving specific models out of the reference model.
- Formalization of the general concepts in order to reduce ambiguity and provide a basis for the development of a sound theory of Collaborative Networks.

Acknowledgements. This work was funded in part by the European Commission through the ECOLEAD project.

4. REFERENCES

1. Bernus, P., Nemes, L., Williams, T.J. (Editors) (1995). Architectures for Enterprise Integration; Findings of the IFAC/IFIP Task Force on Architectures for Enterprise Integration, Chapman & Hall, November 1995
2. Camarinha-Matos, L. M.; Afsarmanesh, H. (2006). Towards a reference model for collaborative networked organizations. In *Proceedings of BASYS'07, Information*

Technology for Balanced Manufacturing Systems (W. Shen, Ed.) (Springer), Niagara Falls, Ontario, Canada, 4-6 Sep 2006. IFIP Series, Vol. 220, ISBN: 0-387-36590-7.

3. Camarinha-Matos, L. M.; Afsarmanesh, H. (2007). A comprehensive modeling framework for collaborative networked organizations, *Journal of Intelligent Manufacturing, Volume 18, Number 5 / October, 2007, pp 527-615.*

4. FEA   (2005).   FEA   Consolidated   Reference   Model,   May   2005, http://www.whitehouse.gov/omb/egov/documents/CRM.PDF

5. Noran, O. (2003). A mapping of individual architecture frameworks (GRAI, PERA, C4ISR, CIMOSA, ZACHMAN, ARIS) onto GERAM, in Handbook on enterprise architecture, P. Bernus, L. Nemes, G. Schmidt (Ed.s), Springer.

6. Vernadat, F., Kosanke, K. (1992). CIM-OSA: A Reference Architecture for CIM. In Proceedings of the IFIP TC5 / WG5.3 Eight International PROLAMAT Conference on Human Aspects in Computer Integrated Manufacturing, IFIP Transactions; Vol. B-3, pp 41-48, (North-Holland).

7. Williams, T.J. (1994). The Purdue Enterprise Reference Architecture. In Computers in Industry, 24, (2-3) pp. 141-58.

8. Zachman, J. A. (1987). A Framework for Information Systems Architecture. *IBM Systems Journal,* vol. 26, no. 3.

PART **3**

MODELING TOOLS AND APPROACHES

3.1
Overview

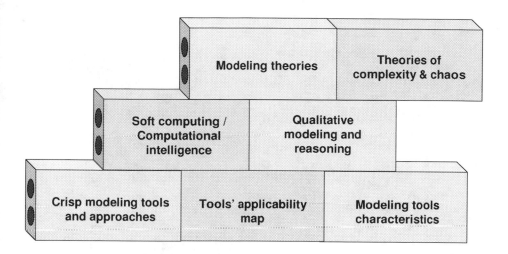

Modeling is one of the key activities in understanding, designing, implementing, and operating software systems. It is at the very heart of any scientific and engineering activity. As such, many disciplines and research fields have developed a large portfolio of modeling theories, approaches, and tools, some of which can be potentially applied in the area of collaborative networks.

This section includes an analysis of the most promising contributions, covering a wide spectrum of modeling purposes. The second chapter introduces an extensive list of modeling tools and theories and, for each one, it offers a brief synopsis and key references. An applicability map is then introduced to help the reader identify which tools / approaches best fit his / her specific modeling needs.

As many reasoning and decision-making problems in collaborative networks have to deal with imprecision and incompleteness of information, the third chapter is devoted to a survey of soft modeling tools. Here a synopsis of tools and methods originated in the soft computing / computational intelligence area is complemented with approaches coming from other sectors such as qualitative reasoning, theories of complexity, theory of chaos, etc. Additionally, examples of potential application to collaborative networks are given.

3.2
A survey of modeling methods and tools

A large portfolio of modeling tools and theories, developed in different disciplines, have a good applicability potential in collaborative networks. A brief survey of those promising approaches and a set of bases references are presented. A map of their application potential is also included.

1. INTRODUCTION

Collaborative Networks (CNs) are complex systems that can be described or modeled from multiple perspectives. In this context there is no single modeling formalism or "universal language" that can cover all perspectives of interest. Since CNs have a clear multidisciplinary nature, it is natural that we search for applicable modeling tools and approaches originated in other disciplines. In fact, Computer Science, Engineering, and Management, among other fields have developed plenty of modeling tools that might have some applicability in CNs.

In addition to modeling tools, systems, and methods there are also some theories as well as several approaches and processes that try to address and describe general complex systems and that might help in getting a better understanding of the CNs, namely in what concerns their variety of endogenous entities and exogenous interaction dimension. The term *modeling construct* will be used to represent each one of these cases.

The remaining of this chapter will first, in section 2, provide a summary table of the modeling constructs with potential applicability in the various dimensions of CNs modeling. Then in section 3, first a detailed description of the considered constructs is included, also providing a few references for each. Then an "applicability map" is introduced, relating all these constructs to different modeling needs in CNs. Section 4 concludes the chapter.

2. PROMISING APPROACHES AND TOOLS

Taking into account the suggestions of a large group of experts with diverse background knowledge involved in projects such as THINKcreative (Camarinha-Matos, Afsarmanesh, 2004a, b) and ECOLEAD, a portfolio of about 30 modeling constructs was selected as potential contributors to a modeling foundation for CNs.

2.1 Modeling Endogenous Elements

Table 1 summarizes the potential applicability of the analyzed modeling constructs with respect to the four indicated dimensions for the Endogenous Elements perspective of the ARCON framework (Camarinha-Matos, Afsarmanesh, 2007) for CNs (see chapter 2.4). In this table, the names **[SD]**, **[CD]**, **[FD]**, **[BD]** stand for Structural, Componential, Functional, and Behavioral dimensions, respectively. This table was developed taking into account both the scope of the modeling dimensions and the practical knowledge about each approach acquired during the various activities of the ECOLEAD project.

Table 1 – Some modelling constructs and their potential applicability in CNs

Construct	Potential contribution to CN Endogenous Elements modeling
Bayesian networks	**[FD]** Use of probabilistic inference to update and revise belief values. Can support complex inference modeling including rational decision making systems, value of information and sensitivity analysis. Causality analysis and support a form of automated learning (parametric discovery, network discovery, and causal relationships discovery).
Benchmarking	**[FD]** Assessment of performance in comparison with a reference (benchmark), including assessment of processes, trustworthiness, and suggestion of best practices.
Complexity theories	**[FD]** Methods for forecasting emergent behavior, trustworthiness, etc. **[BD]** Modeling of emergent behavior in advanced networks. Qualitative (macro) understanding of CN's life cycle.
Decision support	**[FD]** Give a basis for developing methods to assist humans in decision making.
Deontic logic	**[BD]** Represent in a formal way aspects such as "it is obligatory that …", "it is forbidden that …", "it is permitted that …", which can be useful in the governance of behavior.
Distributed group dynamics	**[SD]** Focus on inter-group relationships such as power, leadership, etc, **[BD]** Analysis of leadership behavior, hostility, compliancy, etc.
Diversity in work teams	**[SD]** Characterization of the diversity of individuals and cultures found in CNs and analysis of the potential induced by this diversity.
Evolving ontologies	**[CD]** To capture the evolution of mutual understanding among members of the network, but still is offering limited results.
Federated systems	**[SD]** Providing a vision of the CN as a federation of autonomous, heterogeneous, and distributed sources of resources (data / information, services). Relate roles with authorized access to and visibility of resources. **[CD]** Distributed data / information repositories.

Formal engineering methods	[SD] [CD] [FD] [BD] Rigorous specifications (mathematical-based) with potential application in verification and synthesis of systems. Very hard to apply.
Formal theories	[SD] [CD] [FD] [BD] Solve design problems (architecture, protocols, verification of specifications according to correctness and completeness), but very hard to develop. If developed for specific perspectives / subsystems, can contribute to reduce ambiguities and provide a sound basis for further developments.

Game theory	[FD] Can provide concepts for decision-making, e.g.:
	  - Cooperative game theory: distribution of responsibility and resources.
	  - Non-cooperative game theory: selection of partners, sustaining cooperation and trust building.
	
	[BD] Model interactions with formalized incentive structures.

Graph theory	[SD] Representation of the structure of the network – topology, routing, activity, flow. [FD] Methods to perform computations on flows and optimization.
Knowledge mapping	[CD] Providing visual representations of knowledge which can facilitate analysis of the CN and its resources.
Memetics	[BD] Help understanding some aspects of the dynamics of evolutionary processes (cognitive and business) in multi-cultural contexts.
Metaphors	[SD] [CD] [FD] [BD] Quick description for human communication namely a possible help in expressing complex ill-defined concepts. Can be used in early stages (conceptual design) as long as they are not taken too literally.
Multi-agent systems	[FD] [BD] Model societies of autonomous, distributed and heterogeneous entities, giving insights on how these societies can be organized and their behavior regulated through norms and institutions. [FD] Brokering, coalition formation and negotiation. [BD] Simulation of self-organizing behavior.
Multi-agent dependency theory	[FD] [SD] Representation of social interactions among agents – dependency relations, power relations.
Network analysis	[SD] [FD] Specialized graph theory-based algorithms for application in network management systems (mostly applied in telecommunication networks).
Portfolio theory	[FD] Decision making such as in VO creation (to select the optimal VO from a VBE)
Real options theory	[FD] Decision making, e.g. decision to create a VO for a business opportunity, evaluation of the minimum profitable bid in a call for tenders, etc.
Scopos theory	[FD] Understand transformation of information or knowledge from one cultural and language environment to others in such a

	way that the understanding and conception of the source information or knowledge would be the same for all.
Self-organizing systems	[**BD**] Understanding and simulation of self-organizing behavior. [**FD**] Help in predicting evolution.
Semiotics	[**BD**] Model responsibility relationships and commitments. Prescribe norms and roles – epistemic, deontic and axiologic.
Social network analysis	[**SD**] Analysis of social and organizational structure of CNs, including provision of a number of metrics. Ongoing research may lead to useful results on the inclusion of soft-modeling aspects.
Soft computing	[**FD**] [**BD**] Represent and exploit the tolerance for imprecision, uncertainty, partial truth, and approximation. Particularly important to model human and social aspects.
Synergetics	[**BD**] Help understanding emerging behavior and emerging values.
Temporal and modal logic	[**FD**] [**BD**] Focus on the representation of temporal information within a logical framework. Can be used to model temporal aspects of processes and some aspects of behavior.
Transactions cost theory	[**FD**] Understand and analyze governance structures based on transaction costs.
Trust building models	[**FD**] Organize and systematize the trust building and trust management processes.
Web & text mining	[**FD**] Analysis and knowledge discovery from unstructured data: documents in free text form, web documents. Potential applications include evolution of ontologies, finding business opportunities, etc.

In addition to the above modeling constructs, there are other modeling tools that have a generic applicability or have been already widely used in modeling CNs and therefore are not further discussed in this chapter. Nevertheless they shall be considered as important candidates for some or all of the modeling dimensions of ARCON. These generic formalisms include:

Table 2 - Additional tools and their potential applicability in CNs

Ontology	[**SD**] [**CD**] [**FD**] [**BD**] Representation of the main CN concepts and their relationships.
Petri nets	[**FD**] Modeling or processes and auxiliary processes.
Workflow	[**FD**] Modeling or processes and auxiliary processes.
UML	[**SD**] [**CD**] [**FD**] [**BD**] Generic object-oriented modeling tool (graphical language) with potential application to all dimensions of CN. However, being a generic tool, it does not properly capture all specificities of each dimension.

2.2 Modeling Exogenous Interactions

The main modeling focus of ARCON framework is the Endogenous Elements (considered in previous section) and the Exogenous Interactions. However, regarding the second perspective, the objective is not to model the "world" surrounding the CN but solely the "interface" and interactions between the CN and the surrounding environment. For this purpose, there is no need for very specialized modeling formalism or tools. The concepts and constructs available in general purpose tools, such as UML and ontologies for example, are in principle sufficient.

Nevertheless, if there is a need for more detailed models of interactions, then other tools used in process modeling might be considered.

3. SUMMARY OF MODELING CONSTRUCTS

3.1 Synopsis[*]

A brief synopsis of the selected modeling constructs, including some references to help the reader in finding additional information, is included below:

♦ ***Bayesian networks***. Bayesian belief Networks are becoming an increasingly important area for research and application in the entire field of Artificial Intelligence. Bayesian networks support the use of probabilistic inference to update and revise belief values. They permit qualitative inferences without the computational inefficiencies of traditional joint probability determinations. In doing so, they support complex inference modeling including rational decision making systems, value of information and sensitivity analysis. As such, they are useful for causality analysis and through statistical induction they support a form of automated learning. This learning can involve parametric discovery, network discovery, and causal relationship discovery.

Alternatively, causal relationship discovery is also the topic of link discovery, an emerging area of machine learning at the intersection of relational data mining and text mining.

Some references
- Han, J. and Kamber, M. (2001): Data Mining: Concepts and Techniques. Morgan Kaufman.
- Jensen, F. V. (2001): Bayesian Networks and Decision Graphs. Springer.
- Pearl, J. (2000): Causality. Cambridge.
- Jordan, M. I. (ed) (1998): Learning in Graphical Models. MIT Press.

■ ***Benchmarking***. The term "benchmarking" has its roots in cartography, where bench marks are important orientation points. Nowadays it is mostly applied for setting reference points in evaluating and comparing different systems' performances. A system's performance can be assessed in terms of metrics, e.g. quality of output, efficiency (input / output – ratio), productivity (quantity of output / time unit). To reach a realistic and significant assessment, these data need to be related to the performance data provided by congeneric systems that may act as reference system (benchmark) in that comparison.

Benchmarking is also applied in assessing enterprise processes: different enterprises run different business processes with more or less efficiency. In trying

---

[*] *With contributions from various colleagues, see Acknowledgements section.*

to optimize its own processes, an enterprise may select a reference enterprise running a similar process in an outstanding manner (setting the benchmark). The result of this comparison will be a gap between the reference (benchmark) process and the process to be optimized. In a final step a set of *Best Practices* needs to be developed for bridging the gap between the sub-optimal "as-is" process state and the desired "to-be"-state represented by the reference process.

Some references

- Battaglia, J. Jr and Musar, R. (2000): Picking the right benchmark, *Journal of Accountancy*, 190(2), p. 63.
- Bhutta Khurrum, S. and Huq, F. (1999): Benchmarking ± best practices, an integrated approach, *Benchmarking: An International Journal*, 6(3), pp. 254-68.
- Carpinetti, L.C.R. and De Melo, A.M. (2002): What to benchmark?: A systematic approach and cases, *Benchmarking: An International Journal*, 9(3), pp. 244-55.

- **Complexity theories.** Complexity deals with systems that show complex structures in time or space, often hiding simple deterministic rules. An intuitive notion considers a complex system as a system for which it is difficult, if not impossible, to reduce the number of characterizing variables without loosing its essential global functional properties. The first developments in the area of complexity resulted from the studies in non-linear systems. In fact, more than a single theory, the so-called complexity science represents a set of theories describing how the complex adaptive systems like stock markets, supply chains, ecosystems, and even rain forests work. A complex system can be understood as any network of interacting agents (processes or elements) that exhibits a dynamic aggregate behavior as a result of the individual activities of its agents. According to Phellan, "at the core of complexity science is the assumption that complexity in the world arises from simple rules. However, these rules (which I term 'generative rules') are unlike the rules (or laws) of traditional science. Generative rules typically determine how a set of artificial agents will behave in their virtual environment over time; including the interaction with other agents. The application of these generative rules to a large population of agents leads to emergent behavior that may bear some resemblance to real world phenomena.

Some important characteristics of complex systems include: non-determinism, limited functional decomposability, distributed nature of information, and emergence and self-organization. Emergence is in fact one of the most important properties of complex systems, what makes this paradigm an appealing approach for the analysis of advanced collaborative networks.

Some references

- Phelan, S. E. (2001): What Is Complexity Science, Really?, Emergence: A Journal of Complexity Issues in Organizations and Management, 3(1), pp. 120 - 136. www.utdallas.edu/~sphelan/Papers/whatis.pdf
- Pavard B. and Dugdale J. (2000): The contribution of complexity theory to the study of socio-technical cooperative systems. Nashua Conf.
- Eijnatten, F.M. van (2003): Chaordic systems thinking: Chaos and complexity to explain human performance management. At the First International Conference on Performance Measures, Bench-marking and Best Practices in New Economy, Guimaraes, Portugal, University of Minho, June 10-13. Paper published in: Putnik, G. (Ed.), Proceedings of Business Excellence '03.

- Luis Rocha (1999): Complex Systems Modeling: Using Metaphors From Nature in Simulation and Scientific Models, in BITS: Computer and Communications News. http://mysite.verizon.net/pulsar/Library_Ref/Complexity%20Theory/Complex_Systems_Modeling/Complex_System_Modeling.html

♦ ***Decision support****.* Decision support is concerned with supporting human decision-making. The decision making process typically includes: assessing the problem, collecting and verifying information, identifying alternatives, anticipating consequences of decisions, making the choice using sound and logical judgment based on available information, informing others of the decision and the rationale behind it, and evaluating the effect of the decision. Decision support encompasses a number of more specialized disciplines: operations research, decision analysis, data warehousing, group decision support systems, and even computer-supported cooperative work.
Some references
- Clemen R. T. (1996): Making Hard Decisions: An Introduction to Decision Analysis. Duxbury Press.
- Mallach, E. G. (1994): Understanding Decision Support Systems and Expert Systems. Irwin, Burr Ridge.
- Power, D. J. (2007): Decision Support Systems Glossary, DSSResources.COM, World Wide Web, http://DSSResources.COM/glossary/

♦ ***Distributed group dynamics****.* An area that originates in the work of Kurt Lewin (1947) and focuses on inter-group relationships, such as power, leadership behavior, hostility, compliancy etc. A group is understood as two or more individuals engaged in some social interactions, for the purpose of achieving some goal or goals. Sociometric methods (Moreno 1934, 1951) are examples of techniques used in this area.
Some references
- Lewin, K. (1947): Frontiers in group dynamics. Human relations 1, 5-42.
- Moreno, J.L. (1951): Sociometry, experimental method and science of society. Pacon House, Peagon: New York.
- Interpersonal Configurations and Cliques - http://www.analytictech.com/mb119/chap2c.htm
- Groups and group dynamics - http://www.onepine.info/mgrp2.htm , http://www.onepine.info/mgrp.htm

♦ ***Diversity in work teams****.* Organizations increasingly operate in a global context, needing to align internally the wide diversity of individuals and cultures found in the organization, with the diversity of individuals working in collaborating organizations. This area studies the factors that moderate the relationship between diversity and workgroup effectiveness identifying the advantages and disadvantages of heterogeneous groups, where advantages can be achieved through members' shared common goals and values and increased variance in perspectives and approaches.
Some references
- F.J. Milliken and L.L. Martins (1996): Searching for common threads: Understanding the multiple effects on diversity in organizational groups. Academy of Management Review 21(2): 402-433.
- Lavrac, J. (2003): Creating and Maintaining Commitment in a diverse workforce. PhD Thesis.

- http://www.inform.umd.edu/EdRes/Topic/Diversity/ - comprehensive index of multicultural and diversity resources.

♦ *(Dynamic / evolving) ontologies*. The word ontology first appeared in Aristotle's philosophical essays, where it used to describe the nature and organization of being. Artificial Intelligence (AI) practitioners are adopted the term to formally represent domains of knowledge. Often ontologies are expressed as hierarchal descriptions of the important concepts in a domain, coupled with a description of each one of these concepts. Ontologies consist of various base concepts that include: class, subclass, class hierarchy, instance, slot, value, defaults value, facet, type, cardinality, inheritance, variable and relation. A class represents an object category, and is usually made of a set of subclasses (subclasses by themselves are classes), thus forming a class hierarchy. The most upper class in ontology is referred to as "Thing". All the other subclasses and instances inherit from this "Thing" class. An instance of the class is an object (or example) that belongs to that class.

More recently the idea of dynamic / evolving ontologies became a hot issue. Unlike static ontologies, dynamic ones can capture the evolution of mutual understanding among members of the network. However building them is still more of an art. So far, only first limited experiences on distributed and evolving ontology creation and interoperation have been pursued.

Some references
- Heflin J., Hendler, J. (2000): Dynamic Ontologies on the Web, http://www.cs.umd.edu/projects/plus/SHOE/pubs/aaai2000.pdf
- Viezzer, N. (2001): Dynamic ontologies: how to build agents that can change their mind, http://www.cs.bham.ac.uk/~mxv/report3/report3.html
- Pinto, S., Gomez-Perez, A., Martins, J. P. (1999): Some Issues on Ontology Integration , http://osm.cs.byu.edu/CS652s04/PGM99Some.pdf
- Fensel D., et al, (2001): OIL: an ontology infrastructure for the Semantic Web. IEEE Intelligent Systems, Vol. 16, Issue 2, 38 – 45.
- Gomez-Perez, A., and Corcho, O. (2002): Ontology languages for the Semantic Web. IEEE Intelligent Systems, Vol. 17, Issue 1, Jan.-Feb.
- Gruber, T.R. (1995): Toward principles for the design of ontologies used for knowledge sharing. International Journal of Human-Computer Studies, 43, 907 – 928.
- Smirnov, A.V., and Chandra, C. (2000): Ontology-based knowledge management for co-operative supply chain configuration. American Association for Artificial Intelligence (AAAI) Symposium, 85-92.
- Slade, A.J., and Bokma, A.F. (2001): Ontologies within extended enterprises. Proceedings of the 35th Annual Hawaii International Conference on System Sciences, 496 -505.

♦ *Federated systems*. The concept of federation has been emerging in diverse areas, among which the multi-agent systems (MAS), the database and information management, and the web services communities can be signified. In all these contexts a network of distributed, autonomous, and heterogeneous resources (data/information or services) is considered and the basic principle is to allow authorized and transparent access to remote resources, without the need for the client to be aware or care about the resource distribution or communication mechanisms applied.

Federated MAS. Various federated architectures for MAS have been proposed in the literature. One example is the Facilitator-based approach in which several related agents are combined into a group. Communication between agents always takes place through a specialized interface agent called Facilitator. Another case is the broker-based federation. Brokers are agents similar to facilitators but with some additional functions such as monitoring and notification. While a facilitator is responsible only for a designated group of agents, any agent may contact any broker in the same system for finding its required service / information agents for a particular task.

Federated databases. A federated database system is a distributed multi-database system in which every node in the federation maintains the autonomy on its data and defines a set of export schemas through which the data is made available to other specific nodes. Every node is able to import data from other nodes through their import schemas, and access their data according to the bilaterally pre-defined access permissions. As a consequence of this general interaction facility, the federated database approach allows the cooperation between federated nodes, in order to accomplish common global tasks, while the autonomy and independence of every node is preserved and reinforced. There are 2 main types of federation: loosely coupled and tightly coupled.

Due to its capability to preserve node's autonomy while supporting cooperation and transparent data access via the federated query processing mechanism, the federated database architecture is a strong base approach for information management in CNs. The federated query processing component supports transparent access to the remotely located information (from multiple nodes) for which enterprises are authorized, while preserving the nodes' autonomy, visibility levels, and different access rights for exchanged information among CN nodes.

Services federation. In the service federation approaches, service providers, independently of the way their services are implemented or where they are located, make them accessible within a "virtual market". A client such as a VO creator can "shop" in this market for the best set of services to satisfy the needs of a given business opportunity. The service federation infrastructure provides the basic mechanisms for transparent (remote) access to services according to certain agreed access rules.

Services are registered in a Service Catalogs and various catalogs may be interconnected. Advanced lookup services will support service discovery and selection. Due to the members autonomy (and their legacy systems) there might be a large heterogeneity / diversity in the way services are implemented. However, in order to facilitate services' selection ("shopping") and utilization, a common service interface is agreed among the service providers.

The federated systems approaches are quite promising for CNs and various projects have applied some facets of federation.

Some references

- H. Afsarmanesh, C. Garita, Y. Ugur, A. Frenkel, L. O. Hertzberger (1999): Federated Information Management Requirements for Virtual Enterprises. In Book Infrastructures for Virtual Enterprises - Networking Industrial Enterprises, (L. M. Camarinha-Matos, H. Afsarmanesh, Editors), Kluwer Academic Publishers, Pages 36-48.
- C. Garita, H. Afsarmanesh, and L. O. Hertzberger (2002): A Survey of Distributed Information Management Approaches for Virtual Enterprise Infrastructures, in Managing Virtual Web Organizations in the 21st Century: Issues and Challenges, U. J. Franke, Ed.: Idea Group Publishing.

- Sheth, A; Larson J. (1990): Federated Database Systems for Managing Distributed, Heterogeneous, and Autonomous Databases, ACMCS, 22(3).
- Camarinha-Matos, L.M., Afsarmanesh, H. (2001): Virtual Enterprise Modeling and Support Infrastructures: Applying Multi-Agent Systems Approaches, in Lecture Notes in Artificial Intelligence LNAI Nº 2086, Springer.
- Shen, W. (2001): Agent.based cooperative manufacturing scheduling: an overview, COVE News N. 2, www.uninova.pt/~cove/newsletter.htm.

♦ ***Formal engineering methods***. Formal methods are mathematically based techniques for the specification, development and verification of systems (e.g. software and hardware). They represent a way to enhance the rigor (methodology), comprehensibility (human), and tool supportability (software tools) of systems development process and consequently the quality of the final *product*. In this sense, formal methods are fault avoidance techniques that help in the reduction of errors introduced into a system, particularly at the earlier stages of design. They complement fault removal techniques like testing.
Some examples are: Estelle, RAISE, Petri Nets, Z notation, SDL (see also http://www.imm.dtu.dk/~db/formal-methods/which-fms/).
Some references

- Bowen, J.P. and M.G. Hinchey (1995): Seven More Myths of Formal Methods. *IEEE Software*, p. 34-41.
- Bowen, J.P. and M.G. Hinchey (1995): Ten Commandments of formal Methods. *IEEE Computer*, p. 56-63.
- Hall, A. (1990): Seven Myths of Formal Methods. *IEEE Software*, p. 11-19.
- Wooldridge, M: Introduction to formal methods, http://www.csc.liv.ac.uk/~mjw/teaching/soft-eng/lect06.pdf
- Bjørner, D. (2003): Integrating formal methods - http://www.imm.dtu.dk/~db/formal-methods/challenges/utopia/

♦ ***Formal theories***. Formal theories are based in mathematical tools (e.g. logic, set theory, algebra) that are used for describing system properties, and for producing systems that satisfy those properties. These theories are used to solve design problems like for instance: architecture, protocols, network creation-specify systems, verify specifications according to correctness and completeness. Although formal theories are expressed using a formal language, it shall be noted that the use of a formalism does not guarantee by itself that we have a formal theory. The development of a formal theory is a complex task involving a considerable number of concepts whose representation must be accurate and free from ambiguities. First-order languages seem to have enough expressiveness to be used in different formalization areas in CNs.
Some references

- Formal theories - http://www.math.psu.edu/simpson/papers/philmath/node11.html
- Formal systems - http://hemsidor.torget.se/users/m/mauritz/math/logic/inform.htm

♦ ***Game theory***. Game theory is a branch of mathematics that uses models to study interactions with formalized incentive structures ("games"). It can be applied to a variety of fields, including economics, evolutionary biology and political science. The predicted and actual behavior of individuals (groups or formal organizations) in games is studied, as well as optimal strategies. Game theory has important applications in the field of collective action, which is inline with the problems of CNs. It seeks to find rational strategies in situations where the outcome depends not only on one's own strategy and business environment, but also upon the strategies chosen by other players (i.e. CN members), with possibly different or overlapping goals.

Game theory can provide the concepts for the analysis of decision-making in cases involving multiple decision-makers who interact with each other. In the case of CNs, game theory could offer: tools to manage *cost, risk and profit sharing* among the network participants, and tools to design *optimal incentives* for the VBE, VO, etc.

Some references

- www.gametheory.net (A comprehensive web-resource)
- Gibbons, R. (1992): A Primer in Game Theory. Prentice Hall. (A textbook for economists)
- Czap, H., Becker, M. (2003): Multi-Agent Systems and Microeconomic Theory: A Negotiation Approach to solve Scheduling Problems in High Dynamic Environments. http://csdl.computer.org/comp/proceedings/hicss/2003/1874/03/187430083b.pdf
- Gerding, E.H., van Bragt, D.D.B., La Poutré, J.A. (2000): Scientific Approaches and Techniques for Negotiation A Game Theoretic and Artificial Intelligence Perspective. http://ftp.cwi.nl/CWIreports/SEN/SEN-R0005.pdf
- Norman, T. J., Preece, A., Chalmers, S., Jennings, N., Luck, M., Dang, V., Nguyen, T., Deora, V., Shao, J., Gray, W., Fiddian, N. (2004):Agent-Based Formation of Virtual Organisations. *Knowledge Based Systems*, 17 (Elsevier), http://www.ecs.soton.ac.uk/~nrj/download-files/kbs04.pdf
- General links:
- Stanford Encyclopedia of Philosophy: Game Theory, http://plato.stanford.edu/entries/game-theory/
- Andrew J. Buck "An Introduction to Game Theory with Economic Applications", http://courses.temple.edu/economics/Game Outline/index02.htm
- Drew Fudengerg in Jean Tirole: Game Theory, MIT Press, 1991
- http://www.gametheory.net/ - game theory resource page
- http://plato.stanford.edu/entries/game-theory/ - an introduction.

♦ ***Graph theory***. Graph theory is the branch of mathematics that examines the properties of graphs. Informally, a graph is a set of objects called vertices (or nodes) connected by links called edges (or arcs). If the edges have a direction associated with them (indicated by an arrow in the graphical representation) then it is a directed graph, or digraph. Various networks are conveniently described by means of graphs, which is also the case for networked organizations. In CN several layers of networks exists, which can be, studied holistically or as sub problems (physical network, organizational network, social network, etc.). There are many available algorithms to analyze and extract properties from graphs, what makes it a useful tool.

Some references

- Biggs, N. (1989): Discrete mathematics. Oxford: Clarendon Press.
- Anderson (1974): A first course in combinatorial mathematics. Oxford: Clarendon Press.
- Wilson, R. (1979): Introduction to graph theory. London: Longman.
- Graph theory - http://www.math.fau.edu/locke/graphthe.htm
- http://www.graphtheory.com/ - graph theory resource.

♦ ***Knowledge mapping***. A knowledge map is "a visual representation of a knowledge domain according to criteria that facilitate the location, comprehension or development of knowledge". The process used to gather the information needed for knowledge map construction is called knowledge mapping (direct and indirect methods).

A comprehensive knowledge map about CNs can be seen as a dynamic landscape of explicit knowledge (core competencies, legacy systems, additional expertise, forms, documents, presentations, papers), procedures (guidance, tips, checklists), tools and methods (web services, training, applications) available to the network members.

Some references
- White, D. (2001): Knowledge Mapping and Management. IRM Press.
- Wiig, K. M. (1999): Introducing Knowledge Management into the Enterprise. In Knowledge Management Handbook. J. Liebowitz (Editor). Boca Raton, FL: CRC Press, Chapter 3, pp. 119-158.
- Doignon, J.-P., Falmagne, J.-C. (1999): Knowledge Spaces. Springer Verlag.
- http://www.aleks.com
- http://www.brint.com

♦ ***Memetics***. The 'meme' is one of the most central concepts in evolutionary policy processes. It is defined as a replicator: 'a piece of data that is copied from individual to individual without too much alteration'. In an evolutionary framework a meme is a replicator, a term that was first used for genes.

In human cognitive processes it is quite common that ideas, normative criteria and other entities are copied from individual to individual. Ideas thus transmitted from individual to individual, or from report to report, are called replicators. The acts in which this transmission takes place are called replications. A replicator contains data or, in other words, has a 'coded structure'. Such replicators are called 'memes' when the replication system is the brain. Memes may be ideas, but also ways of thought, complete models of how (parts of) our world works (theories), examples or metaphors to explain things, and so on. Just as genes, memes are replicators, be it in a very different replication environment and process. A meme can also be seen as a contagious information pattern that replicates by parasitically infecting human minds and altering their behavior, causing them to propagate the pattern.

In the case of CN each member could be seen as a meme as well as every process (cognitive and business process) competing with others. According to the memetics theory only those memes that are in-line with the environment (business, cultural, VBE, etc.) have good chances to survive.

Some references
- Dawkins, R. (1991): Viruses of the Mind. In Dennett and His Critics: Demystifying Mind, ed. Bo Dalhbom (Cambridge, Mass.: Blackwell)
  http://www.cscs.umich.edu/~crshalizi/Dawkins/viruses-of-the-mind.html
- Speel, H.-C. (1995): Memetics: On a conceptual framework for cultural evolution. Evolution of Complexity Symposium. http://www.hanscees.com/hcesmem.htm
- Moritz, E. (1990): Memetic Science: I - General introduction. The Institute For Memetic Research, Florida, USA.
- A Brief Overview and History of Memetics - http://jom-emit.cfpm.org/overview.html
- http://pespmc1.vub.ac.be/MEMES.html , - Principia Cybernetica Web by F. Heylighen
- http://users.lycaeum.org/~sputnik/Memetics/ , memetics on-line papers.

♦ **Metaphors**. The essence of a metaphor is support to understanding and experiencing one kind of thing in terms of another. Metaphors and other mental models provide a means for individuals and, ultimately, organizations to create and share their understandings. These mental models establish images, names and an understanding of how things fit together. They articulate what is important and unimportant ...the models must be articulated and accepted in the organization for them to be effective ... In the context of such models, "believing is seeing".

Although not formal, metaphors can provide a quick description for human communication (a possible help in expressing complex ill-defined concepts). They can be used in early stages (conceptual design). There is however the risk of taking metaphors too strictly.

Some references
  - Mental Models, Metaphor, Systems Theory and Theory -
    http://www.chrisfoxinc.com/mentalModels.htm
  - Lawley, J.: METAPHORS OF ORGANISATION - Part 1 & Part 2-
    http://www.devco.demon.co.uk/Metaphors-of-Orgs-1.html ,
    http://www.devco.demon.co.uk/Metaphors-of-Orgs-2.html
  - Rohrer, T. (1997): Conceptual Blending on the Information Highway: How Metaphorical Inferences Work. International Cognitive Linguistics Conference '95 Proceedings. http://philosophy.uoregon.edu/metaphor/iclacnf4.htm
  - Limbeek, C.A. (2001): Metaphors in a Virtual Chat Environment - Selected Readings, IVLA Conference, an international conference in Eskilstuna, Sweden. http://www.idp.mdh.se/forskning/amnen/informationsdesign/publikationer/pdf/carinametaphors2001.pdf

♦ **Multi-agent systems**. The study of multi-agent systems (MAS) focuses on systems in which many intelligent agents interact with each other. Agents are considered to be autonomous entities, for instance as software programs or robots and their interactions can be either cooperative or selfish. AI researchers have devoted considerable attention to understanding and modeling how societies of agents can be organized and their behavior regulated. Coalition formation, negotiation, brokering, contract negotiation, development of concepts related to norms and institutions, are examples of intense research areas in this discipline. On the other hand, researchers in social sciences and complexity science are adopting the MAS paradigm as a simulation tool to develop and evaluate their models of social organizations. MAS can, therefore be an important catalyst in diverse approaches to model and understand collaborative networks.

The potential use of this approach in virtual organizations and their breeding environments has already been recognized by several researchers that represent enterprises as agents and the inter-enterprise cooperation as interactions in a distributed multi-agent system. The initial works however were more focused on the use of MAS as a technology, rather than as a modeling framework. Nevertheless, the recent theoretical work on MAS suggests however its potential contribution to understanding and modeling emerging behavior and in supporting the institutions involved in complex collaborative networks.

Some references
  - Camarinha-Matos, L.M.; Afsarmanesh, H. (2001): Virtual Enterprise Modeling and Support

Infrastructures: Applying Multi-Agent Systems Approaches, in Multi-Agent Systems and Applications, M. Luck, V. Marik, O. Stpankova, R. Trappl (eds.), Lecture Notes in Artificial Intelligence LNAI 2086, pp.335-364, Springer, ISBN 3-540-42312-5, July.

- Marik, V.; Pechoucek, M. (2004): Agent technology for virtual organizations, in Collaborative Networked Organizations - A research agenda for emerging business models, Kluwer Academic Publishers.

♦ **Multi-agent dependence theory.** According to this theory, dependence and power relations between the agents are the basis to explain how agents interact in order to cooperate and accept to help others. This approach tries to understand two fundamental problems: *(i)* The sociality problem, which deals with the question: Why should autonomous agents enter into social interactions? *(ii)* The adoption problem, which deals with the question: How can an agent get his problem to become social, i.e. get it adopted by other agents?

Based on this approach a dependence relation is the informal answer to the sociality problem where there are a number of possible dependency relations (unilateral dependence, mutual dependence, reciprocal dependence, and independence) and power is the answer to the adoption problem where there are three types of power (power of, power over and power to influence). This theory can be useful in capturing aspects of the behavioral dimension of collaborative networks.

Some references

- Sichman, J.S., Conte, R., Castelfranchi, C., Demazeau, Y. (1994): A social reasoning mechanis based on dependence networks. In A.G. Cohn (ed.), Proceedings of the IIth European Conference on Artificial Intelligence - ECAI'94 (pp. 188-92). John Wiley & Sons, UK.
- Sichman, J.S. and R. Conte (2002): Multi-agent Dependence by Dependence Graphs. in 1st International Joint Conference on Autonomous Agents and Multi-Agent Systems (AAMAS'02). Bologna, Italy. http://delivery.acm.org/10.1145/550000/544855/p483-sichman.pdf?key1=544855&key2=7515987801&coll=GUIDE&dl=ACM&CFID=22927676&CFTOKEN=61926431

♦ **Network analysis.** A wide variety of systems of interconnected components are called networks. Specific examples include: transport networks, electric circuits, electricity networks, social networks and business networks, criminal networks, computer networks, telecommunications networks, network externality in economics, neural network.

In mathematics, a network is usually called a graph. General-purpose mathematical models of network structures and associated algorithms have been developed in graph theory. For instance, computer network routing is a direct application of graph theory to the real world. Networks can be characterized in a number of different ways. For example, many networks are observed to be scale-free networks, in which a few network nodes act as "very connected" hubs.

Networks are present in all sectors - in telecommunications as much as in information technology, in the energy as much as in the transportation sector, in the corporate world as much as in public life. Planning networks so as to ideally suit a network operator's business and customer processes is a major success factor.

In telecommunication, network management is the execution of the set of functions required for controlling, planning, allocating, deploying, coordinating, and monitoring the resources of a telecommunications network, including performing functions such as initial network planning, frequency allocation, predetermined traffic routing to support load balancing, cryptographic key distribution authorization, configuration management, fault management, security management, performance management, and accounting management. Network management systems model an entire telecommunications network and make it possible to filter and correlate alarms (traps, poll events) in a useful way. Network management systems are typically made up of subsystems, such as subscriber management, fault management, and performance management. Collaborative networks may benefit from models and algorithms defined in various of these other specialized networks.

Some references
- CONDIS (COmmunication Network Documentation and Information System) - http://www.siemens.at/condis/
- ECANSE - http://www.siemens.at/pse/ecanse/.

♦ ***Portfolio theory***. Portfolio theory was originally introduced by Markowitz (1952), who developed an approach to select the optimal portfolio of financial securities. In general, the problem is to select the in-some-ways optimal subset from a set of alternatives. In the context of CN's, the application could be for instance to *select the optimal VO from a BE*. The optimality criterion/criteria depend on the specific task that the VO needs to carry out. The portfolio approach *may help seeing the VO as a whole*, instead of merely locally optimising the input of each individual partner. Hence, the objective of global efficiency would be inbuilt in the management mechanism.

Some references
- www.moneychimp.com/articles/risk/riskintro.htm (An introductory to modern portfolio theory in the context of finance)
- Luenberger, D. G. (1998): *Investment Science*, Oxford University Press. (A textbook on investment theory)

♦ ***Real options theory***. Real options theory builds on financial theories such as *discounted cash flow* and *net present value*. The objective is to value actions that a decision-maker can either perform or leave undone. The improvement to portfolio theory is that real options theory allows the modeling of dynamic uncertainties. In the CN context such cases could be, e.g. decision on *whether to found a VO* to meet a collaboration opportunity or evaluate the *minimum profitable bid* for a customer's call if a VO would be founded.

Some references
- www.real-options.com (A website supporting a textbook having the same name)
- www.puc-rio.br/marco.ind/ (A comprehensive web-resource on real options)
- Luenberger, D. G. (1998): *Investment Science*, Oxford University Press. (A textbook on investment theory)

♦ ***Scopos theory***. The Scopos theory (Greek word for the "objective of action") deals with the problem of translation and interpretation was set by a German scholar Vermeer two decades ago. The basic goal of here is transformation of the information or knowledge from one cultural and language environment to others in such a way that the understanding and conception of the source information or knowledge would be the same for all cultural and language environments for which the transformation occurred. According to Vermeer, the understanding of the objective defines the character of the whole processing of special lexis since the shape of the original text depends on the specificity of the transposed text as well as its purpose. Therefore, the recipient of the information should take into account not only the original information but also accompanying conditions in terms of specialized areas of the source language and culture.

A basic process in every organization is communication where the machines are involved in the communication or knowledge transfer when there are humans involved in communication. Similarly in CNs. In order to make the knowledge transfer most efficient, the personalization should be taken into consideration. Personalization of the knowledge transfer could be described with Scopos theory.

Some references
  - Vermeer, H. (1990): Skopos und Translationsauftrag – Aufsätze,Heidelberg pp.24 – 32.
  - www.sprog.asb.dk/la/WrittenComBA02/TASkoposIntro.ppt - Scopos introduction.

◆ *Self-organizing systems, autopoiesis.* Realizing that the organizational forms we can identify around us are only a small sub-set of those theoretically possible, the question arises: Why these organizational forms and not the others? Self-organization theory, that is a branch of systems theory also considered one of the development axes of the theory of complex systems, tries to address such question and relates to the process of "order" formation in complex dynamic systems. The essence of self-organization is that system structure often appears without explicit pressure or involvement from outside the system. Self-organization is understood as the spontaneous creation of a globally coherent pattern out of certain local interactions. In other words, the constraints on form (i.e. organization) of interest to us are internal to the system, resulting from the interactions among its components, and usually independent of the "physical" nature of those components. According to the 'self-organization' theory, order in an interconnected system of elements arises around what are called the 'attractors' that help to create and hold stable patterns within the system. These attractors combine to form a dynamic 'landscape', which determines the behavior of the system. The field of self-organization seeks general rules about the growth and evolution of systemic structure, the forms it might take, and finally methods that predict the future organization that will result from changes made to the underlying components.

The term autopoiesis appeared first in the area of biology and provides a foundation for describing and analyzing 'auto-determination', as the central concept of autopoiesis defines living systems as self-producing units which accordingly (self-)maintain their essential form. Autopoiesis is the process whereby an organization produces itself. An autopoietic organization is an autonomous and self-maintaining unity which contains component-producing processes. The components, through their interaction, generate recursively the same network of processes which produced them.

According to its original creators (Maturana and Vilela): "An autopoietic machine is a machine organised (defined as a unity) as a network of processes of production (transformation and destruction) of components that produces the components which: (i) through their interactions and transformations continuously regenerate and realise the network of processes (relations) that produced them; and (ii) constitute it (the machine) as a concrete unity in the space in which they (the components) exist by specifying the topological domain of its realisation as such a network."

These concepts might be used to better understand emerging dynamic CNs.

Some references

- Heylighen, F. (2001): The science of self-organization and adaptivity, The Encyclopedia of Life Support Systems, Vol. Knowledge Management, Organizational Intelligence and Learning, and Complexity" (L. Douglas Kiel, Ed.), EOLSS Publishers.
- Whitaker, R. (1995): Self-Organization, Autopoiesis, and Enterprises, http://bat710.univ-lyon1.fr/~jmathon/autopoesis/Main.html
- Corning, P. A. (1995): SYNERGY AND SELF-ORGANIZATION IN THE EVOLUTION OF COMPLEX SYSTEMS. SYSTEMS RESEARCH, 12(2): 89-12. http://members.aol.com/iscs/synres.html
- Autopoiesis - http://www.cs.ucl.ac.uk/staff/t.quick/autopoiesis.html.
- FAQ - http://www.calresco.org/sos/sosfaq.htm .

♦ **Semiotics.** Semiotics is the science of signs. It is concerned with saying whether and how to use signs to refer to something. As main dimensions, semiotics considers syntax, semantics, and pragmatics (concerned with the relationship between signs and the potential behavior of responsible agents in a social context). Organizational semiotics focuses on the concept of sign as a basis for more complex concepts such as information.

In one of its branches, potentially useful for CNs, semiotics is concerned with modeling responsibility relationships and commitments, prescribing norms and roles, and legal support. It can also be used as a tool to capture system requirements. Particularly in the normative perspective it addresses collaborating individuals that share a number of norms of different types: espistemic, deontic, and axiologic. Also the pragmatic analysis, i.e. the identification of the agent intentions behind the actions of organizational agents is particularly important in conversation analysis and patterns of interaction and coordination. However reasoning in deontic logic may lead to paradoxes; difficult to automate reasoning.

Some references

- Filipe, J. (2004): The organizational semiotics normative paradigm, in Collaborative Networked Organizations – A research agenda for emerging business models, Kluwer Academic Publishers.
- Chandler, D. (2007): Semiotics for beginners. Routledge, 2nd Edition. http://www.aber.ac.uk/media/Documents/S4B/semiotic.html .

♦ **Social networks analysis.** Social network analysis is a methodological approach in the social sciences using graph-theoretic concepts, possibly combined with some statistical analysis, to describe, understand and explain social structures. In other words it is focused on uncovering the patterning of people's interaction. It involves the mapping and measuring of relationships and flows between people, groups, organizations, computers or other information/knowledge processing entities. The nodes in the network are the people and groups while the links show relationships or flows between the nodes. Individuals, groups, and organizations are tied together by interaction patterns, common members, communication exchanges, and resource flows.

The social networks approach to the study of behavior has involved two commitments: (1) it is guided by formal theory organized in mathematical terms, and (2) it is grounded in the systematic analysis of empirical data. For instance, a method to understand networks and their participants is to evaluate the location of actors in the network. Measuring the network location is finding the centrality of a node. These measures help determine the importance, or prominence, of a node in the network. Other metrics used include: degree of a network, betweenness, closeness, Structural Equivalence, Cluster Analysis (cliques and other densely connected clusters), Small Worlds, etc.

Examples of research lines in this area include:

- New concepts, theories, and knowledge about organizing and organization, coordination, adaptation, and evolution.
- Integration of soft computing approaches in graph theory.
- Tools and procedures for the validation and analysis of computational models of distributed agent systems at the group, organization, and social level.
- Simulation and network based tools and metrics.

The results of this area seem fundamental for Professional Virtual Communities and CNs in general. One potential application is to elaborate collaboration-oriented performance indicators.

Some references

- Brandes, U., Wagner, D. (2003): Analysis and Visualization of Social Networks. Proceedings of the 2nd International Workshop on Experimental and Efficient Algorithms (WEA'03), volume 2647 of Lecture Notes in Computer Science, pages 261-266. http://i11www.ilkd.uni-karlsruhe.de/algo/people/dwagner/papers/bw-vavsn-03.pdf
- Barabási, A. L. (2003): Linked: How everything is interconnected to everything else.... Penguin Books.
- Wasserman, S. and Faust, K. (1998): Social Network Analysis. Methods and applications. USA: Cambridge University Press.
- Freeman, L.C. (1997): Uncovering organizational hierarchies. Computational & Mathematical organization theory 3:1:5-18.
- Guide to Online Social Networks, Social Software, and Business Communities - http://www.onlinebusinessnetworks.com/online-social-networks-guide/

♦ **Soft computing.** Soft computing differs from traditional (hard or crisp) computing in that, unlike hard computing, it is tolerant of imprecision, uncertainty, partial truth, and approximation. Soft computing tries to exploit the tolerance for imprecision, uncertainty, partial truth, and approximation to achieve tractability, robustness and low solution cost. The basic ideas underlying soft computing find their roots on fuzzy sets, analysis of complex systems and decision processes, probabilistic reasoning, and the possibility theory and soft data analysis. More recently neural computing and genetic computing where "added" to soft computing.

Considering the growing importance of the human and social aspects in CNs, soft computing approaches, also known as computational intelligence, are likely to play an important role in this area.

Some references
- Engelbrecht, AS. P. (2002): Computational Intelligence: An introduction. Wiley.
- Kusiak, A. (): Soft Computing: Industrial Applications, http://www.icaen.uiowa.edu/~ie238/Lecture/Soft_computing.pdf
- Tzafestas, S G (1999): SOFT COMPUTING IN SYSTEMS AND CONTROL TECHNOLOGY. World Scientific Series in Robotics and Intelligent Systems - Vol. 18. http://www.worldscientific.com/books/engineering/3706.html

♦ **Synergetics**. Applied to the human mind, "synergy" denotes the working together of the enormous variety of functions that comprise the mind, producing a new whole that is greater than the mere sum of its parts. Individual Synergetics, Group Synergetics and Social Synergetics, are three vitally important divisions of this field.

Synergetics is actually a branch of cybernetics and is based on philosophical theory of "connectionism". The theory is related to the Chaos Theory, self-organization and complexity. The theory is mathematically well elaborated and can be used in CNs namely to understand emergence and value creation.

Some references
- Grabec I., Sachse W. (1997): Synergetics of Measurements, Prediction and Control, Springer Verlag, Series in Synergetics, Heidelberg.
- Buckminster Fuller, R. (1979): SYNERGETICS Explorations in the Geometry of Thinking, Macmillan Publishing Co. Inc.
- www.nous.org.uk/synergetics.html ,
- http://spkurdyumov.narod.ru/Start1Engl.htm

♦ **Temporal and modal logic**. Modal logic is the study of the deductive behavior of the expressions 'it is necessary that' and 'it is possible that'. It also includes logics for belief, for tense and other temporal expressions, for the deontic (moral) expressions such as 'it is obligatory that' and 'it is permitted that', and many others.

Temporal logic (also known as tense logic) refers to approaches to the representation of temporal information within a logical framework. It deals with expressions such as "It will always be the case that ...", "It will be the case that ... ", "It has always been the case that ...", "It was the case that..."

Some references
- Garson, J. (2000, 2007): Modal Logic. The Stanford Encyclopedia of Philosophy - http://plato.stanford.edu/entries/logic-modal/
- Galton, A. (1999, 2008): Temporal Logic. The Stanford Encyclopedia of Philosophy - http://plato.stanford.edu/entries/logic-temporal/

♦ **Transactions costs theory**. Transactions costs are generally defined as being the cost for gathering information, negotiation and contracting, and physical transaction of *objects* through a defined interface. According to this theory, enterprises and markets are alternative governance structures that differ in their *transactions costs*. From this point of view cooperation is explained as an organizational "hybrid" form between the market and the enterprise.

Some references

- Williamson, O. E. (1985): The Economic Institutions of Capitalism: Firms, Markets, Relational Contracting, New York: Free Press.
- Williamson, O. E. (1998): Transaction Cost Economics: how it works; Where it is Headed. De Economist 146 1: 23-58.
- Jong, G. Nooteboom, B. (Ed.) (1992):The Causal Structure of a Long-term Supply Relationships: An Empirical Test of a Generalized Transaction Cost Theory.
- Klos, T. and Nooteboom, B. (2001): Agent-based computational transaction cost economics, Journal of Economic Dynamics and Control, 25: 503-526.
- Appel, W.; Behr, R. (1998): Towards the theory of virtual organisations: A description of their formation and figure. Virtual-Organization.Net Newsletter, 2(2):15-36, June. http://virtual-organization.net/news/nl_2.2/nl_2-2a4.pdf

♦ ***Trust building models***. There are many views of trust and there are also many fields, which study this topic, as for instance: sociology, biology, economics, management and philosophy. The definition of trust given by Morton Deutsch in 1992 is the most widely accepted:

If an individual is confronted with an ambiguous path, a path that can lead to an event perceived to be beneficial (Va+) or to an event perceived to be harmful (Va-); He perceives that the occurrences of (Va+) or (Va-) is contingent on the behavior of another person; and He perceives that the strength of (Va-) to be greater than the strength of (Va+). If he chooses to take an ambiguous path with such properties, I shall say he makes a trusting choice; if he chooses not take the path, he makes a distrustful choice.

A second definition is given by Gambetta: "*a particular level of the subjective probability with which an agent will perform a particular action, both before he can monitor such action and in a context in which it affects his own action*".

In a cooperative process between enterprises there is mutual dependence between them and in order to achieve success in a dynamic environment the cooperation agreements, for instance, must be established within an extremely short period of time. Since the traditional ways of collaboration are usually very time and resources consuming and since laws do not change as fast as technology does, a type of cooperation that is based on a trust model might be an efficient alternative to reduce the complexity and time consuming of some steps. The application of a trust model based on socio-cognitive aspects, reputation mechanism, and competencies evaluation could be a good approach.

Some references

- Castelfranchi, C. and R. Falcone (2000): *Trust is much more than subjective Probability: Mental components and sources of trust.* In *Proceedings of the 33rd Hawaii International Conference on Systems Sciences (HICSS 2000).* Maui, Hawaii, USA.
- McKnight, D. and N. L. Chervany, (1996): The Meanings of Trust. University of Minnesota.
- Rahman, A. A. and S. Hailes (2000): Supporting trust in virtual communities. In *Proceedings of the 33rd Hawaii International Conference on System Sciences.*
- Lewis, J.D. (2000): Trusted Partners How companies Build Mutual Trust and win Together. The Free Press.
- Ramchurn, S. D., Sierra, C., Godo, L. and Jennings, N. R. (2003): A Computational Trust Model for Multi-Agent Interactions based on Confidence and Reputation. 6th International Workshop of Deception, Fraud and Trust in Agent Societies, 2003, Melbourne, Australia. http://www.ecs.soton.ac.uk/~nrj/download-files/aamas-trust-ws.pdf
- Wang, Y., Vassileva, J. (2003): Bayesian Network-Based Trust Model. Proc. of IEEE/WIC International Conference on Web Intelligence (WI 2003):372-378,October 13-17, Halifax, Canada. http://www.cs.usask.ca/grads/yaw181/publications/wangy_trust.pdf

3.3 Towards an applicability map

Figure 1 represents a simplified attempt to establish a map relating different addressed modeling constructs to the modeling dimensions of the Endogenous Elements perspective. This map is not exhaustive and certainly not fully accurate, but just a contribution providing a rough idea of the many possibilities that can be considered.

Some of the constructs have a generic nature, others are very specific. For instance, UML or formal engineering methods are quite general and thus potentially applicable to all modeling dimensions; on the other hand, deontic logic is quite specific and potentially useful in the modeling of only some aspects of CN's behavior.

As shown in Figure 1, there are some sub-dimensions for which there is no specialized theory that is particularly suited (e.g. hard/soft resources). Nevertheless there are some generic formalisms (associated to CN modeling framework in the center) that are "good for everything", such as the UML, ontology, etc.

UML, although widely used in industrial applications over the last decade, is still less formal than many others mentioned in this chapter and does not include clear guidance regarding the use of its diverse graphical notations. Some attempts to add more formalization to UML (e.g. pUML – precise UML) are on going. But the methodological aspects in terms of guidance on what notation to use for each case are not yet sufficiently addressed. There are even some "conceptual discontinuities" between these notations.

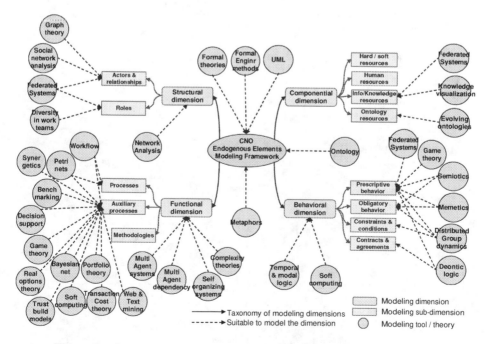

Figure 1 – An attempt to map modelling constructs applicable to CNs

Another aspect to consider is that some modeling constructs might cover, in part, more than one dimension or sub-dimension. For instance, complexity theories can be linked to the functional and behavioral dimensions. Not all these possibilities are represented in Figure 1. The suitability of a theory / tool to be applied to a particular modeling perspective also depends on the experience of the modeler with that theory / tool. There are in fact several "gray areas" of applicability. For instance, self-organizing systems could, in a limited way, also relate to the structure of the network. Therefore, and in order to not make the map too complex, only what currently seems to be the <u>most important and obvious links</u> are represented.

3.3 Main characteristics

The of the studied modelling constructs offer different levels of formalization, present different levels of maturity, and might be supported by specific languages, as summarized in Table 3.

Table 3 – Some characteristics of the considered theories

Modeling construct	Level of formalization	Includes specific modeling language / Examples	Maturity level
Benchmarking		(Statistical methods)	
Complexity theories			
Decision support		Decision Trees Multi-attribute Modeling Bayesian networks	
Deontic logic		Logic-based	
Distributed group dynamics			
Diversity in work teams			
Evolving ontologies			
Federated systems			
Formal engineering methods		Z, VDM, RAISE, Estelle, …	
Formal theories		First order languages, set theory	
Game theory		(Mathematical)	
Graph theory		Mathematical / set theory, graphical	
Knowledge mapping		(Diversity of graphical tools)	
Memetics			
Metaphors			
ML/ Bayesian networks		Probabilities	
Multi-agent systems		(FIPA standards), A-UML	

Multi-agent dependency theory			
Network analysis			
Portfolio theory			
Real options theory		(Mathematical / Probabilities)	
Scopos theory			
Self-organizing systems			
Semiotics			
Social network analysis		(Graph theory + statistics)	
Soft computing		Fuzzy Logic, Probabilistic Reasoning, Neural Computing, Genetic Computing	
Synergetics			
Temporal and modal logic		Logic-based	
Transactions cost theory			
Trust building models			
Web & text mining		Text mining methodologies and techniques; Text-mining applications (e.g. TOKO)	
Other tools			
Ontology		Ontology engineering methodologies & techniques; Ontology representation frameworks (e.g. OWL, RDFS); Ontology editors (e.g. Protégé, Triple20)	
Petri nets		Graphical, algebraic	
UML		Graphical, (Visio, Rat. Rose)	
Workflow		XPDL, WS-BPEL, …	

Level of formalization:

	Informal / descriptive		Semi-formal		Formal

Specific modeling language:

	No (resorts to a variety of "languages")		Yes (Which? examples)

Maturity level:

	On-going research		Mature &still being extended		Stable and mature

Another relevant observation is that some theories also propose a specific modeling language / tool (e.g. the theory of Petri nets suggests a specific graphical modeling language); others don't and leave it up to the modeler to chose a representation formalism.

On the other hand not all theories and modeling approaches are at the same level. In fact some of them are specializations of others or show a strong dependency on others, as illustrated in Figure 2. As the mentioned theories and modeling approaches were originated in different scientific disciplines, it is not easy to fully inter-relate them. Nevertheless this diagram can help the reader in "locating" each theory or modeling approach, i.e. getting a rough idea of what it covers, through association with others. For instance, a reader not familiar with Social Network Analysis can see that this theory is a kind of specialized branch of Graph Theory.

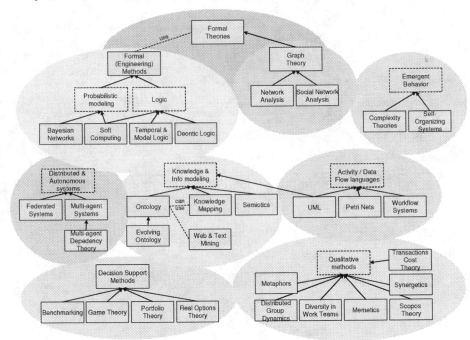

Figure 2 – "Modeling islands" – Some inter-dependencies

3.4 Formal or informal models

A recurrent debate can be found on the appropriate level of formalization to be used in the models. In other words, what is the desired level of formalization to be applied in CNs? From a purely theoretical point of view, it is well known that formal models, due to their strong mathematical foundation, are likely to reduce ambiguity and errors and thus are generally preferable as a basis in consolidated disciplines. However, the actual answer depends on the background of the modeler, the purpose, and the scope of the model, among other factors such as the level of maturity of the knowledge in the considered domain.

Formal methods facilitate automatic verification of the properties of the system being modeled as well as automatic synthesis of system components. But they are quite hard to handle by humans, even those with and engineering background.

Informal and semi-formal methods not always give adequate results in terms of correctness and precision. On one hand, informal methods normally use natural languages which are easier to understand by human interlocutors; they are however problematic when confidence in correctness is desired. On the other hand, semi-formal graphical representations such as data flow diagrams are easily readable, and provide some sort of "organization" or "structure" to the descriptions, but lack precise semantics, which may still lead to some ambiguous interpretations and turn reasoning or "automation processes" more difficult.

Attempts to introduce formal methods have been exercised in the areas of systems automation and software engineering, namely for automatic synthesis and verification. Many researchers in these areas claim that the more formal a model is the more correct, complete, precise, and unambiguous the resulting system remains. Furthermore, some state that formal methods with properly defined semantics can predict potential solutions to the system's behavior resulting in a more efficient and easily maintainable system (Alexander, 1996; Bowen & Hinchey, 2006; George & Vaughn, 2003; Liu, 2005. Nevertheless, difficulties to employ formal methods emerge when one tries to formalize a complex system as a whole. According to (Bowen & Hinchey, 2006), when analyzing the state practice of adoption of formal models in the last ten years, *"many highly publicized projects proclaimed as great formal methods successes formalized only 10 percent or less of the system"*.

Since a complete formalization of the properties of a whole (complex) system is not feasible in practice, it would be interesting to think of combining the best of

Informal Methods

Advantages:
- Specifications are written in a language that both experts and non-experts understand (e.g. natural language)
- Flexibility and ease of use.

Disadvantages:
- Often inaccurate
- Inconsistent
- Ambiguous
- Vague
- Self-contradictory
- Incomplete
- Encourages imprecise thinking
- Hard to handle with abstractions
- Difficult to check completeness

Semi-Formal Methods

Advantages:
- Emphasize the use of graphical representations of the system such as diagrams, tables and simple notation.
- Include structured analysis and object-oriented analysis.

Disadvantages:
- Lack of precise semantics, which may lead to ambiguous interpretation of certain aspects.

Formal Methods

Advantages:
- Early discovery of ambiguities, inconsistencies, incorrectness and incompleteness in informal requirements.
- Easily handle abstractions
- Is concise and encourages rigor
- Use mathematical notation to represent properties.
- Facilitates automatic reasoning.

Disadvantages:
- A non-expert cannot easily understand the specification.
- Even engineers have difficulties with the notation.
- Do not effectively handle large and complex systems development.
- Lack of adequate tools support
- In the real world, getting precise user requirements is a problem.

traditional models with the best of formal methods in order to achieve a "semi-rigid" level of formalization for CNs.

In fact the modeling scope in CNs does not only focus on the software components but rather involves many other perspectives of a socio-organizational nature that are hard to model. There is also a large variety of purposes and users for the developed models.

Therefore, a realistic approach is to consider that most modeling efforts at this stage have to be based on semi-formal approaches. To a lesser extend, and in specific sub-areas, formal models can be progressively attempted in order to facilitate both the scientific progress and the engineering activities.

4. CONCLUSIONS

Collaborative Networks practitioners have at their disposal a large variety of modeling constructs. A few tools (e.g. UML, ontologies) are general purpose (for some level of abstraction). Others are more adequate when the intention is to model some very specific aspects (e.g. deontic logic and contract modeling).

Given the complexity of the CN area, clearly multiple modeling perspectives are needed in different contexts and for solving specific problems. No single tool or theory can cover all these needs and therefore, the modeler might need to use various constructs according to the particular aspects of interested. The "navigational" guidelines introduced in this chapter, combined with the "organizational" properties of the ARCON framework, are proposed as a working basis

Acknowledgements. This work was funded in part by the European Commission through the ECOLEAD project. The authors thank the contributions of their partners Alexandra Klen, Martin Ollus, Nada Lavrac, Mitja Jermol, Falk Graser, Toni Jarimo, António Abreu, and Simon Msanjila.

5. REFERENCES

Alexander, P. (1996). Best of both worlds: Combining formal and semi-formal methods in software engineering. *Potentials*, IEEE, 14(5), 29-32.

Bowen, J. P., & Hinchey, M. G. (2006). Ten Commandments of Formal Methods... Ten Years Later. *Computer,* 39(1), 40-48.

Camarinha-Matos, L.M.; Afsarmanesh, H. (2004). Emerging behavior in complex collaborative networks, in *Collaborative Networked Organizations – A research agenda for emerging business models*, cap. 6.2, Kluwer Academic Publishers.

Camarinha-Matos, L.M.; Afsarmanesh, H. (2004). Formal modeling methods for collaborative networks, in *Collaborative Networked Organizations – A research agenda for emerging business models*, cap. 6.3, Kluwer Academic Publishers.

Camarinha-Matos, L.M.; Afsarmanesh, H. (2007). A comprehensive modeling framework for collaborative networked organizations, *Journal of Intelligent Manufacturing, Volume 18, Number 5 / October, pp 527-615.*

George, V., & Vaughn, R. (2003). Application of Lightweight Formal Methods in Requirement Engineering1. CrossTALK - The Journal of Defense Software Engineering(Jan 2003).

Liu, S. (2005). Formal Engineering Method for Software Development - An Introduction to SOFL. Retrieved February, 2006, from the World Wide Web: http://cis.k.hosei.ac.jp/~sliu/FMlecture1.pdf

3.3
A survey of soft modeling approaches for collaborative networks

A large number of aspects in collaborative networks are difficult to capture with traditional modeling approaches due to the inherent imprecision and incompleteness of information. Soft modeling approaches are specifically developed to handle such cases and thus have a high potential to the establishment of more effective and close to reality models. Computational intelligence methods are complemented with other approaches such as qualitative reasoning, complexity theories, chaos theory, etc.

1. INTRODUCTION

Collaborative networked organizations are complex entities whose proper understanding, design, implementation, and management require the integration of different modeling perspectives and techniques. Perspectives related to behavior and decision making in face of incomplete and imprecise information are particularly difficult to model. In fact, CNs involve a large number of autonomous and heterogeneous entities – organizations and people – often with:

- different value systems, and therefore different perceptions of value and importance / priority of things,
- a behavior influenced by factors such as emotions, preferences, working habits, ethical values, level of trust, competences, etc.

Some of these aspects have a socio-organizational and anthropocentric nature that is difficult to capture with traditional logic modeling approaches. For instance, while to define the past sub-contracting / outsourcing paradigms and simple cooperation forms we could stay at the level of well-defined structures and processes, the collaborative organizational structures are more fluid and their processes less defined, making the role of humans and socio-organizational aspects much more important. In these systems it is necessary to consider that:

- Different entities have their own individual agendas and goals, sometimes conflicting with each other;
- It is difficult to collect / share information on a timely fashion, even though parties might have agreed to do so;
- Some parties might omit relevant information or even lie for their own benefit;
- It is often difficult to make explicit all relationships, roles, and principles followed in a network; also social-networking at personal level often happens in multiple dimensions in background and overlapping (if not dominating over) the foreground (basically explicit) network structures.

Nevertheless, and in spite of these difficulties, entities involved in a CN need to plan and make decisions in scenario cases with incomplete and imprecise information. This raises the need for:
- Modeling approaches and developing models to represent such contexts;
- Reasoning techniques for decision-making in contexts of incomplete and imprecise information.

Other dimensions of this problem area include "complexity", what researchers try to capture with the notions of non-linear models, emergence, self-organization, etc, as well as the "dynamism" of the networks in terms of their "shape / topology" (membership, roles, distribution in case of mobility).

Soft modeling methods can exploit the tolerance for imprecision, uncertainty, and partial truth, and are therefore promising candidates to deal with the issues addressed above.

2. SCOPE OF THE SURVEY

Issue of terminology. The word "soft" appears in related research literature as qualifier of different terms, e.g. soft computing, soft modeling, soft systems, and soft systems methodologies. Some of these terms are originated in different scientific communities, e.g. Artificial Intelligence / Computer Science, Control Engineering, or Operations Research, and have different meanings even when the very same term is used by two distinct communities, as it is the case for "soft modeling". Therefore, this section briefly identifies the main two branches or schools of thought where these terms are used in order to set the context for the interpretation used in this chapter.

Branch 1: *Based in Artificial Intelligence / Computer Science / Engineering*. This community uses mainly the term **soft computing** for describing a collection of methodologies that aim to exploit the tolerance for imprecision and uncertainty to achieve tractability, robustness, and yet low solution cost for reasoning in such context. According to Zadeh (1994): "*…in contrast to traditional, hard computing, soft computing is tolerant of imprecision, uncertainty, and partial truth.*" In his study, Zadeh states the following basic premises of Soft Computing (BISC, 2006; Zadeh, 1994):
- The real world is pervasively imprecise and uncertain.
- Precision and certainty carry a cost.

In fact Soft Computing (SC) is a kind of "umbrella" term encompassing a number of approaches / components such as Fuzzy Systems (FS), Neural Networks (NN) / Neurocomputing, Evolutionary Computation (EC) and Probabilistic Reasoning (PR), with the latter subsuming the rough sets, clustering, chaos theory and parts of learning theory. Soft computing techniques resemble human reasoning more closely than traditional techniques, while the two techniques are often used to complement each other in many applications. In this perspective, the principal constituent methodologies in SC are also complementary rather than alternative. Soft computing may be viewed as a foundation component for the emerging field of *conceptual intelligence* and it is recently known as **computational intelligence**.

The common denominator of these soft computing / computational intelligence methodologies is their departure from classical reasoning and modeling approaches that are usually based on Boolean logic, analytical models, crisp classifications, and deterministic search. Traditional or hard computing systems, in order to be modeled or controlled, are described by complete and precise information. In these cases, formal reasoning systems, such as theorem provers, are used to attach binary truth values to the statements describing the state or behavior of the physical system (Bonissone, 1997). Soft Computing on the other hand relies on approximate models, approximate reasoning mechanisms, and randomized search methods, which try to give a theoretical sound framework so that relevant results can still be achieved in a context of imprecision and uncertainty. This is illustrated in Figure 1.

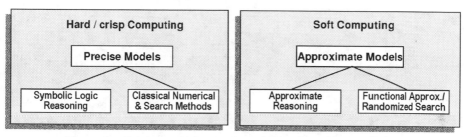

Figure 1 – Bonissone's perception of hard and soft computing

A number of techniques used in this area are inspired in biological systems (Fig. 2).

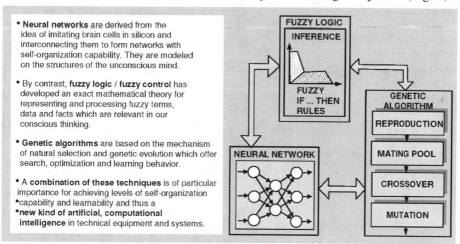

Figure 2 – Information processing inspired by biology (Krogmann, 1997)

One characteristic of soft computing is the intrinsic capability to create hybrid systems, combining two or more SC methodologies to benefit from consequent synergistic effects. Such arrangement provides complementary reasoning and searching methods that allow combining domain knowledge and empirical data (e.g. training data sets) to develop flexible computing tools and solve complex problems.

Figure 3 illustrates a taxonomy of these hybrid algorithms and their components. For further information of this topic consult (Bonissone, 1997; Bonissone, Chen, Goebel, & Khedkar, 1999; Zadeh, 1994).

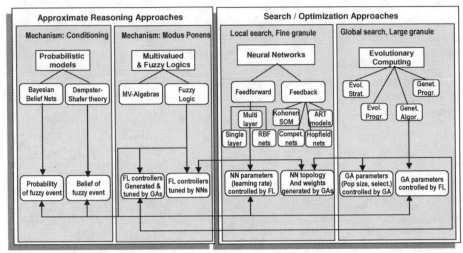

Figure 3 – Bonissone's soft computing overview

Some typical **application areas** of SC are data mining, pattern recognition and classification, optimization, decision support systems, and control systems. For instance, in the financial area, applications of Soft Computing can be found in scoring of mortgage appliances, risk profile analysis, investment consulting, insurance fraud detection, etc. Fuzzy control uses experts' knowledge to generate some form of qualitative rules, instead of differential equations to describe and control a system.

Soft computing includes both the "modeling" of imprecision, partial truth, and uncertainty – also referred to as **soft modeling** – and the "reasoning" and inference based on such models – also referred to as **soft reasoning**:

Soft computing = soft modeling + soft reasoning

Nevertheless some authors take soft modeling as a synonym to soft computing (Rasmy, Tharwat, & Ashraf, 2005; SGZZ, 2006; Wang, 2000).

***Branch 2**: Based in Operations Research / Systems Analysis*. This "school" uses the terms soft system, soft systems methodology, and soft modeling in a rather different perspective, focused on systems analysis. The *soft systems* approach uses social metaphors to build an interpretative understanding of human systems, where meaning is central. The intention is to create a *meta-methodology* that identifies the key elements in the problem to be solved, and then decides which of the available methodologies should be applied to those elements. These include culture, informal interactions, and attitudes – which Checkland calls the 'Human Activity System' (Checkland, 1981, 2000).

Thus, such soft approaches assume that problem definition is not straightforward but is itself problematic. The differences, according to Checkland, between hard and soft approaches can be summarized as shown in Table 1. (Sørensen & Vidal, 2002)

Table 1 – Hard vs. soft approaches (based on Checkland, 1981)

	Hard	Soft
Problem situation	Straight forward	Messy (problematic)
Purpose	Problem solving	Problem structuring
Organization	Given	To be negotiated
Methodology	Logical/mathematical model	Conceptual models
Result	Product/recommendation	Learning process

Peter Checkland (1981) of Lancaster University was one of the first authors that devoted considerable attention to this question in connection with the development of his (soft) approach known as Soft Systems Methodology (SSM). Soft Systems Methodology is based on systems thinking, involving the basic ideas of emergence, hierarchy, control, and communication. SSM views the problem domain in a holistic rather than reductionist way, recognizing that the component parts are interconnected, so that a change to one part will affect the other parts. Not only this, but the problem domain itself is a subsystem of several larger systems – changes in one will affect our domain as well. (Checkland, 1981; Eva, 2004; Sørensen & Vidal, 2002)

Although Checkland coined the term Soft Systems Methodology (SSM), it is not strictly the only methodology applied to soft systems problems. There are a variety of other soft approaches such as the (Checkland, 1981; Finegan, 1994; French, 2003; Sørensen & Vidal, 2002) ·

- The SWOT Analysis
- The Future Workshop
- Rich Pictures Diagrams / Scenario Planning
- Strategic Option Development and Analysis (SODA) / Cognitive Mapping
- Strategic Choice Approach (SCA)
- CATWOE

From all these soft systems approaches the most generic, and as a consequence the most used approach, is the Soft Systems Methodology. In the following sub-section a brief description of this method is presented.

Soft Systems Methodology (SSM)
The Soft Systems Methodology is described as "a seven stage process of analysis which uses the concept of a human activity as a means of getting from *finding out about the situation* to *taking action to improve the situation*" (Checkland, 1981; Wilson, 1984). These seven stages are illustrated in Figure 4.

The Checkland's seven stages embrace some of the soft approaches and consist of (Bustard, He, & Wilkie, 1999; Finegan, 1994; Rose, 1997):
- Finding Out (Stage 1 & Stage 2)
  Use rich pictures and other problem-structuring methods/techniques to explore the problem situation.
- Formulating "Root" Definitions of relevant systems (Stage 3)

It identifies the clients, actors, transformations, worldview, owners and environment (CATWOE) and from this builds definitions of the human activity systems needed to improve the problem situation.
- Building Conceptual Models (Stage 4)

  Based on the root definitions for each defined area, build a conceptual (systems) model of the required capabilities to achieve a given purpose or solve a particular problem.
- Comparing Models and Reality (Stage 5)

  Use gap analysis, compare scenarios, and tables of comparisons and key-players' contrasting opinions to identify what part(s) of the conceptual models are lacking or poorly supported in the existing problem situation.
- Defining Changes (Stage 6)

  The debate on – systematically desirable vs. culturally feasible, to determine what can realistically be done.
- Taking Action (Stage 7)

  The decision to implement the defined changes and assign responsibility through an agenda for action.

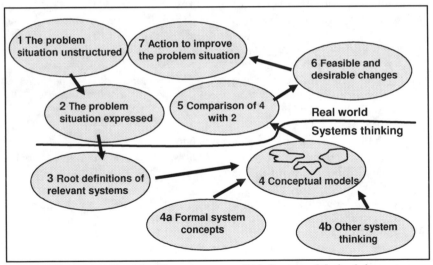

Figure 4 – Checkland's seven-stage Soft Systems Methodology

Furthermore, it should be taken into consideration that these stages represent the pattern of the activities in the methodology; they do not necessarily impose a sequence in which it should be applied.

In the following sections the perspective of the AI / Computer Science / Engineering (Branch 1) will be used, since it is the one that makes a closer match with the needs of the reference models for collaborative networks.

Therefore, Soft Modeling is considered to address a wide range of methods, techniques and tools developed to enhance structured human thinking. Tools are created to support the process of making human reasoning explicit. Soft modeling approaches aim at building a picture which is as close as possible to the real world taking all of its complexities into account. In this respect it is closer to the real-world which is characterized by uncertain, contradictory (or even paradoxical), and conflicting situations that we can refer to as "organized complexity".

Soft models try to depict the reality and how it is actually perceived by individuals or a group of individuals, and provide the following benefits:

- *Flexibility in construct*: Soft modeling creates optimal linear relationships among constructs specified by a conceptual model.
- *Flexibility in measurement:* Manifested (observed) variables in soft modeling may be measured at nominal, ordinal, or interval levels; and models may include variables measured at different levels.
- *Complexity simplification:* Spurious relationships, common in complex models with many variables, are easily identified with soft modeling procedures.
- *Ease of experimentation:* Soft modeling is useful in quasi-experimental designs and observational studies with both very small and very large sample sizes.

3. SURVEY OF METHODS

3.1 The most usual techniques

Fuzzy Logic
Fuzzy logic (FL) is one approach that deals with imprecise concepts (Berthold, 2003) and it is derived from the fuzzy set theory. Its objective is to allow the introduction of degrees of inclusion/relevance of each element in a given set. It means to allow one element to belong in a given set with different (big or small) intensity, also known as degrees of membership or degrees of truth. Please note that in classical set theory every element of a given universe of discourse is uniquely classified as either belonging to the set or not. In contrast to this crisp (precise) notion of set, fuzzy sets theory introduced by L. Zadeh (Zadeh, 1978, 1994), proposes an approach to "vagueness" in which each element can belong to a set to a specific degree μ ($0 <= \mu <= 1$). For instance, in classical set theory one partner is either reliable or not reliable, whereas in fuzzy set theory we can say that a partner is reliable in 75 percent of cases (i.e. with a degree of truth of 0.75).

Degrees of truth are often confused with probabilities. However, they are conceptually distinct; *fuzzy truth represents membership in vaguely defined sets*, not likelihood of some event or condition.

Fuzzy logic allows for set membership values between and including 0 and 1. It means shades of gray as well as black and white, and in its linguistic form, imprecise concepts like "slightly", "quite" and "very".

Fuzzy Logic is thus a type of logic that recognizes more than simple true and false values. Where classical reasoning requires "yes" and "no" values, fuzzy logic values range from an interval of values with associated membership function that states the membership of a value to a certain fuzzy linguistic value. For instance, the concept of *speed* is modeled in a fuzzy way as shown in Figure 5. A value of 65 for speed would be classified as "Low" with membership of 0.7, and as "Medium" with membership of 0.25. Modeled in this way, speed constitutes an example of what it is called a <u>linguistic variable</u>, one of the fundamental concepts in Fuzzy Logic.

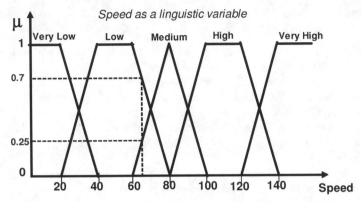

Figure 5 - Fuzzy modeling of capital Rate of Return (ROR).

Another fundamental concept in Fuzzy Logic is the concept of Fuzzy Rule. Fuzzy rules are linguistic IF-THEN- constructions that have the general form "IF A THEN B" where A and B are (collections of) propositions containing linguistic variables. A is called the premise and B is the consequence of the rule. An example of Rule is:

> *If a HIGH flood is expected and the reservoir level is MEDIUM, then water release is HIGH.*

A collection of rules like this one constitute a fuzzy rule base that can feed what is called as Fuzzy rule based inference engine, as shown in Figure 5.

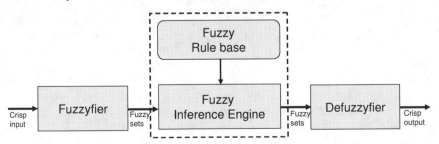

Figure 6 - Structure of a Fuzzy rule-based System.

The interface with the system being modeled is done through two additional components: the fuzzyfication and defuzzification functions. Fuzzification is the operation that converts crisp input values (e.g. ROR if Fig. 7) into fuzzy sets. Defuzzyfication is the operation in which a linguistic value output, induced by the fuzzy inference engine, is translated into a crisp value (Sanches, Pamplona, &

Montevechi, 2005). Figure 7 shows the crisp value of the linguistic variable Net Present Value (NPV) obtained by defuzzification from the fuzzy result.

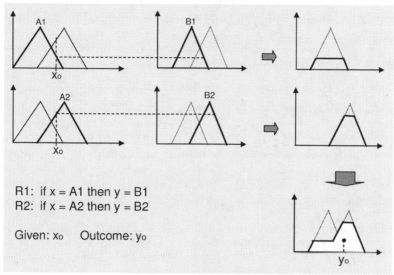

Figure 7 – Fuzzy inference and defuzzification example

There are a number of methods in the literature on how to do the defuzzification as well as various methods for combining rules and their fuzzy terms during an inference process.

Fuzzy logic is controversial in some research circles, despite its wide acceptance and a broad track record of successful applications. It is rejected by some control engineers for questions of validation and other reasons, and by some statisticians who argue that probability is the only rigorous mathematical description of uncertainty. Other critics also argue that it cannot be a superset of ordinary set theory since the membership functions are defined in terms of conventional sets (Klir & Folger, 1988).

Some examples of potential applicability in CNs:
Some early attempts of using fuzzy logic approaches in CNs include: supervision and assessment of performance in CNs, modeling and assessment of enterprise agility, negotiation and decision making in consortia formation, partners' selection, modeling agents' interactions, simulation for analysis of emergent behavior, implementation of auctions, negotiation in resource sharing / access, etc.

Bayesian Belief Networks
A *Bayesian network*, also known as Bayesian belief network or just belief network is based on Bayesian probability theory that captures believed relations (which may be uncertain, ambiguous or imprecise) within a set of variables which are relevant to some problem.

A Bayesian network is commonly represented as a graph, in which the vertices (or nodes) represent the variables, and the edges (or arcs) represent the conditional dependencies in the model.

The *Bayesian probability theory* is a branch of the mathematical probability theory. This theory interprets probability as a degree of belief and by applying the Bayes rule it is possible to infer how the prior probability is replaced by the posterior, after getting extra information e.g. the observed data. The *Bayesian inference* is a process of updating probabilities of outcomes based upon the relationships in the network and the evidences known about the situation at hand.

When the user introduces a new data item (evidence) all variables that are connected to the variable representing the new evidence will be updated. After the inference, the updated probabilities will reflect the new level of belief in (or probabilities of) all possible outcomes in the network.

The original levels of belief in the network are known as prior probabilities, because they are entered before any evidence is known about the situation and the beliefs are updated; after a piece of evidence is entered, they become posterior probabilities, because they reflect the levels of belief after the new evidence.

The construction of a Bayesian network follows a common set of guidelines:
*   *Definition of the set of variables* – Identify all variables that are relevant.
*   *Definition of the states for each variable* – For each variable, define the set of outcomes or states that each one can have. This set is referred to in the mathematical literature as "mutually exclusive and collectively exhaustive", meaning that it must cover all possibilities for the variable, and that no important distinctions are shared between states.
*   *Definition of the graph structure* – In this context, it means connecting the variables in such way that arcs lead from cause to effects. If there is a link from node A to node B, then A causes B, and node A is called the parent and node B the child. On the other hand, the absence of an arc between two variables indicates conditional independence; that is, there are no situations in which the probabilities of one of the variables depend directly upon the state of the other. To define the causal relationships among variables it means, for any variable, to ask the questions:

What other variables (if any) directly influence this variable?  What other variables (if any) are directly influenced by this variable?

As in the probability theory there is no a-priori way of knowing which variables influence other variables one rule is to allow the creator to use common sense and real knowledge to eliminate needless complexity in model.
*   *Definition of the probabilistic relations* – Define these relations according to the number of parent variables defined in the probabilistic relations and the numeric probabilities, based on prior knowledge of each variable.

In order to illustrate an example of Belief Network application let us consider the case shown in Figure 8. According to this network, the two top nodes "Lead Time" and "Competences" are the variables that influence the likelihood of a good "Performance", and the evaluation of "Prestige" level is influenced by the Performance variable. The tables in the figure show, for each child variable, the set of states that each one can have and its belief level (prior probability) expressed as a percentage.

Let us now assume that a VO broker introduces a new data item about another enterprise in terms of lead Time and Competences beliefs. After the inference, the updated probabilities as show in the bar graphs of each child variable, reflect the new level of belief in all allowed stages.

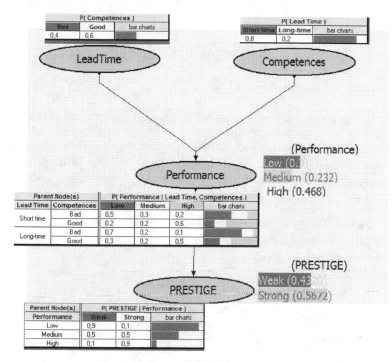

Figure 8 - Example of a Belief Network application for selecting partners

Some examples of potential applicability in CNs:
Belief networks could contribute to model and support inferences in cases of diagnosis and prediction of CN performance, credit assignment, partners' selection, data fusion, decision making in general, etc.

Neural Networks

Neural networks represent an information processing paradigm that is inspired in the way biological nervous systems process information. The basic premise of an Artificial Neural Network (ANN), commonly called Neural Network, is that biological systems perform extraordinarily complex computations without resource to explicit quantitative operations. Organisms are capable of learning a task gradually over time. This learning property reflects the ability of large ensembles of neurons to learn through exposure to external stimuli and to generalize across related instances of the signal (Silipo, 2003).

An ANN is composed of a large number of highly interconnected processing elements (neurons) that combine their activity to solve specific problems (e.g.

pattern recognition or classification). An artificial neuron is a device with many inputs and one output, see Figure 9.a).

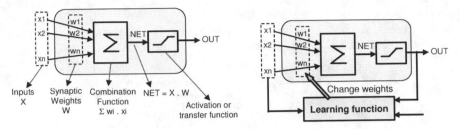

Figure 9 – a) Implementation of an artificial neuron   b) Learning function

The neuron has two modes of operation; the learning mode and the using mode. In the learning mode, the neuron can be trained to fire (or not), for particular input patterns (i.e. finding the right synaptic weights to guarantee that output matches the desired output, see Fig. 9-b)). In the using mode, when an input pattern is detected an output is generated according to the set of weights the network learned in the previous phase.

An example of ANN combining various layers of neurons is shown in Fig. 10. The knowledge in an ANN is thus contained in the variable interconnection weights. The network learns the correlation between vectors of an input quantity and the related vectors of the output quantity.

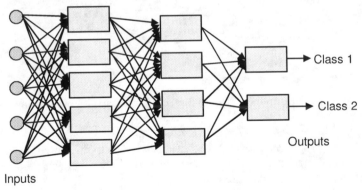

Figure 9 - An example of artificial neural network

In most cases an ANN is an adaptive system that changes its structure based on external or internal information that flows through the network. ANN can be used to model complex relationships between inputs and outputs or to find patterns in data.

In terms of computing, a ANN represents a kind of parallel processing system with:
- simple processing elements
- a high degree of interconnection
- simple scalar messages
- adaptive interaction between elements.

In summary a NN involves a network of simple processing elements which can exhibit complex global behavior, determined by the connections between the processing elements, the weights associated to those connections, and the implemented transfer function. There are various architectures for ANNs and various learning algorithms such as, for instance, the back-propagation algorithm. Genetic algorithms can also be sued to train the network, i.e. to determine an optimal weights vector.

In modern software implementations of artificial neural networks the approach inspired in biology has more or less been abandoned for a more practical approach based on statistics and signal processing. In some of these systems, neural networks, or parts of neural networks (such as artificial neurons) are used as components in larger systems that combine both adaptive and non-adaptive elements.

Some examples of potential applicability in CNs:
ANN can fit well with applications that can be formulated as classification problems. Therefore, examples of potential application could include classification of VBE members regarding their readiness and suitability for a specific collaboration opportunity, exploration of historic data (data mining) on past collaboration cases, assess the likelihood of success of some suggested consortia (assuming historic data is available to train the network), etc.

Evolutionary Computation

Evolutionary Computation is the general term for several techniques used to describe computer-based problem solving systems which are inspired, to some degree, on the theory of evolution of biological life in the natural world. A number of evolutionary computational models have been proposed. The major ones are genetic algorithms, the evolution strategy, evolutionary programming, and artificial life. These approaches use techniques inspired by evolutionary biology such as:

- Inheritance – a process by which an offspring cell or organism acquires or becomes predisposed to characteristics of its parent cell or organism. Through inheritance, variations exhibited by individuals can accumulate and cause a species to evolve.
- Mutation – a genetic operator used to maintain genetic diversity from one generation of a population of chromosomes to the next.
- Natural selection – often illustrated by the notion of "survival of the fittest", occurs when individuals differ from each other in their ability to tackle the challenges posed by their internal biology and by the biological and physical environment. The availability of a function to evaluate the fitness of each chromosome is assumed.
- Recombination (or crossover) – a genetic operator used to vary the "programming" of a chromosome or chromosomes from one generation to the next.

Genetic algorithms (Holland 1992) are typically implemented as a computer simulation in which a population of abstract representations (called chromosomes) of candidate solutions (called individuals) to an optimization problem evolves toward better solutions. Traditionally, solutions are represented in the form of binary strings of 0s and 1s, but different encodings are also possible. Typically the process starts with a population of completely random individuals and evolves in several generations. In each generation, the fitness of the whole population is evaluated, multiple individuals are selected from the current population (based on their fitness), modified (mutated or recombined and reproduced) to form a new population, which becomes current in the next iteration of the algorithm. A key element here is a metric called a *fitness function* that allows each candidate to be quantitatively evaluated (Marczyk, 2004). Domain knowledge is basically included in this function; the genetic operators are (almost) application independent. There are several methods for selecting the individuals to be reproduced for the next generation, e.g. elitist selection, roulette-wheel selection, scaling selection, tournament selection, rank selection. Various methods for implementation of mutation and crossover are also available (Mitchell, 1996).

One of the basic characteristics of these algorithms is that they are intrinsically parallel, being able to explore the solution space in multiple directions at once.

Various works have proposed combinations of Evolutionary Computation and Neural Networks. For instance, evolutionary training of neural networks, i.e. use of genetic algorithms to determine the set of synaptic weights of the neural network, or evolutionary design of network topologies, etc.

Some examples of potential applicability in CNs:
Among the many reported examples of successful applications of genetic algorithms (see Marczyk 2004, for instance), some of them have a direct potential interest for CNs, namely:
- Pattern recognition in data mining with applicability to historic performance data, repository of announcements of collaboration opportunities, etc.
- Scheduling (for distributed business processes) and routing (in problems of logistics).
- Multi-criteria based partners' selection.
- Simulation and forecasting, with application to predict behaviors in a collaborative environment.

Rough Sets theory
Rough sets theory is another approach to model and address vagueness according to which imprecision is expressed by a "boundary region of a set", and not by a partial membership as in the fuzzy sets theory. The main idea of the rough sets is the approximation of a set by a pair of sets that are called the lower and the upper approximation of the set (Pawlak, 1982). The lower approximation of a rough set X is the collection of objects which can be classified with full certainty as members of the set X. The upper approximation of X is the collection of objects that may possibly be classified as members of the set X. The boundary region comprises the objects that cannot be classified with certainty as to be neither inside X, nor outside X, thus the "set difference" between the upper and lower approximation sets (Fig. 11).

In this sense, a particular set X is crisp if the boundary region of X is empty.
The concept of rough set implies the notion of indiscernibility, i.e. the assumption that due to lack of knowledge about some objects of our universe of discourse they are classified as belonging to the same class (or cluster). In other words, the indiscernibility relation is intended to express the fact that due to the lack of knowledge we are unable to discern some objects employing the available information. That means, in general, we are unable to deal with single objects but

we have to consider clusters of indiscernible objects, as fundamental concepts of the theory.

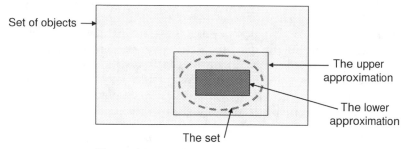

Figure 11 – Intuitive notion of rough set

The notions of lower and upper approximations offer a way to classify objects in cases of noisy or incomplete information.

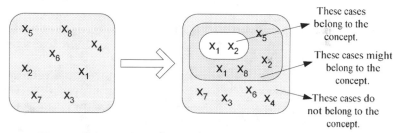

Figure 12 – Rough sets in concept approximation.

In terms of its application to pattern matching and classification problems, objects are supposed to be characterized by a set of attributes. Methods are proposed to determine the minimal set of attributes (called reduct) that allow a partition of objects into a given set of classes, and how to build classification or decision trees (or decision rules) (Hassanien, 2004).

Examples of potential applicability in CNs:
In terms of the CN field, Rough Sets theory can be used to discover characteristics of groups of members from a collaborative network that are of interest. For instance, based on the attributes of the partners, and the way they perform in the network, this methodology may help in discovering properties or patterns that might be considered as emergent behavior. It might be also useful in clustering members in a VBE, based on historic data, for the purpose of selecting partners for a future VO. A similar problem could be defined for the selection of collaboration opportunities.

3.2 Other techniques

In addition to the classical methods of soft computing as the ones mentioned above, there are other approaches with potential applicability in dealing with vagueness in CNs. Some of them are introduced in this section.

Qualitative Reasoning

Qualitative reasoning creates simplified representations for continuous aspects of the world, such as space, time, and quantity, which support reasoning with very little information. It is motivated by two observations.

- People draw useful and subtle conclusions about the physical world without differential equations. In our daily lives we figure out what is happening around us and how we can affect it, working with far less data, and less precise data, than would be required in order to use traditional, purely quantitative methods. Consider, for instance, the reasoning process when driving a car.
- Scientists and engineers appear to use qualitative reasoning:
  - o For initial understanding of a problem.
  - o When setting up more formal methods to solve particular problems.
  - o When interpreting the results of quantitative simulations, calculations, or measurements.
  - o To benefit from the representations and techniques that enable them to reason about the behavior of physical systems, without precise quantitative information needed by conventional analysis techniques such as numerical simulators.
  - o To model cases where **causality** is explicitly represented and used to explain the structure and behavior resulting from interactions among components of a system.

Thus advances in qualitative reasoning should lead to the creation of more flexible software that can adequately help engineers and scientists to deal with complex systems modeling. These systems are characterized by increasing levels of uncertainty, complexity, and heterogeneity.

One well-known example of qualitative modeling is the Allen's interval-based **temporal logic** (Allen, 1983) to represent and reason about temporal knowledge. Thirteen temporal relationships are considered (Figure 13).

Relation	Symbol	Symbol for inverse	Pictorial example
X *before* Y	<	>	
X *equal* Y	=	=	
X *meets* Y	m	mi	
X *overlaps* Y	o	oi	
X *during* Y	d	di	
X *starts* Y	s	si	
X *finishes* Y	f	fi	

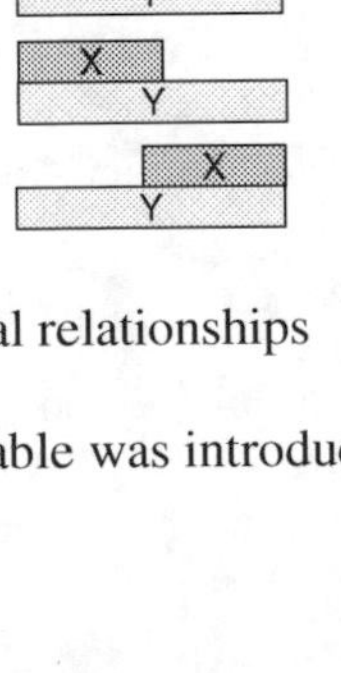

Figure 13 – Allen's temporal relationships

As part of the inference technique a transitivity table was introduced (Figure 14).

B r2 C / A r1 B	<	>	d	di	o	oi	m	mi	s	si	f	fi
"before" <	<	no info	< o m d s	<	<	< o m d s	<	< o m d s	<	<	< o m d s	<
"after" >	no info	>	> oi mi d f	>	> oi mi d f	>	> oi mi d f	>	> oi mi d f	>	>	>
"during" d	<	>	d	no info	< o m d s	> oi mi d f	<	>	d	> oi mi d f	d	< o m d s
"contains" di	< o m di fi	> oi di mi si	o oi dur con =	di	o di fi	oi di si	o di fi	oi di si	di fi o	di	di si oi	di
"overlaps" o	<	> oi di mi si	o d s	< o m di fi	<	o oi dur con =	<	oi di si	o	di fi o	d s o	< o m
"over-lapped-by" oi	< o m di fi	>	oi d f	> oi mi di si	o oi dur con =	>	o di mi	>	oi d f	oi d >	oi	oi di si
"meets" m	<	> oi mi di si	o d s	<	<	o d s	<	f fi =	m	m	d s o	<
"met-by" mi	< o m di fi	>	oi d f	>	oi d f	>	s si =	>	d f oi	>	mi	mi
"starts" s	<	>	d	< o m di fi	< o m	oi d f	<	mi	s	s si =	d	< m o
"started by" si	< o m di li	>	oi d f	di	o di fi	oi	o di fi	mi	s si =	si	oi	di
"finishes" f	<	>	d	> oi mi di si	o d s	> oi mi	m	>	d	> oi mi	f	f fi =
"finished-by" fi	<	> oi mi di si	o d s	di	o	oi di si	m	si oi di	o	di	f fi =	fi

Figure 14 – The Transitivity Table for the Twelve Temporal Relations (omitting "=") (Allen, 1983).

Another major area of development is causal modeling:

Causal modeling and reasoning
Causal modeling (CM) appeared due to the need for a sketching technique to support and facilitate reasoning about cause and effect. It is viewed as the simplified and diagrammatic counterpart of an action language.

CM builds upon a binary relationship, called an *influence relationship*, between two entities that represent named quantitative or qualitative values (or value sets), whereby changes in the influencing entity are conveyed as changes in the influenced entity (Greenland & Brumback, 2002). CM also provides mechanisms for depicting *influence chains* (sequential influence paths), *influence forks* (parallel influence paths), as well as mechanisms for reducing these.

Existing modeling approaches and their diagrammatic representation can be classified into the following categories (Akkok, 1998):

- Structural modeling and sketching which is characterized by hierarchies and depicting things of concern and their composition or organization with respect to each other.
- Behavioral modeling and sketching which is characterized by simple input-

process-output sequences showing how information is processed in steps, or by sketches depicting causes and their effects.

The structural modeling and sketching of CM resembles the Entity Relationship Diagrams, the structure (or class) diagrams of object-oriented modeling methods like UML, etc. Such methods are said to provide a data-perspective of a system in disciplines like Method Engineering (Odell, 1996) and in modeling Information Systems (Olle et al., 1991). The behavioral modeling and sketching approach of CM covers both the process and the dynamic perspectives of a system e.g. resembles methods like Data Flow Diagrams on the one hand (Yourdon & Constantine, 1979), and methods like State Charts (Harel, 1987) on the other hand.

Causal modeling and sketching drives sequences of reasoning. It is characterized by keywords such as 'leads to', 'influences', 'causes' on one hand, and the 'if-then', 'when then', 'on-then', 'as-then' or 'supposing-then' (Akkok, 1998) on the other hand. Typical examples are statements like "when the accelerator is pressed, the speed increases" or "as more fuel flows into the motor, the speed increases" or the "amount of fuel flowing influences the speed", etc. Following are some examples of causal models as applied to a number of different domains:

- **Plant population growth model:** The increase of number of plants in a certain field is causally related to the plants grown (birth rate) and the plants died (death rate). Figure shows a causal model diagram which can be used to support reasoning about population growth of plants.

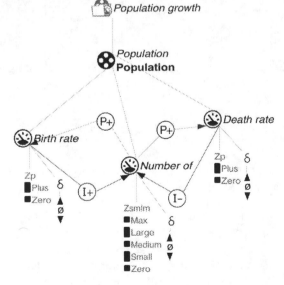

Figure 15 – A causal model for plant population growth (Bredeweg & Salles, 2005).

- **Decision making models:** Decision makers such as those in economics or management must causally analyze the consequences of decisions they make. Decision-makers must explore the chain of entities (concepts) and relationships with constraints and those parts which turn the ultimate outcome to be a negative outcome. As a result, the decision-maker can investigate the reasons for the negative outcome (for example, that tax-cuts cause social stratification somehow, as in the case illustrated in Fig. 16.

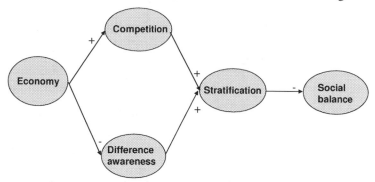

Figure 16 - A causal model for decision making related to economics (Akkok, 1998).

- **Policy analysis models:** The processes of analyzing and formulating policies must consider and understand the influence and causal effect that may lead to their effectiveness or ineffectiveness. In the process of formulating policies, all important values of all stakeholders must be considered. These values can be impacted in one way or another when the policies are in operation. For example, causal analysis has been applied for the formulation of airport policies and their effect to the environment, economic, noisy to neighbors, etc. (Roelen, Bellamy, Hale, van Paassen, & Molemaker, 2000). For instance, at Schiphol airport, a causal analysis was conducted to study the feasibility of constructing a fifth take-off and landing line. The impacts that can result due to the construction were studied based on causal approach (Hale, 2002).

There are four major types of causal models namely (Greenland & Brumback, 2002):

- Graphical models (causal diagrams): Used to model and illustrate qualitative population assumptions and biasness among the variables in a given system. Such diagrams display qualitative assumptions about causal directions and independencies in a population.
- Potential-outcome (counterfactual): Enhances the graphical models details by allowing studying the variables quantitatively.
- Sufficient-component causal models: Support the analysis among factors to understand if two factors can have same causal effects on other factors. These causal models also act as bases for constructing and formulating mathematical equations.
- Structural-equations models: Provide a means of representing causal relations among various factors through mathematical equations.

Examples of potential applicability in CNs:
Analysis of the side effects of collaboration opportunities, analysis of the impact of VBE managerial decisions before they are put into action, trust assessment and reasoning, process planning, supervision and diagnosis of network performance, risk management, etc.

Complex Systems

Complex system is a new field of science that aims to understand how parts of a system give rise to the system's collective behaviors, and how it interacts with its environment. Complex systems are basically formed out of parts so that the behavior of the parts forms the behavior of the whole. It is commonly understood that the term "complex system" refers to "a system of many parts which are coupled in a nonlinear fashion". Complexity is also known as the science of nonlinear dynamics.

Complexity deals with the system of entities and relations between them. It encompasses both distinction and connection and mostly describes a mass phenomenon. The study of this area led to various theories of complexity, in most cases as a result of interdisciplinary research programs. As an example we can refer to the various theories originated in the Santa Fé Institute.

W. H. Roetzheim defines complexity science as the study of emergent behavior exhibited by interacting systems operating at the threshold of stability and chaos. One important focus of attention is the study of complex adaptive systems and self-organizing systems. One central concept here is the notion of emergence. Complexity theory states that critically interacting components self-organize to form potentially evolving structures exhibiting a hierarchy of emergent system properties. In other words, emergence refers to the situation in which complex systems and patterns (e.g. form, behavior) can arise out of a multiplicity of relatively simple interactions.

But the science of complexity does not represent a single modeling tool or approach. Rather it encompasses a large diversity of tools and models (e.g. attractors, fitness landscapes, fractal geometry, 2nd law of thermodynamics, autopoiesis, co-evolution, simulation, etc.) developed in various research fields.

Complexity is also bound to personal perception: Different persons will attribute different degrees of complexity to one and the same system or task according to their personal perception. Managing a project for instance can be a complex task if one does not have the level of experience necessary to do it. At the same time, the same project might be characterized as non-complex by an experienced project manager. Thus, it is difficult to draw the borderline between systems that show technical elements of complexity, but are simple to perceive from a personal point of view, and those that are too complex for even an experienced expert to understand them.

In CNs, elements of complexity can be found at all four levels at the ARCON reference model:
- *Structural dimension*: information- and material flows between the nodes of the network are complex ones,
- *Componential dimension:* Failures of single resources in the operation phase of CN have clear impacts on the other levels of the network. Network response and recovery mechanisms to such failures show complex patterns, and can be better understood by application of complexity theories.

- *Functional dimension:* Even at a small number of processes and tasks, information exchange between them shows complex patterns. False, delayed, ceased, or insufficient information may have effects on various subsequent pieces of information. These effects show complex behavior.
- *Behavioral dimension:* Human behavior is bound to different frameworks: In business situations, it is bound to formal rules and contractual obligations – but also to own beliefs and estimations that may be in line or in conflict with the formal framework. Depending on the human actor's perceptions and propositions, behavior is the result of many of those. Understanding this complexity in human behavior may help to establish formal behavioral frameworks for CN.

Summarizing, these examples show that models on complexity in CN must give the managers clear guidelines how to perceive, illuminate, and master complex mechanisms under specific circumstances.

Chaos Theory

Formally, chaos theory is defined as the study of complex nonlinear dynamic systems. Another definition: "Chaos Theory is the qualitative study of unstable a-periodic behavior in deterministic nonlinear dynamical systems" (Kellert, 1993). Thus chaos theory is, in general terms, the study of forever changing complex systems based on mathematical concepts of recursion, whether in the form of a recursive process or a set of differential equations modeling a physical system.

Among the characteristics of chaotic systems is the sensitivity to initial conditions (popularly referred to as the butterfly effect[1]). As a result of this sensitivity, the behavior of systems that exhibit chaos appears to be random, even though the model of the system is deterministic in the sense that it is well defined and contains no random parameters. Examples of such systems include the atmosphere, the solar system, plate tectonics, turbulent fluids, economics, and population growth (Rae, 2006).

For a dynamical system to be classified as chaotic, it is commonly agree that it must have the following properties:

- it must be sensitive to initial conditions
- it must be topologically mixing.

Sensitivity to initial conditions means that two points in such a system may move in vastly different trajectories in their phase space – the space in which all possible states of a system are represented – even if the difference in their initial configurations is very small. The systems behave identically only if their initial configurations are exactly the same.

Topologically mixing means that the system will evolve over time so that any given region or open set of its phase space will eventually overlap with any other given region. Here, "mixing" is meant to correspond to the standard intuition: the mixing of colored dyes or fluids is an example of a chaotic system.

---

[1] Small variations of the initial condition of a dynamical system may produce large variations in the long term behavior of the system.

Chaotic system behavior often appears to be random. This arises from their characteristic that almost similar initial conditions never lead to the same evolutionary path of the system. Influences that determine the path are assumed to occur irregularly in time and intensity creating patterns that seem to be random. With each of these influences "distracting" the system from its previous path, a series of irregular influences creates a unique system path.

With that, chaos theory can be applied in various scientific fields that describe the evolutionary behavior of social and/ or technical systems. Some examples of applying chaos theories in science are meteorology (weather forecasting and simulation), aerodynamics (simulation of airflows and wake turbulences), biology (hunter-/ prey patterns in animal populations), or economics (predicting or simulating market behavior as aggregate decisions of its actors).

Examples of potential applicability in CNs:
Forecasting behavior / evolution of a collaborative ecosystem, modeling organizational behavior and organizational change, modeling dynamic market systems, etc.

Other approaches and theories ...
Several other approaches to handle uncertainty and imprecision have been developed, either as extensions of the ones described above, or even as different directions. A few examples are included below.

Possibility theory.   This theory was first introduced by L. Zadeh (1998) as an extension of his theory of fuzzy sets and fuzzy logic and was later on extended by Dubois Prade (2001). It is therefore an uncertainty theory devoted to the handling of incomplete information. The rules of possibility theory are similar to probability theory, but use either MAX/MIN or MAX/TIMES calculus, rather than the PLUS/TIMES calculus of probability theory. The notion of possibility can, in fact, have several interpretations, e.g. feasibility (it is possible to do something - physical), plausibility (It is possible that something occurs - epistemic), consistency (compatible with what is known - logical), and permission (it is allowed to do something - deontic). Examples of application include: Exception-tolerant reasoning in rule bases, belief revision and inconsistency handling in deductive knowledge bases, decision-making under uncertainty with qualitative criteria (scheduling), abductive reasoning for diagnosis under poor causal knowledge, etc.

Dempster-Shafer theory of evidence.   This is a theory of evidence that uses *belief functions* and *plausible reasoning*, which is used to combine separate pieces of information (evidence) to calculate the probability of an event and can be regarded as a more general approach to representing uncertainty than the Bayesian approach (Shafer, 19976). It does not require an assumption regarding the probability of the individual constituents of the set or interval, i.e. it allows distributing support for proposition (e.g., this is user A) not only to a proposition itself but also to the union of propositions that include it (e.g., "this is likely either user A or user B"). This is a potentially valuable tool for the evaluation of risk and reliability in engineering applications when it is not possible to obtain a precise measurement from experiments, or when knowledge is obtained from expert elicitation.

Situation theory. Situation theory is a mathematical theory of meaning. According to the theory, individuals, properties, relations, spatio-temporal locations, and situations are the basic ingredients. The world is viewed as a collection of objects, sets of objects, properties, and relations (Tin, Akman, 1994). One of the distinguishing characteristics of situation theory is that information content is context-dependent (where a context is a situation). This theory has been mostly applied in natural language and semantics processing. Although not strongly related to soft modeling methods, this approach can provide some tools to deal with complexity. Nevertheless the concept of uncertain information flow among objects is also addressed (Huibers, Lalmas, Rijsbergen, 1996).

4. SUMMARY

The following table summarizes the characteristics of the discussed methods and theories and gives examples of potential application.

Table 1. Summary of soft modeling approaches

Soft computing techniques	Characteristics	Typical application problems
Fuzzy logic/sets	- Use of Linguistic, imprecise (fuzzy) variables and fuzzy if-then rules to perform human-like reasoning. - Modeling of imprecise/qualitative knowledge. - Simple to design and very easy to interpret.	- Inference - Feedback control - Fuzzy data analysis - Fuzzy cluster analysis -Classification, clustering
Belief networks	- Acyclic graph model that represents conditional dependencies between random variables - Use of the Bayes' rule to update beliefs about states of variables when some other variables are observed (new evidence).	- Classification under uncertainty - Decision making under uncertainty - Forecasting - Diagnosis ...
Neural networks	- A connectionist computation model composed of neurons interconnected by weighted arcs. The knowledge inside the network is encoded in these weights. - Reconfigurable based on learning - Resistance to noise and distorted patterns	- Pattern matching & classification - Learning and curve fitting - Cluster analysis - Forecasting & diagnosis
Evolutionary computing & Genetic algorithms	- Set of techniques inspired by biology, such as inheritance, mutation, natural selection, and recombination. - The information is encoded in the chromosomes in the form of binary strings.	- Search and optimization problems - Pattern recognition - *Data mining*
Rough sets	- Analysis of information composed of cases and their attributes obtained from information tables	- *Data mining* - Classification and decision making

	- Definition of vague concepts, from redundant, contradictory and/or incomplete information - Rough sets are specified via definition of upper and lower approximations of a given set of interest.	- Cluster analysis - Induction of decision rules
Qualitative reasoning	- It allows the creation of simplified representation of continuous aspects of the world. It permits working far less, and less precise, data than quantitative methods. - Qualitative relationships between concepts / variables - Causal diagrams - Graphical sketching of dependencies	- Temporal reasoning, scheduling - Diagnosis - Trust management - Risk management
Complex Systems	- Complexity refers to the amount of information needed to describe a non-linear system - Complexity Theory allows for description of time-invariant cause-/ effect relationships in non-linear systems - It cannot describe system evolution as chaos theory does - Understanding and managing the existence of complexity in a system is also subject to individual perception of the actor confronted with it.	- Process Management - Information Flows Modelling - Forecasting/ Prognosis
Chaos theory	- Chaos Theory provides algorithms for describing evolution of non-linear systems in time - It allows to describe a system's evolution under exogenous impacts - The system status depends on initial conditions that must be known to describe future evolution of the system - Chaos theory is deterministic (although irregularly occurring elements make chaotic behavior seem random)	- Forecasting/ Prognosis - Simulation

This collection of soft modeling tools and theories offers diverse approaches to deal with uncertainty and imprecision and, as such, with a potential applicability in modeling difficult aspects of collaborative networks, as illustrated in other chapters of this book.

Acknowledgements. This work was funded in part by the European Commission through the ECOLEAD project. The authors thank the contribution of their colleagues Alexandra Klen, Filipa Ferrada, Simon Msanjila, João Rosas, Edmilson Klen, and Falk Graser.

4. REFERENCES

Akkok, N. (1998). *The causal modeling technique.* Unpublished Thesis for the degree of Cand. Scient. in informatics, Institute of Informatics, University of Oslo.

Allen, J. F. (1983). Maintaining Knowledge about Temporal Intervals, Communications of

Berthold, M. R. (2003). Fuzzy Logic. In D. J. Hand (Ed.), *Intelligent Data Analysis: An Introdution* (Second ed.): Springer.

BISC. (2006). *Berkeley Initiative in Soft Computing.* Retrieved May 2nd, 2006, from the World Wide Web: http://www-bisc.cs.berkeley.edu/bisc/bisc.memo.html#what_is_sc

Bonissone, P. P. (1997). Soft computing: the convergence of emerging reasoning technologies. *Soft Computing - A Fusion of Foundations, Methodologies and Applications, 1*(1), 6-18.

Bonissone, P. P., Chen, Y.-T., Goebel, K., & Khedkar, P. S. (1999). Hybrid soft computing systems: industrial and commercial applications. *Proceedings of the IEEE, 87*(9), 1641-1667.

Bredeweg, B., & Salles, P. (2005). The Ants' Garden: Complex Interactions between Populations and the Scalability of Qualitative Models. *AI Communications, Vol. 18*(4), 305-317.

Bustard, D. W., He, Z., & Wilkie, F. G. (1999). Soft Systems and Use-Case Modelling: Mutually Supportive or Mutually Exclusive? *Thirty-Second Annual Hawaii International Conference on System Sciences, Vol. 3*, pp. 3055.

Checkland, P. (1981). *Systems Thinking, Systems Practice*: John Wiley & Sons, Chichester.

Checkland, P. (2000). Soft systems methodology: a thirty year retrospective. *Systems Research and Behavioral Science, 17*(S1), S11-S58.

Dubois, Didier and Prade, Henri, "Possibility Theory, Probability Theory and Multiple-valued Logics: A Clarification", Annals of Mathematics and Artificial Intelligence 32:35-66, 2001.

Eva, M. (2004). *Soft systems methodology.* ACCA Global. Retrieved September, 2006, from the World Wide Web: http://www.accaglobal.com/publications/studentaccountant/1073535

Finegan, A. (1994). *Soft Systems Methodology: An Alternative Approach to Knowledge Elicitation in Complex and Poorly Defined Systems.* Complexity International. Vol. 1. Retrieved, 2006, from the World Wide Web: http://journal-ci.csse.monash.edu.au/ci/vol01/finega01/html/

French, S. (2003). *Soft Modelling and Problem Formulation.* Manchester Business School, The University of Manchester. Retrieved, 2006, from the World Wide Web: http://www.sal.hut.fi/TED/slides/Soft_modelling.pdf

Greenland, S., & Brumback, B. (2002). An overview of relations among causal modeling methods. *In international journal of epidemiology.*, ISBN: 31-1030-1037.

Harel, D. (1987). Statecharts: A Visual Formalism for Complex Systems. *In Science of Computer Programming, Vol. 8*, 231-274.

Hassanien, A. E., "Rough Set Approach for Attribute Reduction and Rule Generation: A Case of Patients With Suspected Breast Cancer", Journal of the American Society for information Science and Technology, 55(11):954–962, 2004

Holland, John. "Genetic algorithms." *Scientific American*, July 1992, p. 66-72.

Huibers, T.W.C., Lalmas, M., Rijsbergen, C. J. (1996). Information Retrieval and Situation Theory. ACM SIGIR Forum, Volume 30, Issue 1.

Kellert, S.H. (1993). In the wake of chaos: Unpredictable order in dynamical systems. Chicago: The University of Chicago Press.

Klir, G., & Folger, T. (1988). *Fuzzy Sets, Uncertainty, and Information.*

Krogmann, U., (1997). Techniques for computational and machine intelligence – Soft Computing. In Advances in Soft-Computing Technologies and Application in Mission Systems, AGARD Lecture Series 210.

Marczyk, A. – Genetic Algorithms and Evolutionary Computation, 2004, http://www.talkorigins.org/faqs/genalg/genalg.html

Mitchell, M. – An introduction to genetic algorithms, MIT Press, 1996.

Odell, J. J. (1996). A Primer to Method Engineering. In R. J. Welke (Ed.), *Method Engineering - Principles of Method Construction and Tool Support, proceedings of the IFIP TC8 WG8.1 Working Conference on Method Engineering*: Chapman & Hall.

Olle, T. W., Hagelstein, H., Macdonald, I. G., Rolland, C., Sol, H. G., Van Assche, F. J. M., & Verrijn-Stuart, A. A. (1991). *Information Systems Methodologies - A Framework for Understanding* (2nd ed.): IFIP. Addison-Wesley.

Pawlak, Z., "Rough sets," International Jornal of Computer and Information Sciences, pp. 341–356, 1982.

Rae, G. (2006). *Chaos Theory: A Brief Introduction*. Retrieved, from the World Wide Web: http://www.imho.com/grae/chaos/chaos.html

Rasmy, M. H., Tharwat, A., & Ashraf, S. (2005). *Enterprise Resource Planning (ERP) Implementation in the Egyptian Organizational Context*. Retrieved, 2006, from the World Wide Web: http://uxisweb1.brunel.ac.uk/iseingsites/EMCIS/EMCIS2005/pdfs/21.pdf

Roelen, A. L. C., Bellamy, L. J., Hale, A. R., van Paassen, M. M., & Molemaker, R. J. (2000). *Feasibility of the development of a causal model for the assessment of third party risk around airports*. NLR, Amsterdam: CR-2000-189PT-2.

Rose, J. (1997). Soft systems methodology as a social science research tool. *Systems Research and Behavioral Science, 14*(4), 249-258.

Sanches, A. L., Pamplona, E. d. O., & Montevechi, J. A. B. (2005). *Capital Budgeting Using Triangular Fuzzy Numbers*. V Encuentro Internacional de Finanzas. Santiago, Chile, 19 a 21 de Janeiro. Retrieved, from the World Wide Web: http://www.iem.efei.br/edson/download/ArtAlexFuzzyChile05.pdf

Shafer, Glenn (1976). A Mathematical Theory of Evidence. Princeton University Press.

SGZZ. (2006). *Soft Modelling*. Retrieved September, 2006, from the World Wide Web: http://www.sgzz.ch/?Systems_Thinking_Practice:Soft_Modelling

Silipo, R. (2003). Neural Networks. In D. J. Hand (Ed.), *Intelligent Data Analysis: An Introdution* (Second ed.): Springer.

Sørensen, L., & Vidal, R. V. V. (2002). The Anatomy of Soft Approaches. *Economic Analysis Working Papers, 1*(08).

Tin, E., Akman, V. (1994). Computational Situation Theory. SIGART Bulletin, Vol. 5, No. 4

Wang, P. P. (2000). Soft modeling for a certain class of intelligent and complex systems. *Information Sciences, 123*(1-2), 149-159.

Wilson, B. (1984). *Systems: Concepts, Methodologies, and Applications*: John Wiley & Sons, Brisbane.

Zadeh, L. A. (1994). Soft computing and fuzzy logic. *Software, IEEE, 11*(6), 48-56.

Zadeh, Lotfi, "Fuzzy Sets as the Basis for a Theory of Possibility", Fuzzy Sets and Systems 1:3-28, 1978.

PART 4

MODELING EXAMPLES

4.1
Overview

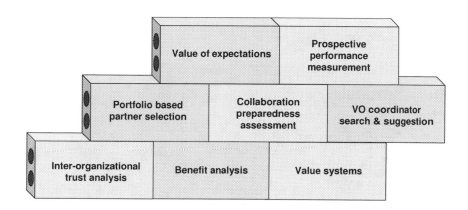

Due to the multi-faceted perspectives of collaborative networks and the wide variety of complex aspects that need to be addressed, there is no single modeling formalism or theory that can properly cover all needed modeling aspects. Very often it is necessary to combine different modeling formalisms and/or theories in order to get a more holistic perspective of CNs.

Each modeling tool / system is usually developed to sufficiently cover certain aspects within its respective discipline(s). Therefore usually several independent modeling tools and/or systems are applied in research, to model different aspects of CNs. Nevertheless, while keeping their independence, some forms of interoperation / composition among these modeling tools and systems are necessary.

Focusing on the modeling of certain aspects in CNs in which multi-modeling tools / systems are needed to be jointly applied, one of the two manners of *interoperability* or *composition* of the modeling tools may be needed to be applied, as addressed below:

i) In some cases, to fully model a certain aspect a number of modeling tools can be applied in a sequential manner, where for example the output of one model constitutes the input for another. Therefore, the modeling tools need to interoperate by sharing and exchanging some input and output elements. In this case some dependencies among the modeling tools / systems exist, and for each case some sequential interoperability of the modeling tools / systems components is required to be developed.

ii) In some other cases, to fully model a certain aspect, a number of modeling tools / systems need to be first integrated with each other into a new compound

/ composite model, which then is implemented to provide the required elements and functionalities.

In the following chapters, a number of cases for modeling different CN aspects are presented, where either the interoperability or the composition of several modeling tools / systems are applied. The purpose here is on one hand to raise awareness on the need for interoperation / composition of several modeling tools / systems applicable to CNs and, on the other hand, to address a number of CN-related aspects that require multi-modeling tools / systems for their proper representation. These two elements are addressed through focusing on some specific example cases. Furthermore in each application area we focus on either the interoperation or composition of the required modeling aspects.

4.2

A multi-model approach to analyze inter-organizational trust in VBEs

S. S. Msanjila, H. Afsarmanesh

The perceptions, preferences and interpretations of trust differ among the organizations depending on their purposes for establishing trust relationships with others. As a result, different organizations consider different aspects when assessing the trust level of other organizations. Thus a number of complex aspects must be addressed to comprehensively cover the trust objectives of organizations which in turn make it difficult to model and analyze these aspects. Consequently, it is hard to thoroughly cover the needed trust aspects by applying a single modeling tool, system or approach. Integrating models and supporting their interoperability, a challenge on its own, is suggested in this chapter for addressing the analysis of inter-organizational trust. This chapter analyzes and proposes a number of specific models that can be applied to comprehensively cover the fundamental aspects related to inter-organizational trust in Virtual organizations Breeding Environments (VBEs).

1. INTRODUCTION

A fundamental prerequisite for setting up a collaborative consortium, such as a virtual organization (VO) within a VBE, is creating trust among its involved organizations. Nevertheless, creating trust among organizations in a large-size VBE, e.g. more than twenty organizations, whose members do not know each other well is challenging (Afsarmanesh et al, 2007). Traditionally, trust among organizations was only established *"bi-laterally"* and subjectively based on reputation and recommendation from others. In large networks such as VBEs however, applying traditional approaches for creating bilateral trust among organizations is difficult, mostly due to the following reasons (Msanjila & Afsarmanesh, 2007a): (1) It is hardly feasible for a trustor organization to collect reputation data or peer opinions about the trustworthiness of a trustee organization, with whom it had never interacted before, and (2) It is hardly feasible to (rationally) reason on the trustworthiness of organizations based on subjective data.

In this paper the following definitions of VO and VBE are applied:

> *A VO is an association of (legally) independent organizations (VO partners) that come together and share resources and skills to achieve a common goal, such as acquiring and executing a market/society opportunity (Camarinha-Matos & Afsarmanesh 2006).*

> *A VBE is defined as an alliance of organizations (VBE members) and related supporting institutions, adhering to a base long term cooperation agreement,*

and adopting common operating principles and infrastructures, with the main goal of increasing both their chances and preparedness towards collaboration in potential VOs [Afsarmanesh & Camarinha-Matos, 2005].

To support the creation of trust among organizations in VBEs, a rational (fact-based) approach is suggested in this research work. In this approach, we suggest applying formal mechanisms to assess trust level of organizations. These mechanisms are formulated applying measurable parameters (called trust criteria) about organizations, such as the past performance, the achieved results, etc. With this approach an organization can trust others rationally and based on facts about their trust level. Thus, trust level of organizations is properly assessed through their trust criteria and can be supported by some rational reasoning based on the mathematical equations. With this approach the VBE administrator can assess the trust level of trustee organizations and provide it to the trustor organization when requested.

In our approach we characterize trust among organizations that participate in the VBEs as a multi-objective, multi-perspective, and multi-criteria subject. As such, the formal mechanisms for assessing trust level of organizations must incorporate and cover all these aspects. It is hardly feasible for a single modeling tool/system or approach to comprehensively cover all these aspects.

To comprehensively cover all the fundamental aspects of trust among organizations therefore, a number of models must be applied each capturing a part of the complexity of the trust system and its main aspects. For this purpose, a number of specific models must be identified and analyzed, specifically addressing their interoperation through which the fundamental trust aspects can be comprehensively covered.

This chapter aims at these analyses of a number of specific models for comprehensive coverage of the fundamental aspects of trust among organizations in VBEs. Here, we primarily focus on the problem area of *"assessment and analysis of trust level of organizations"* applying the *"multi-model approach"* (Figure 1). At the high level this problem area can be broken into four main aspects which constitute the following sub-problems: (1) Identification and analysis of trust criteria that can be applied for measuring trust level of organizations, (2) Formulation of mechanisms for assessing trust level of organizations applying the identified trust criteria for organizations, (3) Analysis of the influences of external factors on the behavior of trust criteria for organizations, and (4) Analysis of sensitivity of mechanisms for assessing trust level when extreme values of trust criteria emerge.

In our approach four sets of specific models were selected each covering one of the mentioned four subspaces. Based on their interoperation (Figure 1) it is feasible to comprehensively cover the fundamental aspects of inter-organizational trust.

The remaining part of this chapter is structured as follows: section 2 addresses specific models that can be applied for identifying trust elements for organizations. Section 3 focuses on specific models which can be applied for formulating and analyzing mechanisms for assessing trust level of organizations. Lastly, section 4 concludes the chapter.

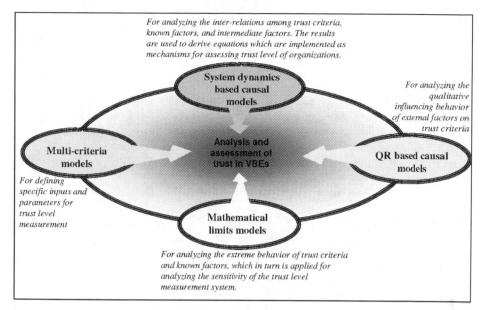

Figure 1: Interoperability among models for the assessment of trust level of organizations (QR refers to qualitative reasoning)

2. IDENTIFYING AND ANALYZING TRUST ELEMENTS

One important aspect of characterizing trust in VBEs is identifying trust elements for its various organizations. We define *trust elements as the hierarchical-related elements from abstract (non measurable) ones which represent the root node to the measurable ones which represent lowest child nodes that together characterize both trust and trust relationships, and form the base for deciding about the data needed for the assessment of trust level of organizations* (Msanjila & Afsarmanesh, 2007c). Some trust elements defined in the literature for organizations are subjective (opinion-based) and thus cannot be measured (Weth, & Bohm, 2006). But performance based trust elements can also be identified for organizations that are rational (fact-based) and thus can be measured.

In (Msanjila & Afsarmanesh, 2007c) the HICI approach for identifying trust elements for organization is presented. This approach constitutes three phases namely: *Hierarchical analysis, Impact analysis and Causal Influences analysis.* Through applying the HICI approach, the hierarchical identification and characterization of rational trust elements for the organizations in VBEs is achieved in the first phase. Hierarchically, trust elements include: *trust objectives, trust perspectives, trust requirements, and trust criteria* (Figure 2).

The identification and characterization of trust elements constitutes the first phase of the HICI approach. A list of trust elements identified by applying this approach and in collaboration with VBE networks, which participated in ECOLEAD project (www.ecolead.org), is published in (Msanjila & Afsarmanesh, 2007c). In brief, the establishment of each trust relationship is for certain objectives. The trust objectives (e.g. for creating trust among member organizations in the VBE) characterize the reason why trust relationships must be established. Each trust objective is further characterized by a number of trust perspectives (e.g. structural perspective, social perspective, etc.). Furthermore, each trust perspective is characterized by a set of trust requirements (e.g. for structural perspective requirement can be structural strength, and business strength). Each trust requirement is also characterized by a set of trust criteria (e.g. for structural strength criteria include size of an organization, personnel experts, etc.). Each trust criterion is specified by its value structure. Figure 2 presents the concept of hierarchies of trust elements and shows an example of trust elements for organizations.

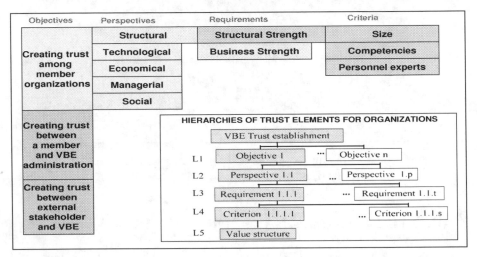

Figure 2: Hierarchies of trust elements for organizations and some examples

As described earlier, we suggest assessing trust level of organizations by applying *rational mechanisms*. Thus only measurable trust elements can be applied; namely only the trust criteria are applied to the mechanisms for assessing trust level of organizations. The formulation of the mechanisms for assessing trust level of organizations is addressed in section 3.

Furthermore, in our approach for assessing trust level of organizations we suggest applying performance data of organizations as the main input. However, the trust level of organizations is measured in terms of values of trust criteria. Therefore, careful analysis is needed to examine the relation between the performance data and their trust criteria. The analysis should also address the possibility of expressing performance data in terms of the values of trust criteria. We apply the impact analysis approach to identify the relations between trust criteria and performance data. Figure 3 visualizes the partial results of our impact analysis, exemplifying the specific trust elements identified specifically for the economical perspective of organizations. Here the impact analysis aims at examining the impact of the changes in values of trust criteria on organizational performance. Thus with this approach it is possible to identify a specific trust criterion whose value must be enhanced, in order to optimize specific aspect of organizational performance. When a specific set of trust criteria is identified which covers all respective specific aspects of organizational performance, it can be said that the performance data can be expressed in terms of values of trust criteria (for example, assume that the profit made by an organization is one aspect of its performance. The profit of an organization can be enhanced by maximizing its "cash in" and minimizing its "cash out"). Thus when all aspects of organizational performance (social, economical, structural, managerial and technological aspects of organizational performance) are expressed in terms of trust criteria, the organizations can focus on enhancing the values of those trust criteria that indirectly optimize their performance, which in turn enhances their trust level.

As described above, the input data (also known as *"trust related data"*) needed for the assessment of trust level of organizations is the performance data expressed in terms of values of trust criteria. To ease and enhance the accessibility of trust related data as well as to ensure its update and consistency, automated management services are required and databases need to be designed and implemented. To develop the databases as part of trust management systems, first different aspects of the trust related data must be modeled.

In our approach, the identified trust elements are modeled applying the record-based formalism. In this formalism the concepts of relational data modeling are applied. The record-based models designed in our research are published in (Msanjila & Afsarmanesh, 2007b). The record-based trust models are applied to build relational database schemas which in turn are used for the automation of management of trust related data. The designed schemas were applied to the implementation of the trust management system.

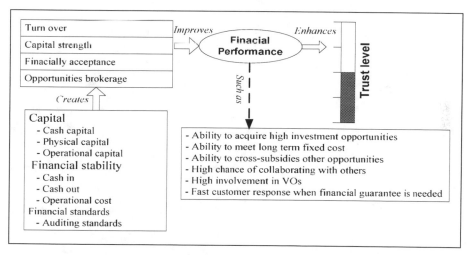

Figure 3: Impact analysis of trust criteria for organizations

Furthermore, the concepts of "trust and trust elements" must be well defined and specified so that these concepts can well be understood by the organizations in VBEs, in order to raise the acceptance and application of the results of the assessment of trust level. To facilitate the understanding of identified trust elements, the trust models are specified using the VBE ontology formalism. This ontology-based trust model provides the VBE actors with the definitions and thus better understanding of the concepts related to trust and trust elements for organizations (Msanjila & Afsarmanesh, 2007b).

3. FORMULATING AND ANALYZING MECHANISMS FOR ASSESSING TRUST LEVEL OF ORGANIZATIONS

This section addresses specific modeling approaches/tools that can be applied to the formulation and analysis of mechanisms for assessing trust level of organizations.

3.1 The base concepts of system dynamics and qualitative reasoning

Causal modeling and analysis approach is applied to different disciplines for the study of the inter-relationships and causal influences among different factors. However, causal modeling is perceived and applied differently in different disciplines. In this work we borrow and adopt the base concepts of *"causal modeling and analysis"*, as applied in the two disciplines of: *"system dynamics"* and *"qualitative reasoning"*. The concepts of causal modeling and analysis are applied in these two disciplines but addressing different aspects. Thus the perception and interpretation of causal models in both disciplines differ as addressed in the next two paragraphs and also visualized in Figure 4.

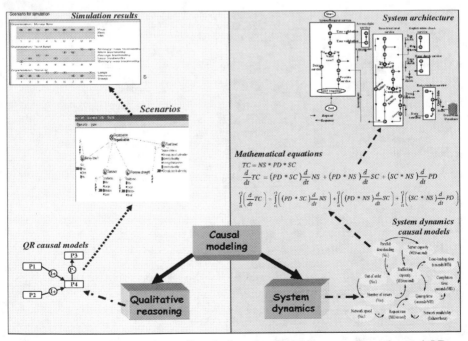

Figure 4: The concept of causal analysis as applied in system dynamics and QR disciplines

In the discipline of system dynamics (Ge at al 2004) it is assumed that a complex system can be broken into smaller measurable elements (criteria). The criteria can then be analyzed using the causal modeling approach to study their causal behavior. The results of causal analysis can be represented in a diagram showing the relations among the criteria. These causal relations can also be translated into mathematical equations. The mathematical equations can be applied to make a formal analysis of the entire system. The right side of Figure 4 represents the application of the causal modeling approach to the system dynamics discipline; namely, first the generation of System dynamics based causal models, followed by the definition of mathematical equations that lead the way to the design of the system architecture (Greenland & Brumback, 2002). In our approach for analyzing inter-organizational trust, the concepts of causal modeling – as perceived in the discipline of system dynamics – are applied for the formulation of mechanisms for assessing trust level of organizations, as further addressed in details in section 3.3.1.

In the discipline of qualitative reasoning (QR) it is assumed that some complex systems are characterized with parameters which are difficult to quantify or their measurable data are hard to collect. However, such systems can be analyzed through developing their QR based models that can be used to identify some values for these parameters with some qualitative degrees (e.g. large, medium, small, etc.). Furthermore, based on these qualitative values, the models can be simulated to analyze the causal influences among these parameters. The results of the causal analysis can then be applied to qualitatively examine the entire system. The left side of Figure 4 shows the application of causal modeling approach in QR; namely first the generation of QR based causal models, followed by the definition of scenario cases that can then be used for simulation (Greenland & Brumback, 2002). In our approach the applications of the concepts of causal modeling and analysis as perceived in the discipline of qualitative reasoning are addressed in section 3.4.1.

3.2 Base concepts related to assessing trust level of organizations

Trust in VBEs is characterized as a multi-objective, multi-perspective and multi-criteria subject. Therefore, trust is not a single concept that can be applied to all cases (Msanjila & Afsarmanesh, 2006) for trust-based decision-making, and its measurements depend on both the purpose of establishing trust relationship and to the specific actors involved. In the past research (Msanjila & Afsarmanesh, 2006) we have shown that trust level of organizations can be measured in terms of quantitative values for a set of trust criteria. Trust level of an organization is complex and can neither be measured with single value for a single parameter nor interpreted with a single metric. Rather, the level of trust of an organization can be specified based on the values for a set of trust criteria applied to measure it.

Proper understanding and interpreting trust level described in terms of values for a set of trust criteria will be complex and difficult to most decision makers, such as managers, directors, etc., who are not trust experts and do not have sufficient knowledge in both mathematics and computer applications. Therefore, trust level must be presented in a format, which is as understandable as possible for the expected users.

We propose that trust level of organizations shall be represented and expressed in terms of a set of qualitative values, and these values can only represent a comparative trust level among organizations, since trust levels cannot be measured with absolute values. For the assessment of the base trust level of VBE members, these qualitative values will be generated by the trust management system (TrustMan system) based on the values that VBE member organizations hold for the set of designated trust criteria, which is a part of each specific trust requirement and perspective. The TrustMan system is designed and implemented in ECOLEAD, to assist the VBE administrator and other VBE stakeholders with semi-automatic services to perform their tasks, related to management of inter-organizational trust in the VBE.

For the specific trustworthiness of member organizations, these qualitative values will be generated for the trustee organization, based on score of its values (on the specific criteria), as compared to those of the other organizations. The set of "qualitative values" for the representation of trust level can include: *Strongly more trustworthy, More trustworthy, Average trustworthy, Less trustworthy, and Strongly less trustworthy.* As an example, the comparative qualitative values of trust level of five compared organizations (ORG-1 to ORG-5) can be graphically represented as in Figure 5 that is here referred to as the "**Trust-Meter**".

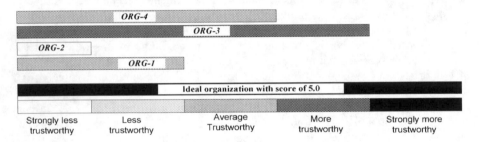

Figure 5: Trust-meter for presenting comparative trust levels of organizations

Please note that for the classification of different comparative measured trust level of the organizations, the *lowest resulted value* will be assigned to the category of "Strongly less trustworthy" and similarly the *highest resulted value* to the category of "Strongly more trustworthy" and the other categories represent a uniform distribution of these values. Furthermore, these resulted qualitative values for the organizations are totally dependent on the trustor's choices/preferences on the measured trust criteria. Similarly, the VBE administrator will decide on the trust criteria for the base trust level assessment.

While the final rating of organizations with Trust-Meter is comparative and thus *relative, the manipulation of performance related values for trust criteria of organizations,* which in turn guides the decisions about the trust level of organizations, is rational (fact-based) and not qualitative. These manipulation mechanisms are based on the mathematical equations, and therefore the comparisons of trust levels among VBE member organizations is also rational (fact-based). The qualitative aspects of the process for assessing trust level and modeling trust are threefold (Msanjila & Afsarmanesh 2007):

* Applying the hierarchical analysis approach for *identifying the trust elements* (section 2) and defining their inter-relations to each other, in order to generate the related mathematical equations (section 3.3.1)

* Applying a learning process in the VBE environment for *defining and updating the rating of trust level based on the values of* trust criteria

* Applying a learning process on the use of the trust criteria, in order to *define new trust criteria* for the VBE environment or for a specific trust objective through applying the HICI approach as addressed in section 2.

3.3 Measurements and assessments of organizations' trust level

For "*rational*" assessment of trust level of organizations in VBEs a series of fact-based trust criteria can be applied. However, the behaviour of these trust criteria changes in time. These changes of behaviours are "*causally*" influenced in two ways, namely through: "*internally initiated influences*" *and* "*externally initiated influences*" as described below.

Trust criteria applied for the measurement of trust level of organizations do causally influence each other's behaviour. The global behaviour of these criteria therefore can be regarded as the behaviour of the system used for measuring trust level. As described in (Ge, et al 2004) these causal influences can be studied by applying concepts from system dynamics discipline. The results of such causal analysis can be represented diagrammatically in a so-called "*causal diagram*". The results can also be translated into mathematical equations reflecting the relations among trust criteria. The formulated mathematical equations comprise the base for our designed formal mechanism for rational assessment of trust level of organizations as addressed in section 3.3.1. The influences on one trust criterion that are initiated by changes of behaviour of one or more other criteria are referred as "*internally initiated influences*".

Trust criteria can also be influenced and their values can change due to a number of other factors that in our research are classified as factors that are external and uncontrollable by the VBE and its member organizations. In other words, while the behaviour of these external factors influences the behaviour of trust criteria in VBEs, they cannot be directly controlled by the organizations or the VBE, for example, the economical related trust criteria (i.e. cash out) can be influenced by changes in tax regulations (i.e. increase in percentage of tax on price of raw materials) which cannot be directly controlled by the VBE and its members (see section 3.4.1). Therefore, when some changes emerge in the values of the external factors, the VBE and its member organizations cannot directly control or influence those changes to meet their favour. Alternatively, organizations can optimize the current values related to their trust criteria, in order to avoid/reduce the impact of changes in the values of external factors on their own trust level. Such causal relations are referred to as "*externally initiated influences*".

3.3.1 Mechanisms for measuring trust level of organizations

Methodologies developed in the discipline of system dynamics can be applied for analyzing causal influences among factors (Kirkwood, 1998, Ge et al 2004). For example, research performed in the discipline of system dynamics has developed methodologies which can be applied to analyze a complex problem and break it into a set of measurable factors. The behavior of these factors, which together represent the global picture of the problem, can then be analyzed.

We apply causal analysis, as perceived in system dynamics discipline, to analyze the "*internally initiated causal influences*" among trust criteria for organizations in VBE. We then apply the results of such analysis to formulate mathematical equations relating the trust criteria. The mathematical equations are applied to formulate the mechanisms for assessing trust level of organizations. Figure 6 shows an example of the causal diagram representing the relations among trust criteria related to the social perspective of the organizations. It should be noted that trust criteria do not directly influence each other, rather through some intermediate factors. Thus the mathematical equations are derived representing these relations, where the intermediate factors become the subject of the equations. Some known factors defined in a specific VBE environment are also applied to the equations.

In the causal diagram, a plus sign (+) on an arrow indicates that the increase or decrease of the source (first) factor causes the increase or decrease of the destination (second) factor, and on the contrary the minus sign (-) indicate that the increase or decrease of the first factor causes the decrease or increase of the second factor (Kirkwood, 1998).

For the formulation of mathematical equations from the causal diagram, primarily the plus sign (+) on an arrow represents either an arithmetic addition or multiplication, and the minus sign (-) represents either an arithmetic subtraction or division, depending on the semantic of each trust criterion and the metric that scales it (Kirkwood, 1998; Ge, et al 2004). The selection of the correct arithmetic operator depends on the balance of dimensions, and when complex relations are involved, dimension analysis can be applied. To put it simply, when several criteria (C1 to Cn) influence an intermediate factor (Ft), then the value metric of Ft is simply used to determine how the value metrics of the C1 to Cn must be inter-related with each other to produce Ft.

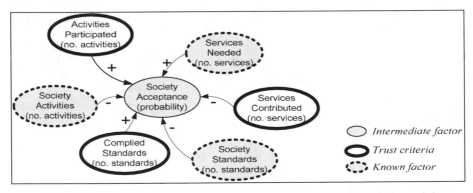

Figure 6: Causal diagram showing influences among trust criteria in social perspective

In principle, three kinds of equations can be formulated, namely: arithmetic, differential, and integral equations. Each of these equations is applied for different purposes in the analysis and assessment of trust level of organizations as further described in (Msanjila & Afsarmanesh, 2007a). To exemplify, the equations related to the social perspective of the organizations, for the intermediate factor of Society Acceptance (SAC) are shown below, where AP refers to Activities Participated, SA refers to Society Activities, SC refers to Service Contributed, SN refers to Service Needed, CS refers to Complied Standards and SS refers to Society Standards.

$$SAC = \frac{AP}{SA} * \frac{SC}{SN} * \frac{CS}{SS} \ldots (1), \quad \frac{d}{dt} SAC = \frac{d}{dt}\left(\frac{AP}{SA} * \frac{SC}{SN} * \frac{CS}{SS}\right) \ldots (2), \quad \int_{t1}^{t2} \frac{d}{dt} SAC = \int_{t1}^{t2} \frac{d}{dt}\left(\frac{AP}{SA} * \frac{SC}{SN} * \frac{CS}{SS}\right) \ldots (3)$$

The mathematical equations derived during our research are applied to the design of the mechanisms for the Trust Management (TrustMan) system (Msanjila & Afsarmanesh, 2007d). In ECOLEAD, the TrustMan system is designed and implemented for the main purpose of supporting the management of trust among organizations and the related processes in the VBE. The subject of derivation of mathematical equations is further discussed in (Msanjila & Afsarmanesh 2007a).

Clearly the use of the different forms of equations presented above differs. The arithmetic equations are used for assessing trust level of an organization at a specific point in time, such as the current time. When trust level of an organization must be assessed by applying a large amount of data from the past it becomes complex. Also, when trust level must be forecasted, the complexity of the assessment process increases. In these two later special cases simulation can be applied. For the simulation case the differential equations are applied to build the simulation models.

3.3.2 Correctness measures for mechanisms of trust level analysis
In TrustMan system, as described above a number of formulas that formally define the inter-relations among trust criteria, the intermediate factors, and the known factors, are applied for the implementation of mechanisms for assessing trust level of organizations. When an organization prefers a number of trust criteria the related predefined formulas that constitute these criteria are invoked. Also the values for selected criteria related to each organization will be used. However, in some cases the predefined formulas might include more trust criteria than those selected. In such cases, mechanisms are implemented to eliminate the influences of the rejected (not selected) criteria in the predefined formulas, thus ensuring that correct results from the assessment of trust level are obtained. A value of either "1" or "0" is assigned to the trust criterion depending on the mathematical operator relating it to others. For example, if the operator is (+) sign or a minus (-) sign then a value of 0 will be assigned to the trust criterion. Moreover, if the operator is multiplication (*) or a division (/) then the trust criterion will be assigned a value of 1.

3.4 Analyzing mechanisms for assessing trust level

In this section we analyze the influence of external factors on behavior of trust criteria for organizations. Trust criteria are applied to the derivation of mathematical equations, which in turn are applied in the formulations of mechanisms for assessing trust level of organizations. Thus the influence of external factors on behavior trust criteria will also impact the variation of trust level of organizations. In this section we also address the sensitivity of mechanisms for assessing trust level of organization whenever extreme values of trust criteria are applied.

3.4.1 Analysis of externally influenced behavior
The external factors are exogenous to the VBE environments and cannot be

controlled by VBE policies. Some example of external factors to the VBE can include changes in: tax regulations (i.e. percentage of tax on prices of products), customer preferences related to services provided by the VBE through VOs (i.e. demand for better quality), prices of raw materials, etc. Thus it is hardly feasible to timely collect related data to enable formal analysis of their behaviour. Consequently, it is difficult to analyze and study externally initiated influences on trust criteria for organizations using "formal methods". Hence, approaches must be identified or developed to support the analysis of these influences with lack (or incompleteness) of quantitative data. In such situation when measurable data is not be available, qualitative analysis approaches can assist by producing possible expected pictures instead of exact answer. We propose to apply qualitative reasoning (QR) to study the (qualitative) causal influences between trust criteria and the external factors (here also called uncontrollable factors).

In this section we address the analysis of externally initiated influences on the behaviour trust criteria. We apply the concepts of qualitative reasoning to analyze the possible trends of behaviour of external factors. Based on the identified trends, possible behaviour of trust criteria can be qualitatively simulated. This will enable to examine possible impacts that can be caused by variation of behaviour of external factors on behaviour of trust criteria which in turn influences the changes in the trust level of organizations.

Previous research on QR has generated techniques that have been applied in several other significant and complex domains and applications, such as autonomous space-craft support, failure analysis and on-board diagnosis of vehicle systems, as well as sensitivity and causal analysis of heterogeneous factors in ecosystems, etc. (Bredeweg & Struss 2003). It is claimed that (Salles & Bredeweg 2006) QR provides approaches to model systems behaviour as close to the exact model as possible, specifically addressing the following three aspects:

+ *Incompleteness of data:* QR compliments the inapplicability of pure mathematical modelling approaches whenever the quantitative data is missing or incomplete,
+ *Inaccuracy of system output:* Support qualitative interpretation of system behaviour and its output, and thus compares what was expected and what is achieved, i.e. improving the accuracy of equations,
+ *Unavailability of data*: QR compliments the insufficient causal analysis that can be handled through mathematical models whenever measurable data is missing.

Based on the above aspects as well as considering the achieved results in application of QR to previous complex system, we have chosen to apply QR in analyzing and assessing trust level of organizations and specifically due to the following points among others:

Point 1 – *Analyzing the need for enhancing/extending the set of trust criteria:* From time to time the set of trust criteria which is customized for a specific VBE shall be tuned (such as extended) to enhance the performance, accuracy and efficiency of Trust Management system. However, the tuning can be externally influenced by following among others:

* Variations of trust preferences, acceptance of results of trust level assessment, variations of trust perceptions, etc.
* Changes in the environments, e.g. VBE operating rules, VBE policies, etc.
* Market evolutions: raw materials, production costs, etc. in relation to trust perceptions.
* Government and political influences, e.g. imposition of new rules.

Point 2- *Analyzing causal influences between trust criteria and external factors*: The trends in change of behaviour of trust criteria are causally influenced by external factors. Mathematical analysis of such kind of influences can be performed when all the *quantitative* data is available. However, it is hardly feasible to measure and collect quantitative data for external factors. Some influences can include: changes of behaviour of fundamental market elements (e.g. money flow), emergence of new technologies, etc.

Point 3- *Complementing rational assessment of trust level of organizations*: There are parameters that are difficult to measure and thus cannot be included in formal mechanisms for assessing trust level of organizations. However, they do influence trust level and trustworthiness picture of organizations. Qualitative reasoning approaches can be applied to analyze the influences of these parameters on the trust level of organizations. Among others the following can be considered for applying the QR approach:
* Public support and confidence in the organization,
* The image of the organization in public,
* The benefits to the public which is resulted from the existence of the organization.

Point 4- *Analyzing the influence of trust antecedents on trust level*: Antecedents are crucial cardinals that unless met, they can have a negative impact on the process of creating trust among organizations, such as the shared values, the previous interactions, and the practiced behaviors (Msanjila & Afsarmanesh 2007e).

Shared values can range from business objectives to internal management processes. They occur when the trustor organization and the trustee organization have common understanding on important issues that might influence the creation of trust to each other, i.e. missions, goals, policies, interpretation of right or wrong etc.

Previous fruitful interactions between the trustor organization and the trustee organization either directly or indirectly (through other intermediate organizations) enhances the effectiveness of the established trust relationships. The interactions can be formal as well as informal, i.e. sharing meaningful and up-to-date information.

Practiced (moral and/or ethical) behaviours basically refer to acting against the opportunistic behaviour. It refers to taking immediate advantage, often unethically, of any circumstance that may generate possible benefit. It also refers to ungentle action taken by VBE members for the purpose of benefiting themselves unethically more than others (e.g. quitting the collaboration once they gain, or if they expect for the risks of the collaboration to arise).

Thus if these antecedents are not met by some involved organizations they may encourage other organizations to be reluctant to trust them. However, the relation between these antecedents and trust level of organizations is not clear and it is difficult to mathematically represent. We suggest applying QR to analyze and reason about these relations and their impacts on the perceived trust level of organizations.

Point 5- *Analyzing the relation between trust level and past performance:* The trust level of an organization is causally related to the past performance it has achieved, actions and events it had performed, or in which it participated, etc. There are a number of elements that influence the performance of organizations that cannot be measured or controlled by the organization. Thus these elements can be thoroughly analyzed using qualitative approaches.

To properly analyze the complex relations between trust criteria and external factors a number of QR models must be designed and implemented using simulation systems such as the Garp system (Garp 2007). The implemented models can then be simulated to analyze possible external influences on trust criteria that can emerge during the operation stage of the TrustMan system. However, several scenarios need to be simulated addressing the possible behavior of the implemented model of the system, in order to thoroughly present the expected behavior of TrustMan system. The results of these simulations can then be applied to enhance the efficiency of mechanisms developed for the TrustMan system.

To exemplify the analysis of external influences on trust criteria we consider the economical trust perspective of organizations. Further information on the trust criteria for organizations in VBEs is presented in (Msanjila & Afsarmanesh 2007a). In this example a large number of trust criteria associated with the economical perspective need to considered, but for simplicity purposes here Figure 7 shows that only one influence path is considered. The two criteria (Cash in and Cash out) are presented here as examples. The "Turnover" and "Financial strength" are considered here as intermediate factors.

In this example the "Market money flow" into and out of an organization is considered as the external factor. The behaviour of market money flow cannot be directly controlled by organizations. Its behaviour depends on some parameters that are beyond the organization's control, such as the price of raw materials, increase in the number of customers, etc.

There are two important aspects that must be carefully considered when applying QR for analyzing the causal influences, as follows:

1. *Influences (I) and propagations (P):* There are also two kinds of causal influences, namely: direct influences (I+, I-) and propagation (indirect influences) (P+, P-) (Salles & Bredeweg 2006). I+ and I- refer to the influences between two factors, (the source of factor and the destination of factor), where the changes are one to one and can be represented mathematically without major assumptions. In most cases these two factors do have compatible measurement units. For P+ and P-, in most cases, there is no clear picture of the nature of influence, though the direction of influence can be qualitatively observed. Figure 7 shows an example of a causal diagram for some aspects of the economical perspective.

2. *Ambiguities among influences:* In some cases the influences can be hard to reason about. These happen when a destination factor is influenced by at least two source factors and the influences are contradicting. The contradiction happens when at least one influence has an opposing sign as compared to those of others.

Such contradicting influences are referred to as *ambiguity influences* (e.g. cash in and cash out as source factors, and turnover as destination factor as shown in Figure 7). It becomes more challenges when propagations are involved in the ambiguity relations. These ambiguities become too complex to manually analyze when the magnitude of the influences absolutely differ. In this example the analysis of such ambiguities is done using the **Garp system** (Garp, 2007).

The results of analysis of causal influences between trust criteria and external factors are shown in Figure 7.

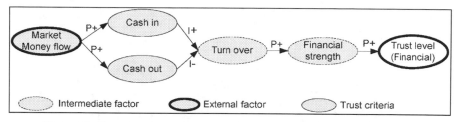

Figure 7: Causal diagram indicating direct and propagation influences

Through scenarios, it is possible to identify some possible behavioural trends of elements being analyzed. Figure 8 shows one of the possible scenarios indicating the possible value of each parameter. As indicated in Figure 8 all parameters are at the level of an organization.

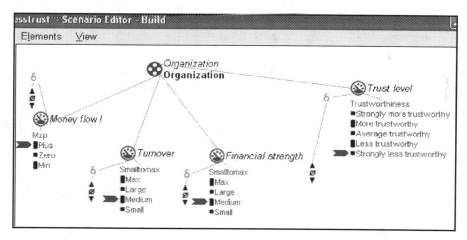

Figure 8: Screenshot of one of the scenarios in Garp system

To experiment with our scenario in Garp system, it is assumed the qualitative values of the parameters as shown in Table 1.

Table 1: Assumed values applied for simulation of the model

	Money flow	**Turnover**	**Trust level**
Possible values	Min, zero, plus	Small, medium, large	Strong less trustworthy, less trustworthy, average trustworthy, more trustworthy, strongly more trustworthy
Starting values	Zero, plus	Small, medium	Strongly less trustworthy
Behavior	Steady, increasing, decreasing, Random,	Dependent	dependent

As an example case the Garp system is used to implement and simulate the suggested scenario. Garp system has a qualitative modelling engine which supports defining scenarios and simulating them for the purpose of qualitatively studying the complex system.

While simulating a scenario in Garp system different states that can occur until the system is stabilized can be analyzed. A state in real practice is related to time and thus with these results we can predict the possible behaviour of trust criteria and their influences on the trust level as shown in Figure 9 indicating the possible values of states 1 and 9. Figure 9 shows a state transition graph indicating the possible paths (possible behaviour) that a system can experience before it is stabilized, such as the state number 12 in Figure 9.

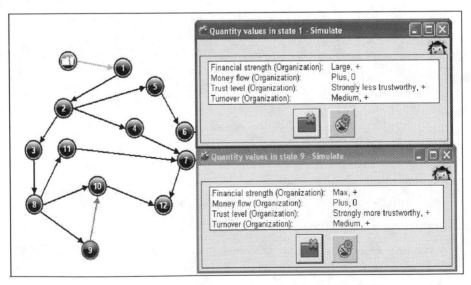

Figure 9: Screenshot of possible states from the simulation in Garp system

A state in this diagram represents a particular situation of the modelled system. A state contains information about the structural organisation, the current values of quantities, inequalities, and the active model fragments. A state can be interpreted, terminated, ordered, or closed. A state graph consists of a set of states and state transitions. A state transition specifies how one state may change into another state. A sequence of states, connected by state transitions, is called a behaviour path (a behaviour trajectory of the system). A state graph usually captures a set of possible behavioural paths because multiple state transitions are possible from certain states.

Figure 10 shows that trust level of an organization increases as the money flow in the organization remain positive and steady. Thus it indicates that the change of "trust level" of an organization can be influenced by (is dependent on) the rate of "money flow" into an organization.

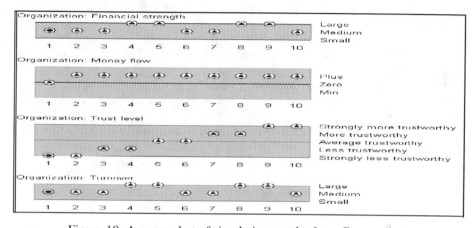

Figure 10: A screenshot of simulation results from Garp system

Thus the more the money flow into the organization the higher its financial trustworthiness. The simulated scenario has applied the value of money flow as "plus & steady. However, as stated earlier the money flow cannot be directly controlled by the respective organization as it is influenced by customers, market conditions (such as prices of raw material), etc.

   In other words, by the varying qualitative values of factors (such as small, medium, and large) that constitute the source of influences in the model, the sensitivity of trust level can be analyzed, using these simulation results. Assuming similar scenarios can happen in real life, the "sensitivity" of trust level results produced by the trust management system can thus be studied. This in turn will facilitate the tuning of the trust management system to meet and preserve the VBE requirements independent (in spite of) of changes of behavior of external factors.

3.4.2 Analysis of sensitivity to changes behavior

The assessment of trust level of organizations applies values of trust criteria as its main input data. As explained earlier, the mechanisms that manipulate these values to provide the trust level of organizations are based on mathematical equations. In section 3.4.1 we have shown how the influences initiated by external factors on the trust criteria can alter the trust level of organizations. Furthermore, some internally initiated influences among trust criteria may incorrectly or unexpectedly alter the trust level of organizations. For example, if an extreme value is applied to a trust criterion (e.g. a very large number is applied for technological standards) it will cause inaccurate results from the assessment of trust level of organizations. Therefore, the resulted trust level might not represent a correct picture about the trustworthiness of organizations. Such extreme values can, for example, occur when the value of one trust criterion becomes too large (in mathematics referred to as infinity).

To exemplify, consider the equation (1). When the value of Service Contributed (SC) becomes arbitrarily large the calculated value of society acceptance (SAC) will also become arbitrarily large. This is because the influences of other parameters in the equations become negligible. Furthermore, when the value of Service Needed (SN) becomes arbitrary large the calculated value of SAC approaches to zero. The sensitivity analysis enables the stakeholders to set some limits for values of trust criteria that can be applied in the TrustMan system.

The analysis addressing such extreme behavior is necessary to enhance the accuracy of the applied mechanisms for assessing trust level of organizations. For the development of TrustMan system we applied the concepts of mathematics limits (ML) to analyze the behavior of mechanisms when some extreme values of trust criteria emerge.

The concept of *"limit"* is used in mathematics to describe the behavior of a function as its argument either gets *"close"* to some point, *popularly close to zero*, or as it becomes arbitrarily large, *popularly close to infinity*.

4. CONCLUSION

Trust level of organizations can neither be measured using one criterion nor be interpreted using a single unit that can comprehensively cover all aspects of inter-organizational trust as characterized so far for VBEs (Msanjila & Afsarmanesh 2007a). Consequently, no single model can be suitable or comprehensively cover all fundamental aspects of trust among organizations. The approach suggested in this chapter proposes the needed interoperation among specific models that can comprehensively cover the fundamental aspects of trust in VBEs. Thus to properly support the modeling of trust among organizations in VBEs, a number of different models must be applied to thoroughly cover its fundamental aspects.

This chapter addresses application of four sets of specific models for modeling and analyzing inter-organizational trust, namely: (1) Set of multi-criteria models which are applied for identifying, analyzing and modeling trust elements for organizations, (2) Set of causal models based on concepts adopted from system dynamics discipline which are applied to develop mechanisms for assessing trust level of organizations. The mechanisms are developed based on the results of analysis of causal inter-relations among trust criteria, known factors and intermediate factors, (3) Set of QR based models which are applied for analyzing the influences on trust criteria caused by external factors, and (4) Set of mathematical limits models which are applied for analyzing possible extreme behavior of trust criteria.

As stated earlier trust is a complex subject and its concepts are differently addressed and applied in real life and business. The presented example cases in this chapter aim at supporting and enhancing the explanation of the application of the presented set of models for analyzing trust in VBEs. However, to verify the applicability of these sets of models in daily practice some real data is needed. The solutions presented in this chapter are currently being applied and validated by industry based VBE networks. The results from the validation will enable as to verify the applicability of these sets of models as well as guides us to tune and enhance their coverage of emerging trust aspects, which will be reflected in our future publications.

Acknowledgement: This work was supported in part by the ECOLEAD project funded by the European Commission. The authors acknowledge contributions from partners in ECOLEAD.

5. REFERENCES

Afsarmanesh H., & Camarinha-Matos L.M. (2005). A framework for management of virtual organization breeding environments In *Proceedings of PRO-VE'05 – Collaborative Networks and their Breeding Environments*, Valencia, Spain, 26-28 Sept 2005, (Springer: Boston).

Afsarmanesh, H., Camarinha-Matos, L. & Msanjila, S.S. (2007). Virtual organizations breeding environments: key results from ECOLEAD. *In the proceedings of International conference on Cost Effective Automation in Networked Product Development and Manufacturing* - IFAC-CEA'2007, Monterey, Mexico.

Bredeweg, B. & Struss, P. (2003). Current topics in qualitative reasoning. *In AI magazine on qualitative reasoning*. ISBN: 0738-4602-2003.

Camarinha-Matos, L. M. & Afsarmanesh, H. (2006). Collaborative Networks: Value creation in a knowledge society. *In knowledge enterprise: Intelligent strategies in product design, manufacturing and management*. Springer, page 26-40.

Garp: (2007) http://hcs.science.uva.nl/QRM/software/, accessed on July 2007.

Ge, Y., Yang, J.B., Proudlove, N. & Spring, M. (2004). System dynamics modeling for supply-chain management: A case study on a supermarket chain in the UK. *In the International Transactions in Operational Research*, Vol. 11, pg. 495-509.

Greenland S., & Brumback, B. (2002). An overview of relations among causal modeling methods. *In international journal of epidemiology*. ISBN: 31-1030-1037.

Kirkwood, C. W. (1998). System Dynamics Method. Ventana System Inc.

Msanjila, S.S. & Afsarmanesh H. (2007a). Trust Analysis and Assessment in Virtual Organizations Breeding Environments. *In the International Journal of Production Research; Special issue: Enhancing performance in industrial collaborative networks*. ISSN (Print): 0020-7543, Taylor & Francis, Vol. 46, No.5 pg. 1253-1295.

Msanjila, S.S. & Afsarmanesh H. (2007b). Modeling Trust Relationships in Collaborative Networked Organizations. *In the International Journal of Technology Transfer and Commercialisation; Special issue: Data protection, Trust and Technology*; Inderscience. ISSN (Print): 1470-6075. Vol. 6, issue 1. pg. 40-55.

Msanjila, S.S. & Afsarmanesh H. (2007c). HICI: An approach for identifying trust elements – The case of technological perspective in VBEs. *In proceedings of International conference on availability, reliability and security* (ARES-2007), Vienna.

Msanjila, S.S. & Afsarmanesh H. (2007d). Specification of the TrustMan System for Assisting Management of VBEs. *In Lecture Notes in Computer Science* (LNCS: 4657), Springer. pg. 34-43.

Msanjila, S.S. & Afsarmanesh H. (2007e).Towards Establishing Trust Relationships among Organizations in VBEs. *In Establishing Foundation of Collaborative Networks (proceedings of 8th PRO-VE2007)*, Guimarães, Portugal. pg. 3-14.

Msanjila, S. S. & Afsarmanesh, H. (2006). Assessment and creation of trust in VBEs. *In proceedings of PRO-VE2006* conference, IFIP, Vol. 224, Network-Centric Collaboration and Supporting Frameworks (Camarinha-Matos, L., Afsarmanesh, H. & Ollus, M.-editors),Springer, pg. 161-172.

Salles, P. & Bredeweg, B. (2006). Modeling population and community dynamics with qualitative reasoning. *In journal ecological modeling*, vol. 195, page 114-128, Elservier B. V.

Weth, C. V. D. & Bohm, K. (2006). A unifying Framework for Behavior-Based Trust Models. OTM 2006, In Lecture Notes in Computer Science, LNCS 4275, , pg. 444-461, Springer.

4.3
Networked partner selection with robust portfolio modeling

T. Jarimo, K. Korpiaho

This chapter illustrates the applicability of mathematical decision-analysis in VO partner selection. The approach allows for multiple criteria, which can also relate to inter-organizational issues such as collaboration history between partner candidates. Moreover, the approach is soft in the sense that it allows interval parameter data, instead of point estimates. Using the RPM method, Pareto-efficient VO configurations can be identified and the robustness of the candidates can be analyzed. The results suggest that the models are very useful in practical decision-making situations.

1. INTRODUCTION

For some time, competition has changed from the level of individual firms towards rivalry among company networks (Jarillo, 1988). Through networking, companies can focus on their niche core competences, which may contribute to increased global efficiency (Hamel and Prahalad, 1990). Networking, however, involves transaction costs, which partly result from partner search and selection (Williamson, 1975). Therefore, several methods have been proposed for the reduction of these costs. Most notably, multi-criteria approaches to partner selection have attracted the interest of researchers and practitioners in the field.

A Virtual Organization Breeding Environment (VBE) in particular is in good position for utilizing semi-automated approaches to support the partner selection in Virtual Organizations (VO). The repeated creation of VOs allows the collection of data on the VBE members. This data can be further used to evaluate the suitability of the candidates in specific VOs. (Camarinha-Matos and Afsarmanesh, 2003)

This chapter models the partner selection problem as a multi-objective binary program. In multi-criteria problems it is typically more beneficial to identify the set of Pareto-efficient solutions rather than a unique solution (Steuer, 1976). Here, we employ the Robust Portfolio Modeling (RPM, Liesiö et al. 2007) method for identifying the Pareto-efficient configurations of a partner selection case. The advantage of RPM is that the model parameters need not be point estimates, which in many cases is too restrictive. Instead, the model can contain interval values as input data. The modeling approach allows for candidate-specific criteria, as well as network criteria that need to be measured for the configuration as a whole.

The rest of this chapter is organized as follows. Section 2 reviews earlier soft methods for partner selection. Section 3 formulates a multi-criteria mathematical programming model, which is operationalized in the partner-selection case of Section 4. Section 5 discusses the approach and Section 6 concludes with topics for future research.

2. ROBUST METHODS FOR NETWORK FORMATION

In multi-criteria decision-making, the decision-maker (DM) can aggregate the different objectives, e.g., by way of a subjective *value function* which reflects his or her preferences for the relative importance of the selection criteria. This method is based on multi-attribute value theory (MAVT, Keeney and Raiffa, 1976). The value function is typically additive, and the preferences are captured through criteria weights, which can be elicited using systematic approaches, such as SMART (Edwards, 1977), SWING (von Winterfeldt and Edwards, 1986), SMARTS or SMARTER (Barron and Edwards, 1994). Another method, which has become popular among practitioners, is the *analytic hierarchy process* (AHP, Saaty, 1980). It relies on pairwise comparisons of the alternatives and selection criteria, but its theoretical foundations differ from that of MAVT (Dyer, 1990; Saaty, 2005).

A common case in decision-making is that no perfect information is available on the decision alternatives and/or the DM's preferences over the selection criteria. Therefore, several methods, based on MAVT or AHP, have been suggested to cope with imperfect information (Arbel, 1989; Mikhailov, 2000; Salo and Punkka, 2005). Using such methods can help evaluate the robustness of decisions under imperfect information, often referred to as *soft modeling*.

VO partner selection is essentially a multi-criteria decision-making problem which involves several factors, such as corporate culture and social relations (Meade et al., 1997). Moreover, perfect data on such factors is hardly ever available, thus VO partner selection has been the subject of some soft modeling techniques. Since partner selection itself is a precise problem, the ambiguity is usually related to the partner candidates' expected performance, or the preferences of the decision-maker. In many works, this ambiguity has been captured by fuzzy approaches.

One of the earliest soft partner selection studies is that of Mikhailov (2002), who develops a fuzzy programming method for incorporating uncertain attribute weights and candidate scores into the AHP framework. A somewhat different one-criterion model is that of Ip et al. (2003), who maximize the probability of success of a virtual enterprise. Because their model is neither linear nor convex, they develop a genetic algorithm for solving it. Li and Liao (2004), in turn, use trapezoidal fuzzy numbers to express parameters related to various kinds of risk factors that they use to analyze risks in dynamic alliances. Since risk factors are difficult to measure quantitatively, the fuzzy approach helps the DM compare the risks of different alliances. The decision support tool of Crispim and Sousa (2005) allows the DM to use interval and linguistic variables in describing the candidates' performance. Such variables are useful if no exact data on historical performance is available.

3. MATHEMATICAL MODEL OF PARTNER SELECTION

3.1 Decision Variables and Objective Function

The partner selection problem can be mathematically formulated as follows. Following commonly used notation (e.g. Liesiö et al. 2007), let there be m partner candidates $X = \{x^1, \ldots, x^m\}$. From these candidates a configuration p is formulated by selecting partners into it. The x^js are used as the decision variables, if $x^j \in p$ then $x^j = 1$, otherwise $x^j = 0$. Each candidate is evaluated with regard to the n decision criteria $i = 1, \ldots, n$, and the resulting score vector for x^j is $v^j = [v_1^j, \ldots, v_n^j]$. The relative importance of the decision criteria are captured through criteria weights $w_1, \ldots, w_n$, which are non-negative and scaled to sum up to one. The value of a configuration p is the weighted sum of the scores

$$V(p) = \sum_{x^j \in p} \sum_{i=1}^{n} w_i v_i^j. \tag{1}$$

Usually, partners are selected with respect to specific competences or project tasks, to which the above scores typically connect.

3.2 Optional Constraints

Without any constraints, the objective function (1) could prefer selecting all the candidates. Thus, the following types of restrictions are common and can be modeled as linear inequalities (Stummer and Heidenberger, 2003).

Resource constraints: These are the most commonly used constraints. A candidate j consumes or produces different kinds of resources l denoted by r_l^j, which are positive for consumption and negative for production. The resource limit for resource l is c_l. The following linear inequality determines the feasible configurations:

$$\forall l: \quad \sum_{x^j \in p} r_l^j \leq c_l. \tag{2}$$

Positioning constraints: With these constraints we can ensure that at least or at most a certain number of partners from a subset $X' \subseteq X$ will be chosen to our configuration. If at most m' partners are wanted, we create a new positioning resource constraint $\hat{l}$ and set $r_{\hat{l}}^j = 1$ $\quad \forall x^j \in X'$ and $r_{\hat{l}}^j = 0$ for the rest. The following inequality ensures that at most m' partners from X' are chosen:

$$\sum_{x^j \in p} r_{\hat{l}}^j \le m'.\tag{3}$$

In contrast, if we multiply both sides of the inequality (3) by -1 and keep the less than or equal sign as it is, the inequality ensures that at least m' partners are chosen from X'. Positioning constraints are used to ensure e.g. that at least one partner is selected for each required competence.

Logical constraints: As the name states, we use these constraints to build logical requirements to our configuration. If, for example, x^k can be selected only if at least m' partners from X' are selected, we create constraint $\tilde{l}$ and set $r_{\tilde{l}}^j = -1$ $\forall x^j \in X'$ and $r_{\tilde{l}}^j = 0$ to the rest, except $r_{\tilde{l}}^k = m'$. The following inequality ensures that x^k is in the configuration only if the requirement holds:

$$\sum_{x^j \in p} r_{\tilde{l}}^j \le 0.\tag{4}$$

If at most m' candidates can be chosen, both sides of the inequality should be multiplied by -1 while the less than or equal sign remains as it is. If both of these inequalities are used at the same time either all the candidates in X' and x^k are chosen or none of them are chosen. The logical constraints can be used to ensure that x^k is chosen if exactly m' partners are chosen from X', but it is possible to choose less than m' partners from X'. These inequalities are used to model inter-organizational dependencies.

Threshold constraints: These constraints can be used as balancing constraints, to ensure certain performance levels or to reject otherwise high value configurations where too low performance on some criterion has been compensated by other criteria. If we require that the resulting configurations earn at least $h_{\bar{i}}$ points from the i th criterion, we create constraint $\bar{l}$ and set $r_{\bar{l}}^j = -v_i^j$ $\quad \forall j$. The following inequality ensures that the required performance levels are reached:

$$\sum_{x^j \in p} r_{\bar{l}}^j \le -h_{\bar{i}}.\tag{5}$$

The inter-organizational dependencies can be modeled into the selection problem with the help of logical constraints and dummy partners. For example, we gain synergy value $v^{\tilde{j}}$ if partners x^k and $x^{k'}$ are chosen to our configuration. We create a dummy partner $x^{\tilde{j}}$ and set its score vector to be $v^{\tilde{j}}$. In addition, we create new constraints $\tilde{l}$ and $\tilde{l}+1$ and set $r_{\tilde{l}}^k = r_{\tilde{l}}^{k'} = -1$, $r_{\tilde{l}}^{\tilde{j}} = 2$, $r_{\tilde{l}+1}^k = r_{\tilde{l}+1}^{k'} = 1$, $r_{\tilde{l}+1}^{\tilde{j}} = -2$ and $r_{\tilde{l}}^j = r_{\tilde{l}+1}^j = 0$ for all the other partners. The following inequalities ensure that the dummy partner $x^{\tilde{j}}$ is selected if and only if partners x^k and $x^{k'}$ are selected, too:

$$\sum_{x^j \in p} r_{\tilde{l}}^j \le 0$$
$$\sum_{x^j \in p} r_{\tilde{l}+1}^j \le 1. \tag{6}$$

Partner synergies are illustratively modeled through a network of project proposals. With ten candidates there can be at maximum 45 edges between the 10 vertices, thus to model this network with the help of dummy candidates and inequalities which we already used for synergy requires only at worst case 45 dummy candidates. Each edge defines one dummy candidate, which is chosen only when both its end-point vertices are chosen. The edges can be weighted with the scores of the dummy candidates.

Finally, some of the tasks can be more important to the completion of the project than the others. We can model this with additional criteria for all the tasks and by giving scores to candidates depending on how important they are to a certain task.

3.3 Solving the Partner Selection Model

In summary, the model (1)-(6) comprises a binary linear program (BP), where the binary x^js are variables, the objective function is in (1), and the optional constraints are in (2)-(6). Linear models are favorable in that they can be readily solved using for instance Simplex (Dantzig, 1963) and Branch-and-Bound algorithms (Land and Doig, 1960), which solve the problem with exact parameter values.

The recently developed RPM method (Liesiö et al., 2007) is particularly suitable for solving multi-criteria portfolio-selection problems, where a subset of elements is to be chosen from a larger set, with respect to multiple criteria. The above partner selection model fits into this category. The advantage of RPM is that it allows interval-values for model parameters and criterion weights. Given the parameter space, the result of the RPM algorithm is the set of Pareto-efficient solutions, which offers good grounds for further analysis of the decision alternatives.

4. ILLUSTRATIVE CASE EXAMPLE

We applied the model to a partner selection case of Virtuelle Fabrik (http://www.vfeb.ch), which is an operative VBE located in Switzerland (Jarimo et al., 2006). The results suggest that relevant criteria can be taken into account and reasonable configurations are identified.

4.1 Project Description

The aim of the project was to construct a prototype magnetic clutch to be used in trucks. The project was broken down into nine tasks, which were 1) Grinding, 2) Gear milling, 3) Metal sheet forming, 4) Milling and turning of bigger parts, 5) Welding, 6) Bending of pipes, 7) Engineering, 8) Milling and turning of smaller parts, and 9) Project management. For each task, there were two to five partner candidates, some of which were candidates for several tasks (Table 1).

Table 1 – Tasks and partner candidates of the case project

Tasks	Candidates
Grinding	Sulzer AG, Brunner
Gear milling	Okey AG, Humbel
Metal sheet forming	Beni Butscher, Unima AG
Milling bigger parts	SMA, Knobel, OMB AG, SIG
Welding	Beni Burtscher, Amsonic
Bending of pipes	Fornara, SMA
Engineering	Schuler, AE&P AG, Schär Engineering
Milling smaller parts	Innotool, SIG, Wiftech, Bühler, Alwo AG
Project management	VF AG, Schär Engineering, AE&P AG, CCB

The partners were to be selected according to the following criteria: 1) Punctuality, 2) Partnership synergy, 3) Reliability, 4) Cost, and 5) Economical situation. The Customer of the project was a large German auto manufacturer, and a very important reference to Virtuelle Fabrik. The project had a tight schedule and the Customer's top priority was to finish the project in time. Thus, punctuality and reliability were the most important criteria in partner selection. Moreover, it was assumed that a successful collaboration history contributes to finishing the project in time. The Cost and Economical situation do not directly influence the schedule of the project, therefore they were less important. However, this only means that in the additive model the weights of the less important criteria do not exceed those with higher importance – Costs and Economical situation are not ignored. In general, the criteria need to be selected and weighted case-specifically; in another case for instance Costs or some completely new criteria could be the most important ones (Baldo et al., 2007).

Data concerning Punctuality, Reliability, and Economical situation consisted of Virtuelle Fabrik's managerial assessment of the candidates' performance, evaluated on a 1-6 scale. No exact estimates were required, but instead the score could be an interval within the 1-6 scale. The costs were given as the total price in Euros for performing the task for which the candidate is attached. Partnership synergy was modeled through a network that described the candidates' collaboration history (Figure 1).

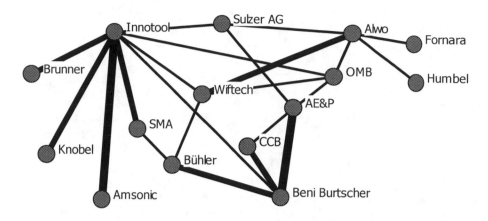

Figure 1 – Intensity of past collaboration between the partner candidates

In Figure 1 each circle represents a partner candidate of the case and the links between the candidates represent the number of past joint projects; a thicker line between two candidates represents a greater number of joint projects in the past. Also here, the score related to links need not be exact; intervals are allowed. Candidates that had no earlier collaboration with the others are excluded from the figure.

4.2 Case Analysis

With this data, the problem is that of selecting a good partner for each task, with respect to minimizing Cost and maximizing Punctuality, Partnership synergy, Reliability, and Economical situation. This can be modeled as a multi-criteria binary programming problem as described above. Using the novel RPM-algorithm (Liesiö et al. 2007) developed for this kind of selection problems, the model was solved as follows.

First, we defined that Punctuality, Partnership synergy, and Reliability are more important than Cost and Economical situation. The minimum weight of a criterion was 0.1. Solving the problem with this information resulted in 129 various Pareto-efficient configurations, which is too much to consider for a DM.

Second, we made our preference information more accurate by raising Punctuality and Reliability to be the most important criteria, leaving Partnership synergy as the second important and Cost and Economical situation as the least important ones. This increase of information reduced the number of Pareto-efficient configurations to 109, which is still too much.

Finally, we defined that the weights of Punctuality and Reliability are close to each other, which results in configurations with good scores in both of the most important criteria. Consequently, six Pareto-efficient configurations remained, listed in Table 2. It is worth noting that making the information more accurate reduces the set of Pareto-efficient configurations so that the DM can finally end up with a manageable number of solutions.

Table 2 – Performance of six Pareto-efficient configurations

Configuration	Punctuality	Reliability	Partnership synergy	Economical situation	Cost (€)
#74	48	52	29	45	123710
#76	48	52	28	45	123010
#80	48	52	27	47	126270
#73	46	53	29	44	123110
#75	46	53	28	44	122410
#79	46	53	27	46	125670

With a closer look at Table 2, the most interesting one is Configuration #74, which has the highest scores on Punctuality and Partnership synergy, and the second highest score on Reliability. It is also estimated as one of the least expensive configurations.

An interesting measure for the robustness of the partner candidates is the percentage of Pareto-efficient configurations in which the candidates are involved. Table 3 shows these robustness scores for those candidates that are involved in at least one Pareto-efficient configuration. Candidates with a score of 100 are robust choices within the parameter space, irrespective of the relative importance of the selection criteria.

Table 3 – Sensitivity analysis on the efficient partner candidates

Task	Candidates and their robustness scores			
Grinding	Sulzer	67	Brunner	33
Gear milling	Humbel	50	Okey AG	50
Metal sheet forming	Beni Burtscher	100		
Milling bigger parts	Knobel	100		
Welding	Beni Burtscher	100		
Bending of pipes	SMA	100		
Engineering	AE & P AG	100		
Milling smaller parts	Innotool	67	Bühler	33
Project management	AE & P AG	100		

Selecting the candidates that have the highest robustness scores leads to Configurations #73 (Gear milling: Okey AG) or #74 (Gear milling: Humbel). Configuration #73 outperforms #74 in terms of Reliability and Cost, but has lower scores with respect to other criteria. Neither Okey AG nor Humbel had earlier collaboration with the other partners of Configurations #73 and #74, thus these configurations have the same score on Partnership synergy. In conclusion, through the score table together with robustness analysis we have come up with two interesting configurations, namely #73 and #74, on which the decision-maker can focus in further analysis and negotiations.

5. DISCUSSION

The multi-criteria approach has several advantages:

- The methods are theoretically sound, relying on multi-attribute value theory and mathematical optimization. This facilitates for instance efficient identification of Pareto-efficient configurations and flexibility in that additional linear constraints and objectives can be formulated.
- No point estimates on parameter values of criterion weights are required. Instead, interval values can be given as input, which is practically favorable. For a decision maker it may be difficult or overly expensive to collect exact information. Therefore, the softness of the model indeed contributes to the practicality of the approach.
- The robustness of the partner candidates can be analyzed easily. Calculating the percentage of Pareto-efficient configurations in which each partner candidate is involved divides the candidates in three categories: 1) candidates that are selected in each Pareto-efficient configuration, 2) candidates that are selected in at least one Pareto-efficient configuration, and 3) candidates that are not selected in any of the Pareto-efficient configurations. Category 1) candidates are the most robust choices, since they are selected irrespective of the uncertainty in parameter values or the relative importance of the selection criteria.

We model partner selection as a centralized decision-making problem. This is reasonable if one entity is fully responsible for selecting the network partners. In the above Virtuelle Fabrik case the customer wanted that the broker company takes responsibility of the project, hence it was natural that the broker selected the partners unilaterally. Indeed, centralized decision making typically fits cases that involve a hierarchical topology.

However, there are situations where the decision-making is in fact decentralized. This is the case if the partner candidates themselves decide with whom to collaborate. An example of a decentralized partner selection process is the formation of inter-organizational research projects. In this case, the formation of the final consortium is a multi-party negotiation process between research teams at universities, research institutes, and companies.

Another decentralized partner selection case could be that of selecting a new partner into the VO, whereby the original partners may be willing to influence the selection process. For such cases the candidates that were not originally selected but who were part of some Pareto-efficient configurations provide a good starting point for searching. The use of decision-support tools increases transparency in group decision-making, too.

A prerequisite for the use of decision support tools in partner selection is the availability of data for parameter estimation. The long-term VBE cooperation structure supports parameter estimation because it enables the collection of longitudinal performance data. Moreover, longitudinal data helps VBE management in identifying trends for instance in individual members' performance.

6. CONCLUSIONS AND FURTHER CHALLENGES

This chapter illustrated the use of multi-criteria mathematical programming methods for robust partner selection in collaborative networks. The objective of the model is to match the core competencies of partner candidates with the requirements of a project and thereby select the optimal VO to serve the customer. The analysis and the realistic case study suggest that the methods are both theoretically sound and practically useful.

Solving the models with RPM allows the decision makers to give interval parameter-estimates. The more imprecise the information the larger is the set of Pareto-efficient solutions. Thus, the decision maker can gradually increase the accuracy of the parameter estimates until a manageable number of Pareto-efficient solutions remains. From the remaining set, the decision maker can select the most preferred configuration and make possible manual modifications to it.

The models are potentially useful in cases where one decision maker selects network partners. Such cases occur in a VBE that repeatedly creates VOs whenever there is potential for value creation through collaboration. Customers often wish that only a single partner – the broker – is responsible for the operations of the VO. It is therefore natural that the broker has the control over the VO and partner selection. In group decision-making, the models can improve the common understanding of the case at hand and increase transparency of the decision criteria and their assessment.

Topics for future research are manifold. First, our optimization model could be improved by several features. These include for instance dynamic decision-making and uncertainties, interdependent risks, hedging against capacity risk, etc. Second, the effect of incentives, e.g. profit sharing rules, on VO creation should be studied. Third, VBE member performance measurement models are needed in order to most efficiently use operative models. For instance, our model raises the need to measure factors related to cooperative efficiency.

ACKNOWLEDGEMENTS

The work was funded by the European Commission through the Sixth Framework Programme Integrated Project ECOLEAD. The authors thank the project partners for collaboration.

REFERENCES

1.   Arbel A., 1989. Approximate articulation of preference and priority derivation. European Journal of Operational Research 43, 317–26.

2. Baldo, F., Rabelo, R. J., Vallejos, R. V., 2007. An Ontology-Based Approach For Selecting Performance Indicators For Partners Suggestion. In: Camarinha-Matos, L. M., Afsarmanesh, H., Novais, P., Analide, C. (Eds.), IFIP International Federation for Information Processing, Volume 243, Establishing The Foundation Of Collaborative Networks, Springer, 187-196.

3. Barron, F. H., Edwards, W., 1994. SMARTS and SMARTER: Improved simple methods for multiattribute utility measurement. Organizational Behavior and Human Decision Processes 60 (3), 306–325.

4. Camarinha-Matos, L. M., Afsarmanesh, H., 2003. Elements of a base VE infrastructure. Computers in Industry 51, 139–163.

5. Crispim, J., A., Sousa, J., P., 2005. A Multi-criteria Decision Support System for the Formation of Collaborative Networks of Enterprises. In: Camarinha-Matos, L. M., Afsarmanesh, H., Ortiz, A. (Eds.), IFIP International Federation for Information Processing, Volume 186, Collaborative Networks and their Breeding Environments, Springer, 143-154.

6. Dyer, J. S., 1990. Remarks on the analytic hierarchy process. Management Science 36 (3), 249–258.

7. Edwards, W., 1977. How to use multiattribute utility measurement for social decision making. IEEE Transactions on Systems, Man and Cybernetics 7 (5), 326–340.

8. Hamel, G., Prahalad, C. K., 1990. The core competence of the corporation. Harvard Business Review 68 (3), 79–91.

9. Ip, W. H., Huang, M., Yung, K. L., Wang, D., 2003. Genetic algorithm solution for a risk-based partner selection problem in a virtual enterprise. Computers & Operations Research 30, 213–231.

10. Jarillo, J. C., 1988. On strategic networks. Strategic Management Journal 9 (1), 31–41.

11. Jarimo, T., Salkari, I., Bollhalter, S., 2006. Partner Selection with Network Interdependencies: An Application. In: Camarinha-Matos, L. M., Afsarmanesh, H., Ollus, M. (Eds.), IFIP International Federation for Information Processing, Volume 224, Network-Centric Collaboration and Supporting Frameworks, Springer, 389-396.

12. Keeney, R. L., Raiffa, H., 1976. Decisions with Multiple Objectives: Preferences and Value Tradeoffs. Cambridge University Press.

13. Land, A. H. and Doig, A. G. 1960. An Automatic Method for Solving Discrete Programming Problems. Econometrica 28, 497-520.

14. Li, Y., Liao, X., 2007. Decision support for risk analysis on dynamic alliance. Decision Support Systems 42 (4), 2043-2059.

15. Liesiö, J., Mild, P., Salo, A., 2007. Preference Programming for Robust Portfolio Modeling and Project Selection. European Journal of Operational Research 181 (3), 1488-1505.

16. Meade, L. M., Liles, D. H., Sarkis, J., 1997. Justifying strategic alliances and partnering: a prerequisite for virtual enterprising. Omega 25 (1), 29–42.

17. Mikhailov L., 2000. A fuzzy programming method for deriving priorities in the Analytic Hierarchy Process. Journal of the Operational Research Society 51, 341–9.

18. Mikhailov, L., 2002. Fuzzy analytical approach to partnership selection in formation of virtual enterprises. Omega 30, 393–401.

19. Saaty, T. L., 1980. The Analytic Hierarchy Process. McGraw-Hill, New York.

20. Saaty, T. L., 2005. Making and validating complex decisions with the ahp/anp. Journal of Systems Science and Systems Engineering 14 (1), 1–36.

21. Salo, A., Punkka, A., 2005. Rank Inclusion in Criteria Hierarchies. European Journal of Operational Research 163 (2), 338-356.

22. Steuer, R. E. 1976. Multiple Objective Linear Programming with Interval Criterion Weights. Management Science 23 (3), 305–316.

23. Stummer, C., Heidenberger, K., 2003. Interactive R&D Portfolio Analysis With Project Interdependencies and Time Profiles of Multiple Objectives. IEEE Transactions on Engineering Management, 50 (2), 175–183.

24. Williamson, O. E., 1975. Markets and Hierarchies: Analysis and Antitrust Implications. New York: Free Press.

25. von Winterfeldt, D., Edwards, W., 1986. Decision Analysis and Behavioral Research. Cambridge University Press.

4.4
Modeling collaboration preparedness assessment

J. Rosas, L. M. Camarinha-Matos

Information incompleteness and imprecision are typical difficulties when assessing the collaboration preparedness of a candidate to join a collaborative network. Bayesian belief networks and Rough Sets are examples of modeling approaches that can be used in these cases. The use of these approaches depends on the type of collaborative network considered, namely long term or goal oriented, and on the available data necessary to perform the assessment. Combination of different modeling techniques is also useful in this context. In order to illustrate the suggested approach, a number of modeling experiments are described and achieved results are briefly discussed.

1. INTRODUCTION

A number of decision making problems in collaborative networks involve the assessment of network members. Examples include the estimation of the preparedness level of a candidate to join a virtual organization breeding environment (VBE) (Afsarmanesh, Camarinha-Matos, 2005) or the selection of partners to form a virtual organization (VO) in response to a business opportunity.

In such assessment cases, multiple criteria are typically used and the decisions are often based on incomplete and / or imprecise information. This chapter discusses some approaches to handle this problem, namely resorting to Bayesian belief networks and Rough Sets. A combination of various modeling techniques in order to achieve better results is also discussed. In order to illustrate the concepts and suggested approach, a number of modeling examples or experiments are introduced along with the introduction of base concepts and definitions.

The collaboration preparedness concept has lately received some attention. For instance, it is referred that a way to increase the preparedness to work in collaboration is to be part of a VBE, as it provides a common ICT infrastructure, mechanisms and guidelines for collaboration, letting members to be able to agilely grasp business opportunities. In this sense, the level of preparedness would be measured taking in attention several technical, economical and reliability indicators (Camarinha-Matos, Afsarmanesh, 2006). In (Baldo, 2007) a methodology is presented to help finding the appropriate performance indicators to be used when searching for suitable sets of organizations to fulfil specific collaboration opportunities. In (Jarimo et al, 2005), the concept of preparedness is organized in an attribute hierarchy, constituted by node and network preparedness attributes, over which a mathematical optimization methodology for optimal VO configurations is applied as a multi-attribute decision making problem. However, most of the previous works addressing this issue remain at a qualitative and informal level of analysis.

2. COLLABORATION PREPAREDNESS ASSESSMENT

2.1 Estimation of preparedness to join a VBE using Belief Networks

This modeling example proposes the use of Bayesian belief networks in order to predict whether a member has adequate characteristics for collaboration and thus be considered a good candidate to join a VBE. A number of attributes are used to characterize members, such as their prestige, reliability, size and tolerance to risk.

A model based on belief networks is particularly useful when there is little information to perform an accurate assessment. This typically happens whenever there is a new candidate to join a VBE, for which the available information concerning this candidate is usually low as the example described below illustrates.

The Bayesian belief network concept. A Bayesian belief network is a kind of probabilistic model that represents causal relationships on a set of variables (Fig. 1). It is composed of two parts: (i) the structural part, which consists of a direct acyclic graph, in which nodes stand for random variables and edges for direct conditional dependences between them; and (ii) the probabilistic part that quantifies the conditional dependence between these variables.

Each variable can have state values (such as, 'no', 'yes' or 'low', 'high'). If the value of a variable in a node is known, then that node is said to be an evidence node. In Fig. 1, the arc pointing from node A to node E can be perceived as "A causing or influencing E". Each of the children nodes have an associated conditional probability table that quantifies the effects that the parents have on them. For nodes without parents, the corresponding table only contains prior probabilities. Due to these conditional dependences, if a node becomes an evidence node, then the probabilities (or likelihood) of the other nodes change. More on belief networks can be found in (Jensen, 1996).

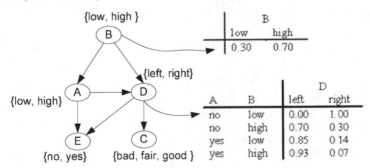

Figure 1 – An example of a Bayesian belief network

For any node of the network in Fig. 1, the computation of conditional probabilities is done using the Bayes' rule, as exemplified in the modeling example below. Belief networks can be used to perform queries in distinct ways:

- To perform predictions. This is useful whenever some causes are known and it is necessary to determine the probability of possible effects/consequences. For instance, when A=low and D=left, the probability of E=yes is given by the query $P(E$=yes $| A$=low, D=left).
- To perform diagnostics. For instance, when the fact C=bad is known, it is necessary to determine the likelihood of eventual causes, e.g. $P(D$=right$| C$=bad).

It is also possible to make queries on the joint distributions, without providing evidences. For instance, the probability of C=fair, without further evidence, is given by $P(C$=fair).

In simple cases, a Bayesian network can be specified by an expert and used to perform inferences. In other cases, the task of defining the network is too complex to be done by hand. Therefore, both the structure (nodes and arcs) and parameters of the local distributions must be learned from data using Machine Learning techniques (Pearl, 1996), (Cheng, Greiner, 2001), (Friedman, 1997). This process can be summarized by the following steps:

1. Acquire sufficient information from data repositories and take it as the learning / training sample data.
2. Use Belief Network Learning in order to obtain the structure of the Belief network.
3. Use probabilistic/statistical methodologies to compute the local probability tables on every node of the belief network.
4. Use examples out-of-the-sample data to test the model.

After this process, and if the network is considered good enough, it can be used to support decision making. Moreover, during the utilization phase of the belief network model, the conditional probabilities can be adjusted (through learning) as more cases and corresponding decisions are observed (Wang & Vassileva, 2003).

For the example described below, due to the difficulty in obtaining historic data concerning situations of collaboration preparedness assessment, the belief network was specified by hand. Nevertheless, this does not undermine the intents of the modeling exercise, as its primary objective is to reveal the potential application of this approach in the context of CNs.

Modeling Example. This example illustrates a situation where a candidate is being considered to join a network, namely a VBE. Let us suppose that, at the very beginning, little information is known about the candidate's profile, though it might present attractive technological skills.

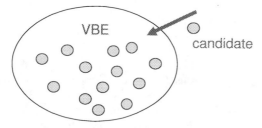

Figure 2 – A candidate wants to get in the network.
Little information on its profile is available

In order to better illustrate the potential use of belief networks, the modeling exercise is built up in two phases, as illustrated in Fig. 3.

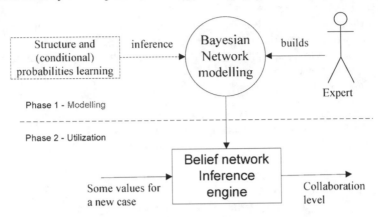

Figure 3 – Phases followed in the modeling exercise

Phase 1. In this phase, the expert structures the belief network by first identifying and specifying its probabilistic variables and corresponding conditional dependencies. He then quantifies these dependencies in the so called conditional probability tables. For this example, the expert creates a kind of prediction model to help estimate the probability of the candidates to be ready to join a collaborative network. When designing the belief network (by hand), a few assumptions related to members' behavior were made in order to guide the design process. These assumptions, among potential many others, should be taken as merely illustrative. Therefore, we conjecture that:

- An organization in a difficult economical condition, in order to benefit from others' competences (that usually it cannot afford to own) and have access to others' business opportunities, is more willing to accept the risks of collaboration. On the other hand, due to its fragile condition, it tends to be less reliable.
- An organization in good economical conditions might be more reliable, but does not feel the same pressure, as the previous case, to collaborate and therefore tend to be more risk conservative considering collaboration/partnerships.
- An organization might become less reliable if it has a weak adaptability to newer situations.
- A small size organization (e.g. a SME) might possess fewer competences and, in order to complement them, accepts to be more exposed to the risks of collaborating with other organizations.
- The prestige of an organization, which is an attribute that is perceived by its peers, is fundamental in collaboration and has a positive contribution to the preparedness level.
- The creativity of an organization, which can be roughly estimated by evaluating its rate of generated innovations, might also be important for collaboration, and adds to the preparedness level.

A belief network, modeled using the above guidelines, is shown in Fig. 4 and can be used to perform some testing as described below. It shall be noted that Belief networks models do not live by themselves, but are rather integrated as sub-components in larger (reasoning) systems.

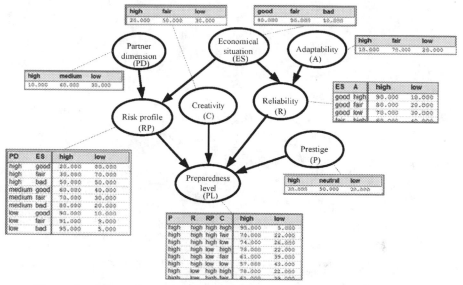

Figure 4 – A Bayesian network example to assess the preparedness level

For this belief network, the joint probability distribution, from which the analysis can be made, is the following (showing only the initials for the nodes names):

$$P(PD,ES,A,RP,R,C,P, PL) = P(PD) \times P(ES|PD) \times P(A|ES,PD) \times P(RP|PD,ES,A)$$
$$\times P(R|PD,ES,A,RP) \times P(C|PD,ES,A,RP,R) \times P(P| PD,ES,A,RP,R,C) \times$$
$$P(PL|PD,ES,A,RP,R,C,P)$$

This function can be simplified by considering the conditional independence statements implied in the belief network. For instance, the 'Partner Dimension' and 'Risk Profile' variables do not influence the 'Reliability', as 'Economical Situation' and 'Adaptability' do. This is because $P(R|PD,ES,A,RP)=P(R|ES,A)$, so *PD* and *RP* can be removed from the above expression. The same approach can be applied to the other conditional probabilities, helping remove more variables (the shaded ones) from the above expression. This results in the function:

$$P(PD,ES,A,RP,R,C,P,PL) = P(PD) \times P(ES) \times P(A) \times P(RP|PD,ES)$$
$$\times P(R|ES,A) \times P(C) \times P(P) \times P(PL|RP,R,C,P)$$

As illustration for the given problem, and assuming most of the nodes as evidences (to reduce calculations), the probability of collaboration level *PL=high*, given that *PD=high*, *ES=fair*, *A=fair*, *C=high* and *P=high* is given by

$$P(PL_{high} \mid PD_{high}, ES_{fair}, A_{fair}, C_{high}, P_{high}) = \frac{P(PL_{high}, PD_{high}, ES_{fair}, A_{fair}, C_{high}, P_{high})}{P(PD_{high}, ES_{fair}, A_{fair}, C_{high}, P_{high})}$$

The steps for the calculation of this probability are the following:

$$P(PL_{high}, PD_{high}, ES_{fair}, A_{fair}, C_{high}, P_{high})$$

$$= \sum_{rp\in\{high,low\}} \sum_{r\in\{high,low\}} P(PL_{high}, PD_{high}, ES_{fair}, A_{fair}, RP_{rp}, R_r, C_{high}, P_{high})$$

$$= P(PL_{high}, PD_{high}, ES_{fair}, A_{fair}, RP_{high}, R_{high}, C_{high}, P_{high})$$

$$+ P(PL_{high}, PD_{high}, ES_{fair}, A_{fair}, RP_{high}, R_{low}, C_{high}, P_{high})$$

$$+ P(PL_{high}, PD_{high}, ES_{fair}, A_{fair}, RP_{low}, R_{high}, C_{high}, P_{high})$$

$$+ P(PL_{high}, PD_{high}, ES_{fair}, A_{fair}, RP_{low}, R_{low}, C_{high}, P_{high})$$

$$= P(PD_{high}) \times P(ES_{fair}) \times P(A_{fair}) \times P(RP_{high}|PD_{high}, ES_{fair})$$

$$\times P(R_{high}| ES_{fair}, A_{fair}) \times P(C_{high}) \times P(P_{high}) \times P(PL_{high}| RP_{high}, R_{high}, C_{high}, P_{high})$$

$$+ P(PD_{high}) \times P(ES_{fair}) \times P(A_{fair}) \times P(RP_{high}|PD_{high}, ES_{fair})$$

$$\times P(R_{low}| ES_{fair}, A_{fair}) \times P(C_{high}) \times P(P_{high}) \times P(PL_{high}| RP_{high}, R_{low}, C_{high}, P_{high})$$

$$+ P(PD_{high}) \times P(ES_{fair}) \times P(A_{fair}) \times P(RP_{low}|PD_{high}, ES_{fair})$$

$$\times P(R_{high}| ES_{fair}, A_{fair}) \times P(C_{high}) \times P(P_{high}) \times P(PL_{high}| RP_{low}, R_{high}, C_{high}, P_{high})$$

$$+ P(PD_{high}) \times P(ES_{fair}) \times P(A_{fair}) \times P(RP_{low}|PD_{high}, ES_{fair})$$

$$\times P(R_{low}| ES_{fair}, A_{fair}) \times P(C_{high}) \times P(P_{high}) \times P(PL_{high}| RP_{low}, R_{low}, C_{high}, P_{high})$$

The final step is to replace every conditional (or prior) probability in the expression by the values taken from the conditional (or prior) probability tables that are in the belief network. This results in:

$$\sum_{rp\in\{high,low\}} \sum_{r\in\{high,low\}} P(PL_{high}, PD_{high}, ES_{fair}, A_{fair}, RP_{rp}, R_r, C_{high}, P_{high})$$

$$= 0.1 \times 0.5 \times 0.7 \times 0.3 \times 0.5 \times 0.2 \times 0.3 \times 0.95$$

$$+ 0.1 \times 0.5 \times 0.7 \times 0.3 \times 0.5 \times 0.2 \times 0.3 \times 0.78$$

$$+ 0.1 \times 0.5 \times 0.7 \times 0.7 \times 0.5 \times 0.2 \times 0.3 \times 0.78$$

$$+ 0.1 \times 0.5 \times 0.7 \times 0.7 \times 0.5 \times 0.2 \times 0.3 \times 0.61$$

$$= 0.001567$$

The calculation of the denominator is similar to the previous steps:

$$P(PD_{high}, ES_{fair}, A_{fair}, C_{high}, P_{high})$$

$$= \sum_{rp\in\{high,low\}} \sum_{r\in\{high,low\}} \sum_{cl\in\{high,low\}} P(PL_{cl}, PD_{high}, ES_{fair}, A_{fair}, RP_{rp}, R_r, C_{high}, P_{high})$$

$$= 0.00209$$

The corresponding probability is therefore

$$P(PL_{high} | PD_{high}, ES_{fair}, A_{fair}, C_{high}, P_{high}) = \frac{0.001567}{0.00209} = 0.75$$

Phase 2. In order to test the belief network, the model obtained in the first phase was implemented with the help of the NETICA tool. This is a program used to create diagrams encoding knowledge or representing decision-making problems. The corresponding API (Application Program Interface) provides the same functionality as NETICA application, but designed for programmers to embed in their programs (NorSys, 1997).

The result is shown in the Fig. 5, where the gray nodes (Partner dimension and Economical situation) stand for variables that, at that instant, are evidences. The way to use the belief network is to provide some evidences (if available) and place queries for the probability or likelihood of the other unknown values: P(query | evidences).

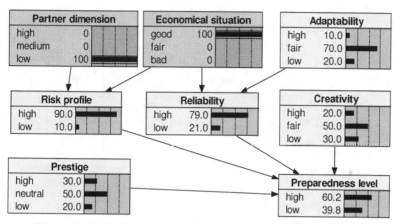

Figure 5 – Belief network with two nodes taken as evidences

This model can now help estimate the probability of a candidate to be prepared for collaboration. For instance, given the evidence that a certain candidate is in good economical situation and is of low dimension (Fig. 5), the probability of that member being prepared for collaboration is given by

P("Collaboration level"=high | "Partner dimension"=low, "Economical
situation"=good)=60.2%.

If more information is known about this candidate, the certainty of the performed classification increases. For instance, if it is also known that it has high creativity and high prestige (Fig. 6), then the collaboration level is:

P("Collaboration level"=high | "Partner dimension"=low, "Economical
situation"=good, "Prestige"=high, "Creativity"=high)=89.7%.

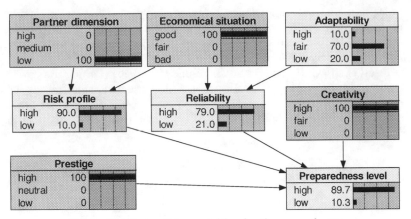

Figure 6 – State of the variables for the second case

Naturally, the more information is available, the more accurate is the classification. Even when the available information is (quite) scarce, belief networks appear to offer a reasonable model, as they can still provide helpful outputs.

Benefits and Limitations. In summary, belief networks are particularly suited for modeling and decision making in contexts of uncertainty and insufficient information. They can be used both for prediction and for diagnosis. They are easy to maintain and modify, particularly if a tool like NETICA is available. The structure and corresponding cause-effects in a belief network are easy to understand. They can be obtained using learning processes (Friedman, 1997).

As main limitation, it might be difficult to collect initial data for building up (learning) the belief network. Most often expert knowledge is used instead. Collecting knowledge for modeling a belief network can be very difficult and time consuming.

2.2 Improving partners' evaluations with Rough Sets

Rough Sets provide a way to do concept approximations for concepts of interest. In the following example, this theory is used to define the concept of "Excellent partner". By applying the Rough Sets theory, this definition is obtained through the utilization of both the indiscernibility relation and the reducts concepts. From the obtained model, it is possible to generate a rule-based decision support system that can be used to perform the classification of CN members.

Contrary to the belief network model previously described, the utilization of Rough Sets is usually applied in situations where there is a significant amount of information. The aspect of uncertainty still exists, but the principal concerns here are the imprecision and vagueness of information. Typically, there is a repository of cases characterized by many attributes, which are specified with imprecision. Moreover, some cases might contradict other cases. Such cases can be found in a VBE composed of members that have been participating in VOs. Assuming that during the lifecycle of the VBE, the collaboration opportunities, formation of VOs, obtained performance and outcomes are recorded in a VBE repository, the Rough

Sets methodology can be applied on this repository for knowledge extraction, as the example below illustrates.

The Rough Sets concept. Rough sets theory is an approach to model and address vagueness according to which imprecision is expressed by a "boundary region of a set", and not by a partial membership as in the fuzzy sets theory. The main idea of the rough sets is the approximation of a set by a pair of sets that are called the lower and the upper approximation of the set (Pawlak, 1999). The lower approximation of a rough set X is the collection of objects that can be classified with full certainty as members of the set X (Fig. 7). The upper approximation of X is the collection of objects that may possibly be classified as members of the set X. The boundary region comprises the objects that cannot be classified with certainty as to be neither inside X, nor outside X, thus the "set difference" between the upper and lower approximation sets.

This theory was proposed in early 1980s by Pawlak (Pawlak, 1991) as a way to deal with the needs in the analysis and classification of large data/decision tables taken from information systems. As a Soft Computing method, whose typical uses are found in the Knowledge Discovery and Data Mining areas, it is applied in situations where the available information is characterized by vagueness, ambiguity and uncertainty – therefore, to characterize concepts not easily defined in a crisp way. Rough Sets is used to synthesize approximations for the concepts of interest, using the referred upper and lower approximations, as illustrated in Fig. 7. More about Rough Sets can be found in (Pawlak, 1991, 1995) and (Pawlak and Skowron, 1999).

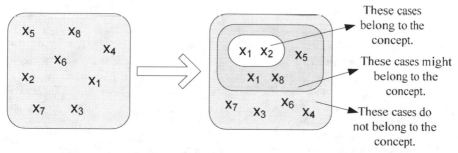

Figure 7 – The Rough Sets' concept approximation approach

Adopted methodology. This section applies the rough sets methodology on an illustrative modeling example. Basically, it begins with historic data taken from a VBE repository. In practice, such data may be organized in a (possibly) large decision table with (possibly) tens of attributes. But, for illustrative purposes and in order to keep this example simple and clear, the used table was made smaller.

As in the belief networks example, the experiment is developed in two separate phases, as shown in Fig. 8. In the first phase, an expert builds an information table from the repository. Then he selects the decision attribute (e.g. Partner grade) for the concept of interest, which in this case is the concept of "Excellent Partner". The result is the concept approximation for "Excellent Partner" or, in other words, its Rough Set definition. Finally, the obtained concept can be transformed into a set of decision rules.

In phase 2, the rough sets technique is applied to evaluate the members of the VBE to see whether they can be considered excellent partners or not.

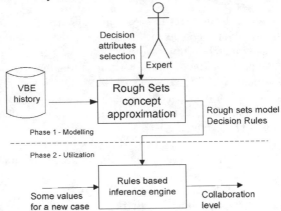

Figure 8 – Phases of the rough sets modeling experiment

Modeling example. When selecting a new member for a VO, it is not possible to foretell whether this candidate will turn out to be a good partner or not. A VBE manager would typically pick up the candidate's profile and, based on the history of previous selections, use his/her best judgment to make the decision. However, this manager could benefit if there was a model, obtained from the history of previous collaboration cases that would provide some support to his /her decision.

The modeling example follows the two phases as mentioned above.

Phase 1. The table in Fig. 9 shows a number of records taken from a VBE repository of past collaborations. It is assumed that during the lifetime of the network, members participated in several VOs. As time passed, they were given a "Partner grade" quantifying their performance as partners in collaborative projects. Therefore, each member was classified as an "excellent", "good" or "fair" partner.

	Past Activity	Prestige	Reliability	Risk _profile	Respect other partners	technological background	Localization distance	Partner dimension	Economic situation	Partner grade
1	high	high	good	high	high	high	far	big	good	excellent
2	low	fair	good	low	fair	medium	near	big	fair	fair
3	high	low	bad	prudent	high	low	far	medium	good	fair
4	low	low	fair	high	fair	low	near	small	fair	fair
5	low	high	good	low	high	high	near	big	fair	good
6	high	fair	good	prudent	fair	high	far	medium	good	excellent
7	low	low	bad	prudent	high	low	near	small	good	fair
8	high	fair	fair	high	fair	medium	near	big	fair	good
9	high	fair	good	prudent	high	low	far	medium	good	good
10	low	high	bad	high	fair	high	near	small	fair	fair
11	low	fair	fair	low	high	high	near	big	good	fair
12	low	high	good	prudent	fair	low	far	medium	fair	fair
13	low	high	good	prudent	high	medium	near	small	fair	fair
14	low	fair	fair	prudent	fair	medium	far	big	good	fair
15	high	high	good	prudent	high	high	near	medium	fair	good
16	low	high	good	prudent	fair	low	near	small	fair	fair
17	low	high	fair	low	high	low	far	big	good	fair
18	high	fair	good	prudent	fair	medium	near	medium	fair	good
19	low	high	good	prudent	high	low	near	small	fair	fair

Figure 9 – Examples with characteristics and grading for the members of a VBE.

When observing the partners characteristics, and corresponding grades, one would wonder if there was any pattern in the values, or any dependencies that might be of interest. Just by looking at the table, it seems that it is possible to discover some patterns in the data. Therefore, it is worth exploring whether these patterns provide some insights on how to classify a candidate.

In this phase, the utilization of Rough Sets to identify the aspects that are important for candidates' classification is described. The Rough Sets theory not only identifies these attributes, but it also provides a classification model, in the form of a rule-based decision system for further utilization. This model can then be used to classify the candidates for new VOs.

The exercise is performed using the ROSETTA tool (Komorowski et al., 2002), as illustrated in Fig. 10. It begins with the sample data given as input and selecting the decision variable "Partner Grade" amongst the table's attributes, as Fig. 9 illustrates. Then, using the concept of indiscernibility, the reducts are determined. In order to illustrate this concept, any two or more cases in Fig. 9 are considered indiscernible if for a chosen set of attributes, they share the same values. Considering the attributes set {'past activity', 'prestige', 'risk profile, 'respect other partners', 'technological background'}, then cases 12 and 16 are indiscernible, as spotted by the squares in the referred figure. Reducts are, therefore, minimum sets of attributes that preserve the contents of the decision table, while removing the redundant attributes. The indiscernibility relation, in turn, allows the elimination of the redundant cases. The resulting decision table, composed of the reduct's attributes and the non-redundant cases, expresses the same knowledge as the original table. For the proposed modeling example, one of these reducts is the set {Past activity, Prestige, Risk profile, Respect other partners, Technological background}, which according to the Rough Sets technique, are just the necessary attributes to classify a candidate. As such, a VBE manager can pay more attention to these characteristics of the candidates when considering and classifying the VBE members.

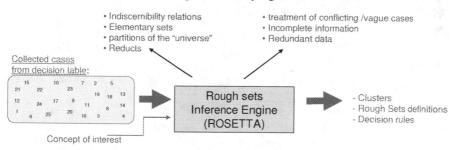

Figure 10 – Using the Rough Sets methodology in concept approximation

The results of applying this technique are shown in Fig. 11. The cases 1, 23 and 6 correspond to "Excellent" partners. This means that any new candidate with similar characteristics (i.e., with the same values in the attributes of the reducts) will be definitely considered as an excellent partner. Regarding partners 15 and 21 it is uncertain whether they are excellent or just good partners. This means that, there will be uncertainty when classifying new cases with similar attribute values. The outer region represents partners that do not belong to the concept of "Excellent partner".

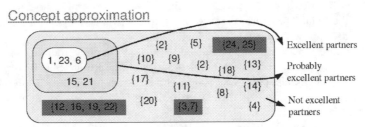

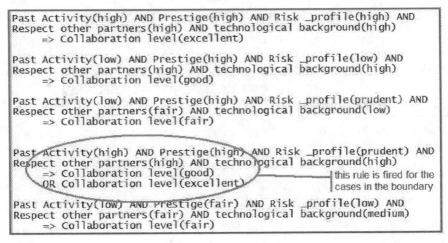

Figure 11 – The lower and upper approximations for the concept "excellent partner". Other clusters in this figure might represent other concepts

With Rosetta tool, we can convert these concepts into decision rules (Fig.12), which can be integrated in a larger reasoning system.

```
Past Activity(high) AND Prestige(high) AND Risk _profile(high) AND
Respect other partners(high) AND technological background(high)
     => Collaboration level(excellent)

Past Activity(low) AND Prestige(high) AND Risk _profile(low) AND
Respect other partners(high) AND technological background(high)
     => Collaboration level(good)

Past Activity(low) AND Prestige(high) AND Risk _profile(prudent) AND
Respect other partners(fair) AND technological background(low)
     => Collaboration level(fair)


Past Activity(high) AND Prestige(high) AND Risk _profile(prudent) AND
Respect other partners(high) AND technological background(high)
     => Collaboration level(good)                    ┐ this rule is fired for the
     OR Collaboration level(excellent)               ┘ cases in the boundary

Past Activity(low) AND Prestige(fair) AND Risk _profile(low) AND
Respect other partners(fair) AND technological background(medium)
     => Collaboration level(fair)
```

Figure 12 – Decision rules for the concept of "Excellent partner"

Phase 2. Before performing the tests with the model obtained in previous phase, the corresponding decision rules must be converted into some computable format. The ROSETTA tool can perform such conversion and these rules were translated to Prolog predicates, as shown in Fig. 13.

If a query is performed for case o1, the model classifies it as "excellent", and so any candidate similar to this case. Similarly, for case o10 the model yields a "fair" classification. These cases correspond to unambiguous classifications.

Prolog shell	Rough Set predicates

?- 'collaboration level'(o1, Class, _, _, _).
 Class = excellent
 	
 ?- 'collaboration level'(o10, Class, _, _, _).
 Class = fair ;
 	
 ?- 'collaboration level'(o15, Class, _, _, _).
 Class = good ;
 Class = excellent ⬅
          Case in the boundary
	'collaboration level'(X, excellent, 1, 1.0, 1.0) :-
	      'past activity'(X, high),
	      prestige(X, high),
	      'risk _profile'(X, high),
	      'respect other partners'(X, high),
	      'technological background'(X, high).
	
	 'collaboration level'(X, fair, 1, 1.0, 1.0) :-
	      'past activity'(X, low),
	      prestige(X, fair),
	      'risk _profile'(X, low),
	      'respect other partners'(X, fair),
	      'technological background'(X, medium).

Figure 13– A partial view of the decision rules tried in a Prolog shell

Now, let us consider member o15 as a potential partner. Some information available about its profile is shown in Fig. 14.

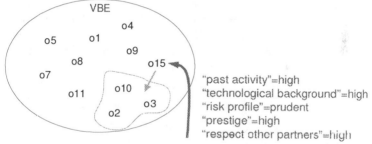

"past activity"=high
"technological background"=high
"risk profile"=prudent
"prestige"=high
"respect other partners"=high

Figure 14 – Member o15 is a candidate for a new VO

The classification for the case o15 is not like the others tested before. For this case, the decision rules cannot unequivocally classify whether it is a "good" or "excellent" partner, as it yields these two results. However, there is a reason for this kind of classification. Although case o15, in a previous collaboration, was classified as "good" (as the table of Fig. 9 shows), its profile resembles the profiles of other cases that were classified as "excellent". Due to the incongruence between the o15's profile, its corresponding classification and the classifications given to similar cases, the model places case o15 in the boundary between the upper and lower approximation of the Rough Set obtained in phase 1. Perhaps there was a mismatch in the classification, or maybe something did not go totally well in a previous collaboration with member o15, which might mean that it did not performed as well as what was expected, given its (perceived) profile.

Benefits and limitations. In summary, the Rough Sets approach allows dealing with problems characterized by incomplete information, which may also be redundant, and even ambiguous and vague. Using the Rough Sets approach allows the construction of a concept from a possibly large historic record table (with thousands of rows and tens of attributes). The resulting concept uses only a minimal set of the original attributes, which allow decision making with fewer decision variables.

A comparison between Rough Sets and other decision tree classifier algorithms as ID3 was presented in (Hassanien 2004). Rough Sets test results were much better in terms of the number of rules and classification accuracy. In decision trees, more robust features are required to improve the performance of decision tree classifiers. Moreover, ID3 cannot handle contradictory data, whereas Rough Sets deal well with it (through their approximations to the concepts). ID3 is also very sensitive to small modifications on the data. This does not occur with Rough Sets.

One limitation found in this experiment is that, if the information about some candidate is not sufficient to assign values to the reduct's attributes, then the classification cannot be performed, because no decision rule will be fired. This drawback is better handled using Bayesian Belief Networks, as illustrated in the modeling approach previously presented.

3. MODELING A PARTNERS SUGGESTION MECHANISM

3.1 The concept of collaboration preparedness

The last modelling experiment illustrates how different modeling methodologies, "crisp" and "soft", can be combined in the resolution of a problem and how we can benefit from such combination in collaborative networks modeling.

The next modeling exercise is focused on a situation where a collaboration opportunity is identified and a virtual organization (VO) has to be formed. Therefore, possible sets of VBE members are suggested for the corresponding consortium formation. The process of partners' suggestion is traditionally based on a matching performed between the requirements of the collaboration opportunity and the competences provided by the potential candidates.

In this modeling experiment, this matching process is improved by considering the concept of organization's character. An organization's **character** can be defined as a composition of a set of traits. A **trait** represents relatively stable predisposition to the manifestation of a certain pattern of behaviour. As illustrated in the example below, these traits are often described in a rather imprecise, incomplete and uncertain way. In this example, the assumption is that if an organization's behaviors can be predicted from its traits, then collaboration preparedness assessment can also be performed using these traits. Additionally to character's preparedness, the concept of competences fitness should also be considered in a collaboration readiness assessment concept, as described in section 3.3.

3.2 Partners' suggestion based on the concept of preparedness

For modeling a partner's suggestion mechanism using the principle of collaboration preparedness based on organization's character, we reuse the belief network model described in section 2.1, which is combined with the concept of competences fitness, as described below. For each suggestion of candidates (or rough VO coalition), a model of the VO together with its business process plan for the collaboration opportunity is simulated in a simulation engine for obtaining estimated performance measurements.

This framework was implemented using a rule-based knowledge base, developed in Prolog. The belief network inference engine is provided by NETICA tool, whose access is done through its API. For undertaking the experiment, some concepts of Project Management modeling and Simulation techniques were also used. Therefore, a combination of various modeling techniques is used in this example, as shown in Fig. 15.

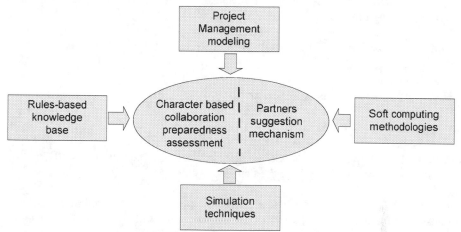

Figure 15 – Theories and tools used in this experiment

3.3 An axiomatic model for partners' suggestion

The first step is to define basic sets, such as organizations, competences and traits, which are necessary for the specification of the partners' suggestion axioms. To adequately distinguish the concepts, it is assumed that all single attributes are named in small letters, while sets are named in capital letters. These sets are defined as:

- $O=\{o_1, o_2, \ldots \}$ – the set of organizations of a VBE.
- $T=\{t_1, t_2, \ldots\}$ – the set of traits identifiers that can be used to characterize an organization's character.
- $V_i=\{v_{i,1}, v_{i,2},\ldots\}$ – the set of values that trait t_i can assume.
- $OP=\{op_1, op_2, \ldots \}$ – the set of comparison operators. The operator op_i performs comparisons between the values of the set V_i (e.g. 'near(v_1,v_2)').
- $C=\{c_1, c_2,\ldots\}$ – the set of competences required for the achievement of a given collaboration opportunity (CO).

Just as an example, these sets can be instantiated with the following values:
O={net1, org2, university3}, T={flexibility, creativity, reliability}, $V_{reliability}$={low, fair, high}, C={DBA, logistics, ICT, CAD},and OP={'<', '>', '=', about, near, reliability_op, prestige_op}.

For the purposes of this experiment, the collaboration opportunity (CO) already appears organized as a business process plan, which is constituted by a set of activities, each one having time and precedence constraints, and requiring specific competences for their execution.

These activities are specified in a PERT-like approach. The duration of each activity is specified by three estimated values: the most optimistic (to), the most likely (tm), and the most pessimistic (tp). From these values and following the PERT approach, the duration of an activity is calculated by the formula Te = (to +

4*tm + tp) /6, with standard deviation s = (tp - to)/6, which already incorporates the underlying uncertainty for the activity durations (Martinich, 1997).

For the definitions presented below, we abstract from many details that, although important, are irrelevant for our illustrative purposes in this experiment. For instance, our definition of collaborative business process plan is rather simplistic and is better explained in (Camarinha-Matos et al, 2005).

Definition 1 (**Activity**) – An activity, a component of the collaborative business process plan for the CO, is defined as a tuple Act=(id, d, C) in which:

- *id* - is the name of the activity.
- *d*=(*to*, *tm*, *tp*) - is a tuple that specifies the time duration, using a *PERT* modelling approach. The attributes *to*, *tm* and *tp* stand for the most optimistic, the most likely and the most pessimistic time duration, respectively.
- $C=\{c_1,c_2...\}$ - corresponds to the set of competences required for the satisfaction of the goals of the activity.

Definition 2 (**Collaborative business process plan**) – A collaborative business process plan for a given CO is defined as a project based plan composed of a set of activities and corresponding precedences. This plan is defined as a tuple *Plan*=(*co*, *A*, *Prec*), in which

- co is the collaboration opportunity.
- $A=\{(act_1,d_1,C_1),\quad(act_2,d_2,C_2),...\}$ - is a set of activities as specified in *definition 1*.
- $Prec=\{(a_i,a_k)|\ a_i,a_k \in A\}$ - is the set that specifies the precedences between the activities of set *A*.

Definition 3 (**Organization's Character**) – An organization's character can be seen as a composition of a set of traits that determine the way it behaves. It can be modeled as a tuple *OC*=(*o*, *TV*), in which:

- o - is the organization being characterized;
- $TV = \{(t_i, v_{i,k}) \mid t_i \in T, v_{i,k} \in V_i\}$ – is the trait set constituted of tuples, each one composed of a trait and a corresponding trait value.

Definition 4 (**Character-related Preparedness Conditions**) – The preparedness conditions related to the organization's character are represented by a set *PC* of preparedness items. Each item is a tuple that specifies the condition or value required for a given character trait of an organization. The preparedness conditions set is defined as:

$PC = \{ (t_i, v_{i,k}, op_i, p_i) \mid t_i \in T, v_{i,k} \in V_i, p_i \in [0,1], op_i \in OP \}$, in which

- t_i - is the trait name;
- $v_{i,k}$ - is the trait (linguistic) value, such that $v_{i,k} \in V_i$;
- op_i - is the comparison operator that is used for comparing the values of V_i ;
- p_i - expresses the desired probability/likelihood of the attribute t_i having the value $v_{i,k}$.

Definition 5 (**Competences fitness**) – An organization fits in some collaboration scenario if it possesses the adequate (or required) competences.

The competences' adequacy depends on whether the context is a *VBE* (bringing competences that fit the general scope of the VBE) or a *VO* (providing or complementing required competences for the achievement of the *VO goals*).

Definition 6 (**Preparedness for collaboration**) – An organization is considered prepared to collaborate if it both satisfies a set of character's conditions (definition 4) and possesses adequate competences (definition 5).

With the definitions above it is now possible to state the axioms for the partners' suggestion model. Such axioms are formally presented below, together with their corresponding descriptions. The process of partners' suggestion in VO creation is a complex task (Camarinha-Matos et al, 2005), (Camarinha-Matos, Afsarmanesh, 2006). In this modeling experiment we consider only a simplified version of this process by defining a few axioms that establish the correspondence, or matching, between the CO's necessary competences and the competences provided by candidate partners. This process is illustrated in Fig. 16.

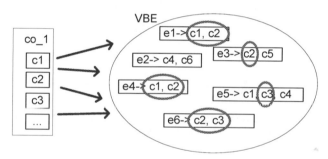

Figure 16 – Illustration of the matching between the CO needed competences and the candidates' competences

Axiom 1 – Any VO is an acceptable suggestion for a given *CO*, if it satisfies the requirements *C* of the *CO* and also complies with a specified preparedness conditions *P*.

$$\forall_{co} \forall_P \forall_{VO} \left((suggest\_vo(co, P, VO) \leftarrow \right.$$
$$\left. \exists_C \left(requiremen\,ts(co, C) \wedge satisfy\,(C, VO) \wedge preparedne\,ss(VO, P) \right) \right)$$

For this axiom, the predicate "requirements" grabs the needed competences from the *CO* and puts them into the set *C*.

Axiom 2 - A *VO* satisfies a set of required competences *C* if, recursively, for each competence in *C* there is an organization in the *VO* that satisfies it.

$$(\forall_C \forall_{VO} ((\textit{satisfy } (c_i.C, (o_j, c_i).VO) \leftarrow$$
$$\textit{satisfy } (C, O) \wedge \text{competence } (o_j, c_i)) \vee \text{satisfy}(\{\}, \{\}))$$

In this axiom, the operator '.' unifies or *grabs* the first element of the set (assuming sets modeled as lists). For instance, c_i represents the first element of C. The 'competence' predicate verifies whether a competence c_i is owned by organization o_j.

Axiom 3 – A *VO* satisfies the given preparedness conditions *P* if all its members are prepared according to *P*.

$$\forall_P \forall_{VO} ((\textit{preparedness}(VO, P) \leftarrow$$
$$\forall org((\textit{belongs}(org, VO) \rightarrow is\_prepared(org, P)))$$

In axioms 3 and 4, the predicate *belongs* performs the usual set membership operator.

Axiom 4 - An organization *org* is prepared according to the given preparedness conditions *P* if for each preparedness item *t* in *P*, there is a corresponding belief *b* in *org*'s character, such that *b* complies with *t*.

$$\forall_{org} \forall_P ((is\_prepared(org, P) \leftarrow$$
$$\forall_t ((belongs(t, P) \wedge (\exists_b belief(org, t, b)) \rightarrow complies(t, b)))$$

The predicate *complies* compares the desired probability or likelihood of the trait in item *t* with the obtained belief *b*, using the comparison operator inside *t* (see definition 4).

The predicate *belief* deserves more attention. It provides the probability that the preparedness item *t*, in axiom 4, has a corresponding trait in the organization's character. Let us suppose that t = (reliability, high, '>', 70) and let us observe the vbe_1 in table 1 of section 3.5. The predicate *belief* would provide values for belief *b* in the axiom, as illustrated by the following cases:

- For enterprise *e1*, the belief that reliability=*high* is b=100%, because *e1* has the trait 'reliability' defined with value "high" in its character profile. It would be represented by an evidence node in the belief network of Fig. 6.
- For enterprise *e3*, the belief that reliability=*high* is b=0%, because *e3* has low reliability in its character profile. It would be represented by an evidence node in the belief network of Fig. 6, but with different evidence (low reliability).
- For enterprise *e2*, the belief is b=53.6%. This is because, the reliability of this enterprise is unknown and, therefore, this value is obtained using the query b=P('reliability=high'| known_traits(o_2)) on the belief network of Fig. 6. The predicate '*known_traits(org)*', provides the known values of an organization's traits.

These axioms can be translated into Prolog predicates, as shown in Fig. 17.

```
suggest_vo(CO_id, P, VO):-
  co(CO_id,Act,Links), requirements(co(CO_id,Act,Links),Lcomp),
  satisfy(Lcomp,VoList), preparedness(VoList,P), VO=vo(VoList).

satisfy([],[]).
satisfy ([Comp|Tail],Orgs):-
  satisfy (Tail,Orgs2), competence(Org,Comp), append([(Org,Comp)], Orgs2,Orgs).

preparedness( VO,P):-
  forall( member( (Org,C), VO) , is_prepared(Org, P)).

is_prepared(Org,PrepList):-
  forall(( member((Trait,Value,Comparator,Probability), PrepList),
           belief(Org,Trait,Value, Probability2)
         ), complies(Comparator,Probability2, Probability)).
```

Figure 17 – Prolog predicates for partners' suggestion axioms

These axioms can be invoked using the query below. The shaded argument is the preparedness pattern required for the suggested organizations. The characters and competences of organizations are modeled as facts in the memory of the Prolog's inference engine.

```
suggest_vo(co_1,{(creativity,high,'>',60), (preparedness_level,high,'>',70)}",VO).
```

3.4 The simulation component

Simulation is employed in this modeling example to work as a kind of verification process for the VOs obtained using the axioms modeled above. Hence, it is used to 'animate' the inferred VOs along the corresponding CO's business process, in order to measure the performance of each VO and, eventually, select the ones that appear more suitable for the given CO.

The simulation component was specified using a similar axiomatic approach as just described for the partners suggestion presented above. Hence, this component is composed of a set of axioms that were also translated into Prolog. During a simulation cycle, the generated events and corresponding states are kept as facts in the knowledge base. The complete axiomatic model for the simulator (e.g., the predicates *has_events* and *start_activities* used in axiom 5) is not presented here. The axiom 5 specifies a simulation recursively in the following way:

Axiom 5 – At any simulation instant T, if there are pending events, finish the corresponding activities, start new ones and advance simulation to next time step. Otherwise, display the simulation results.

$$\forall_T (run(T) \leftarrow (has\_events(T) \rightarrow finish\_activities(T) \land start\_activities(T))$$
$$\land run(T+1) \lor (\neg has\_events(T) \rightarrow write\_simulation\_state(T))$$

The simulation can be started at any initial time by invoking this axiom using the term "run(initial_time)", e.g., "run(0)".

3.5 The structure of the partners' suggestion mechanism

The way the partners' suggestion mechanism works is illustrated in Fig. 18. The business process needed to satisfy the CO, the required preparedness conditions and preparedness level are provided at the beginning. Then the partners' suggestion function selects candidates according to competences' fitness. This might provide several solutions, as illustrated in the example below. Then, taking into account the character of the candidate organizations, the mechanism refines the suggestions to only select candidates that appear to be more prepared to the context of the CO, accordingly to the required preparedness conditions. For instance, if the CO is characterized by strict deadlines, selected candidates must be highly reliable, and so, less reliable candidates would not be selected. The suggested set(s) of candidates would be organized as a VO, taking into consideration the CO's business process. Finally, the VO and CO's business process are given to the simulation module. More on this process is illustrated through the example below.

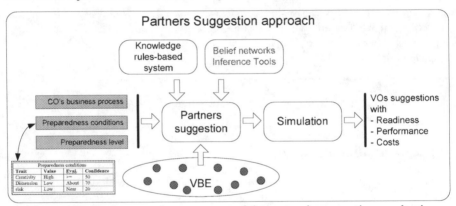

Figure 18 – Structure and components of the partner's suggestion mechanism

3.6 Application example

For the purpose of a modeling example, we can consider the existence of a virtual organization breeding environment (VBE) composed of a group of enterprises (or organizations). These enterprises, together with corresponding competences and character traits, are defined as shown in table 1. One important aspect to emphasize here is that some traits are undetermined.

Table 1 - Competences and traits of the VBE's members.

VBE_1 composition							
		Organization traits					
Enterprise	**Competences**	PD	ES	RP	R	C	P
e1	c1, c2	high	high	?	high	high	high
e2	c4, c6	med	?	high	?	low	high
e3	c2, c5	med	fair	high	low	high	high
e4	c1, c2	?	high	high	low	?	?
e5	c1, c3, c4	high	bad	high	high	high	low
e6	c2, c3	high	fair	high	?	?	?
...	...						

(PD: partners dimension; ES: economical situation; RP: risk profile; R: reliability; C: creativity; P: prestige).

Let us assume that at a given instant, a collaboration opportunity was identified, for which the corresponding business process plan is shown in Fig. 19.

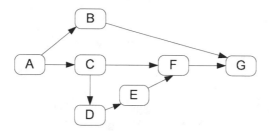

Figure 19 – Example of a business process plan for a given collaboration opportunity

The details of this plan, as specified by definitions 1 and 2, are shown in table 2.

Table 2 – Example of time and precedences

Time and precedences for project "co_1"					
Activity	Necessary Competences	Durations			Precedences
		Most Optimistic	Most Likely	Most Pessimistic	
A	c3	8	16	20	-
B	c2	10	20	30	A
C	c1	12	18	24	A
D	c2	12	16	18	C
E	c4	6	9	12	D
F	c1	10	15	20	C, E
G	c3	5	7	9	B, F

As specified by axiom 2, the suggestion mechanism for partner's selection is initially based on the traditional matching of competences or, in other words, competences fitness. These suggestions are then enhanced when the mechanism uses the preparedness conditions. In the simulations phase, the organizations characters are also important. For instance, a very reliable member expectedly tends to perform better its assigned activities. Consequently, we can tell that activity durations are influenced according to the entities that perform it, and that a reliable organization tends to faster and promptly perform its assigned activities.

Therefore, the simulation model computes the activities' durations that run at each instant, using the following rule of thumb: "If the member that performs an activity has high probability of having high 'collaboration level', the duration Te of the assigned activity will slightly decrease, and it will increase otherwise".

Now using the partners' suggestion model for the given CO, only the correspondent business process is provided, at the first try, without specifying any preferences for the candidate members (Fig. 20). As referred before, the mechanism is invoked by the predicate 'suggest_vo' of axiom 1.

Figure 20 – Suggestions without preparedness restrictions

The initial VO suggestions, as shown in table 3, are based on a simple competences' matching approach, according to axiom 2. For each suggestion, the simulation module provides the duration of the simulated business process plan, helping spot the best suggestions. In order to restrict the number of provided suggestions, it is imposed that each member can be assigned to only a single competency otherwise the number of suggestions would be much bigger.

Table 3 – Example of VO suggestions

Virtual Organization Possibilities								
Solution	e1	e2	e3	e4	e5	e6	e7	Duration
1	c1	c4	c2		c3			38
2	c1	c4		c2	c3			39
3	c1	c4			c3	c2		39
4	c2	c4		c1	c3			40
5		c4	c2	c1	c3			40
6		c4		c1	c3	c2		41
7	c1	c4	c2			c3		38
8	c1	c4		c2		c3		39
9	c1			c2	c4	c3		38
10	c1			c2	c4	c3		39
11	c2	c4		c1		c3		40
12		c4	c2	c1		c3		40
13	c2			c1	c4	c3		40
14			c2	c1	c4	c3		40
15	c2	c4			c1	c3		40
16		c4	c2		c1	c3		40
17		c4		c2	c1	c3		41

In the previous solution, we did not consider any preparedness conditions. Some suggestions may in fact be composed of members with low reliability and the VO might fail in achieving its goals. On the other hand, as shown in Fig. 21, if we now provide desirable preparedness conditions to the suggestion mechanism (see definition 6 and axiom 4), the suggestions would be those in table 4. As the preparedness conditions restrict the number of suggestions, each partner can now be assigned with more than one competence.

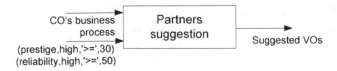

Figure 21 – Suggestions influenced by preparedness conditions

For this case, the mechanism selected only organizations with both high reliability and prestige. Organizations with these traits undefined are also selected, provided that the likelihood of having a high value is at least 30% and 50% respectively. As mentioned in a previous section, this likelihood is determined by the predicate *belief* of axiom 4, using the belief network of Fig. 6.

Table 4 – Another example of VO suggestions

Virtual Organization Possibilities								
Solution	e1	e2	e3	e4	e5	e6	e7	Duration
1	c1 c2	c4				c3		38
2	c1	c4				c3 c2		39

Finally, the mechanism can be told to only consider organizations with a high preparedness level, this time without specifying any preparedness conditions, as they are implicit in the preparedness level. The likelihood of any organization to have a high level of preparedness is determined using the *belief* predicate and associated belief network mentioned before. If we impose a collaboration level of value "high" with likelihood of 60% (Fig. 22), then just one suggestion shows up (table 5).

Figure 22 – Selection of organizations with high preparedness level

With the corresponding solution:

Table 5 – Another example of VO suggestions

Virtual Organization Possibilities								
Solution	e1	e2	e3	e4	e5	e6	e7	Duration
1	c1	c4	c2		c3			38

After performing the simulation for this suggestion, the Gantt diagram appears as it is shown in Fig. 23. This diagram illustrates how the business process plan's activities are executed and how they were assigned to the VO members. For instance, activities 'b' and 'd' were assigned to enterprise 'e3'.

For the offered suggestion, the project duration is 38, which is the minimum possible duration. Nevertheless, duration does not make the whole story, as it could be longer. The point is that the suggested VO is composed of partners with higher likelihood of a "high" collaboration level, which accounts for a lower risk of working together.

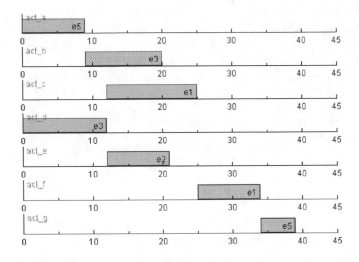

Figure 23 – Simulation of the collaboration opportunity with the suggested VO
(Source-code obtained from Chris Beck, University of Toronto, 1995)

3.7 Results analysis

Through this modeling experiment, it was shown that, to a certain degree, through a combination of different methodologies may result in improved solutions for the example presented. Based on a traditional approach, the partners' suggestion model proposed several VOs, some of which presented longer project durations during the simulation phase. With the inclusion of preparedness conditions, the partners' suggestions model yielded improved results.

Several aspects of this experiment require further research. The collaboration preparedness was based on the utilization of a belief network, which was used to predict the collaboration level of a candidate. In practice, the correct approach for an adequate preparedness assessment should be based on several indicators. Furthermore, the situations and contexts in which collaboration occurs must be considered, which is also an aspect being currently researched, and not included in this experiment.

4. CONCLUSIONS AND FURTHER CHALLENGES

Although not yet widely used in the collaborative networks research area, soft computing / computational intelligence methods are potentially useful when dealing with reasoning and decision making under situations of incomplete and imprecise information. Given the nature of these networks, composed of autonomous, distributed, and heterogeneous nodes, this is a frequent situation.

The set of modeling experiments discussed in this chapter illustrate how Bayesian belief networks and Rough Sets can be applied to assess the preparedness of a candidate to join a collaborative network. Furthermore, in some problems it is convenient to combine various modeling techniques in order to capture different facets of the problem at hands, as illustrated by the last example of partners' suggestion for a VO.

It shall be noted that the introduced examples have only an illustrative purpose and therefore several simplifications were made. The application of the suggested methods to more realistic scenarios certainly needs further research and evaluation.

Acknowledgements. This work as funded in part by the European Commission through the ECOLEAD project.

5. REFERENCES

Afsarmanesh H, Camarinha-Matos LM. A framework for management of virtual organization breeding environments. In: Collaborative Networks and their Breeding Environments; eds. Camarinha-Matos, L., Afsarmanesh, Ortiz, A.;(Springer), pp. 35-48, 2005.

Baldo F, Rabelo RJ, Vallejos RV. An Ontology-based Approach for selecting performance indicators for partners suggestion. In Establishing the Foundation of Collaborative Networks, (PRO-VE'07), Springer, Guimaraes, Portugal, 10-12 Sep 2007.

Camarinha-Matos LM, Silveri I, Afsarmanesh H, Oliveira AI. Towards a Framework for creation of Dynamic Virtual Organizations. In: Collaborative Networks and their Breeding Environments; eds. Camarinha-Matos, L., Afsarmanesh, Ortiz, A.;(Springer), pp. 26-28, 2005.

Camarinha-Matos LM, Afsarmanesh H. Creation of Virtual Organizations in a Breeding Environment. In: Proceedings of INCOM'06 - St. Etienne, France - 17-19 May 2006.

Cheng J, Greiner R. Learning Bayesian Belief Network Classifiers: Algorithms and System. In: Lecture Notes in Computer Science, page 141-151, vol. 2056, 2001.

Friedman N. Learning belief networks in the presence of missing values and hidden variables. In: D. Fisher, ed., Proceedings of the Fourteenth International Conference on Machine Learning, Morgan Kaufmann, San Francisco, CA, pp. 125-133, 1997.

Hassanien AE. Rough Set Approach for Attribute Reduction and Rule Generation: A Case of Patients With Suspected Breast Cancer. In: Journal of the American Society for information Science and Technology, 55(11): 954–962, 2004.

Jarimo T, Ljubič P, Salkari I, Bohanec M, Lavrač N, Žnidaršič M, Bollhalter S, Hodik J. Hierarchical multi-attribute decision support approach to virtual organization creation. In: Collaborative Networks and their Breeding Environments; eds. Camarinha-Matos, L., Afsarmanesh, Ortiz, A.;(Springer), pp. 135-142, 2005.

Jensen, FV. Bayesian Networks basics. In: AISB Quarterly, 94:9-22, 1996.

Komorowski J, Øhrn A, Skowron A. The ROSETTA Rough Set Software System, In: Handbook of Data Mining and Knowledge Discovery, W. Klösgen and J. Zytkow (eds.), ch. D.2.3, Oxford University Press. ISBN 0-19-511831-6, 2002.

Martinich JS. Production and Operations Management: an applied modern approach, John Wiley & Sons, 1997.

Netica application for Belief Networks and Influence Diagrams Users Guide, Norsys Software Group, 1997,http://www.norsys.com.

Pawlak Z. Rough Sets: Theoretical Aspects of Reasoning about Data, Kluwer Academic, 1991.

Pawlak Z. Vagueness and Uncertainty: a Rough Set Perspective. In: Computational Intelligence 11: pp. 277-232, 1995.

Pawlak Z, Skowron A. Rough Sets Rudiments. In: Bulletin of IRSS 3/3, pp 67-70, 1999.

Pearl J. Decision Making Under Uncertainty. In: ACM Computing Surveys, Vol. 28, No. 1, March 1996.

Wang Y, Vassileva J. Bayesian Network-Based Trust Model in Peer-to-Peer Networks. In: Proc. Workshop on Deception, Fraud and Trust in Agent Societies at the Autonomous Agents and Multi Agent Systems 2003 (AAMAS-03), Melbourne, Australia, July 2003.

4.5
A benefit analysis model
for collaborative networks

A. Abreu, L. M. Camarinha-Matos

The identification and characterization of collaboration benefits is an important element for the wide adoption of the collaborative networks paradigm. In order to establish a basis for analysis of benefits in collaborative networks (related to the behavioral dimension in the ARCON reference model) this chapter introduces an approach for the analysis of benefits in collaborative processes for enterprise networks. The potential application of some suggested indicators and the emergence of a "collaborative spirit" based on the reciprocity mechanism derived from this analysis are also discussed in a VO breeding environment context.

1. INTRODUCTION

The sustainable development of collaborative networks requires a clear understanding of the potential benefits and their structure. Collaborative networks (CNs) are frequently referred to as a survival mechanism for organizations in face of turbulent markets due to the implicit agility of these organizational forms (Camarinha-Matos, Afsarmanesh, 2004).

However, it is also recognized that collaboration introduces high overheads due to the higher coordination costs, diversity of working methods and corporate culture, which induces higher transaction costs, loser control structures, etc (Williamson, 1985). Is the balance between the potential benefits and the increased overheads substantially positive? Literature in the field as well as a growing number of practical case studies seem to indicate that the answer is yes. It is however difficult to prove it. For instance, it is difficult to find some objective indicators in order to show to a small and medium enterprise that there are potential benefits in joining a collaborative network.

Furthermore it is not always easy to determine the contribution of each partner to value generation. For instance, in innovation projects the contribution of each partner to the value generation is not necessarily proportional to the involved resources.

In order to address this problem, the issue of performance measurement and benefit analysis in collaborative networks has been attracting attention (Seifert, Eschenbaecher, 2004) (Brewer, Speh, 2000). Being able to measure the performance of a collaborative network as a whole, as well as the performance of each of its singular members, could represent an important boosting element for the wide acceptance of the paradigm. However performance indicators tailored to collaborative networks or even an adequate conceptual basis for benefit analysis are not available yet.

On the other hand, in CNs the continuous and repetitive interactions among partners make that the value benefits generated by a collaboration process is no more determined only by its tangible assets (given by products/services supplied), but also by its intangible assets (e.g. relationship value, or "social capital").

In order to establish a basis for the analysis of benefits in collaborative networks, it is necessary to consider multiple aspects that can better be captured by a combination of soft and crisp modeling approaches. This chapter discusses the nature of collaborative benefits, and their role in the sustainability of a "collaborative spirit" based on the reciprocity mechanism. It also suggests some indicators focused on collaborative networks, and discusses their measurability.

2. BENEFITS CONCEPT

From the traditional literature on virtual enterprises / virtual organizations (Camarinha-Matos, Afsarmanesh, 2004), (Saiz, Rodriguez, Ortiz, 2005) a number of variables related to the identification of collaboration benefits have been suggested as illustrated in Fig. 1.

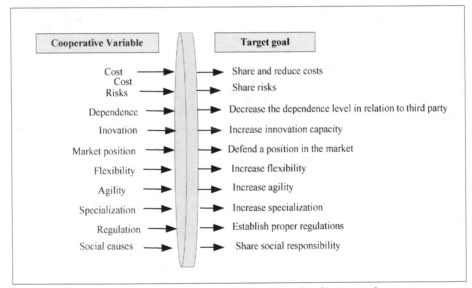

Figure 1 – Cooperation variables and associated target goals

Table 1 shows, for each target goal, some examples of associated (intuitive) advantages of collaboration (Camarinha-Matos, Abreu, 2004).

Table 1– Examples of some advantages in CNs

Target goal	Example of some advantages associated to collaboration
Share and reduce costs	• Have access to new markets and/or businesses without the need to make high investments. • Share R&D costs. • Financial stability. • Ability for SMEs to compete with large competitors.
Share risks	• Companies operate in changing environments and with limited, therefore imperfect, knowledge. Consequently in some cases the level of uncertainty may have a negative impact on the decision-making processes. Sharing knowledge among several partners allows a reduction of this uncertainty level. • When several partners are involved in a collaborative project there is a partition of the responsibilities among them (co-responsibility). • In some cases solidarity mechanisms can be established among partners. • Also enabling the competition of SMEs with large companies.
Decrease the dependence level in relation to third party	• All companies depend on others to some extent for products, services, raw materials, tangible and intangible resources and competencies. Through cooperation companies can reduce this dependence by creating privileged links to other firms in an attempt to reduce transaction costs that arise when uncertainty increases. • Also enabling the competition of SMEs with large companies.
Increase the innovation capacity	• Increase the capacity of generating new ideas through the combination of the existent resources and diversity of cultures and experiences (critical mass). • Emergence of new sources of value. • Reduction of the life cycle of the products and technologies. • Possibility of developing more robust products fitting the customers' expectations and therefore contributing to an increase of the quality.
Defend a position in the market	• Achievement of economies of scale by sharing resources. • Establishment of defensive coalitions with the purpose of building entry barriers in order to defend themselves against a dominant firm or a new player. • Establishment of offensive coalitions with the purpose of developing competitive advantages and strengthening their position by diminishing the other competitors' competitiveness. • Increase the negotiation power in relation to suppliers and/or customers that are outside of the collaborative network. • Also enabling the competition of SMEs with large companies.
Increase flexibility	• Share of resources and combination of skills among partners. • Use the core competences from other partners. • Increase the adaptation capacity towards several business environments simultaneously. • Offer a broader range of products / services. • Grow for new segments in a stable way reaching a larger stability.
Increase agility	• React in a short period of time to a business opportunity through the establishment of more agile procedures. • Increase the interoperability between several processes and products (establishment of norms)
Increase specialization	• Let companies concentrate their resources on the critical activities.
Establish proper regulations	• Definition of rules to avoid opportunistic behaviors and to avoid conflicts. • Increase common culture of trust.
Share social responsibilities	• Obtain recognition from others (intangible value). • Develop social responsibility. • Altruism. • Reinforce values that are common.

At a macro-level, these potential benefits can be regarded from two perspectives:
- *Survival capacity* – Reflecting the capacity of an actor (e.g. company) or a group of actors to stay in operation "alive" when confronted by forces that tend to destroy them.
- *Performance capacity* – Reflected in the capability of an actor or group of actors to better accomplish their tasks.

However, for the purpose of this analysis these perspectives are assumed as independent although in some cases the performance capacity can be regard as one aspect of the survival capacity.

Based on a small survey conducted among a number of experts[1], Table 2 illustrates the potential relation among the mentioned benefits of collaboration and their potential impact in a situation of survival or performance improvement.

Table 2 – Contribution of benefits to survival and performance increase

Target goal	Level of benefits impact on	
	Survival	Performance
Share and reduce costs	Moderate	Moderate
Share risks	Strong	Moderate
Decrease the dependence level in relation to third party	Moderate	Moderate
Increase innovation capacity	Moderate	Strong
Defend a position in the market	Moderate	Moderate
Increase flexibility	Strong	Strong
Increase agility	Strong	Strong
Increase specialization	Strong	Strong
Establish proper regulations	Moderate	Moderate
Share social responsibility	Weak	Moderate

The adopted scale considers the following:
- *Strong relationship* - When the distribution of most answers in relation to the variable is in the interval of 75% to 100% of relevance.
- *Moderate relationship* - When the distribution of most answers in relation to the variable is in the interval of 25% to 50% of relevance, or in the interval of 50% to 75% of relevance.
- *Weak relationship* - When the distribution of most answers in relation to the variable is in the interval of 0% to 25% of relevance.

From these results one can conclude that there is a clear (intuitive) perception that collaboration benefits are related to the two strategic goals perspectives – survival or

[1]The survey was conducted by email, involving 45 experts from industry and academia from Portugal, Italy, Spain, Germany, UK, Denmark, Turkey, Austria, USA, Canada, and Japan.

performance increase.

It is also visible that if the primary goal of a company is to stay "alive" it would likely be motivated to find cooperating partners with the purpose of sharing risks. On the other hand, if the strategic goal is to improve performance, the motivation for partnership will be more related to increasing innovation capacity. Increasing flexibility, agility, and specialization are equally important in both cases.

However, the actual meaning of a benefit depends on the underlying value system that is used in each context. It is commonly accepted that the behavior of an individual, society, or ecosystem is determined by the underlying value system (Abreu, Camarinha-Matos 2006). It is intuitively understood that the values considered in a business-oriented collaborative network are different from the ones in a non-profit context (e.g. disaster rescue network). A value system is in essence the ordering and prioritization of a set of values (e.g. prestige, profit, recognition, trust, etc.) that an actor or a society of actors holds.

Taking the simplified view that the goal of a CN is the maximization of some "attribute" of its value system, in a business context the dominant value is the profit (in economic sense), while in other cases the objectives are altruist and compensated by the amount of prestige or social recognition.

In general, the structure of a value system, and therefore the drivers of the CN behavior, might include multiple variables / aspects. Complementarily there are other elements that strongly influence or determine the behavior of the network and its members, such as the schema of incentives, trust building and management, ethical code, the collaboration culture, and the contracts and collaboration agreements. The concept of "benefit" depends on the specific context.

3. METHODOLOGY AND SOFT TECHNIQUES ADOPTED

Since the concept of benefit is multifaceted, there are several perspectives that must be analyzed. Fig. 2 shows the three models / theories proposed to be used in this analysis that contribute each one to cover different aspects or perspectives of analysis of collaboration benefits in CNs.

Game theory - A mathematical model designed for analyzing the interaction between several actors whose decisions affect each other. An interactive situation is described as a *game* including an abstract description of the players (actors), the courses of actions available to them, and their preferences over the possible outcomes. From this perspective, the collaborative benefits can be seen as a measure of the *utility* of players in a collaborative or cooperative game and its value depends on several variables such as: actors' behaviors, past interaction and distribution schemes such as the Shapley value.

The Shapley value provides a usefulness index for distribution of benefits in collaborative networks. The basic assumption is that the benefits obtained by a certain number of enterprises will be lower than the benefits obtained when incorporating a new element in the coalition. The Shapley value determines the average value of each enterprise's contribution to the coalition.

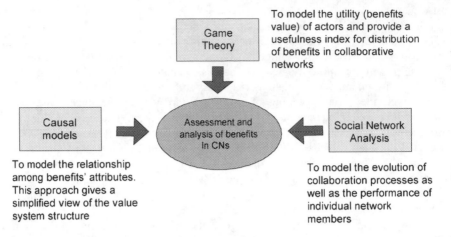

Figure 2 – Models/theories contributing to the assessment and analysis of benefits in CNs.

Causal Model – It is used to represent influence relationships that might be positive or negative among a set of variables. Based on this model the concept of benefit can be defined in terms of a set of values and can be measured as an abstract aggregated value.

Social network analysis (SNA) – Based on graph-theoretic concepts and basic statistics analysis it is used to model and explain social structures. In other words it is focused on uncovering the patterning of actors' interaction. It involves the mapping and measuring of relationships and flows between actors. The nodes in the network are the actors while the links show relationships or flows between the nodes (Wasserman and Faust, 1994). Based on SNA concepts it is possible to establish a list of benefits-based indicators tailored to collaborative networks and model the evolution of the collaboration process.

In order to address the benefits analysis in CNs the following four steps are followed in this modelling experiment:
    Step 1 – Modelling the concept of benefit
    Step 2 - Modelling the distribution of collaboration benefits
    Step 3 – Development of a benefits model
    Step 4 - Modelling the evolution of collaboration based on benefits analysis.

Step 1 – Modelling the concept of benefit
In general, as mentioned above, the concept of benefit for the context of networks of enterprises most likely represents a measure of the economic benefits (in the sense of net profit), while in the context of a not-for-profit organizations it could represent a more abstract notion of acquired social prestige or peer recognition. Nevertheless, in most cases this concept could be expressed as a combination of multiple variables, and might be represented as an abstract aggregated value as illustrated in Fig. 3.

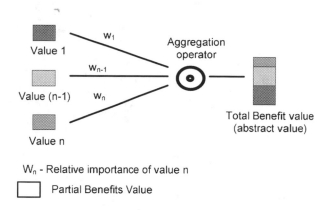

W_n - Relative importance of value n

☐ Partial Benefits Value

Figure 3 – The benefit concept as a combination of multiple values

However, the values that have influence on the concept of "benefit" depend on the underlying value system that is used in each context. In order to capture relations of influence among values, causal models can be used, as illustrated in Fig. 4.

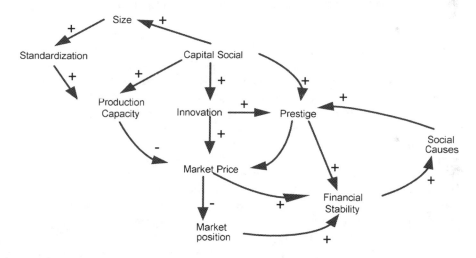

Figure 4 – An example value system structure

Departing from the value system model that is used in each context it is possible to express any benefit concept as a combination of multiple values. To illustrate this idea, let us consider the value system model illustrated in Fig. 4 to express the concept of "Financial Stability" benefit as a combination of multiple variables. In this case, as illustrated in Fig. 5 the concept of Financial Stability benefit depends on Prestige, Market Price and Market Position and its total value depends on the relative importance of each of these variable.

Figure 5 – Example of Financial Stability benefit concept
as combination of multiple values

A better understanding of the concept of benefit is an important element to support
collaborative processes. Furthermore, to demonstrate that the participation in a
collaborative network brings valuable benefits to the involved entities it is necessary
to assure a fair distribution of benefits. The next step is devoted to illustrate the
applicability of the Shapley value in determining a fair distribution of benefits from
collaboration.

Step 2 - Modelling the distribution of collaboration benefits
The development of common mechanisms and rules for a fair distribution of benefits
is an important step to support the sustainability of collaborative behavior over time.
When partners apply different rules, which typically leads to different values of
benefits, non-collaborative behaviors are likely to develop. In order to overcome this
problem, the Shapley value provides a useful index to decide on a fair distribution of
collaboration or cooperation benefits when it is possible to estimate the added
(marginal) value of each new partner joining a coalition.

The basic assumption is that the benefits obtained by a certain number of
enterprises will be lower than the benefits obtained when incorporating a new
element in the coalition. The Shapley value determines the average value of each
enterprise's contribution to the coalition. In order to better understand the concept,
let us consider the following metaphor (Myerson, 1997) :

Suppose that we plan to assemble a coalition of three partners (a_1, a_2, a_3) in a
room, but the door to the room is only large enough for one actor to enter at a time,
so the actors randomly line up in a queue at the door. There are |A|! (3! in this
example, as illustrated in Fig. 6) different ways that the actors might be ordered in
this queue.
For any set S that does not contain the actor (a_i), there are:

$$|S|!(|A|-|S|-1)!$$

different ways of ordering the actors so that S is the set of actors who are ahead of
actor a_i in the queue.

$$A = \left\{ \underbrace{a_1, a_2, \dots, a_{i-1}}_{|S|}, a_i, \underbrace{a_{i+1}, \dots, a_n}_{|A|-|S|-1} \right\}$$

Thus, if the various orderings are equally likely, the following equation,

$$\frac{|S|!\left(|A|-|S|-1\right)!}{|A|!}$$

gives the probability that, when actor (a_i) enters the room, he will find the coalition S there ahead of him.

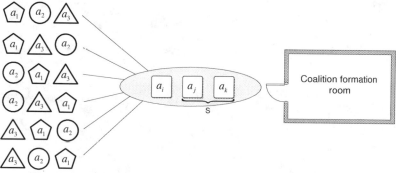

Figure 6 – Different ways of ordering the 3 partners in a queue

If a_i finds S ahead of him when he enters the room, then his marginal contribution (v) to the worth of the coalition in the room is:

$$\left(v\left(S \cup \{a_i\}\right) - v(S)\right)$$

The Shapley value of any actor is the expected marginal contribution of that actor when it *enters* the coalition. This metaphor also helps in implementing a practical algorithm for computing the Shapley value, as illustrated in Fig. 7.

The Shapley value, $\phi_{a_i}(v)$ for an actor a_i in a coalition of value v is given by the following equation:

$$\phi_{a_i}(v) = \sum_{S \subset A\backslash\{a_i\}} \frac{|S|!\left(|A|-|S|-1\right)!}{|A|!} \times \left(v\left(S \cup \{a_i\}\right) - v(S)\right)$$

where:

    $\phi_{a_i}(v)$ - Shapley value for actor a_i in a coalition of value v

    A - Set of actors members of the coalition

S - All subsets of A that do not contain the actor a_i

In order to illustrate this idea, let us consider the following case:

Three tourism operators – a hotel chain (H), a flight company (F), and a bus transportation company (T) - decide to establish a cooperation agreement in order to increase their competitiveness and improve their position in the market by offering integrated holiday packages. In this case none of the enterprises knows a priori the relative weight of each partner. They can however estimate what would be the expected added-value to their current business (benefits of cooperation) for each coalition case as shown in Fig. 7.

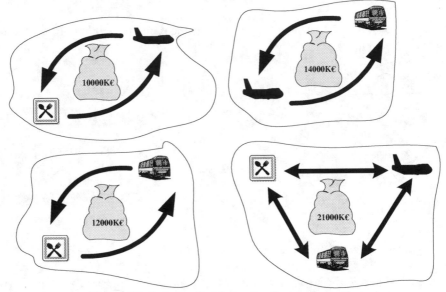

Figure 7 – Estimated added value from cooperation
in case of bi-lateral or tri-lateral consortia

Based on these estimates, we can then calculate the Shapley value. Fig. 8 illustrates the calculation of the Shapley value for this example. Let us consider the first row (F-H-T): column (F) is the expected added-value when flight company (F) works alone; column Hotel (H) represents the expected added-value when Hotel joins to flight company (F); column Transportation Company (T) represents the additional added-value when Transportation company joins the coalition of flight company and hotel chain. The following rows apply the same principle for the other possible orderings of F, H, and T. The last row shows the average of each column.

Based on this approach the flight company could get 6000K€ (28.57%) of the benefits, the hotel chain 7000K€ (33.33%), and the transportation company 8000K€ (38.09%).

Coalition	Marginal Contribution			TOTAL (K€)
	Flight (F)	Hotel (H)	Transportation (T)	
F – H – T	0	10000	11000	21000
F – T – H	0	9000	12000	21000
H – F – T	10000	0	11000	21000
H – T – F	7000	0	14000	21000
T – F – H	12000	9000	0	21000
T – H – F	7000	14000	0	21000
Shapley value	*6000*	*7000*	*8000*	21000

Figure 8 – Estimated benefits and Shapley value

The development of mechanisms and rules for a fair distribution of benefits is an important way to ensure that every member of the network understands the measurements in the same way. However, it remains difficult to find some objective indicators to show a partner that there are potential benefits in joining a collaborative network. In order to address this problem, the next step introduces an approach to model collaboration benefits and a preliminary set of performance indicators inspired in concepts from the Social Networks analysis and game theory.

Step 3 – Development of a benefits model
The wide adoption of the collaborative networks paradigm in its various manifestation forms requires the establishment of proper performance indicators to be used in decision making processes at various levels: VO breeding environment management, VO brokering, VO management and VO breeding environment membership.

For the purpose of the following discussion, let us consider Task Performance Benefits (TB) as the combined benefits that result from the performance of a task in the context of a collaborative process. A collaborative process is understood as a set of tasks performed by the collaborative network members towards the achievement of a common goal (e.g. the business goal that motivates the creation of a Virtual Enterprise). For reasons of simplicity we also consider a level of granularity of tasks such that each task is performed by a single member of the network (single actor).

As discussed in step 1, the actual meaning of benefit depends on the underlying value system and, in general, represents a combination of multiple variables. The term benefit is used here with the same meaning as net profit and in this model benefits are assumed as abstract quantifiable measurements (Camarinha-Matos and Abreu, 2005). Based on this assumption we define the following set of intuitive concepts:

Self-benefit - benefits for actor a_i as a result of performing the task t_l (Fig. 9.a).

Received benefits - benefits received by actor a_i when actor a_j performs the task t_l (perspective of a_i) (Fig. 9.b).

Contributed benefit – benefits from actor a_j to actor a_i as a result of performing the task t_l (perspective of a_j) (Fig. 9.b).

Figure 9 – a) Self benefits for actor a_i b) Actor a_i receives benefits from actor a_j

However, in the context of a collaborative network it is also important to distinguish two set of tasks benefits - dependent (DTB) and independent (TB) tasks benefits. There is a task dependence when the realization of a task by one actor, and therefore the respective benefits, depends on other actors that are not involved in the execution but have an influence on that execution. An example of task dependence occurs when an actor with a good reputation in the market is present as member of a collaborative network and this fact helps others to acquire a contract (task) that otherwise would be lost. For all other cases, the tasks are considered independent. Based on this assumption the total *self-benefits*, *received benefits or contributed benefits* for a actor a_i in a given collaborative process is given by the sum of the benefits obtained from all tasks performed inside of the collaborative network, as shown in Table 3.

Table 3 – Classes of benefits

Name	Formula	Explanation of variables
Self-benefits (SB)	$(SB_{ii}) = \sum_{l=1}^{L} TB_{ii}(t_{il}) + \sum_{m=1}^{M} DTB_{ii}(t_{im})$	TB_{ii} - Task performance benefit for actor a_i. t_{il} – Description of an independent task t_l performed by actor a_i. DTB_{ii} - Dependent task benefits for actor a_i. L – Total of independent tasks performed by a_i. M – Total of dependent tasks performed by a_i
Received Benefits (RB)	$(RB_{ij}) = \sum_{l=1}^{L} TB_{ji}(t_{jl}) + \sum_{m=1}^{M} DTB_{ji}(t_{jm})$	TB_{ji} - Task performance benefit from a_j to a_i DTB_{ij} - Dependent task benefits from actor a_j to actor a_i. t_{jl} – Description of an independent task t_l performed by actor a_j L – Total of independent tasks performed by actor a_j M – Total of dependent tasks performed by a_j
		TB_{ij} - Task performance benefit from actor a_i to an actor a_j.

Contributed Benefits **(CB)**	$(CB_{ij}) = \sum_{l=1}^{L} TB_{ij}(t_{il}) + \sum_{m=1}^{M} DTB_{ij}(t_{im})$	DTB_{ij} - Dependent task benefits from actor a_i to actor a_j. t_{jl} – Description of an independent task t_l performed by actor a_i L – Total of independent tasks performed by actor a_i M – Total of dependent tasks performed by a_i.

Combining these concepts with concepts from the Social Network Analysis area, a useful tool to analyze benefits in collaborative processes can be obtained (Camarinha-Matos, Abreu, 2007).

Table 4 – Mapping between SNA and Benefits Analysis Model

Social Network Analysis (SNA)	Benefits Analysis Model
Key concepts	
Node - A social discrete entity such as: enterprises, actors, corporate or collective social units	Enterprises, organizations, people (i.e. CN members or "actors" in general)
Relational tie - Type of ties or links between nodes	Benefits flow
Dyad – consists of a pair of actors and the possible ties between them	Received benefits Contributed benefits
Structural Variables – measure ties of a specific kind between pairs of actors.	Value of exchanged benefits
Composition variables – are measurements of actors' attributes.	Self-benefit Social Contribution benefits $(SCB_i)^2$ External Benefits $(EB_i)^3$ Reciprocity index $(RI)^4$
Basic Analysis	
Nodal Degree – is a measure of the activity of the actor it represents. • Out-degree • In-degree	Define **indicators** in order to measure: ▪ Actor degree centrality ▪ Group degree centralization ▪ Actor closeness centrality ▪ Group closeness centralization ▪ Actor betweenness centrality ▪ Group betweenness centralization ▪ Degree of prestige ▪ Proximity prestige ▪ Status or Rank prestige
Density of network	Social capital of the CN
Network Size	Number of members of the CN
Connectivity of network • Cutpoints	Measures the concept of reachability between pairs of nodes.

[2] This concepts is defined in table 5.
[3] This concepts is defined in table 5.
[4] This concepts is defined in table 5.

• Bridges • Walks • Trials • Tours • Cycles	
Cohesive Subgroups Clique n-cliques n-clans n-clubs	Identification of subsets of actors among whom there are relatively strong, direct, intense and frequent ties

Based on this mapping, table 5 shows an example of basic indicators that can contribute to establish a list of performance indicators tailored to collaborative networks.

Table 5 – Indicators of collaboration

Indicator	Short Description	Expression
Social Contribution Benefits (**SCB$_i$**)	The sum of benefits contributed by an actor a_i to all its partners as a result of its performance in the collaborative process.	$SCB_i = \sum_{j=1}^{N} CB_{ij} \quad i \neq j$ N – Number of actors involved in the collaborative process
External Benefits (**EB$_i$**)	The sum of benefits received by an actor a_i as a result of the activity of the other actors involved in the collaborative process.	$EB_i = \sum_{j=1}^{N} RB_{ij} \quad i \neq j$ N – Number of actors involved in the collaborative process
Total Individual Benefits (**TIB$_i$**)	The sum of external benefits plus self-benefits of an actor a_i	$TIR_i = SB_i + EB_i$
Individual Generated Benefits (**IGB$_i$**)	The sum of social contributed benefits plus self-benefits of an actor a_i	$IGB_i = SB_i + SCB_i$
Total Received Benefits (**TRB**)	The sum of external benefits achieved by a set of actors	$TRB = \sum_{j=1}^{N} EB_i$ N – Number of actors involved in the collaborative process
Total Contributed Benefits (**TCB**)	The sum of social contributed benefits generated by a set of actors	$TCB = \sum_{j=1}^{N} SCB_i$ N – Number of actors involved in the collaborative process
Total Network Benefits (**TNB**)	The sum of benefits achieved by a set of actors in a specific collaboration process or over a period of time.	$TNB = \sum_{i=1}^{K} (SB_i + SCB_i)$ K – Number of actors involved
Progress Ratio (**PR**)	This ratio is a macro indicator that represents the variation of the global benefits over a period of time. If: $PR_{[t_1,t_2]} \begin{cases} = 1 \text{ there is no change} \\ > 1 \text{ TNB increase} \\ < 1 \text{ TNB decrease} \end{cases}$	$PR_{[t_1,t_2]} = \dfrac{TNB_2}{TNB_1} \quad t_2 > t_1$

Social Capital **(SC)**	Social capital can be defined as the sum of resources, that accrue to an individual or a group by virtue of possessing a durable network of more or less institutionalized relationships of mutual acquaintance and recognition. In the context of a collaborative network, SC can be seen as the density of the network benefits relation.	$$SC = \frac{2R}{K \times (K-1)}$$ R – Number of collaborative relations in the network K – Number of actors involved
Collaborative Development Ratio **(CDR)**	The aim of this ratio is to measure the progress of collaborative benefits for a set of actors over a period of time. If: $CDR_{[t_1, t_2]} \begin{cases} =1 \ there \ is \ no \ change \\ >1 \ cooperation \ benefits \ increase \\ <1 \ cooperation \ benefits \ decrease \end{cases}$	$$CDR_{[t_1, t_2]} = \frac{\left(\sum\limits_{i=1}^{N} SCB_i\right)_2}{\left(\sum\limits_{i=1}^{N} SCB_i\right)_1} \quad t_2 > t_1$$
Individual contribution index **(ICI$_i$)**	Normalized contribution of an actor a_i to the collaborative network	$$ICI_i = \frac{SCB_i}{\sum\limits_{j=1}^{N} SCB_i}$$ N – Number of actors involved in the collaborative process
Apparent individual contribution index **(ACI$_i$)**	An indicator based on the number of contribution links (i.e. the *out degree* of the actor in the graph representing the collaboration benefits). This index gives an apparent and simple to compute measure of the involvement of an actor as a contributor to the collaboration process. An actor with an ACI close to zero is not perceived as a good contributor to the network (although the real value of its contribution is better expressed by ICI).	$$ACI_i = \frac{N° \ out \ links \ leaving \ a_i}{N-1}$$ N – Number of actors involved in the collaborative process
Individual external benefits index **(IBI$_i$)**	Normalized external benefits received by an actor. This index expresses the *popularity* or *prestige* of the actor in the sense that actors that are prestigious tend to receive many external benefits links.	$$IBI_i = \frac{EB_i}{\sum\limits_{j=1}^{N} EB_i}$$ N – Number of actors involved in the collaborative process
Apparent individual benefits index **(ABI$_i$)**	An indicator based on the number of received contribution links (i.e. the *in degree* of the actor in the graph representing the collaboration benefits). Similarly to IBI, this index also expresses the *popularity* or *prestige* of the actor.	$$ABI_i = \frac{N° \ links \ arriving \ at \ a_i}{N-1}$$ N – Number of actors involved in the collaborative process
Reciprocity index **(RI)**	The balance between benefits credit (the sum of benefits contributed by an actor a_i to all its partners (or one specific partner)) and benefits debit (the sum of benefits received by an actor a_i as a result of the performance of all actors (or one specific partner) involved in the collaborative process). If: $RI \begin{cases} <0 \ selfish \ behavior \\ =0 \ null \ balance \\ >0 \ altruistic \ behavior \end{cases}$	$$RI = \sum\limits_{j=1}^{N} CB_{ij} - \sum\limits_{j=1}^{N} RB_{ji}$$ N – Number of actors involved in the collaborative process

Since the proposed benefits related concepts can be represented graphically through a graph, it is possible to apply several graph properties and relating them to emergence of collaboration. In order to illustrate the potential application of graph properties let us consider some simple examples in this discussion. Assuming the degree of a node is a measure of the "involvement/activity" of the actor in the network, it may be relevant to analyze the collaborative process based on this perspective. According this approach, a network can be classified as decentralized or centralized. A network is decentralized when all nodes have equal value of nodal degree (in-degree and out-degree), otherwise the network is centralized.

Fig. 10 A) illustrates an example of decentralized benefits network supported by a mechanism of indirect reciprocity and Fig. 10 B) shows an example of centralized benefits network supported by a mechanism of direct reciprocity. However, comparing these two types of network, a collaborative process supported on a decentralized benefits network might be more attractive, since the number of provided/received task benefits is identical for all actors.

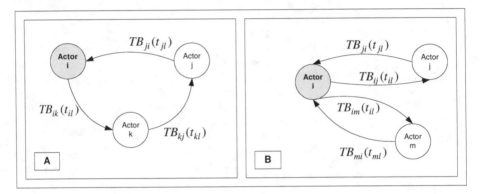

Figure 10 – Decentralized *vs.* centralized benefits network

Based on analyse of network connectivity Fig. 11 A) shows an example of acyclic network. This type of network is characterized by a weak connectivity among actors. However, according to the benefits analysis model, the existence of acyclic benefits network means that there are actors that provide/receive a task's benefits to/from someone and do not receive/provide help from/to others. As a result, for some actors (in this case, actors a_j and a_m) the participation in a collaborative process supported by acyclic benefits network might not be advantageous, unless one of the following assumptions is verified:

- The actors believe that their actions can be perceived as an investment and later on, they can get some services from others.
- The actors that receive benefits recognize a "social debit" as a result of contributions received in the past.

On the other hand, Fig. 11 B) shows an example of cyclic network. A cycle is a closed walk of at least three nodes in witch all links are distinct, and all actors except the beginning and ending actors are distinct. Consequently, the development of a collaborative process based on a cyclic benefits network assumes that actors provide/receive a task benefits to/from someone and simultaneously receive/provide help from/to others. As a result, the participation in a collaborative process supported by cyclic or closed walk benefits network is usually more attractive.

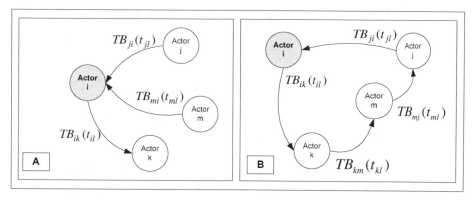

Figure 11 – Acyclic *vs.* Cyclic network of benefits

Since, the most favourable network of benefits for promotion of collaboration is dependent on the existence of cycles or close walk benefits, it is useful to analyse in detail the conditions that drive the emergence of this type of structure.

In order to establish a close walk benefits it is necessary to satisfy the following three conditions:

- **Provide condition** - Actors must provide task benefits. For each actor a_j, there is at least another actor a_k to which a_j provides task benefits.

- **Receive condition** – Actors have to receive task benefits. For each actor a_k there is at least another actor a_j from which a_k receives a task benefit.

- **Identity condition** – Actor $a_k \neq a_j$.

However, due to the capacity of influence that each actor may have inside the collaborative network, it is possible to identify three distinct types[5] of close walk benefits networks:

- Close walk benefits of type "*xor*",
- Close walk benefits of type "*and*"

Fig. 12 shows two examples of close walk benefits of type "*xor*" with distinct levels of impacts. For instance, in Fig.12A) it is shown a kind of structure, where the impacts are null for the decision-maker. In this case, actor a_i receives a task

---

[5] Close walk benefits of type "*or*" will not be analyzed because this case is included in the previous ones.

benefits from actor a_l independently of to whom it provides a benefit, either a_j or a_k. In Fig 12 B), on the other hand, the decision that actor a_i makes in relation to whom it provides a task benefits has impact in its received benefits. As illustrated, if the decision-maker, actor a_i, performs an action that benefits actor a_j then it will receive benefits from actor a_v, otherwise it will receive benefits from actor a_m as a result of having helped actor a_k.

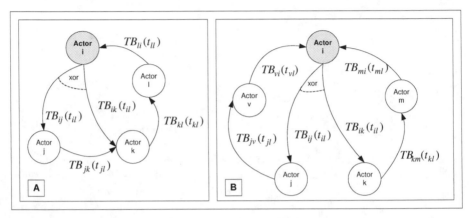

Figure 12 – Close walk benefits of type *"xor"*

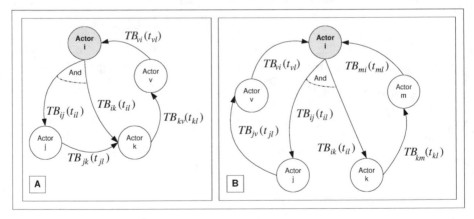

Figure 13 – Close walk benefits of type *"and"*

In relation to close walk benefits of type *"and"*, Fig. 13 A) shows an example of unbalanced structure in terms of nodal degree. In this case, actor a_i receives only one contribution from actor a_v, although it performs an action that benefits two distinct actors a_j and a_k. On the other hand, Fig 13 B) shows an example of balanced structure. Now, there is a balance for actor a_i in terms of the number of actors that were helped by him and benefits received from distinct actors. Assuming that the values of contributions are identical, from the perspective of actor a_i this case might be probably more advantageous than the previous one. However, it shall be noted that this is just a simplistic analysis based on nodal degree analysis. In fact, the balance should consider the weights associated to each arc of the benefits network.

The combination of quantified performance indicators with a graphical visualization based on concepts of social network analysis contributes to the development of a model that allows a better understanding of the evolution of the collaboration processes as well as the performance of individual network members. The next step discusses the potential applicability of the suggested approach.

Step 4 - Modelling the evolution of collaboration based on benefits analysis
In the context of a VBE, the definition of a collaboration benefits model and the corresponding set of indicators can be a useful instrument for the VBE manager, VO broker, and VBE member.

Let us suppose that a record of the past cooperation processes (performance catalogue), represented as collaboration benefits graphs is kept at the VBE management level. Using simple calculations, as illustrated in previous sections, and some simple statistics / data mining (performance and link analysis), it is possible to extract several macro and micro indicators regarding the performance of the VBE and its members as a collaborative network. These indicators can be determined for a particular collaboration process (a particular VO occurrence) or over a period of time (average values) and can be used in decision-making processes, such as the planning of a new VO.

In order to illustrate the applicability of this model let us consider the following experiment based on a VBE of small and medium enterprises (input data based on Swiss Microtech network). Fig. 14 shows the turnover matrix in K€ for 2005 regarding collaborative actions.

Benefits contributions FROM partner TO	1	2	3	4	5	6	7	TOTAL
1	0	5	0	0	22	0	0	27
2	0	0	0	0	126	0	4	130
3	0	0	0	3	96	6	3	108
4	0	0	9	0	26	0	63	98
5	0	0	0	0	0	0	0	0
6	0	0	0	0	16	0	0	16
7	2	4	0	55	0	0	0	61
TOTAL	2	9	9	58	286	6	70	440

Figure 14 – Example of benefits matrix regarding collaborative actions.

Based on these benefits data, the figures below (using the UCINET tool, see (Borgatti, Everett, and Freeman, 2002)) show some examples of indicators for this VBE.

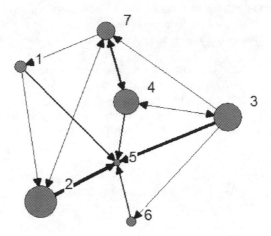

Figure 15 - Social contribution benefits

The nodes' size in Fig. 15 represents the contribution value (i.e. what an actor contributed to others) and the link's width represents the value of the benefit supplied. Hence, the major contributors are enterprise 2, 3 and 4 and if we look for links between enterprises we can easily identify, for instance, a strong exchange of benefits from enterprise 2 to 5.

At the same time, we can also analyze the impact of the enterprise's position in the network based on the concept of **prominent** enterprise. Since, the prominence of an enterprise can be viewed as the capacity of involvement in collaborative process, in this case we are not particularly concerned with whether this prominence is due to the received or supplied benefits, but rather in analyzing how the enterprise is or is not involved in collaborative processes. As the focus on involvement leads us to consider no directional relations in the network, we will assume in this analysis there is no distinction between received and supplied benefits and the **centrality degree** of each enterprise may be used as indicator.

The determination, for each enterprise, of the centrality degree index can be a "soft indicator" for understanding the differences among enterprises in terms of opportunities and constrains they have as a result of their "position". Those enterprises that have high centrality index might have, in the future, more opportunities to participate in collaborative processes than those who have a low centrality index. As shown in Fig. 16, departing from collaborative participation data, it is possible to determine the centrality degree for the set of enterprises members of this VBE.

Analyzing this chart, the variance across the enterprises in terms of the centrality degree may be a basis for differentiation and even stratification in terms of enterprise relevance for the sustainability of this network. For instance, we can conclude the enterprise 7 has a strong involvement in collaborative processes followed by enterprises 3, 4, and 5. On the other hand, supposing that enterprise 6 leaves the network its absence probably will not be significantly felt. However, we need to be careful with these conclusions as these enterprises, although having a small prominence in terms of centrality, might contribute with some particular skill that is vital for some products / services.

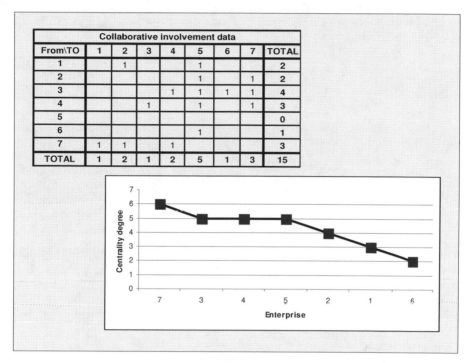

Collaborative involvement data								
From\TO	1	2	3	4	5	6	7	TOTAL
1		1			1			2
2					1		1	2
3				1	1	1	1	4
4			1		1		1	3
5								0
6					1			1
7	1	1		1				3
TOTAL	1	2	1	2	5	1	3	15

Figure 16 – Example of centrality degree

On the other hand, in a VO breeding environment (VBE) context, the reciprocity index can be used as a mechanism to promote a collaborative behavior in a sustainable way (Abreu, Camarinha-Matos, 2008).

When $RI_j < 0$, the actor a_j may be seen, by its partners, as having a potentially "selfish" behavior in the period of time under analysis, in the sense that it received more benefits than it contributed. If this balance remains negative in the long term, the actor would most likely be considered selfish and probably not an appreciated partner. On the other hand, when $RI_j > 0$, the actor a_j might be seen, by its partners, as having a potentially "altruistic" behavior and it would be considered altruist if it holds this behavior in the long term.

In order to illustrate the basis of this mechanism, let us consider the following scenario. Suppose that actor a_j performs a task that benefits actor a_i. From the perspective of actor a_j, this action is perceived as an investment (contributed benefit (CB)) in actor a_i. If the two actors share the same value system then they will have the same perception of the generated benefit value. Based on this premise, actor a_i will value the received benefits (RB) (its satisfaction) to the same amount (RB=CB). As result of actor's a_i satisfaction, actor a_i recognizes a "debt of gratitude" to actor a_j (a kind of "social debit"), and actor a_j gets a "credit" from actor a_i. As both actors have the same perception of the benefit value the total sum of benefit variations is null for a full cycle (Fig. 17).

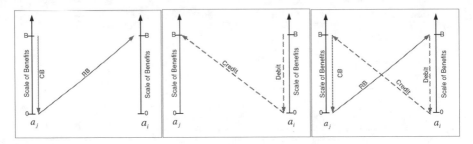

Figure 17 – Contribution of actor a_j to actor a_i

Later on, let us suppose actor a_j needs something to be done by others. As actor a_j has a social credit from a past exchange it can now expect, from the reciprocity principle, to get some service from actor a_i (direct reciprocity) or from any other actor member of VBE (indirect reciprocity). The assumption here is that sharing a common understanding of the benefits leads the two actors to perceive the value of a benefit in the same way. In this context the principle of reciprocity can be a good general governance rule for promoting collaboration.

Applying the reciprocity index, the graph in Fig. 18 A) shows the positive Reciprocity Index (social credits), i.e. the balance between the sum of benefits contributed by an actor to all its partners and the sum of benefits received by an actor as a result of the performance of all actors involved in the collaborative process. According to this example, enterprises 2, 3 and 4 exhibit an altruistic behaviour.

On the other hand, Fig. 18 B) shows the negative Reciprocity Index (social debits). Here, enterprise 5, exhibits a potentially "selfish" behaviour in the sense that it received much more benefits than it contributed.

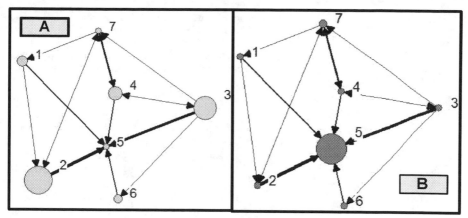

Figure 18 - Social credits and debits

4. CONCLUSIONS

The identification and understanding of collaboration benefits is a key pre-condition for the wide adoption of the collaborative networks paradigm. This understanding is also the starting point for the establishment of proper performance indicators to be used in decision making processes.

Furthermore, the use of common indicators and graphical tools that allow the visualization of these indicators of collaboration for all actors at the same time could be a good approach to increase the transparency in the network. However, it might also have a negative effect if the set of indicators is not properly defined and a good set of indicators is not introduced in the governance principles of the VBE.

The main difficulty is naturally the identification and evaluation/assessment of the benefits corresponding to each collaborative task/process. To collect and record those values without being intrusive in the network members' "life" requires further research. The development of a full practical framework for performance measurement and benefits analysis in collaborative networks also requires further work.

Some preliminary steps in this direction inspired by combination of soft and crisp modeling approaches were presented. Initial results illustrate the applicability of the suggested methods.

Acknowledgments – This work as funded in part by the European Commission through the ECOLEAD project. The authors also thank their project partners Michel Pouly and Francis Monnier for the provision of some example data.

5 REFERENCES

1. Abreu, A., Camarinha-Matos, L. M. - On the role of value systems to promote the sustainability of collaborative environments. International Journal of Production Research, Vol. 46, No. 5, 1 March 2008, 1207–1229.

2. Abreu, A., Camarinha-Matos , L. M. - On the role of value systems and reciprocity in collaborative environments, in Proceeding of PRO-VE 2006 - Network-centric collaboration and supporting frameworks, Springer, ISBN 0-387-38266-6, pp.273-284, Helsinki, Finland, 2006.

3. Alfaro Saiz, J.; Rodriguez, R.; Ortiz, A. – A performance measurement system for virtual and extended enterprises, in Proceedings of PRO-VE 2005 – Collaborative Networks and their Breeding Environments, Springer, pp. 285-292, Valencia, Spain, 2005.

4. Borgatti, S.P., Everett, M.G. and Freeman, L.C. - Ucinet for Windows: Software for Social Network Analysis. Harvard, MA: Analytic Technologies.

5. Brewer, P. C.; Speh. T. W. – Using the balanced scorecard to measure supply chain performance, Journal of Business Logistics, Vol. 21, N° 1, 2000, pp 75-94.

6. Camarinha Matos, L. M., Abreu, A. - Performance indicators for collaborative networks based on collaboration benefits. Journal of *Production Planning & Control*, Volume 18, Issue 7, October 2007 pages 592 – 609.

7. Camarinha-Matos, L. M.; Abreu, A. - A contribution to understand collaboration benefits, in Proceedings of BASYS'04 - Emerging Solutions for Future Manufacturing Systems, Springer, ISBN 0-387-22828-4, IFIP Vol. 159, pp. 287-298, 2004.

8. Camarinha-Matos, L. M.; Abreu, A. - Performance indicators based on collaboration benefits, in Proceedings of PRO-VE'05 – Collaborative Networks and their Breeding Environments, Springer, pp. 273-282, Valencia, Spain, 26-28 Sept 2005.

9. Camarinha-Matos, L. M.; Afsarmanesh, H. (Ed.s) - Collaborative Networked Organizations – A research agenda for emerging business models, Kluwer Academic Publishers, 2004.

10. Myerson, R. B. - Game Theory Analysis of Conflict, Harvard University Press, 1997.

11. Seifert, Marcus; Eschenbaecher, Jens - Predictive performance measurement in virtual organisations - Emerging solutions for future manufacturing systems, Springer, ISBN 0-387-22828-4, 2004.

12. Wasserman, S.; K. Faust. - *Social Network Analysis - Methods and Applications*. Cambridge University press, 1994.

13. Williamson, O. E. - The Economic Institutions of Capitalism: Firms, Markets, Relational Contracting, New York: Free Press, 1985.

4.6
An approach in value systems modeling

P. Macedo, L. M. Camarinha-Matos

Although Value Systems play an important role in collaborative networks, the concept is still ill defined. This chapter contributes to a formal model and analysis of value systems using various modeling formalisms. Examples of applicability of these models are also given.

1. INTRODUCTION

Value Systems play an important role in Collaborative Networks (CNs) as they determine or strongly influence the behavior of the network members.

Value Systems have been studied in distinct scientific areas, such as economy sociology, psychology and knowledge management. Each area developed a different concept of Value System, based on distinct assumptions about value. Social sciences consider a Value System as the ordering and prioritization of the ethical and ideological values that an individual or society holds, while economical sciences defend that a Value System describes the activity links among the firm and its suppliers, other businesses within the firm's corporate family, distribution channels and the firm's end-user customers (Porter,1985).

Goguen and Linde have developed, since 1978 several works on studies about value and Value System in organizations (Goguen,1994, Goguen,1997, Goguen,2004). They proposed a method for using discourse analysis to determine a Value System for an organization from a collection of stories told by members of the organization among themselves on informal occasions. Another contribution to the study of Value Systems comes from the Distributed Artificial Intelligence discipline, which has developed some Value Systems theories using agents (Filipe,2003) (Antunes,2000) (Rodrigues,2003). During the last years some works on Value Systems in networked environments have been developed by two groups of researchers, Katzy (Katzy,1998) and Gordijn, Tan, Kartseva (Gordijn,2000, Tan,2004), (Kartseva,2004).

In Organizational Sociology Alle, Hall and Hebel (Alle,2000b, Hall,1995, Hebel,1998) studied the corporate-identity in organizations. These studies show how relevant it is to specify the corporate-identity of an organization in order to manage organizations. In the last decade, several studies inside the knowledge management discipline led to the development of frameworks to classify the value's elements inside an organization according to their nature. Sullivan (Sullivan,2000), and Alle (Alle, 2000) demonstrated the importance of managing intangible issues for the sustainability of the organization. The Virtual organization's (VO) and VO Breeding Environment's (VBE) decision-making process is naturally influenced both by the common value system of the network and the individual value systems of each partner. Therefore the identification and characterization of these value systems is an important issue when attempting to improve collaborative processes. As partners have different value systems, they might have different perceptions of the outcomes of the collaboration processes, which might lead to non-collaborative behavior and inter-organizational conflicts. Therefore, the development of a common value system is a significant element for the sustainability of collaboration.

The aspects that must be considered for the specification and analysis of Value Systems in VBEs and VOs include different perspectives, so they can hardly be comprehensively covered by a single model or modeling approach. For that reason, the development of a hybrid approach, where some entities of the model are represented using crisp techniques and others using soft computing ones seems to be an interesting possibility worth exploring. This chapter illustrates such approach.

2. VALUE SYSTEM BASE CONCEPTS

The terms *Value* can have two different meanings: *Value* as referring to the qualities, attributes or characteristics that an individual or group believe as being worthwhile or desirable, and *Value* as referring to *the relative worth, utility or importance of something*.

In order to better understand the value concept and how it can be applied in the Value System definition, the concepts of object of evaluation, evaluator, and evaluation have to be introduced.

Let us consider the following statement: this bike costs 100 Euros. The bike has a value assigned to it, but the bike is not the value itself; bike is the object of evaluation. The value of the bike is 100 euros that is the result of the process of calculating the amount of money that the bike costs. Who performs this calculation is the evaluator. An object of evaluation (something) can be a resource, a service, a behavior, or a belief. The evaluator is the entity that performs the evaluation. This entity can be an individual person, a social group (organization, government, Virtual Organization), or an instrument.

The term value is often used to designate the object of evaluation in spite of the value itself. When it is stated: *My values are safe on the bank*, this mean that the objects, which have a specific value assigned to them, are safe in the bank.

The term *"evaluate"* means to judge, measure or calculate the quality, importance or amount of something. Judgment, measurement and calculation are made essentially through two basics forms:

- In an objective way, applying rules and formulas to the data that characterize the object of evaluation.
- In a subjective way, using mental perception about the importance, the quality or the quantity of something.

In others terms, the value of something depends on the function used to evaluate it. This function can be:

- A **numeric function,** that assigns a number to an object. This number represents the *value* of the object in one dimension. This numeric function can implement the calculation formula of an indicator (like annual profit, market average price), an estimation method, or a measurement function of an instrument. The process of measuring involves estimating the ratio of the magnitude of a quantity to the magnitude of a unit of the same type (e.g. length, time, mass, etc.). This measurement is the result of such a process, expressed as the product of a real number and a unit, where the real number is the estimated ratio.

- A **qualitative function** that represents a mental process or a qualitative judgment. This function assigns a qualitative *value* to something.

The example introduced about the value of a bike is, to a certain extent, a simplification of the reality. Often, when we make an evaluation, we are evaluating not the overall object but a specific characteristic of the object. Products, services and behaviors have several characteristics and each characteristic can be evaluated independently.

In order to specify the evaluation of a particular characteristic, the expression evaluation dimension is used. This term seems to embrace the second meaning for the term "value". However the term "value" is more restrictive than evaluation dimension, since it implicitly presumes that values are not just related to simple characteristics but to characteristics that the evaluator believes that are worthwhile and desirable. The term "core-values" of an organization is used to designate the set of evaluation dimensions that are of significant importance to those inside the organization and thus guide their actions.

The different characteristics of an object may have different degrees of importance to the actor that performs the evaluation (Note: Sociologists usually use the term priority to denominate the concept of degree of importance of a dimension, Rokeach's (Rokeach,1973) work demonstrates the importance of the priorities in the valuing process). This idea is represented by associating to each evaluation dimension a weight that represents its degree of importance.

Depending on the objective of the evaluation, a different set of dimensions of evaluation can be considered to evaluate an object, as it is illustrated in Fig. 1. The set of dimensions of evaluation selected to evaluate an object will be denominated as *"evaluation perspective"*. Examples of possible perspectives:

- The **business perspective**, where a set of characteristics related to the business are considered.
- The **social perspective**, where a set of characteristics related to social, moral and cultural aspects are considered.
- The **collaboration perspective,** where a set of characteristics such as: trustiness, reliability, agility are considered.

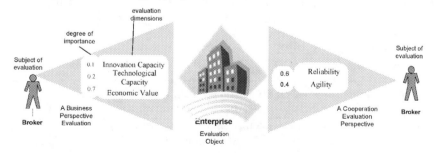

Figure 1- Evaluation Concepts

From the concepts introduced above of value, evaluation and evaluation dimension, some components for the Value System are identified:
- o Object of Evaluations
- o Evaluation Functions
- o Evaluation Dimensions
- o Evaluation Perspectives.

These elements can be subdivided in two sub-groups:
1. Entities that can be evaluated: Object of evaluations.
2. Evaluation mechanism: Functions, Dimension and Perspectives.

According to this, a Value System is composed of a set of valuable things for an organization and a set of functions used for its evaluation on different perspectives, where each perspective is composed of a weighted set of evaluation dimensions.

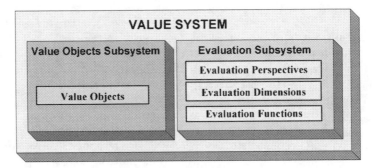

Figure 2 - Value System Model.

3. ADOPTED METHODOLOGY AND MODELING TECHNIQUES

In this chapter three modeling approaches are considered to represent and analyze value systems in collaborative environments (see Figure 3): Unified Modeling Language (UML) models, algebraic models and, causal models.

UML is a standard modeling language used fundamentally in software engineering for software modeling and organizational engineering for modeling organizations and business process. UML diagrams have the advantage of visual/graphics orientation which is easy to adopt/understand and promote the communication between interested parties without the need of in depth technical skills. For these reasons this modeling language was chosen in order to provide an holistic view of Value System and to promote a shared understanding of the main components of the Value System.

However the consistency of the model across all its diagrams and the correctness achieved when transposing from modeling to design is still worth some attention because UML provides only a semi formal approach without sound semantics. So, a formal specification using the algebraic theory can provide a basis for the design of inter-organizational information systems that better support collaborative networked organizations. Moreover formal conceptual models allow for a sounder analysis of value objects and evaluation mechanisms.

In a collaborative network there is the involvement of different types of stakeholders, representing different interests and concerns, raising the risk of misunderstandings. For this reason, it is also important to formalize the *value system* concept in order to promote a shared understanding.

Causal modeling techniques have naturally grown due to a need for a sketching technique supporting and facilitating reasoning about cause and effect. A causal model builds upon a binary relationship, called an *influence relationship*, between two entities that represent named quantitative or qualitative value or value set. Whereby changes in the influencing entity are conveyed as changes in the influenced entity (Greenland,2002). Causal models have been applied inside organizations to specify conceptual maps. Banket and Scavarda (Banket,2007), (Scavarda,2006) had developed some methodologies to construct conceptual maps in a collaborative way. This technique seems to be a good tool to represent and analyze the influence relationship among core-values.

The development of a common Value System in a CN context is an important step to support the sustainability of a collaborative behavior over time (Abreu,2006). Incompatible Value Systems typically lead to conflicts and reduction of the collaboration spirit. In order to overcome this problem, mechanisms to reason about the compatibility among Value Systems should be developed. The first step is to specify forms of comparison or identification of relationships between Value Systems of different members and between a member and the network itself. In collaborative processes, the type of relationships between values can be seen as the seed and ingredient of a successful co-working. Considering the premises that a member's behavior depends on:

- the way its main values are related, and/or
- potential partners having strategic values that makes the member consider as advantageous collaborating with them (i.e. values that provide positive impact on its own values).

Under this assumption the alignment can be analyzed in terms of the structural similarity or impact inter-relationships between value systems. For this purpose causal models can be used to model relationships among values.

To address the interactions among the different models for analysis of value systems in a VBE context, the modeling experiment here described includes the following main steps:

1. Define the value system of each organization using a UML Model.
2. Formalize the value system of each organization, that comprises the *core values* and respective degrees of importance, as identified in step1, using algebraic models.
3. Define the individual *core values* Influence Map using a Causal Modeling approach.
4. Analyze the alignment between two Value Systems, using the Value Influence Maps defined in step 3.

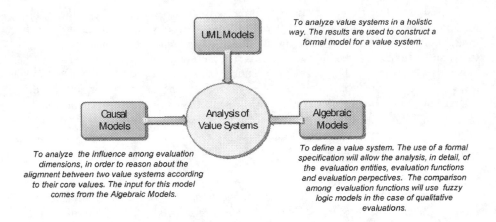

Figure 3- Types of models applied in the experiment.

4. VALUE SYSTEM MODELING

4.1 Algebraic specification of Value System

The Value System definition and analysis deal with several main concepts that were previously introduced (Camarinha-Matos, Macedo, 2007). In order to avoid ambiguity an algebraic specification is proposed for each concept in Table 1.

Table 1-Value System concepts definition

Concept	Short Description	Algebraic expression
Object of evaluation	The entity x that is evaluated	$x \in S$ where: S is the set of things that can be evaluated. *if x belongs to S then x is an object of evaluation.*
Evaluator (actor)	The entity (actor) that performs the evaluation	$a \in A$ A is the set of actors.
Evaluation function	The function used to evaluate an object in order to reason about its *value*.	$f \in F : F = NF \cup QF$ Where NF is the set of numeric functions, and QF the set of qualitative functions
Numeric function	Function assigns a quantitative *value* to something.	*without unit* $f : S_f \rightarrow \Re$ where $S_f \subset S$ *with unit* $f : S_f \rightarrow \Re \times U$ *where* U is the set of unit of measurements.
Qualitative functions	Function that assigns a qualitative value to something.	$f : S_f \rightarrow Y$ *where* $S_f \subset S$ and $Y = \{y1, y2..yn\}$: y_i is a qualitative ordinal

Value	The result of the evaluation of an object by the evaluator	Quantitative values: without unit $$y = f(x) : x \in S_f \wedge f \in NF \wedge y \in \Re$$ with unit $$y.u = f(x) : x \in S_f \wedge f \in NF \wedge y \in \Re$$ Qualitative values: $$y = f(x) : x \in S_f \wedge f \in QF \wedge y \in Y$$ $$Y = \{y1, y2..yn\}$$
Evaluation dimension	Characteristic of an object that is evaluated.	$D = \{d_1, d_2, ...d_n\}$ is the set of evaluation dimensions. The operator Φ express the statement: *the function f permits to evaluate the dimension d.* $f_i \Phi d_i$, f_i evaluates the dimension d_i of an object where $d_i \in D \wedge f_i \in F$ $$\forall d_i \in D \; \exists f \in F : f_i \Phi d_i$$
Degree of importance	Level of importance of an evaluation dimension for a given evaluator.	*If* wv represents the weights -vector and dv$_x$ expresses the set of dimensions of an object that is evaluated, where: $$dv_x = [d_1, d_2, ...d_n] : d_i \in D.$$ $$wv = [w_1, ...w_n] : w_i \in [0..1] \wedge \sum_{i=0}^{n} w_i = 1$$ so, $wv[i]$ is the degree of importance of $dv_x[i]$
Evaluation perspective	A selected subset of evaluation dimensions and the corresponding weights chosen to evaluate an object from a given point of view	$ep_x = <dv_x, wv>$ where $x \in S$ and P is the set of perspectives. For each *dimensions-vector* an *evaluation-vector* can be specified as: $$fv_d = [f_1, f_2, ...f_n] : f_i \in F \text{ where}$$ $$i \in [1..n] \wedge fv_d[i] \Phi dv_x[i]$$ In order to represent the fact that an object can *be evaluated through different* perspectives, the operator Ξ is defined as: $x \Xi ep$, meaning **x** is evaluated through the perspective ep, where $x \in S \wedge ep \in P$
Value Object Subsystem	Value objects subsystem (OS) is a system composed of the objects that can be evaluated	OS = <S, RS> where: • S is the set a valuable things ; • *RS is the set of relationships among the elements of S, which can be essentially of two types: composition and specialization.*

Evaluation Subsystem	A system composed of all elements that represent "mechanisms" of evaluation (functions, dimensions and perspectives)	$ES=<EF, RE>$ where: EF represents all the elements that belong to the evaluation subsystem and is defined as a triple: $EF=<F,D,P>$ where o F is the set of evaluation functions; o D is the set of evaluation dimensions o P is the set of evaluation perspectives. RE is the set of relationships among the elements of EF. These relationships can be categorized as: o Composition-relation – One function is defined by aggregation of two or more functions. o Evaluates-relation – The relation is specified by the operator Φ, that specifies that a function can be used to evaluate a specific dimension. o Priority-relation – The relation that specifies the degree of importance of a characteristic in an evaluation perspective.
Value System	A Value System is composed of a set of valuable things for an organization and a set of functions used for its evaluation on different perspectives, where each perspective is composed of a weighted set of dimensions of evaluation	$VS=<EVS, RVS>$ where $EVS=<OS,ES>$ is the aggregation of the two subsystems that compose the value system. RVS - represents the set of relationships between the two sub-systems. These two subsystems are related by two categories of relationships. • Value-relation – What relates a function and an object is the value resulting from evaluating the object using that function. • Perspective-relation - The relation that is defined by the operator Ξ, that specifies that an object is evaluated through a given evaluation perspective.

4.2 UML specification of Value System conceptual Model

The aim of representing the Value System Conceptual Model using a UML class diagram (see Figure 4) is to give an holistic view of the concepts that have been introduced previously. In order to understand the relationships among entities modeled on this diagram and the formal algebraic specification done above a brief explanation is needed:

- The notion of algebraic set is represented in UML class Diagram as class.
- The relations defined among elements of the same set or of distinct sets are implemented in this diagram as class-associations and as UML-relations: associations, compositions and specializations.

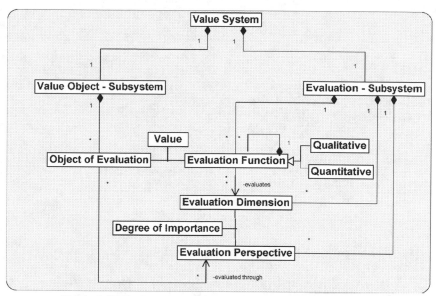

Figure 4- UML Class Diagram of the Value System conceptual model

4.3 Value Influence Map Specification

Core-Values are the main characteristic of the organization that are of significant importance to those inside the organization and that guide their actions. The set of Core-values that characterize an organization should be specified in their Value System. The structural aspects of core-values can be specified through an evaluation perspective, but for decision-making purposes, often managers may need to also study the dynamic aspects of Value Systems. In order to show how the core-values influence each other, and how they are influenced by internal and external factors a causal modeling approach can be applied. So, the specification of a Value Influence Map is proposed, where each node of the graph is a core-value or an influence factor and each link represents the influence relationship between two core-values.

In Table 2 the used notation is summarized and an example is modeled in Figure 5.

Table 2-Graphical representation of influence-relationships

Graphical representation	Description
(X) ⟶ (Y)	If the level of the core-value X (evaluation dimension) increases, the level of the core-value Y will increase too. Example: If the Quality level increases, Customer satisfaction will increase too.
factor1 ⟶ (Y)	If the level of factor1 increases, the level of the core-value Y will increase too. Examples: If sales increase, profit will increase. If suppliers flexibility increases, network flexibility will

	increase too.

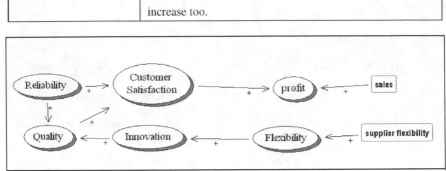

Figure 5 - Example of a Value Influence Map

5 - MODELING EXAMPLES AND RESULTS

As an illustrative example, let us consider the scenario shown in Figure 6. This example does not intend to specify which characteristics a network should satisfy. It only serves to illustrate how the set of core-values can be specified and analyzed using several modeling approaches.

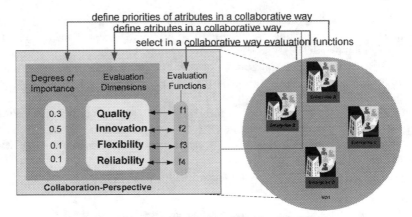

Figure 6- Core-values definition in a CN

The definition of the set of evaluation dimensions that are important to the members of the collaborative network and that guide their actions should be specified during the CN's initial setup. Imagine that a CN defines that the most relevant attributes for collaboration inside the network are: *quality, reliability, flexibility, innovation*. Probably these four attributes do not have the same degree of importance. Thus the CN should specify the degree of importance of each attribute and all members of the CN should be aware that all decisions and behaviours would be "judged" in accordance to this evaluation perspective.

For each evaluation dimension (each attribute) an evaluation function should be defined in a collaborative way (in the case of non-hierarchical networks) and accepted by all. The definition of methods to evaluate *innovation*, *quality*, *reliability* and *flexibility* are not standard, and several studies proceed in these areas.

In the considered example the following elements are considered:
- **Evaluations Objects**: Network, Network Members
- **Evaluation Dimension**: quality, innovation, flexibility, reliability are the characteristics to be evaluated. These characteristics are considered core-values .
- **Evaluation Perspective**: Collaboration perspective, where a set of characteristics related to collaboration relationships, such as: quality, reliability, flexibility and innovation are considered. To each characteristic a relative degree of importance is associated. For instance, quality has a relative degree of importance of 0.2.
- **Evaluation Functions** – f1, f2, f3, and f4 are defined as functions that assign a value to the object of evaluation. These functions can be quantitative or qualitative functions. The selection of the evaluation functions (by the CN manager) is an important issue, but not discussed in this work.

Step1- *Build the UML model in order to provide a holist view to all the stakeholders of the network.*

The diagram of Figure 7 shows the UML object diagram of the Collaboration-perspective definition. This object diagram is an instantiation of the UML Class diagram presented in Figure 4, for the example describe above.

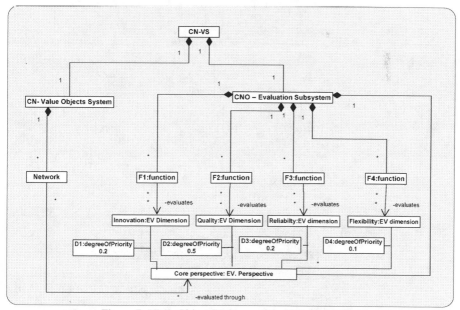

Figure 7- UML Object Diagram of the CN - Value System

The CN Value System is composed of two subsystems: the CN Value Objects Subsystem and the CN Evaluation Subsystem. The CN Evaluation Subsystem represents the Collaboration Perspective, which it is composed of a set of Evaluation Dimensions and each of them has a function to evaluate the Evaluation Dimension. Each Evaluation Dimension is related to the Collaboration Perspective through the degree of importance. For instance, for the collaborative perspective, the innovation has a degree of importance of 0.2.

Step 2 -*Define the Value System using an algebraic modeling approach.*

The Value System conceptual model was used to formally specify the collaborative evaluation perspective of our scenario.

The *value system* of a CN1 (VS_{CN1}) is defined as:

- $VS_{CN1} =< EVS_{CN1}, RVS_{CN1} >$ where $EVS_{CN1} =< OS_{CN1}, ES_{CN1} >$
    - $OS_{CN1}= <S_{CN1}, RS_{CN1}>$ where:
        - $\{CN1, E1, E2, E3, E4\} \subset S_{CN1}$ *where E_x are the members of CN1.*

            $\{mbsh1, mbsh2, mbsh3, mbsh4\} \subset RS_{CN1}$

            $mbsh_{px}$ = Enterprise$_x$ *belongs_to* $CN_{1.}$ _ Composition relation that defines the relationship between an enterprise and the network.

    - $ES_{CNO1} = <EF_{CN1}, RE_{CN1} >$
        - $EF_{CN1=}<D_{CN1}, P_{CN1}, F_{CN1}>$
        - D_{CN} _ Set of evaluation dimensions of CN1
        - P_{CN} _ Set of evaluation perspectives of CN1
        - F_{CN} _ Set of evaluation functions used to make evaluations inside CN1
        - $\{QUALITY, INNOVATION, FLEXIBILITY, RELIBILITY\} \subset D_{CN1}$
        - Collaboration perspective is defined as :

            $ep_{collaboration} =< dv, wv >\in P_{CNO1}$ where:

            $dv=[$ QUALITY, INNOVATION, FLEXIBILITY, RELIABILITY$]$ and (e.g.) $wv=[0.3, 0.5,\ 0.1, 0.1]$.

        - $\{f_1, f_2, f_3, f_4\} \subset F_{CN1}$ and $fv=[f_1, f_2, f_3, f_4]$ is a functions' vector that contains the evaluation functions selected to evaluate the four evaluation dimensions defined in *dv*.

            For our example, the following functions are considered:

            $f_1 : S_{x1} \rightarrow \{high, medium, low\}$ $f_1=$ *level of quality, attributed by external auditing.*

            $f_2 : S_{x1} \rightarrow R_o$ $f_2=$ *Average of patents per year , in the last five years.*

            $f_3 : S_{x1} \rightarrow \Re_0$ $f_3=average\ period\ of\ time\ to\ develop\ or\ change\ a\ logistic\ process\ (unit\ of\ measurement:\ days)$

$$f_4 : S_{x1} \to \Re_0 \quad f_4= \textit{percentage of time without process faults.}$$

- RE_{CN1} is composed of the relations among evaluation functions and evaluation dimensions, and the relations among evaluation dimensions and evaluation perspectives.

$RE_{CN1} =$

$\{ f_1 \phi QUALITY, f_2 \phi INNOVATION, f_3 \phi FLEXIBILITY, f_4 \phi RELIBILITY \} \cup$
$\{ ((QUALITY, 0.3) \in ep_{colaboration}), ((INNOVATION, 0.5) \in ep_{colaboration}),$
$((FLEXIBILITY, 0.1) \in ep_{colaboration}), ((RELIBILITY, 0.1) \in ep_{colaboration}))) \}$

- RVS_{CN1} is composed of the relations among the two subsystems.

$$\{ (CN_1 \, \Xi \, ep_{collaboration}) \} \subset RVS_{CN1} .$$

This relation specifies that the CN_1 is evaluated through the evaluation perspective $ep_{collaboration}$.

The use of the collaboration perspective to evaluate the network will generate a value for each evaluation dimension (see Figure 8). This value represents the relative worth of this characteristic of the network.

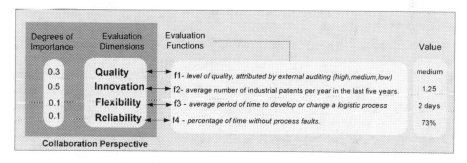

Figure 8 -Evaluation of the network using the collaboration perspective.

Step 3 - *Define the values influence map using causal diagrams.*

For decision-making purposes, often managers also need to study the dynamic aspects of a value system. In order to show how the core -values influence each other, and how they are influenced by internal and external factors, a Values Influence Map was built. For this purpose the Decision Explorer software was used.

The influence relations among core-values are specified by the CN managers during the CN start-up process. The core-values belonging to the collaboration perspective are influenced by other network's core-values. On the considered example the network core-values selected are listed o the next table. The general Values Influence Map is presented in the Figure 9.

Table 3- Example of Core-Values of the network.

Network Core-Values
Employee satisfaction.
Innovation
Quality

| Customer satisfaction |
| Power |
| Profit |
| Reliability |
| Flexibility |

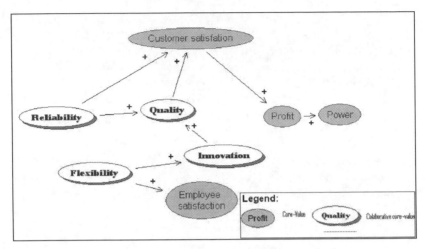

Figure 9- Core-Values influence map

According to this view, we can easily visualize how collaborative core value influence the others core values. In the example shown in Figure 9, we can notice that Quality and Reliability influence positively the level of Customer's Satisfaction and Employee's satisfaction level is positively influenced by the Flexibility level.

The application of causal diagram analysis techniques (Eden,1992) can provide a deeper analysis. In Table 4 the results obtained for the Values Influence map of Figure 9 are presented.

Table 4- Causal Map Analysis.

Analysis technique	Result	Description
Identification of headers	Employee satisfaction Power	*End core-values*. Core-values that do not influence others. Goal core-values
Identification of tails	Reliability Flexibility	Core-values that just influence other values and that are not influence by any.
Identification of central concepts	Customer satisfaction Quality	Core-values that have a great relevance to the network in the way they influence and are influenced by several core-values.
Identification of co-tails	Reliability Flexibility	These core-values influence more than one core-value. The investment on the increase of one such core-value will influence positively several other core-values

Calculate potent concepts	Flexibility	This core-value is the one that influence indirectly more *end core-values*. So if the level of this core-value changes this will imply that several branches of the map will change too. (Note: if the level of flexibility value increases all others core-values-levels, except Reliability will increase too)

Values management can also use causal maps in order to analyze how core-values are influenced by external and internal factors. Figure 10 shows an example where internal factors and external factors that influence core-values are represented.

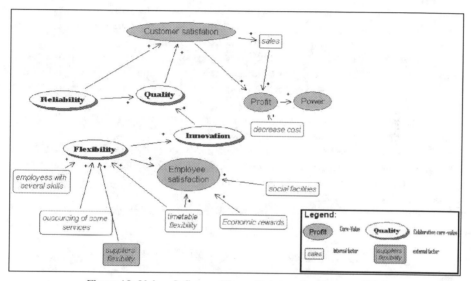

Figure 10- Values Influence Map with internal and external Values

Let us take a partial view of the Values Influence map (see Figure 11) where only the factors that influence the level of Flexibility are shown. From this view, the management staff can easily see what are the external and internal factors that influence the Flexibility level.

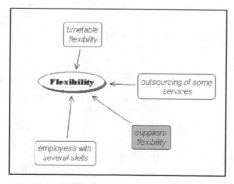

Figure 11- Flexibility Value Influence Map.

Step 4 – *Analysis of the Value System alignment.*

Another important application of the Values Influence Maps is the study of the value systems alignment among network members, or between the network and potential partners. If different members valuate different characteristics this may induce non-collaborative behaviors. If all members define their conceptual map about core-values a comparative analysis could then be performed.

One possible way to perform this analysis is to compute the parameters presented in Table 4 and compare the results achieved for each map. This analysis will provide an easy way to check if a potential partner has the same perceptions about core-values. This procedure can also be applied to network members, but in this case, this should not be applied in order to evaluate members, but rather to promote a shared understanding about values inside the network.

Two types of analysis are presented: the analysis of the similarity between the core-values of the network and potential partner's core-values and the analysis of the influence of the core-values of a potential partner in the core-values of the network.

Case 1. Let us suppose that we want to analyze the similarity between the CN Value System and a potential partner's Value System.

The Influence Value Map of the candidate partner can be specified and a Causal Map analysis can be performed as it was done in step 3 (see table 5). Comparing the results, we can reason about the similarity among Value Systems. This analysis can be performed for all values or for the values belonging to specific perspectives. In this example the analysis is done for the collaboration perspective.

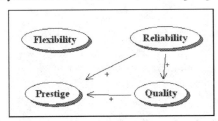

Figure 12- Potential Partner - Values Influence Map for collaborative perspective

Table 5- Analysis of Influence Map for the Collaborative Perspective

Analysis technique	Results for CN – Influence Value Map	Results for Potential Partner-Value Map
Identification of headers	Quality	Prestige
Identification of tails	Reliability	Reliability
Calculation of central concepts	Quality, Innovation	Quality, Prestige, flexibility
Identification of independent cocnepts	-----------	Flexibility
Identification of co-tails	-------------	Reliability

From the analysis of the two Values Influence Maps (see Figure 9, Figure 12 and Table 4) we can conclude that:

- The potential Partner considers Prestige has a relevant value for collaboration and CN does not.
- The potential partner does not consider Innovation has a relevant attribute for collaboration.
- The potential Partner considers Flexibility has an independent Value in terms of collaboration, that is, the level of the flexibility does not change with the change of the level of another collaborative attribute. The CN consider that Flexibility is positively influenced by innovation
- Reliability is a base value. Both the CN and the potential partner consider that the increase of the reliability level will influence positively several other collaborative attributes.
- Both consider that Quality has a great relevance to the network in the way that is a central core-value.

Case 2- Let us suppose that the broker wants to analyze the impact of a new partner in a network in terms of core-values.

The representation of the influences among values allows analyzing how potential partner core-values can influence CN values. The example shown in Figure 13 illustrates four inter-relations of influence between core values of the two Value Systems:

- *Partner-Prestige* influences positively the *CN-Power*. If a prestigious Organization joints a CN then the level of power of the network tends to increase.
- *Partner-reliability* influences positively the *CN-reliability*. If a reliable organization joints a network then the level of reliability of the network tends to increase.
- *Partner-flexibility* influences positively the *CN-flexibility*. If a flexible organization joints a network then the level of flexibility of the network tends to increase.
- *Partner-knowledge* influences positively the *CN-innovation*. If a organization with a high level of knowledge joints a network then this member tends to "transfer" its knowledge to the network and potentiate an increase in innovation level.

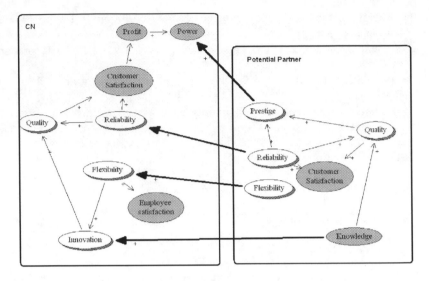

Figure 13- Values Inter-influence Map

Results

In Figure 14 the results of this experiment are summarized, where the points of interconnection between the several approaches are underlined and the outputs provided by each model are presented.

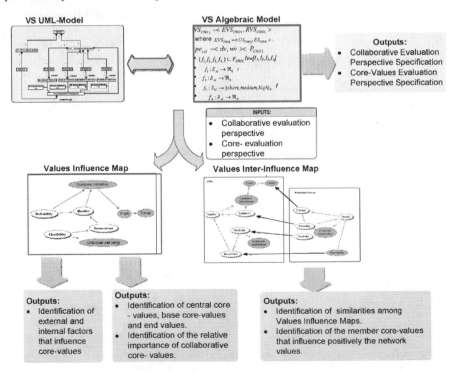

Figure 14 -Summary of the interoperability experiment results

From the Value System's Algebraic Model it is possible to obtain the UML Model and vice-versa because there is a direct relationship between the elements of each model. Each set in the Algebraic Model is represented by a class in the UML model. The UML model will provide a first approach to the modeling process and a holistic view of the components of the value system. On the other hand, the algebraic model gives a detailed view of the objects of evaluation and the mechanism of evaluation.

The Values Influence Map provides the identification of the internal and external factors that have more influence on the variation of the level of each-core value. This model also identifies which are the most central core-values, most end-values and most potent core-values. The core-values specified in that map were previously defined in the UML Model or Algebraic Model.

The Values Influence Map will also provide forms to compare evaluation perspectives between members or between a network and a potential partner. The representation of the influences among values allows the analysis of the impact of a new partner in a network in terms of core-values.

5 CONCLUSIONS

The characterization and understanding of *value systems* is a key condition for improving the sustainability of collaborative networks. The value systems of organizations and networks can neither be represented nor be analyzed using a single modeling approach because no single model can be suitable or comprehensively cover all aspects of value and values among organizations and networks. Thus to properly support the modeling of Value Systems in collaborative environments a combination of a number of models must be applied to cover distinct aspects.

The approach suggested in this chapter proposes the needed interoperation among three sets of specific models that can comprehensively cover all the main aspects of Value Systems in CN. The applicability of the suggested approach was illustrated through the example presented. From the development of this example two additional research challenges can be raised: which methodology to be applied in order to promote a consensus among CN members on the network core-values; and how to manage the CN Value System during CN operation phase.

Acknowledgments – This work as supported in part by the ECOLEAD integrated project funded by the European Commission.

6 REFERENCES

1.Abreu A, Camarinha-Matos LM. On the Role of Value Systems and Reciprocity in Collaborative Environments. In: Spring, ed. IFIP, Volume 224, Network-Centric Collaboration and Suporting Frameworks: Boston Springer, 2006.
2.Alle V. Reconfiguring the Value Network. Journal of Business Strategy 2000a;21:36-39.
3.Alle V. The Value Evolution. Journal of Intellectual Capital 2000b;1:17-32.
4.Antunes L, Coelho H, Faria J. Improving choice mechanisms within the BVG architecture. In: Lesprance CCaY, ed. Agent Theories, Architectures, and Languages - ICMAS 2000; 2000: Springer-Verlag, 2000: 209-304.

5.Banket DK, Shankar R, Faisal MN. Quantification of risk mitigation environment of supply chains using graph theory and matrix methods. European Journal of Industrial Engineering 2007;1.
6.Eden C. The Analysis of Cause Maps. Journal of Managemnet Studies 1992;29.
7.Filipe J. The organisational semeiotics normativa paradigma In: Collaborative Networked Organizations. London: Springer, 2003: 261-272.
8.Goguen J. Requirements Engineering as the Reconciliation of Technical and Social Issues. In: Requirements engineering: social and technical issues, 1994: 162-199.
9.Goguen J. Towards a Social, Ethical Theory of Information. In: Georey Bowker, Les Gasser, LeighStar, Turner W, eds. In Social Science Research, Technical Systems and Cooperative Work: Beyond the Great Divide: Erlbaum, 1997: 27-56.
10.Goguen J. Semiotics, compassion and value-centered design. In, 2004.
11.Gordijn J, J.M. Akkermans, Vliet JCv. Value based requirements creation for electronic commerce applications. In: In Proceedings of the 33rd Hawaii International Conference on System Sciences; 2000; Hawai, 2000.
12.Greenland S, Brumback B. An overview of relations among causal modeling methods. international journal of epidemiology 2002.
13.Hall B. Values Shift: A Guide to Personal and Organizational Transformation: Resource Publications, 1995.
14.Hebel M. Value Systems-A way to Greater Understanding. Systemic Pratice and Action Research 1998;11.
15.Kartseva V, Gordijn J, Akkermans H. A Design Perspective on Networked Business Models: A Study of Distributed Generation in the Power Industry Sector. In: 12th European Conference on Information Systems; 2004, 2004.
16.Katzy B. Value System Redesign. ACM SIGGROUP Bulletin archive, 1998;19: 48-50.
17.Porter M. Competitive Advantage. : New York: The Free Press, 1985.
18.Rodrigues MR, Costa R, Bordini R. A System of Exchange Values to Support Social Interactions in Artifical Societies. In: AAMAS; 2003; Melboune Australia, 2003.
19.Rokeach M. The nature of human values. New York: Free Press. 1973.
20.Scavarda AJ, Bouzdine-Chameeva T, Goldstein SM, Hays JM, Hill AV. A Methodology for Constructing Collective Causal Maps Decision Sciences 2006;37:263-283.
21.Sullivan PH. Value Driven Intellectual Capital: How to Convert Intangible Corporate Assets into Market Value. New York,: John Wiley & Sons, Inc, 2000.
22.Tan Y-H, Thoen W, Gordijn J. Modeling Controls for Dynamic Value Exchange in Virtual Organizations. In: Berlin S, ed. Trust Management, 2004: 236-250.

4.7
Selection of a virtual organization coordinator

A. A. Pereira-Klen, E. R. Klen, L. Loss, J. A. Crispim, J. P. Sousa

Collaborative Networks (CNs) have created new needs from technological, organizational and human viewpoints in terms of models, methodologies, methods and work techniques, as well as in what concerns the involved resources – mainly the human ones. The modeling example presented in this work analyses the process of searching and selecting an individual to act as coordinator in an environment that results from this new business model. The example is also meant to support decision-making - 'what to do' and 'how to do' in order to guide an oriented search for individual competences to achieve an adequate management for a Virtual Organization (VO) that is being created or that has recently been created.

1. INTRODUCTION

The selection of a coordinator is a very important step in the Virtual Organization (VO) life cycle, occurring normally in the Creation phase and, sometimes, in the Evolution phase. The VO coordinator, a role usually performed by an individual from a company in a given Virtual Breeding Environment (VBE), has the assignment to coordinate a VO during its life cycle in order to fulfill the goals set for the collaboration opportunity that triggered the VO (Camarinha-Matos et al., 2005).

A VO takes place in an environment where different organizations and persons collaborate, sometimes relying on quite different cultures, technologies or management styles, in order to achieve a set of common goals. In each single case much of the success of the VO depends on the way in which it is managed. For this reason it is becoming clearer that the role that the VO coordinator (also known as VO manager) plays is not only important but also fundamental for adequately achieving the objectives set for the VO. In fact, during the whole VO life cycle, the VO coordinator is a key element whose specific competences should be carefully taken into account.

Considering that each VO is unique, one can say that the required core competences for both VO members as well as for the VO coordinator are also VO-oriented. Additionally, VO coordinators and their individual competences should significantly contribute to the success of the VO they are involved in. The individual competences (based on 3 dimensions: knowledge, skills and attitude (Durand, 1997 and 1998)) associated with the VO coordinator functional competences will help to achieve the organizational requirements of the VO. The alignment of those competences with the VO requirements or needs will contribute to leveraging the VO results and the performance of individuals. Competences serve to fulfill the needs; and the needs serve to instigate competences (figure 1).

In this sense the modeling example described in this chapter is guided by some organizational governance principles and based on individual competences which are described in section 2. Supporting the modeling example there is a structured procedure for searching and selecting coordinator(s) for a VO based on already existing and available resources in the VO environment. This procedure, described in section 3, is a 3-step process supported by a competence map that serves as an analysis basis for the individual competences. Section 4 presents the modeling techniques used to classify the profile of the candidates for VO coordinators, according to their individual competences, and to support the search and selection of VO coordinators. Finally, section 5 provides an illustrative example where different soft modeling techniques are applied in order to solve such a complex problem and section 6 presents some preliminary conclusions. It is worth mentioning that this approach is particularly useful for VOs whose members do not necessarily know each other (either because it is a large VO composed by several members or because it is originated from a considerable broad VBE) or even for VOs adopting an off shoring strategy.

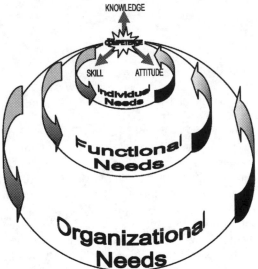

Figure 1 – Competences and needs

2. COMPETENCES IN A VO ENVIRONMENT

In order to choose an adequate coordinator for a given VO many aspects have to be taken into consideration as it is the case of the characteristics of the VO such as its topology and governance principles (Klen, 2007) as well as the required competences. Furthermore the process of searching and selecting a VO coordinator should be fast, simple and effective. Therefore the modeling example proposed in this work strongly relies on the human resources already available in the VO environment that naturally concentrates several professionals with competences in the domain.

The term "competence" can be somehow confusing because each organization normally interprets it in a particular way. Along time many researchers have studied this concept. One of the well-established definitions of competence is provided by (Durand, 1997 and 1998) who states that competence is the ability to coordinate activities to the standards and rules required in the organization using an appropriate mix of <u>knowledge,</u> <u>skills</u> and <u>attitude</u>. According to this author, these three dimensions must be present if someone wants to be effective in the coordination role. This understanding of competence is the one that will be used in this work.

As the VO coordinator has to deal with a distributed, dynamic and sometimes complex organizational environment, he/she should be able to adequately balance these dimensions of knowledge, skills and attitude in order to contribute to the achievement of the VO goals. Accordingly, individual competences are object of a special attention in this modeling example.

Based on (Fleury & Fleury, 2004), in the context of a VO environment, it is possible to define some essential competences for the VO coordinator (Table 1).

Table 1 – Some essential competences of a VO coordinator (adapted from Fleury and Fleury, 2004)

COMPETENCES	
(KNOW HOW TO)	(TO)
Act	judge, choose, make decision (what to do and why)
Mobilize	create synergy among human, financial, and material resources
Communicate	understand, process, and transfer/exchange information and knowledge, assuring that the message was understood by the others
Learn	work the knowledge and the experience; review mental models; develop him/herself and stimulate the development of others
Compromise	engage and compromise with the VO objectives
Take responsibilities	be responsible assuming risks and consequences of the acts
Have Strategic Vision	know and understand the VO business, its environment, identifying opportunities and alternatives

These competences can be extended and detailed in line with the interests of the VO Planner and the VBE or PVC (Professional Virtual Community) Administrator. The data related to these competences can be gathered in a Competence Map, and classified according to three dimensions (Knowledge, Skills and Attitude) aiming at facilitating the recognition of an adequate candidate in the search and selection process. A very crucial issue for the construction of the Competence Map is the use of an adequate Competence Common Ontology as well as the availability of mechanisms for using and evolving this ontology during VBE/VO management. It is outside the scope of this work to go deeper into this subject.

3. SCENARIO DESCRIPTION

For the scenario under analysis the involvement of human resources should be adequately modelled and understood. For this purpose a methodology was developed, making use of the human resources available in the VO environment. The VBE can be an important source for this kind of resources. Its members are organizations that have the knowledge of how to work in a Collaborative Network and, in some cases, already have persons with the competences required to manage a VO. Besides the tangible goods or the traditional support services offered in a VBE, it is often also possible to find this specific service for VO coordination. In some cases organizations may be selected to act in a business "just" as VO coordinator (following the off shoring strategy where management services are provided by "outsiders" if the VO/VBE lacks adequate internal resources or skills). Furthermore the trust environment in force in a VBE cares for the quality and the accuracy of the information provided by the VO candidates.

The methodology developed for searching and selecting a VO Coordinator is a 3-step process. This process is summarized in figure 2 (where some VO coordinator candidates are represented inside the dotted circles) that can be detailed as follows:

Stage 1: Registration of VO Coordinator candidates
The circle on the right-side of the figure represents manifestations of the CNs world where a VBE and a PVC are already established. Potential VO coordinators are highlighted inside the small dotted circles. These potential candidates may belong to the inside or the outside VBE/PVC world.

Stage 2: Information Management
The VO candidates' Competence Maps are stored in a Data Base for future use by the VBE Administrator and/or by the VO Planner. If necessary, and depending on the agreement of the VBE Administrator, the VO candidates information can also be made available to other interested persons (to the Broker for instance).
At this stage a validation of the self evaluation (field "Skills") executed in Stage 1 can be done. External evaluators can analyze the skill rate given by each candidate to each of their competences. They can then transmit their impressions to the VBE Administrator who will take this analysis into consideration in order to have a wider view about each candidate. At this stage the candidates are classified according to their profiles (daring, moderate, conservative).
Information privacy policies are applied according to the operating principles (working and sharing principles) defined in the VBE.

Stage 3: VO Coordinator search and selection
The VO Coordinator search and selection process normally takes place during the Creation (or Evolution) phase of the VO. For each business opportunity a different VO is created. Consequently each VO has its own specific needs and requirements which are identified and analysed by the VBE Administrator and the VO Planner. Based on the VO needs some organizational competences are identified. These competences form the basis for the VBE Administrator/VO Planner to search for the specific VO Coordinator profile (one of the attributes to consider).

It is important to highlight that this modeling example is directed to VBE administrators that have to make decisions in their daily routines, based on a number of aspects ranging from very concrete information up to imprecise and uncertain data. Another critical point besides the synergy among the competences is the environment where the VO operates. In some cases this environment may determine a VO coordinator work-style where a specific profile (conservative, moderate, daring, and so forth) is desired – or even mandatory. Trying to match the interdependent competences with the VO environment requirements may constitute an alternative to identify the VO Coordinator profile that best suits a given VO. Individual competences may be cross-related with organizational competences seeking for the establishment of the VO Coordinator profile. However, all these data are very subjective, imprecise, uncertain and, sometimes, randomly changing. Soft computing emerges as an ad-hoc alternative to work with these approximations and low precision data.

In this specific example, the decision that the VBE Administrator has to make concerns the choice of a VO Coordinator, namely a person to manage the VO. This choice will be based on the person's profile which in turn may be difficult to classify given the "soft" nature of the subject (defining people profiles is not only a matter of checking their abilities and skills but also taking into account the way they react to a given situation, for instance. This has a direct influence in the way coordinators manage a given VO). The rationale is therefore to use some type of soft modeling in order to classify the profile of the candidates for becoming VO coordinators (Stage 2). The classification will be done according to the competences of the candidates. The classified profile (daring, moderate, conservative) will be used as one of the inputs for a multi-attribute model (or a multi-criteria decision analysis process, Stage 3) that will serve as a supporting tool to search and select VO coordinators. The next sections will present more details on the modeling techniques used, as well as an illustrative example.

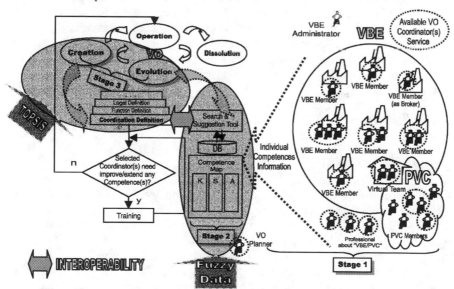

Figure 2 – Searching and selecting a VO Coordinator in a 3-step process

4. DECISION MAKING SUPPORT

4.1 Criteria for VO coordinator selection

VO coordinator selection can be viewed as a multi-criteria decision making problem that involves assessing trade-offs between conflicting, tangible and intangible criteria, and stating preferences based on incomplete or non-available information. Evaluation criteria should account for all factors that impact VO performance and should be chosen to clearly support the selection process.

A good VO coordinator assessment process must identify and track performance along all dimensions that affect VO coordinator selection: knowledge, skills and attitude. Based on Toney (2002) research, there are five main characteristics that make a great project manager, namely: interpersonal skills (the ability to manage people), organizational skills (the ability to assign resources, prioritize tasks, etc.), communication skills (the ability to clearly communicate with members of different organizations in order to clearly inform project objectives, challenges or problems, scope changes, project status reports, etc.), problem-solving skills (the ability to effectively handle unexpected problems or challenges) and professional training/formation.

To assess these characteristics we may have to take into consideration aspects such as character, educational/experience background, honesty and truthfulness or leadership capacity, which are quite difficult to quantify and to evaluate precisely. Therefore, in order to cope with the subjectivity of the information and to facilitate the expression of the preferences or assessment of all involved actors (the VBE/PVC Administrator, the Broker, the VO Planner) about potential candidate characteristics, we allow several types of information (numerical, interval, qualitative and binary) and make use of fuzzy theory (see e.g. Lin, H-Y. et al., 2007). This is an important requirement in practice as the multiplicity of factors considered when selecting a VO coordinator (see e.g. table 1) cannot be expressed in a single measure or scale. Moreover, one should also be able to express some organizational competences in terms of indicators or objectives that can be vague or imprecise.

In this context, qualitative information may be represented by "linguistic variables" (Herrera et al., 2004) based on words or sentences, in a natural language, making the preferences expression easier. Since linguistic variables are not directly mathematically operable, each linguistic variable is associated with a fuzzy number characterizing its meaning.

4.2 Problem description

Assume a network A representing all VO company managers that are VO coordinator candidates. A specific entity (the VBE/PVC Administrator) is responsible for the VO coordinator selection process. The candidates are characterised/evaluated by a set of M attributes. Suppose also that the attributes can be partitioned according to the three dimensions considered (knowledge, skills and attitude). For example, educational/experience background (c_i) is associated to knowledge, ability to assign resources (c_{i+1}) to skills and honesty (c_{i+2}) to attitude, with $c_i \in M$. Part of the M attributes can be used to distinguish the candidates in terms of their behaviour in risky situations, classifying them in daring, moderate or conservative candidates.

Consider a project P, resulting from a detected business opportunity that triggers the formation of a given VO. This project is characterized by a set of attributes that act as constraints, corresponding to some of the functional competences of the candidates. In this way we first need to solve a matching problem to determine the potential candidates that can execute the role of coordinator for this specific project. These attributes can be classified as *critical* since they must be present in the candidates' characteristics and meet some boundary values so that the candidates' "applications" are not rejected. Assume also that the VBE/PVC Administrator selects a group of attributes O (organizational competences) that act as objectives for the project P. In resume the network comprises a set of attributes and some of them are used as constraints or objectives.

The first step in the modeling process is to carefully define what attributes to consider in all subsets (individual, functional and organizational competences). VBE/PVC Administrators can assign weights to the objectives according to their assessment of their relative importance for the project under consideration. Therefore, the VO coordinator selection problem consists in choosing the best company manager to coordinate the VO created to perform project P, taking into account a set of evaluation criteria based on the attributes chosen for project P. Given the multi-criteria nature of the problem, there is generally no "optimal" alternative, and a good "trade-off" solution must be identified.

4.3 Methodology

According to the literature (see e.g. Ng, 2008), the multiple criteria selection problem can be found in many different situations, and experts agree that there is no best way to evaluate/select candidates. Therefore, organizations use a variety of different approaches in their evaluation processes: categorical methods (Timmerman, 1986), DEA (Liu et al., 2000), cluster analysis (Xu et al., 2006), Particle swarm optimization (Gao et al., 2006), mathematical programming (Dotoli et al., 2006), simulation (Kim et al., 2006), artificial intelligence-based models (Li and Liao, 2007) and multiple attribute decision-making methods, such as MAUT (Sha and Che, 2005), SAW, AHP (Sari et al., 2007), TOPSIS (Crispim and Sousa, 2007), ELECTRE and PROMETHEE (Araz et al., 2007).

In this work we use cluster analysis to classify the candidates according to their risk profiles (Daring, Moderate or Conservative) and use fuzzy TOPSIS, as developed by Hwang and Yoon (1981), to obtain the candidates ranking within each cluster. In each cluster we identify dominated candidates (candidates for which the classification obtained in all criteria is worse in comparison with the other candidates), in order to eliminate them from the best candidate search, thus increasing the algorithm's efficiency.

Algorithm steps

Step 1: Divide the candidates in three clusters through the use of k-means cluster analysis

Step 2: Scan all candidates in order to obtain a feasible group according to the functional competences criteria

Step 3: Eliminate dominated candidates

Step 4: Rank the candidates in each cluster through the use of fuzzy TOPSIS

4.3.1 Cluster analysis

Cluster analysis (CA) is a popular data mining technique (see e.g. Olafsson et al., 2008) that involves the partitioning of a set of objects into a set of mutually exclusive clusters such that the similarity between the observations within each cluster (i.e. subset) is high, while the similarity between the observations from the different clusters is low.

Clustering may be categorized in various ways such as hierarchical or partitional, deterministic or probabilistic, hard or fuzzy. The general approaches to clustering are: hierarchical clustering and partitional clustering (e.g. Samoilenko and Osei-Bryson, 2008). Hierarchical clustering form clusters through agglomerative or divisive methods. The agglomerative method assumes that each data point is its own cluster, and with each step of the clustering process, these clusters are combined to form larger clusters, which may be combined to form a single cluster. The divisive method of the hierarchical clustering, on the other hand, starts with one single cluster containing all data points within the sample and proceeds to divide it into smaller dissimilar clusters. In partitional clustering, k-means clustering requires the number of resulting clusters k, to be specified prior to analysis. Thus, k-means clustering will produce k different clusters of greatest possible distinction. In our work we will use k-means clustering to identify the candidate profile.

The k-means procedure (Kim and Ahn, 2008) is a simple way to classify a given data set through a certain number of clusters (assume k clusters) fixed a priori. The main idea is to define k centroids, one for each cluster. The centroid of a cluster is the average point in the multidimensional space defined by the criteria, i.e., the cluster's center of gravity. These centroids should be placed as much as possible far away from each other. The next step is to take each point belonging to a given data set and associate it to the nearest centroid. After all points have been grouped, new centroids are re-calculated and the points are grouped again. This process is repeated until centroids do not change. The k-means algorithm aims at minimizing an *objective function*, in this case the euclidian distance between each data point and the cluster centre.

4.3.2 Fuzzy TOPSIS Procedure

Fuziness is inherent to most decision making processes when linguistic variables are used to describe qualitative data. In fact, in real-word decision problems most decisions are made in the presence of some information that is uncertain, incomplete and/or missing (Li and Liao, 2007). In this context, we will use an extension of the TOPSIS method for fuzzy data (see e.g. Jahanshahloo et al. 2006). This procedure follows a series of steps:

(1) identification of the evaluation criteria
(2) generating alternatives
    (i) take 3 candidates as initial group centroids
    (ii) assign each candidate to the group that has the closest centroid
    (iii) when all candidates have been assigned, recalculate the positions of the 3 centroids
    (iv) repeat Steps 2 and 3 until the centroids no longer move
(3) evaluating alternatives in terms of criteria (the values of the criterion functions which are fuzzy)
(4) identifying the weights of the criteria
(5) constructing the fuzzy decision matrix
(6) calculating the normalized fuzzy decision matrix
(7) constructing the weighted normalized fuzzy decision matrix

(8) identifying a fuzzy positive ideal solution and a fuzzy negative ideal solution
(9) calculating the distance between each alternative *i* to the fuzzy positive ideal solution (eq. 1, 2)
(10) defining a closeness coefficient to determine the ranking order of all alternatives (eq. 3)

$$\tilde{d}_i^+ = \sum_{j=1}^{n} d(\tilde{v}_{ij}, \tilde{v}_{ij}^+), \qquad i = 1,..., m \qquad (1)$$

$$\tilde{d}_i^- = \sum_{j=1}^{n} d(\tilde{v}_{ij}, \tilde{v}_{ij}^-), \qquad i = 1,..., m \qquad (2)$$

where $\tilde{v}_{ij}^+ = (1, 1, 1)$ is the fuzzy positive ideal solution and $\tilde{v}_{ij}^+ = (0, 0, 0)$ is the fuzzy negative ideal solution *n* for each criteria (benefit or cost criteria).

$$\tilde{R}_i = \tilde{d}_i^- / (\tilde{d}_i^+ + \tilde{d}_i^-), \qquad i = 1,..., m \qquad (3)$$

5. ILLUSTRATIVE EXAMPLE

In order to illustrate the proposed approach, consider the following "academic example": a network with 225 VO coordinator candidates, taken from the management positions of the companies belonging to the VBE network, and characterized by 30 attributes expressed in four different types of information: numerical, percentage, binary and linguistic (table 2).

Table 2: VO coordinator candidate's criteria

criterion	type	max (+) / min (-)	cardinality (for linguistic)	risk attitude
c1	percentage	+	-	-
c2	number	-	-	-
c3	percentage	+	-	-
c4	number	+	-	-
c5	linguistic	+	7	-
c6	percentage	-	-	✔
c7	binary	+	-	-
c8	percentage	-	-	-
c9	percentage	+	-	-
c10	binary	+	-	-
c11	linguistic	-	3	-
c12	percentage	-	-	-
c13	percentage	+	-	-
c14	percentage	+	-	-
c15	linguistic	+	3	✔
c16	percentage	+	-	✔
c17	binary	+	-	

c18	percentage	+	-	✔
c19	percentage	+	-	-
c20	linguistic	+	7	✔
c21	binary	-	-	-
c22	number	+	-	✔
c23	linguistic	+	7	-
c24	number	+	-	✔
c25	percentage	+	-	-
c26	binary	+	-	-
c27	number	+	-	✔
c28	linguistic	+	5	-
c29	number	+	-	-
c30	linguistic	+	3	✔

We may want to maximize an attribute (for benefit criteria) or minimize it (for cost criteria). If the attribute is a linguistic variable, the scale cardinality will be defined with the following term sets: {none, more or less, perfect}, {none, low, more or less, high, perfect} or {none, very low, low, more or less, high, very high, perfect}. Some attributes contribute to define the attitude of each candidate in terms of risk behavior (table 2). It is important to notice that only some of the criteria are useful to characterize the candidate risk attitude, so one key task of the decision maker is to carefully define what criteria are going to be considered (e.g. overconfidence, willingness to take risks, intelligence, etc.). For illustration purposes, figures have been randomly generated.

Assume we would like to form a VO to perform a given project. As Organizational Competences, this VO will consider 10 attributes (table 3) chosen from the whole attribute set (table 2) and the associated weights.

Table 3: Organizational competences criteria

Criterion	c5	c25	c1	c27	c26	c11	c2	c13	c21	c28
Weight (%)	1	17	11	7	17	2	9	10	16	10

Assume also that the criteria used to illustrate the functional competences are those described in table 4. The limit value represents the maximum or minimum value accepted, depending if it is a benefit criterion, to be maximized (+), or a cost criterion, to be minimized (-). For example we only accept candidates with at least 50% of evaluation to c9.

Table 4: Functional competences criteria

criteria	limit value	type	example
c23	more or less	linguistic	capacity to face challenges or problems
c9	50	percentage	ability to communicate
c13	65	percentage	trust
c15	more or less	linguistic	leadership capacity
c25	60	percentage	ability to manage people

c30	good	linguistic	character
c24	4	number	classification for educational background
c27	5	number	n° years project manager
c4	2	number	n° of previosly VO coordinations
c7	1	binary	honesty

Notes: a) capacity to face challenges or problems = {none, very low, low, more or less, high, very high, total}

b) leadership capacity = {low, more or less, high}

c) character ={bad, neutral, good} in terms of responsibility, modesty, individuality, ethic morality and confidence.

5.1 K-means cluster analysis

The first step of our algorithm consists in obtaining three different groups of candidates according to their behavior in risky situations. Through the use of a software package (SPSS), using the criteria previously chosen (table 2), we have partitioned the candidates in three clusters (daring, moderate, conservative). Since in this illustrative example we have no concern with the details of each attribute (label and meaning) we assume that cluster 1 comprises all daring candidates, cluster 2 comprises moderate candidates and cluster 3 comprises conservative candidates. Otherwise, we would have to carefully identify the profile of each group according to the candidate's descriptions of the attributes considered. Analysing figure 3 we notice that the clusters are, in this case, very clear. The composition of each cluster is described in table 5.

Table 5: Clusters composition

Candidates		
Cluster 1	Cluster 2	Cluster 3
4	30	20
33	51	38
54	75	45
73	85	47
86	112	61
95	126	70
99	128	76
206	177	80
	187	116
	207	145
	217	169
	220	190
	224	225

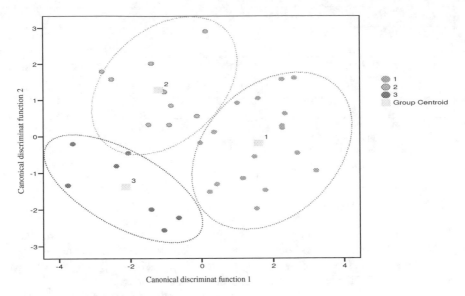

Figure 3 – Candidates divided in clusters

5.2 Fuzzy TOPSIS approach

We have used the TOPSIS technique to obtain the ranking of the non-dominated alternatives set for each cluster (table 6). First we have to transform all the inputs into fuzzy sets. Then we weight the information in order to obtain the normalized fuzzy decision matrix. Finally, we compute the distances between each alternative and the fuzzy positive/negative ideal, as well as the "closeness coefficients".

Table 6: Closeness coefficients / ranking of the alternatives

Cluster 1				Cluster 2				Cluster 3			
d_i^+	d_i^-	R_i	Rank	d_i^+	d_i^-	R_i	Rank	d_i^+	d_i^-	R_i	Rank
116.594	366.592	0,0305	95	116.589	363.657	0,0302	128	116,6	368.100	0,0306	38
116.589	363.291	0,0302	4	116.594	362.354	0,0301	220	116.599	363.868	0,0303	47
116.588	360.762	0,0300	86	116.594	36.071	0,0300	126	116.589	363.636	0,0302	145
116.590	348.762	0,0290	54	116.589	348.028	0,0290	224	116.900	353.530	0,0294	20
116.588	347.277	0,0289	206	116.592	34.563	0,0288	85	116.590	352.877	0,0294	70
116.581	326.933	0,0273	73	116.586	338.493	0,0282	112	116.591	352.545	0,0294	116
116.577	326.346	0,0272	33	116.584	336.208	0,0280	51	116.584	348.527	0,0290	76
116.587	326.153	0,0272	99	116.579	333.694	0,0278	207	116.587	340.476	0,0284	45
				116.579	333.133	0,0278	177	116.579	332.680	0,0277	190
				116.588	332.050	0,0277	217	116.584	332.342	0,0277	61
				116.582	325.827	0,0272	30	116.588	331.540	0,0277	80
				116.581	324.638	0,0271	75	116.584	331.389	0,0276	225
				116.580	323.322	0,0270	187	116.577	327.810	0,0274	169

Analyzing the results obtained from the ranking approaches we are able to recommend candidate 95 if the VBE Administrator prefers a daring person, candidate 128 if he/she prefers a moderate one and, finally, candidate 38 if a conservative candidate is preferred.

6. CONCLUSIONS

The selection process of a coordinator for an emerging VO is a critical issue in its life-cycle. The basic problem consists in choosing the most suitable candidate according to a multi-criteria set of parameters as well as to the global perspective and attitude of the decision makers. Aspects to be considered in this selection process include educational/experience background, character, honesty and truthfulness, ethical values, leadership capacity and so forth. This kind of criteria is sometimes very subjective, imprecise and uncertain and rather difficult to quantify and to precisely evaluate. As a direct consequence crisp modeling approaches are not enough for capturing those aspects. Soft modeling approaches arise to help capturing perspectives related to incomplete or imprecise information and thus to support the modeling of complex systems such as CNs.

In this work, characterized as being a multiple criteria selection problem, two modeling techniques were used: Fuzzy Logic (soft) and Cluster Analysis (crisp). For the integration of these modeling techniques an approach has been developed that can be viewed as a 2-phase algorithm where we first group a set of potential VO coordinators in clusters through the use of a K-means clustering procedure. In the second phase we generate a ranking of potential VO coordinators through a fuzzy TOPSIS based procedure. This efficient quantitative tool seems to provide an adequate support to simulate different alternatives in the VO coordinator selection problem (through the introduction of different attributes or values/perceptions about the characteristics of the candidates) and hence demonstrates the high potential of the modeling techniques used for the envisaged problem. The whole approach can be viewed as a tool for supporting decision making, but not to replace the critical role played by the problem stakeholders in the selection process.

Acknowledgments. This work was funded in part by the European Commission through the ECOLEAD project and by the Brazilian Council for Research and Scientific Development (CNPq) with scholarships as well as through the IFM project.

7. REFERENCES

1. Araz C., Ozfirat M.P. and Ozkarahan I. An integrated multicriteria decision-making methodology for outsourcing management. Computers & Operations Research, 34 (2007), 3738 – 3756.
2. Camarinha-Matos, L.M., Afsarmanesh, H., Ollus, M. A Holistic Approach to Creation and Management of Dynamic Virtual Organizations, In: Collaborative Networks and their Breeding Environments. ISBN 0-387-28259-9. Springer, (2005).
3. Crispim, J. and Sousa, J.P. Multiple criteria partner selection in virtual enterprises. *In* Camarinha-Matos, L.M., Afsarmanesh, H., Novais, P. and Analide, C., eds. IFIP International Federation for

Information Processing. *Establishing the Foundation of Collaborative Networks*. Boston, MA, Springer. 243 (2007), 197-206.

4. Dotoli M., Fanti M. P., Meloni C. and Zhou M. C. Design and Optimization of Integrated E-Supply Chain for Agile and Environmentally Conscious Manufacturing. *IEEE transactions on systems, man, and cybernetics—part a: systems and humans*, 36, 1 (2006), 62-75.

5. Durand, T. Strategizing for innovation: competence analysis in assessing strategic change. In: Competence-based strategic management. Edited by Ron Sanchez and Aimé Heene. Chichester, England: John Wiley & Sons, (1997).

6. Durand, T. Forms of incompetence. In: Fourth International Conference on Competence-Based Management. Oslo: Norwegian Scholl of Management, (1998).

7. Figueira, J., Greco, S., Ehrgott, M. (eds). "Multiple criteria decision analysis: state of the art surveys".Springer, New York (USA), 2005.

8. Fleury, A., Fleury, M.T.L. Estratégias Empresariais e Formação de Competências – Um Quebra-cabeça Caleidoscópico da Indústria Brasileira. ISBN 85-224-3807-2. 3ª ed. Editora Atlas, (2004), in Portuguese.

9. Gao F., Cui G., Zhao Q. and Liu H. Application of Improved Discrete Particle Swarm Algorithm in Partner Selection of Virtual Enterprise. IJCSNS International Journal of Computer Science and Network Security, 6, 3A, (2006) 208-212.

10. Herrera F., Martiınez L., Sanchez P.J. Decision Aiding Managing non-homogeneous information in group decision making. European Journal of Operational Research 166, 1 (2004), 115-132.

11. Hwang C.L., Yoon K. "Multiple attribute decision making: Methods and applications". Springer, Berlin, 1981.

12. Jahanshahloo G.R. a, Hosseinzadeh Lotfi F., Izadikhah M. Extension of the TOPSIS method for decision-making problems with fuzzy data. Applied Mathematics and Computation 181 (2006) 1544–1551.

13. Kim T-Y, Lee S., Kim K. and Kim C-H. A modeling framework for agile and interoperable virtual enterprises. Computers in Industry 57 (2006), 204–217.

14. Kim K-J. and Ahn H. A recommender system using GA K-means clustering in an online shopping market. Expert Systems with Applications, 34, 2 (2008), 1200-1209.

15. Klen, E.R. Methodology for Virtual Organizations Managers Search and Suggestion based on Individual Competences. Florianópolis, (2007), 216p. Ph.D Thesis - Post-Graduate Program in Production and Systems Engineering, UFSC, Florianópolis – SC, Brazil (in Portuguese).

16. Li Y., Liao X. Decision support for risk analysis on dynamic alliance. Decision Support Systems 42 (2007) 2043– 2059.

17. Lin H-Y., Hsu P-Y., Sheen G-J. A fuzzy-based decision-making procedure for data warehouse system selection. Expert Systems with Applications 32 (2007), 939–953.

18. Liu F., Ding F.Y., Lall V. Using data envelopment analysis to compare suppliers for supplier selection and performance improvement, Supply Chain Management 5, 3 (2000) 143–150.

19. Ng W. L. An efficient and simple model for multiple criteria supplier selection problem. European Journal of Operational Research 186, 3 (2008), 1059-1067.

20. Olafsson S., Li X., Wu S. Operations research and data mining. European Journal of Operational Research, 187, 3 (2008), 1429-1448.

21. Samoilenko S. and Osei-Bryson K-M. Increasing the discriminatory power of DEA in the presence of the sample heterogeneity with cluster analysis and decision trees. Expert Systems with Applications, 34, 2 (2008), 1568-1581.

22. Sari B., Sen T. and Kilic S. E. AHP model for the selection of partner companies in virtual enterprises. International Journal of Advance Manufacturing Technology. (2007) DOI 10.1007/s00170-007-1097-6.

23. Sha D.Y. and Che Z.H. Virtual integration with a multi-criteria partner selection model for the multi-echelon manufacturing system. International Journal of Advance Manufacturing Technology, 25 (2005), 793–802.

24. Timmerman E. An approach to vendor performance evaluation. Journal of Purchasing and Materials Management 22, 4 (1986), 2–8.

25. Toney, F. "The Superior Project Manager: Global Competency Standards and Best Practices". Marcel Dekker publisher, New York, USA, 2002.

26. Xu S., Shen L., Zhai J., Yang Z. and Li Y. Research on Virtual Logistic Enterprises Partners Selection Method Based on CLIQUE. 10th International Conference on Computer Supported Cooperative Work in Design, May 2006, 1 – 5.

4.8
Modeling the Value of Expectations in Collaborative Networked Organizations

S. Wiesner, F. Graser, K.-D. Thoben

The goal of modeling the value of expectations in Collaborative Networked Organizations (CNO) is to review the project behind that CNO and have a basis to decide on whether to go on, to optimize, or to stop the project. In Virtual Organizations, where several actors work on common projects, expectations may differ widely: while one actor might believe in the chances of a project, others might see or face critical factors that may prohibit the project from succeeding. A schema on how to gather, cluster and evaluate expectations in a Virtual Organization can create an input for the decision process on the future of the target project.

1. INTRODUCTION

Human expectations are a powerful indicator for motivation, commitment, and eventually the success of a project. In Virtual Organizations (VOs), where many different human actors from different companies with different corporate cultures, values, and visions join forces for a common objective, expectations on the outcome of a common project may widely divert. Especially, when it comes to collaborative innovation project outcomes are all but certain: important success variables like R&D costs, stakeholders actions, market acceptance of the new artifact, etc. may change rapidly and dramatically (Fig. 1). Capturing a broad spectrum of expectations from VO actors may help to gain a realistic image on the project's chances.

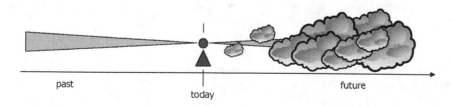

past   today   future

Figure 1 – Uncertainty of expectations

An expectation denotes a personal estimation on what is most likely to happen under uncertain conditions. Several aspects of the term expectation can be identified:

1. Expectations are referring to an uncertain future: Expectations represent a glance into the future; based on the information the actor has on the present situation. Independently from quality and quantity of information available, glances in the future will always present more than one thinkable situation. In a variety of thinkable situations the actor will rank them according to the probability s/he expects this situation to occur. The situation s/he estimates most likely to happen is the expected one.
2. Expectations are context-oriented: Expectations comprise an assessment of the recent situation and of things to happen in the future. Changes in the recent situation and in assessment of things to happen may change expectations.
3. Expectations are subjective: Assessment of the recent situation and of things to happen is related to two aspects. First, to the quality and quantity of information the actor has at hands. Second to the personal interpretation of this information by the actor. Depending on the personal experiences, different actors will draw different images of the future, making expectations subjective.

Formation and fulfillment of partners' expectations are a necessary condition for trust in a Virtual Organization (Msanjila & Afsarmanesh, 2007). Previous positive expectations that have been fulfilled increase the chance that partners will have positive expectations about joint actions in the future. Negative expectations that are not fulfilled have the same effect. Therefore it is vital for the VO that the expectations of the partners can be measured and used to predict and influence the success of a project. In that way, a cyclic process of increasing trust and more fulfilled expectations can be started (Vangen & Huxham, 2003).

In foresight, expectations appear in various shades of gray from "most likely" to "unlikely". This implies a double aspect of softness to the concept of expectations. First, personal expectations can hardly be calculated by an algorithm, and – second – the result of determining an expectation will remain subjective and thus uncertain. The main momentum of uncertainty in expectations derives from the fact that the level of information and knowledge, such as the ways human beings link new information with their existing experiences and knowledge cannot be externalized by mathematic models. Still, it remains up to the individual to express its expectations in terms of qualitative descriptions or rankings (for instance "good" to "bad", "high" to "low", "1" to "x", and so on).

Integrating the expectations of a wide number of actors shall be done by means of combining the data with Fuzzy Logic. Applying Fuzzy Logic is often useful when there is no mathematical description of a problem, but a verbal one (Bothe, 1995). This is especially true for modeling expectations in Virtual Organizations. Through usage of Fuzzy Logic, linguistic variables like "low", "medium" or "high" can be used. The experiment is designed considering the seven steps of data clustering suggested by Jain and Dubes (Jain & Dubes, 1988):

- Data Collection
- Initial Screening
- Representation
- Clustering Tendency
- Clustering Strategy
- Validation
- Interpretation.

Figure 2 outlines, how the stages in clustering data are incorporated into the experiment and how Fuzzy Logic can be applied:

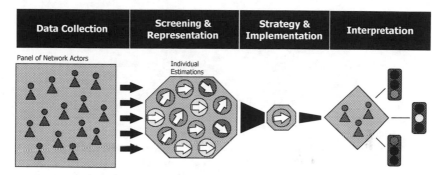

| Data Collection | Screening & Representation | Strategy & Implementation | Interpretation |

Figure 2 – Schema of the modeling experiment

Data Collection is used for extraction of relevant data objects from the underlying data sources. Data objects can be distinguished by their individual values for a set of attributes (or measures). In this phase, actors within the networks are requested to place a vote on a nominal scale. In Screening and Representation, the data are subjected to a first validity test and prepared for the utilization in an algorithm. During Strategy and Implementation Fuzzy Logic is applied to combine the collected data and assign the partners to different sets. In Interpretation the results are subject to analysis of their impact for the Virtual Organization. The combined and interpreted data will be used as one input to the decision process that has to be made on the future of the project. Additionally, the long-term development of expectations can be tracked by means of chart analysis, which is not part of this experiment.

2. MODELING EXAMPLE

In each innovation project, reviews are a common means to assess the project status, and to evaluate on whether to carry-on the project, to reconsider schedules and objectives, or to even stop the entire project. Doing the prognosis depends upon expectations that – by definition – are subject to uncertainty: for instance, it can only be assumed if a competitor will come-up with a more efficient and lower prices solution – but no one knows for sure. Usually, projects are assessed by a small panel of actors that are more or less stakeholders to the project; thus the decision on how to proceed with the project depends only upon the panel's expectations. This is neglecting the expectations of all the other actors in the network that may significantly deviate from the broad majority of actors (Surowiecki, 2004).

According to Eric Bonabeau (Bonabeau, 1999), a large group of actors, each with a limited information horizon put together in a large group may reach smarter and more efficient conclusions than a panel of just a handful but better informed actors
(Fig. 3).

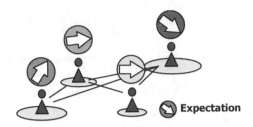

Figure 3 – Differing expectations

In the Experiment, a review of a Virtual Organization based on the expectations of the partners shall create a basis to decide on how to proceed with a project. The options are to continue the project, rework it to achieve greater benefit for all partners or to stop the project. Using the schema presented in the methodology section, the first step for this is Data Collection.

2.1 Data collection

For the experiment, we have three actors of a Virtual Organization with different expectations regarding the financial and strategic benefit of a project as shown in Figure 4:

Actor	Expectations on Financial Benefit	Expectations on Strategic Benefit
A	◓	◔
B	◓	◓
C	◔	◒

Figure 4 – Expectations of actors

Let's suppose a questionnaire regarding the two different expectations towards the project is distributed to Actors A, B and C. At the end of the design phase partners A and B come to the conclusion that their financial expectations to the project will not fulfill, while partner C gives a positive rating. A is also expecting a significant strategic benefit from collaborating with partner C, who itself is ambivalent on this.

The actors have to rate their expectations in an interval from 1 to 10, where one is the worst and ten the best.

2.2 Screening and representation

After the data collection has been completed, the results are checked for valid answers and stored in a matrix. Table 1 is the representation of the subjective expectations of the actors towards selected aspects of the Virtual Organization.

Table 1 – Collected data

Actor	Financial Benefit	Strategic Benefit
A	2	8
B	3	3
C	9	5

2.3 Strategy and implementation

Having structured the data, an algorithm for combining the data has to be defined. As explained beforehand, the expectations of the Actors are subjective and thus uncertain. The algorithm used has to consider this "softness" of data. A method to achieve this is the use of Fuzzy Logic (Hönerloh, 1997). For the experiment, the modeling of the fuzzy inference system is done using the Fuzzy Logic Toolbox of the Matlab software environment. The first step of allocating the actors to different clusters is to translate the numerical data into fuzzy sets. This process is called fuzzification of the input values and is done by applying so called membership functions to the data. These functions can e.g. be derived from statistical surveys or expert knowledge. For the example, three levels of expectation ("low", "medium" and "high") were modeled using the Matlab Membership Function Editor, each of them approximated by a Gaussian distribution of expectations. A simplified illustration of the membership function is given in Figure 5. A value of 2 would equal a degree of membership to low level of expectation of approximately 0.6 in this case.

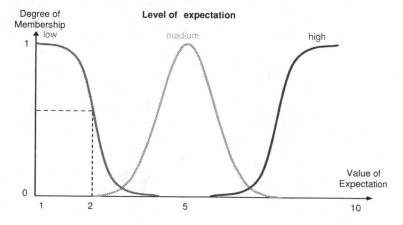

Figure 5 – Fuzzification of expectation values

In a further step to build a fuzzy inference system, a set of rules is applied to the fuzzified input data. For the experiment, a set of simple IF/AND/THEN rules is created. As the system shall help in reviewing the project, the rules define if it is likely that a partner leaves the VO. Using the Rule Editor, the following rules were defined:

IF "Financial Benefit" is low AND "Strategic Benefit" is low THEN "Likelihood of leaving the VO" is high

IF "Financial Benefit" is high AND "Strategic Benefit" is high THEN "Likelihood of leaving the VO" is low

IF "Financial Benefit" is high AND "Strategic Benefit" is medium THEN "Likelihood of leaving the VO" is low

Those rules are applied to the fuzzified input data for all degrees of membership to the different expectation levels. The results of this fuzzy inference process are linguistic values describing the likelihood of the actor leaving the VO. In the last step of Fuzzy Logic, the linguistic values have to be converted to numerical values again. This is done in a process called "defuzzification". In principle that means the reverse appliance of a membership function. For the experiment, a membership function has been created mapping "low", "medium" and "high" likelihoods of leaving the VO to a percentage, again using Gaussian distribution. An example of defuzzification is presented in Figure 6.

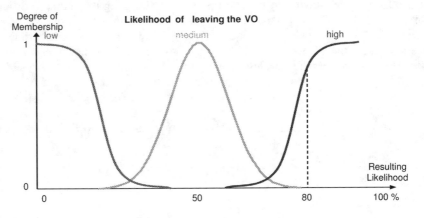

Figure 6 – Calculating the likelihood of leaving the CNO

The application of the fuzzy inference system to the actors of the example by using the Fuzzy Logic Toolbox of Matlab yields the following results. Likelihood of leaving the VO for the different actors:

Actor A: 59.3%
Actor B: 83.4%
Actor C: 13.9%

2.4 Interpretation

Looking at the percentages of likelihood for the single partners of leaving the Virtual Organization, it can be clearly seen that in the current Situation actor C is very likely to further collaborate, while actor B quite certainly withdraws. The position of actor A is fairly ambivalent, with a slight bias towards leaving.

Interpretation of the single values for the future of the whole project depends on the specific VO. Simply taking the average of the values (52.2% in this case) might work if all partners are equally important for the project. If some actors (e.g. leading partners) are more important, their values can be weighted higher by multiplying them with an additional factor. If for example actor C would be weighted double, the average would then be 42.6%. In both cases, reworking of the project is suggested.

3. CONCLUSION

The expectations of the partners are a crucial criterion for evaluating on how to proceed with a project. Measuring and comparing the actual results against the expectations are necessary to take the appropriate actions to keep the VO on track (Salkari et al., 2006). If the average likelihood for the actors leaving the Virtual Organization is low, the project may be continued as it is. A project where the average likelihood of leaving the VO is medium can be enhanced by reworking. Projects that do not seem to provide enough benefit for the partners to stay should be checked if they have to be terminated. The percentile boundaries of these options are fuzzy as well, and may be determined by statistical means by subsequent experiments.

Fuzzy Logic provides an opportunity to model the value of expectations in a VO and to cluster the data. Using rule sets and linguistic variables helps in interpreting the expectations of the actors for the decision process on the future of a Virtual Organization.

There are also certain limits in using methods of soft modeling to interpret the expectations of VO actors. Although it is possible to get a crisp value as a result of the method, it should be remembered that it is derived from uncertain data. To render the functions and rules of the Fuzzy Logic, previous experiences have to be provided as training data.

Acknowledgments – This work as supported in part by the ECOLEAD integrated project funded by the European Commission.

4. REFERENCES

1. Bonabeau E., Dorigo M., Theraulaz G. (1999): Swarm Intelligence from Natural to Artificial Systems. Oxford University Press.
2. Bothe, Hans-Heinrich (1995): Fuzzy Logic. Springer-Verlag.
3. Hönerloh, Albrecht (1997): Unscharfe Simulation in der Betriebswirtschaft. Unitext.
4. Jain, Anil K. and Dubes, Richard C. (1988): Algorithms for Clustering Data. Prentice-Hall.

5. Msanjila, Simon S. and Afsarmanesh, Hamideh: Modelling trust relationships in Collaborative
Networked Organisations. International Journal of Technology Transfer and Commercialisation
2007; 6; 1.

6. Salkari et al.: An Approach to Configuration of Virtual Organisation Management Services. In:
Exploiting the Knowledge Economy: Issues, Applications and Case Studies. IOS Press, 2006.

7. Surowiecki, J.: The Wisdom of Crowds – Why the Many are Smarter than the Few. ISBN 0-349-
11707-1; Abacus, London, 2004.

8. Vangen, Siv and Huxham, Chris: Nurturing Collaborative Relations: Building Trust in
Interorganizational Collaboration. Journal of Applied Behavioral Science 2003; 39; 5.

4.9
Prospective performance measurement in Virtual Organizations

M. Seifert, S. Wiesner, K.-D. Thoben

The goal of prospective performance measurement is to support consortium building in Virtual Organizations. Through identification of possible partners and their potential contributions for realizing an order and comparison of possible consortia, the performance measurement can be used to identify and to evaluate the optimal network configuration. On the other hand, potential alternatives for partner selection can be identified and assessed, for example to guarantee the capacity to act, even if a partner omits. The crisp part of prospective performance measurement lies in recording well defined past performance data. This data is then used to forecast future performance by means of soft modeling. In a final step the forecast can be interpreted by traditional methods again.

1. INTRODUCTION

Traditional Performance Measurement approaches base on the evaluation of executed processes. The results of the last measured period are the basis for process improvements. To be able to learn from history requires that the future keeps the same conditions. In Virtual Organizations, processes as well as consortia are highly dynamic. Cooperation cases are built to serve in some cases exactly one order. The short life cycle of Virtual Organizations requires a new approach to evaluate its performance - one main success factor is already the partner selection: The set of partners which are foreseen to realize the next order pre-defines the performance to be carried out. For this reason, the performance prediction approach has been developed. The principle is shown in figure 1.

The aim is to evaluate the performance of a VO in a very early phase of its life cycle to predict potential weaknesses and strengths of the foreseen consortium. Due to the fact that a certain business opportunity can only be served once, the chance of this approach is to ensure that the best team can be identified and set up to realize the next order. While the cooperation is dynamic, the single contributions of the participating partners base on their specific core competencies. These single parts of the entire process chain in the VO are more stable.

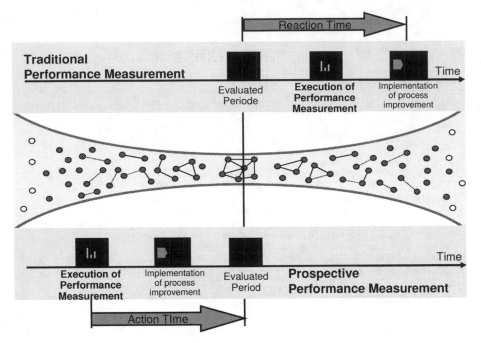

Figure 1 - Traditional vs. Prospective Performance Measurement (see Thoben 2001)

2. APPLICATION OF SCOR IN VIRTUAL ORGANISATIONS

To measure and predict the performance of partners in a Virtual Organization (VO), several methods of performance measurement may be applied. The usage of an artificial neural network in this experiment is not bound to a specific approach in performance measurement. In this example, for modeling the process chain of the Virtual Organization, the SCOR model is used. SCOR has originally been developed for stable supply chains, but may in parts be adapted for use in enterprise networks: Process chains basically represent the structure of the product to be realized. If the final product is fixed and the realization is done by an unchanging consortium, the process chain is static and forms a stable supply chain, which can be described via the SCOR model (Seifert, 2007). This is shown in Figure 2:

The SCOR model has been developed for modelling and evaluating inter-organizational process chains in stable supply chains. It features a three level hierarchy for description and decomposition of inter-organizational processes and follows particularly the material flows of production processes. The main components of the SCOR model are five reference central processes "Source", "Make", "Deliver", "Return" and "Plan", which can be used to model the internal processes of a company in a first step. By connecting the "Deliver" processes of a company to the "Source" processes of its customers, the processes can be combined to inter-organizational process chains.

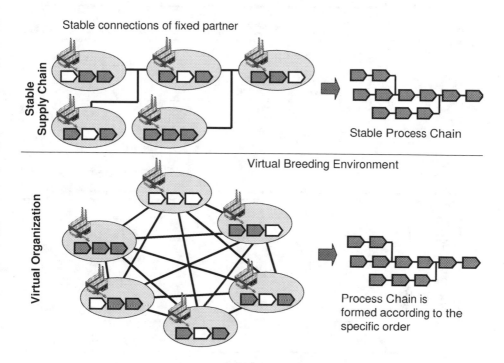

Figure 2 – Process Chains of Virtual Organizations

Evaluation of the SCOR process performance is done by using pre-defined performance indicators, which are associated with the different processes. At the moment, SCOR offers five performance perspectives: "Reliability", "Responsiveness" and "Flexibility" are customer oriented, "Cost" and "Assets" focus on the internal processes of a company (Zeller, 2003). Presentation of analysis results is done with so called "SCOR-Cards". An example of a SCOR-Card is shown in Figure 3.

For the indicators covered by the SCOR-Card, the current performance of the company is recorded. As a benchmark, the Median and Best-in-class are given for every indicator. The last column records the current performance deficit for every Indicator. This deficit is the percentile discrepancy between the current performance and the value for best-in-class.

Performance Perspectives	SCOR Level 1 Indicators	Current Value	Median	Best-in-class	Deficit
Customer-Oriented Perspectives					
Reliability	Perfect Order Fulfillment				
Responsivenss	Order fulfillment Cycle time				
Flexibility	Upside Supply Chain Flexibility				
	Upside Supply chain Adapability				
	Downside Supply chain Adapability				
Internal Perspectives					
Cost	Cost of goods sold				
	Supply Chain Management Cost				
Assets	Return on Supply Chain Fixed Assets				
	Cash-to-cash Cycle Time				
	Return on Working Capital				

Figure 3 – Example of SCOR-Card (Supply Chain Council, 2008)

If the process chain is static and can be described by a stable supply chain, SCOR indicators for performance measurement can be applied. To be able to use SCOR indicators for prospective measurement of partner performance in Virtual Organizations, methods of forecasting performance values for future periods have to be applied. A suitable method for prognosis is Artificial Neural Networks (ANN) (Zurada, 1992). Figure 4 shows the schematic representation of such an ANN:

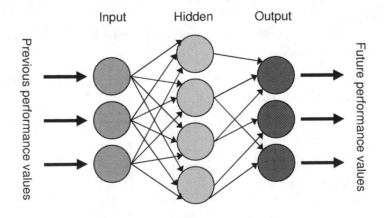

Figure 43 – Artificial Neural Network forecasting future performance

The Artificial Neural Network is trained with partner performance data of previous periods. After that it can be used to forecast future performance values for a specific period of time (Haykin, 1994).

3. MODELING EXAMPLE

In this modeling experiment, the future performance of the leading company of a Virtual Organization will be forecasted. The company is assumed to have been recording performance values for five indicators using the SCOR-Card regularly for a certain time. The result is shown in Table 1.

Table 1 – Performance values for previous periods

	Performance Perspectives	SCOR Indicator	n-2 period	n-1 period	Current period
Customer-Oriented Perspectives	*Reliability*	Delivery Performance to Commit Date	77%	90%	93%
	Responsiveness	Order fulfillment Lead time	3 days	1 day	2 days
	Flexibility	Upside Supply Chain Flexibility	60 days	52 days	55 days
Internal Perspectives	*Cost*	Cost of goods sold	67%	60%	62%
	Assets	Inventory Days of Supply	80 days	111 days	41 days

The example holds performance data for the current, the previous (n-1) and the period prior to that. The length of a period can be e.g. a day, a month or a year and has to be defined regarding the process cycle time.

The collected data is then being used as input for an Artificial Neural Network, modeled in Matlab and trained with previously collected data, which is used to forecast performance values for the planned collaboration. The result is shown in Figure 5.

By specifying benchmarks for performance in form of ideal and minimal values for every indicator, it is possible to generate percentile degrees of performance from absolute indicator values. The median is chosen as the minimal value, while the best-in-class value is regarded ideal. In a second step, the averaged degrees of performance can be aggregated to a Company Indicator. The Company Indicator is a two-dimensional vector and includes a value for customer-oriented performance and internal performance. It can be used as an aggregated performance value for a collaboration partner as a decision basis, founded on a forecasting of performance.

Performance Perspectives		SCOR Level 1 Indicators	Forecast Value	Median	Best-in-class	Deficit	Degree of Perform.
Customer-Oriented Perspectives	Reliability	Delivery Performance To Commit Date	92%	77%	94%	2%	**88.2%**
	Responsivenss	Order fulfillment Lead time	2.5 days	5 days	1 day	60%	**62.5%**
	Flexibility	Upside Supply Chain Flexibility	75 days	68 days	47 days	37%	**-33.3%**
Internal Perspectives	Cost	Cost of goods sold	65%	82%	56%	14%	**65.4%**
	Assets	Inventory Days of Supply	128 days	73 days	30 days	77%	**-127.9%**

$$\text{Degree of P.} = \frac{\text{Forecast Value} - \text{Median}}{\text{Median} - \text{Best-in-Class}}$$

Figure 5 – Forecast SCOR-Card

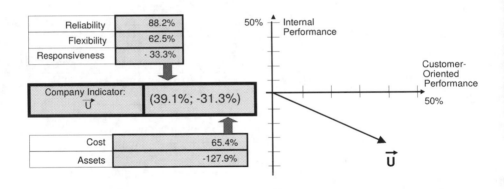

Figure 6 – Calculation of the Company Indicator

Figure 6 shows that the performance of the company aggregated as the Company Indicator well beats the median of the selected branch in the customer oriented view by 39.1%. The internal performance is below average by 31.3%.

In a final step of analysis, for all possible consortia the overall performance is determined by aggregating the Company Indicators of all involved partners, as shown by example in Figure 7. The overall performance of a consortium from the perspective of customer orientation is defined by the lowest performance value of all involved partners (Reiner, 2002). From the view of internal performance, the overall performance is the mean average of the values of all involved partners.

Partner	Company indicator	
	Cust. orient.	Intern.
Lead-Comp.	39.1%	-31.3%
Partner 1	97%	89%
Partner 2	86%	69%
Partner 3	82%	90%
Partner 4	90%	94%
Partner 5	79%	91%
Partner 6	29%	91%
Partner 7	81%	29%
Partner 8	92%	79%
Partner 9	94%	89%

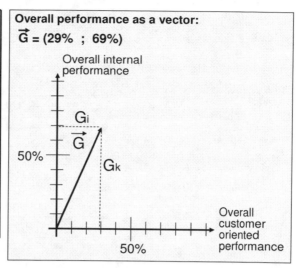

Figure 7 – Overall performance of a possible consortium

All possible Consortia can now primarily be ordered by customer-oriented performance and secondly by internal performance, as a basis for decision.

4. CONCLUSION

Precondition for applying the method in a Virtual Organization is the description of the processes of all members by the same systematic approach. The combination of crisp performance values, e.g. recorded by using the SCOR-Card, and a soft forecasting method like Artificial Neural Networks provides a chance to prospectively measure performance of a VO and its partners. Thus Prospective Performance Measurement can be used as a tool to evaluate alternatives in the course of consortium building. This is an important aspect, as the success of a Virtual Organization considerably depends on providing the capability to bid and deliver even in complex networks.

The method finds its limits in the requirement of the willingness of companies to share performance data inter-organizational in the Virtual Organization. This data is on the one hand needed to train the ANN and on the other hand to have a basis to forecast the future performance. For application of the method in normally sized VO's, performance data would have to be collected automatically, as manual recording would be too time-consuming.

Acknowledgments – This work as supported in part by the ECOLEAD integrated project funded by the European Commission.

4. REFERENCES

1. Haykin, S. (1994): Neural Networks: A Comprehensive Foundation, Macmillan.
2. Reiner, T. (2002).: Supply Chain Management – Drei einfache Weisheiten. Packaging Journal, Ausgabe 9.
2. Seifert, M. (2007): Unterstützung der Konsortialbildung in Virtuellen Organisationen durch prospektives Performance Measurement, Bremen.
3. Zeller, Andrew J. (2003): Controlling von Unternehmensnetzwerken: Bestandsaufnahme und Lückenanalyse. Erlangen-Nürnberg.
4. Zurada, J.M. (1992): Introduction to Artificial Neural Systems, PWS Publishing Company.
5. Supplc Chain Council (2008): SCOR 8.0.
6. Thoben, K.-D, Jagdey, H., (2001): Typological Issues in Enterprise Networks.

Annex.
Biographies

Luis M. Camarinha-Matos

Prof. Dr. Luis M. Camarinha-Matos is currently head of the Robotics and Integrated Manufacturing Group at the New University of Lisbon. He is also the leader of the Collaborative Networks and Distributed Industrial Systems (CoDIS) research group at the UNINOVA institute. He has participated in many international and national projects, both as a researcher and as a project coordinator. Currently he is the scientific director of the EC-funded integrated project ECOLEAD, a major European initiative on collaborative networks. His main areas of current research include: virtual enterprises, virtual organizations, and professional virtual communities, coordination and workflow for distributed business processes, multi-agent systems, intelligent manufacturing systems, systems integration, machine learning in supervision. He has been involved in the organization and program committees of many international conferences, has edited various issues of Journals and books, and he has more than 270 publications in Journals and conferences proceedings. He started the series of conferences BASYS (on balanced automation systems) and PRO-VE (Infrastructures for Virtual Enterprises) and is the founder and president of the international Society of Collaborative Networks (SOCOLNET) as well as the chairman of the IFIP Working Group on Virtual Enterprises. He is also founder and current chairman of the IFIP WG 5.5 on virtual enterprises.

Email: cam@uninova.pt - New University of Lisbon, UNINOVA - PORTUGAL

Hamideh Afsarmanesh

She is an Associate Professor in Computer Science at the University of Amsterdam (UvA), and the director of the Collaborative Networks (COLNET) group at UvA's Informatics Institute. She received her PhD in Computer Science from the University of Southern California (USC) in 1985, and joined University of Amsterdam in 1990, where she has directed the research in more than twenty National, European and International funded projects. Her current research focuses on the areas of federated cooperative databases, object-oriented and semantic information management, virtual organizations / virtual laboratories / virtual communities, and their application to a wide variety of domains from: bio-diversity and bio-informatics, to manufacturing and distributed control engineering. She has co-edited twelve books and various issues of international Journals, and has more than 150 publications in books, journals and conference proceedings. She is a member of the IFIP COVE - WG5.5, and the Dutch representative at the IFIP TC5. She has served as a consultant to both academic and industrial organizations, as an expert reviewer for several EC funded Projects, and evaluator of proposals submitted to several international funding organizations. She is active in professional organizations, has been involved with organizing and founding of several International conferences, and has served as a program chair and Panel chair in several technical International events focused on advanced databases, virtual organizations, and other information technology areas.

Email: hamideh@science.uva.nl - University of Amsterdam – NETHERLANDS

Other contributors:

António Abreu
Dr. António Abreu is currently Assistant Professor at the New University of Lisbon. In 2000, he jointed the UNINOVA – Institute for the Development of New Technologies, Group of Collaborative networks and Distributed Industrial Systems (CoDIS) as a PhD student. Since 2001 he has been involved in several European research projects such as VOmap, Thinkcreative and ECOLEAD. He concluded his PhD in March 2007 in Industrial Engineering at the New University of Lisbon with a thesis entitled "A contribution for the development of a theory for Collaborative Networks". His current research focuses on the conception of methodologies and development of tools to support the promotion of collaborative networked organizations (CNO) namely a formal model to represent the network of benefits, the development of performance indicators for CNO based on concepts from game theory (GT), social network analysis (SNA) and transactions cost theory (TCT). Email: ajfa@fct.unl.pt - New University of Lisbon, UNINOVA - PORTUGAL

José António Crispim
José António de Almeida Crispim graduated in Management at University of Beira Interior in 1995. He took a MSc. (Master) degree in Applied Quantitative Methods for Management at Porto School of Management (EGP), in 2003. Presently, he is a PhD student at the Engineering School of University of Porto. He is a teaching assistant at the Management Department of University of Minho since 1997 on the operations management area. His research interests have been vehicle routing, supply chain design and virtual enterprises.
Email:crispim@eeg.uminho.pt - University of Minho - PORTUGAL

Ekaterina Ermilova
Ekaterina Ermilova received her Master degree in Applied Mathematics and Computer Science from the Pereslavl University, Russia in June 2004. Since December 2004 she has been working on her PhD thesis at the Computer Science Department of the University of Amsterdam. Her research interests include knowledge modeling and management for Collaborative Networks, and specifically competency management and semi-automated ontology engineering.
Email: ermilova@science.uva.nl – University of Amsterdam – NETHERLANDS

Falk Graser
Dipl.-oec. Falk Graser, born in 1975, achieved his diploma in economics in 2001. Having been employed as an assistant researcher at the BIBA since mid-2000, he eventually became research scientist after finishing his studies. Focusing his activities on structures and processes within enterprise networks, he got involved into the EC-funded R&D-projects WHALES (Web-linking Heterogeneous Applications for Large-scale Engineering and Services), MOMENT (the Mobile Manufacturing Enterprise), and ECOLEAD (European Collaborative Network Leadership Initiative). Mr. Graser has been employed at the department "Collaborative Business in Enterprise Networks" of the research division "Applied

Information and Communication Technology for Production" until May 2007, when he left BIBA to work for the industry.

Filipa Ferrada
Filipa Ferrada received the MSc degree in Science in Computer and Electrical Engineering from the New University of Lisbon in September 2006. Currently, she is a PhD student and researcher in the Collaborative Networks and Distributed Industrial Systems (CoDIS) research group at the UNINOVA institute. Her research interests are Collaborative Networked Organizations (CNOs) in particular, virtual organizations, virtual communities and professional virtual communities; risk management applied to CNOs, affective computing and soft modeling. She has been involved in the European research projects TeleCARE and ECOLEAD and she is also a member of the international Society of Collaborative Networks (SOCOLNET).
Email: faf@uninova.pt - UNINOVA - PORTUGAL

Toni Jarimo
Toni Jarimo (MSc 2003, LicSc 2006) is research scientist at VTT Technical Research Centre of Finland with research interests in operations research and management science. In his studies at the Helsinki University of Technology he had a major in operations research and minors in nuclear physics and strategy and international business. Recently his work has focused on value networks, R&D management, and technology valuation. Jarimo is the author of several refereed articles in international journals and conferences.
Email: Toni.Jarimo@vtt.fi – VTT - FINLAND

Kalle Korpiaho
Kalle Korpiaho (MSc 2007) is a software specialist at Innofactor Ltd. His major and minor at the Helsinki University of Technology were, respectively, 'computer and information science' and 'computational science and engineering'. Recently his work at Innofactor has focused on development of European Union Emissions Trading Scheme –related asset-management software.
Email: kalle.korpiaho@innofactor.com – INNOFACTOR - FINLAND

Leandro Loss
Dr. Leandro Loss received his PhD in Electrical Engineering from the Federal University of Santa Catarina, Brazil in 2007. Currently he is researcher at the Intelligent Manufacturing Systems Group (GSIGMA) and Assistant Professor at Faculdades SENAC - Florianópolis. He is member of the SOCOLNET – Society of Collaborative Networks – and has participated in national projects (funded by Brazilian agencies) and several international co-operation projects with Europe (funded by the European Commission). His main areas of interest include: collaborative networks, knowledge management techniques, organizational learning, risk analysis, and decision support systems.
Email: loss@gsigma.ufsc.br – Federal University of Santa Catarina - BRAZIL

Patrícia Macedo
Patricia Macedo is a PhD student in the Electrical Engineering department of the

New University of Lisbon (UNL). She graduated from the Computer Science department of Instituto Superior Técnico (IST) in 1994 and received the MSc degree from IST in 2004. She is a teaching assistant at systems and informatics department at Polytechnic Institute of Setubal (IPS). Her main interests are: collaborative networks, organizational modeling and software engineering.
Email: pmacedo@est.ips.pt – UNINOVA - PORTUGAL

Simon Msanjila
Simon Samwel Msanjila has graduated BSc. in Computer Science in 2001 from the University of Dar es Salaam, Tanzania and MSc. in Systems Engineering in 2004 from Delft University of Technology, The Netherlands. On September 2004 he started his PhD research at the Computer Science department of the University of Amsterdam. His PhD research topic is focused on the management of trust for collaborative networks of organizations. He has published a number of papers in areas of trust management for collaborative networks of organizations, web-services, and modeling and simulation of web-service based business processes.
Email: msanjila@science.uva.nl – University of Amsterdam - NETHERLANDS

Alexandra Pereira-Klen
Dr. Alexandra Augusta Pereira-Klen received her Ph.D. degree in Manufacturing Automation from the Federal University of Santa Catarina (UFSC), Brazil in 1996 after working from 1991 to 1994 at BIBA (Bremen Institute of Industrial Technology and Applied Work Science at the University of Bremen) in Germany as a guest researcher. She is co-founder and coordinator of the Intelligent Manufacturing Systems Group (GSIGMA) and UFSC and, besides her research activities, also works as an independent consultant. Her main areas of interest include: collaborative networks, enterprise modeling, systems and information integration, information and communication technology, agile scheduling, shop-floor monitoring and control, decision support systems for manufacturing, socio-organizational issues as well as research and development in international cooperation. She has participated in national projects (under the CNPq agency) and several international cooperation projects with Europe (under the ESPRIT, IST, INCO and KIT Programmes as well as German agencies). She has written articles for publication on a number of conference proceedings, journals, book chapters and technical reports. She has also served as evaluator and rapporteur on ESPRIT / INCO IiM / IST project proposals, as reviewer of IST projects and as broker for the @LIS Programme (Alliance for the Information Society). She is the General Assembly Secretary of the international Society of Collaborative Networks (SOCOLNET)
Email: klen@gsigma.ufsc.br – Federal University of Santa Catarina - BRAZIL

Edmilson Ramazzo Klen
Dr. Edmilson Rampazzo Klen received his MSc degree in Industrial and Scientific Metrology from the Federal University of Santa Catarina (UFSC), Brazil, in March 2000. His PhD degree in Production Engineering was in the area of Collaborative Networks (CN) and was received from UFSC in March 2007. He is currently lecturer at the Department of Graphical Expression at UFSC and since 2000 works at the Intelligent Manufacturing Systems Group where he has been involved in

international cooperation research projects in the CN area (ECOLEAD, MyFahion.eu, DAMASCOS). He has also worked 5 years at CERTI Foundation, UFSC, as Manager of the Coordinate Measuring Laboratory as well as of the Quality System. He has worked 8 years as Senior Engineer for Mercedes-Benz in São Bernardo do Campo, Brazil (four years) and Bremen, Germany (four years) in the areas of new technologies and design. He is a member of the international Society of Collaborative Networks (SOCOLNET).
Email: erklen@gsigma.ufsc.br – Federal University of Santa Catarina - BRAZIL

João Rosas

João Rosas has been working at the New University of Lisbon, as a teaching assistant, on the Robotics and CIM areas. He also belongs to Uninova, from which he has been making research since 2001 in the TeleCARE and ECOLEAD projects. He is currently working on his PhD, on which he is developing a collaboration readiness assessment model to be used in Collaborative Networks. He graduated in Industrial Electronics at University of Minho in 1995. He had his MSc. Degree in Computer Integrated Manufacturing in 2000, also from University of Minho. His current research focus is on Collaborative Networked Organizations, multi-agent systems and Soft-Computing.
Email: jrosas@uninova.pt - New University of Lisbon, UNINOVA - PORTUGAL

Marcus Seifert

Dr.-Ing. Marcus Seifert, born in 1974, studied Production Engineering at the University of Bremen between 1994 and 1999 and finished his studies with the diploma. In 2007 he received a PhD in the context of consortium building in Virtual Organizations. He is employed as research scientist at BIBA since 1999. Since 2004, Marcus Seifert is head of department for "Collaborative Business in Enterprise Networks" in the division "Applied Information and Communication Technology for Production" of Prof. Thoben. In this function, he oversees numerous European joint projects in the contexts of Performance Measurement and consortium building in co-operative production. At the University of Bremen he is lecturer for the course "Production Systematics" in the faculty of Production.
Email: sf@biba.uni-bremen.de - BIBA – GERMANY

Jorge Pinho de Sousa

PhD in Operations Research (Université Catholique de Louvain, Belgium, 1989). He is currently Associate Professor in the Faculty of Engineering of the University of Porto (FEUP) and a researcher at INESC Porto, where he coordinates the Manufacturing Systems Engineering Unit. Main research areas: Operations Research, Combinatorial Optimization, Decision Support Systems, Public Transportation Services, Production and Operations Management, Enterprise Networks and Virtual Organizations. He has more than 50 publications in international journals and conferences proceedings. He has actively participated in several R&D projects in the area of Operations Management (in sectors such as shoes, automotive, and cork) and Operational Planning for Transportation Systems (scheduling of vehicles and drivers, mobility). He has been involved in several European projects closely related to collaborative networks. In the MIT Portugal Program, he is involved in the areas of Transportation Systems, and Engineering

Design and Advanced Manufacturing. He is currently the President of the Portuguese Operations Research Society (APDIO).
Email: jsousa@inescporto.pt – INESC Porto - PORTUGAL

Klaus-Dieter Thoben
Prof. Dr. Ing. Klaus Dieter Thoben, is professor in Production Engineering at the University of Bremen, Germany. He received his Doctor of Engineering degree in CAD applications in 1989 at the University of Bremen. In the same year he joined BIBA as Manager of the CAD/CAM Lab. From 1991 until 1996 he was in charge of the Department of Computer Aided Design, Planning and Manufacturing. He has been responsible for several research projects and lectures on various design and production-related themes. From 1997 he has been responsible for preparing a new curriculum for industrial engineering and economics at the University of Bremen. Since 2003, he is head of BIBA-IKAP. His special interests are organisational issues and applications of information and communication technologies in co-operative environments.
Email: tho@biba.uni-bremen.de - BIBA - GERMANY

Stefan Wiesner
Dipl.-Wi.-Ing. Stefan Wiesner graduated in Industrial Engineering and Management from the University of Bremen in 2007. He is employed at the Bremen Institute of Production and Logistics (BIBA) at the department "Collaborative Business in Enterprise Networks" of the research division "Applied Information and Communication Technology for Production". From May 2007 onwards he has been responsible for the BIBA contribution to the VBE section of the project ECOLEAD. He is also working on the transnational project ESKALE, which will support knowledge-based manufacturing for traditional SMEs. In addition to the project work he supervises student projects and theses from industrial engineering and economics students at the University of Bremen. In his research he is concentrating on topics in the field of Enterprise Networks.
Email: wie@biba.uni-bremen.de - BIBA - GERMANY

Subject Index